A Case Study and Tutorial

Fallingwater in 3D Studio

Laura Sanchez and Alex Sanchez

ONWORD ®
P R E S S

Published by:
OnWord Press
2530 Camino Entrada
Santa Fe, NM 87505-4835 USA

First Edition, 1994
SAN 694-0269
Printed in the United States of America

10 9 8 7 6 5 4 3 2 1

Library of Congress Cataloging-in-Publication Data
Sanchez, Laura and Sanchez, Alex
   Fallingwater in 3D Studio: A Case Study and Tutorial

   Includes index.
   1. Architecture   2. 3D Studio (computer software)
   3. Fallingwater   I. Title

94-65058
ISBN 1-56690-051-4

Trademarks

3D Studio and AutoCAD are registered trademarks of Autodesk. OnWord Press is a registered trademark of High Mountain Press, Inc. Many other products and services are mentioned in this book that are either trademarks or registered trademarks of their respective companies. OnWord Press and the authors make no claim to these marks.

Warning and Disclaimer

This book is designed to provide information about 3D Studio, AutoCAD, and Fallingwater. Every effort has been made to make this book as complete and accurate as possible; however, no warranty or fitness is implied.

The information is provided on an as-is basis. The authors and OnWord Press shall have neither liability nor responsibility to any person or entity with respect to any loss or damages in connection with or rising from the information contained in this book.

About the Authors

Alex and Laura Sanchez met at the University of New Mexico art department back in prehistoric times, and have been working on mutual projects ever since.

Alex has served as department coordinator for the CAD program at the UNM-Valencia Campus since he initiated the program ten years ago. He is currently teaching both AutoCAD and 3D Studio classes, and trying to keep area A/E firms from snatching up his students before they graduate. Alex has also co-authored a CAD users' guide and rendering documentation.

Laura spent fourteen years running an architectural design and drafting service. She called it quits sometime after the 250th set of plans to concentrate full-time on writing and editing. She is currently a project editor at OnWord Press.

Acknowledgments

We would like to thank the people at Autodesk, first for producing a great program, and second for quickly providing beta and final versions of 3D Studio Release 3. Special thanks go to Bob Bennett, Garth Chouteau, and Laura Kawazoe for resources, suggestions, and review.

At Fallingwater, the entire staff has been gracious, professional, and helpful. Particular thanks go to Director Thomas Schmidt and Curator/Administrator Lynda Waggoner for support and review comments. Education Coordinator Sarah Larsen served above and beyond the call of duty tracking down photographs for the book.

We would like to express appreciation to Donald Hoffmann, both for his luminous and scholarly writing, and for his comments, corrections, and photographs; and to Bill Allen of *3D Artist Magazine* for stealing time from his own deadlines to review the manuscript.

At OnWord Press, thanks go to publisher Dan Raker for liking the idea in the first place, to acquisitions editor David Talbott for a perceptive overview, to project editor Margaret Burns for pulling it all together, to artist Lynne Egensteiner for a dynamite cover, to Carol Leyba, Michelle Mann, and Patrice Werner for outstanding book design in spite of killer schedules, to Kris Smead for copy editing and David Heiret for indexing, and to the production team of Carol Leyba and Tierney Tully for standing firm in the middle of the hurricane.

Thanks also to Kim at See-Mor Video, Normalville, PA, for letting two complete strangers come in one rainy night and mess around with her VCR.

Book Production

This book was produced by Patrice Werner using Ventura 4.1.1 using a 486-33 personal computer. The cover was produced by Lynne Egensteiner using QuarkXPress 3.1.1 and Adobe Photoshop 2.5.1 on a Macintosh Quadra. The color insert was produced by Lynne Egensteiner and David Rohr.

OnWord Press

OnWord Press is dedicated to the fine art of professional documentation.

In addition to the authors who developed the material for this book, other members of the OnWord Press team helped make the book end up in your hands.

Thanks to Margaret Burns (Project Manager), David Talbott (Acquisitions Director), Carol Leyba (Production Manager), Michelle Mann and Patrice Werner (Production Editors), Lynne Egensteiner (Cover Designer), David Rohr (Design Director), Gary Lange (Manager of Contracts and Administration), Kate Hayward (Director of Operations), Dan Raker (Publisher), Kris Smead (Copyeditor), David Heiret (Indexer), and the other members of the OnWord Press team who contributed to the production and distribution of this book.

Table of Contents

Chapter 5
Lights, Cameras, and Rendering   131

Chapter 6
Fallingwater in Motion

Chapter 7
Modeling Details with 3D Studio 217

Chapter 8
Using 3D Studio Materials   **287**

Chapter 9
A Fallingwater Walkthrough   323

Appendix A
3D Studio Pull-Down and
Screen Menu Maps   353

Appendix B
3D Studio Materials   361

Appendix C
Minimum Hardware and Software   373

Appendix D
References   375

Index   377

A Case Study and Tutorial

Fallingwater In 3D Studio

Laura Sanchez and Alex Sanchez

ONWORD®
PRESS

Introduction

This book began with the authors' long-standing involvement with architecture and computer graphics, and evolved toward two goals:

❑ To discover what could be learned by using new tools to look at a familiar building. Fallingwater has been documented many times in many ways, but the power of PC graphics can explore the building in ways not available before.

❑ For beginning and intermediate users, to trace a route through 3D Studio's complexities to the production of useful architectural graphics. Many computer manuals demonstrate specific operations on simple models—the "how to draw a board" approach—but give little help in pulling a project together. This book offers broader guidelines for the user faced with organizing and carrying out a typical modeling, rendering, and animation job.

Why Fallingwater?

Fallingwater was built in the late 1930s for the Kaufmann family of Pittsburgh. Frank Lloyd Wright was 67 years old when he designed the house, and only two of his projects had been built in the preceding seven years. A lesser figure might have drifted gracefully into obscurity, but the Fallingwater years began Wright's second career. He went on to design extraordinary buildings until his death at the age of 92.

Fallingwater is acknowledged as the greatest work of 20th century American architecture. Since it opened to the public in 1964, it has drawn more than two million visitors to its isolated site.

In spite of its fame, in many ways the house remains a mystery. Anyone casually interested in architecture has seen the classic view of Fallingwater, its cantilevered terraces surging out over the stream with the assurance of a mother ship landing. Less well known are the other elevations, the interior, the numerous and complex structural systems. Even a complete collection of photographs fails to convey the entirety of the house. It may be the most complicated small building in the world.

A computer can't tease out the mental processes that led to the design of the house, nor can it reproduce for you the experience of actually being there. What it can do is show you a new way of looking at the house as a physical assembly of parts—no sacrilege intended.

The two principal sources of information about Fallingwater used for this book were Edgar Kaufmann junior's generously illustrated *Fallingwater: A Frank Lloyd Wright Country House* and the recent second edition of Donald Hoffmann's detailed study of the house's construction, *Frank Lloyd Wright's Fallingwater: The House and Its History*.

Due to constraints of time and accessibility, we were unable to study the original working drawings at Columbia University's Avery Library. Therefore, for scaling and dimensioning the model, we used the excellent as-built drawings in the Kaufmann book, done by L.D. Astorino & Associates, Ltd., Architects.

Why 3D Studio?

Modeling, rendering, and animation (MRA) software for personal computers makes possible a qualitative change from traditional methods of design visualization. From the available graphics programs, we chose Autodesk's 3D Studio because of its versatility, power, and popularity.

Many programs are good at one or two aspects of modeling, rendering, and animation, but few perform all three well. 3D Studio covers the broadest possible range of operations. The package is actually five programs in one. The 2D Shaper, 3D Lofter, and 3D Editor modules provide several methods of modeling; the Materials Editor handles surface appearances; and the Keyframer module controls animation. We constructed the basic architectural model in AutoCAD, and then used 3D Studio for modeling details, rendering, and animation.

The power and flexibility of 3D Studio, particularly in animation, go far beyond the scope of this book. Release 3 of the program includes networking functions that match or surpass the capabilities of workstation graphics. However, these exercises and discussions focus on methods possible for one user with one computer.

Instead of attempting to discuss every command and function, this book concentrates on operations most likely to be used in a typical architectural rendering project; it is organized more as a tutorial than as a user's guide. Both the *Reference Manual* and *Tutorial Guide* included with 3D Studio Release 3 are excellent, and the reader should consult them closely when using the program.

How this Book Is Organized

The book concentrates on four types of information:

❑ A brief background of, and new graphic information about, Fallingwater

❑ Approaches and strategies for real-world MRA projects

❑ Exercises that give detailed instructions for using 3D Studio

❑ Tips and traps for using 3D Studio

Chapter 1 briefly describes Fallingwater's design and construction. Chapter 2 discusses general principles of MRA, in the context of how visiting the house focused our assumptions about both the building and the project. The working chapters, 3 through 9, follow the sequence of operations used to model, render, and animate the house, and by extension, other buildings. Each working chapter begins with information about the features of the house addressed in the procedures, discusses strategies for carrying out a particular phase of the project, takes a look at the program features to be used, and includes detailed exercises and specific tips.

Readers and Routes

The three potential audiences for this book can follow different routes:

❑ Students of Fallingwater will find material focusing on the house in the first two chapters, the beginning sections of the working chapters and, most importantly, in the many illustrations throughout the book.

❑ Design professionals interested in MRA concepts and procedures can find useful information in the discussions of strategies, and get an idea of how 3D Studio works in the program overviews and exercises.

❑ 3D Studio users can find both general and specific information about effectively using the program in the working chapters and in the appendices.

Terminology

Because of the varied audience for this book, the problem of specialized vocabularies arose. Rather than include multiple glossaries, we have tried to adjust the language in each section for its most probable audience. Thus, the first chapter and earlier parts of the following chapters avoid computer jargon. The discussions of MRA strategy and specifics of 3D Studio avoid the more delirious flights of architecturalese. In discussing 3D Studio, we have used terminology consistent with the documentation.

Typographical Conventions

❑ Text that you type into the computer is shown in boldface:

Type **50** for the first radius and **60** for the second.

❑ Messages from the program are shown in a monospaced typeface:

`No vertex found.`

❑ Keyboard selections are enclosed by brackets:

Hold down the [Alt] key and press [W] to scroll directly to entries beginning with that letter.

❑ Menu items, dialog box buttons, and command names are capitalized. If the full path to a command is given, each command is separated by a slash:

Choose Create/Tube/Faceted from the screen menu.

❑ File names are shown as they appear on the display screen. File extensions without prefixes are shown in lowercase italics:

Pick the *.lft* wildcard button and select the TABLE2.LFT file.

❑ Tips, notes, and warnings are preceded by **Tip:**, **Note:**, or **Warning:**.

The Disk

The distribution disk includes a complete three-dimensional model of Fallingwater and various files containing geometry and textures used in the exercises. Instructions for installation are located on a README file included on the disk.

An Historical
Sketch

The efforts of four extraordinary people combined to create Fallingwater, and their presence lingers there. The house was commissioned by E.J. and Liliane Kaufmann in the 1930s; entering the house today, there is no sense of visiting a museum, but the impression that the Kaufmanns will be back any minute from a stroll through the glen. That visitors are there at all results from Edgar Kaufmann junior's stewardship and generosity. And the house itself, of course, symbolizes the career of Frank Lloyd Wright.

The Kaufmann Family and Bear Run

The family arrived in western Pennsylvania in the 1860s, when Morris, Isaac, Henry, and Jacob Kaufmann immigrated from Viernheim, in Hessen, Germany. The four brothers—tailors and merchants—established a clothing store in Pittsburgh. Known as "The Big Store," it prospered and became a city landmark.

In 1885, Morris Kaufmann's first son, Edgar Jonas (E.J.), was born. E.J. grew up working in the Pittsburgh store and training in Germany and Chicago. In 1909 E.J. and Lillian Sarah (later, Liliane) Kaufmann were married. These two first cousins were wed in New York City because they could not legally marry in Pennsylvania. By 1913, after one of the original brothers had died and another been bought out, E.J. took active control of the store (Hoffmann, p. 8).

By all accounts, E.J. Kaufmann was a dynamic, unconventional, and convivial man. Beyond the successful running of a business, his interests were wide-ranging: the arts, travel, conservation, civic projects, and building—always building.

Liliane Kaufmann, and Edgar J. Kaufmann in front of a wall of the office designed for him by Wright. (Photos courtesy of Western Pennsylvania Conservancy.)

The couple's only child, Edgar junior, inherited a love of art and travel from both parents. In 1934, the younger Kaufmann returned from a four-year stay in Europe. He had been studying painting and drawing in Vienna and Florence, but the serene glory of Florence's Renaissance buildings triggered an interest in architecture that would eventually prove stronger than the pull of other, smaller art forms.

Back in the United States, Edgar junior settled in New York City to continue his art education, but the twenty-four-year-old would-be painter felt adrift and dislocated. He could find no connection between his native country and the ideas that he had absorbed in Europe until a friend recommended that he read Frank Lloyd Wright's *An Autobiography*. The book impressed Edgar junior deeply. Years later, he recalled, "…his [Wright's] story flowed into my mind like the first trickle of irrigation in a desert land" (Hoffmann, p. 12).

Even though he had no plans to become an architect, Edgar junior was so caught by Wright's vision that, in October of 1934, he applied for an apprenticeship in Wright's Taliesin Fellowship, located near Spring Green, Wisconsin. Wright accepted the new apprentice into the community of students, who spent as much time farming, chopping firewood, and sawing and quarrying materials for the buildings at Taliesin as drafting. The Fellowship was organized more as an opportunity to absorb the aura of the Great Man through association than as a formal college of architecture.

Paradise Regained

While Edgar junior was at Taliesin, E.J. and Liliane Kaufmann continued to divide their lives between business and social duties in Pittsburgh and weekends in the country at Bear Run.

Located about 70 miles from Pittsburgh, Bear Run flows for only four miles through the low Allegheny mountains before emptying into the Youghiogheny River. In its short course, the stream drops over 1,400 feet, cutting through ancient strata of sandstone, forming waterfalls where the layers have eroded unevenly into rock shelves.

The second edition of Donald Hoffmann's detailed account, *Frank Lloyd Wright's Fallingwater: The House and Its History,* traces the evolution of Bear Run back 600 million years. The most surprising information, in view of the area's present beauty, is the almost complete destruction of the watershed in the late nineteenth century. The land had been ravaged by timbering and mining, the stream fished out. Tramways crossed the area where Fallingwater now stands, hauling logs to a sawmill near the mouth of the stream.

Today, much of the damage has healed, and the rest is concealed by the dense vegetation. Rhododendron, mountain laurel, and white and red oak cover the steep, cutover hills. Much of the credit for restoring and preserving the watershed belongs to E.J. Kaufmann.

Weekends in the Country

In spite of its earlier mistreatment, Bear Run began a new incarnation as a recreational retreat in 1890 when a group of Masons from Pittsburgh bought 135 acres from local people and built a country club. The club flourished at first, but within fifteen years it failed and the land was sold. It passed through several other hands, accumulating over a dozen buildings, including a cottage where the guest wing of Fallingwater now stands.

Beyond the original bridge across Bear Run, the road turns and rises to where an old cottage stood, at the site of the present guest wing. (Photo courtesy of Western Pennsylvania Conservancy.)

In 1916 E.J. inaugurated "Kaufmann's Summer Club" on land leased at Bear Run. The facility was to serve as a wholesome and healthful vacation retreat where the store's female employees could enjoy weekends of bathing, sunning, camping, hiking, and other recreation. Hoffmann notes that a concern for working women—or rather what they might be doing when not at work—was typical of American cities in the decades around the turn of the century (Hoffmann, pp. 7–10).

In 1921 the club took a second 5-year lease on the property, and the Kaufmanns built for themselves a small cabin about 500 yards southeast of the falls. Within a few years this original cabin proved inadequate; it was too close to the recently paved road, too lacking in modern conveniences such as plumbing and electricity, and too small to accommodate their frequent guests.

The store employees' association bought the 1,600-acre Bear Run property in 1926, but in a few years their visits to the summer camp began to dwindle, discouraged by labor problems and Depression belt-tightening. However, the Kaufmanns' own involvement with the site increased, and in 1933 they took personal title to the place.

The next year, Edgar junior's enthusiasm for Wright piqued his parents' interest, and E.J. began corresponding with Wright about the possibility of his designing various civic projects in Pittsburgh. In November 1934, the elder Kaufmanns went to Taliesin to visit Edgar junior and meet Wright.

Wright in 1934

In 1934 Frank Lloyd Wright was as becalmed as his volatile temperament would allow. The personal scandals and tragedies of the previous 25 years had receded, though debt continued to plague him. In *Many Masks: A Life of Frank Lloyd Wright*, Brendan Gill states,

> *After the Second World War, the term brinkmanship became a common descriptive term; before the word existed, Wright embodied the activity not only throughout his middle years but—at least in respect to his finances—on into old age as well, with a perverse skill born of long practice. (Gill, pp. 292–293)*

Not that Wright was idle. Settled at Taliesin with his third wife Olgivanna, he wrote, lectured, and oversaw the architectural, farm, and construction work of the Fellowship apprentices. During this period he was developing concepts and plans both for the moderately priced, "democratic" Usonian houses and for Broadacre City, the Wrightian utopia which, for better and worse, foreshadowed the American suburb.

Money, however, was slow to come in. Taliesin was in debt; the fees and work of the apprentices did not cover expenses of the large holding. Only two of Wright's commissions had actually been built in the preceding seven years, one of which was for his cousin. At 67, Wright needed a patron.

Conceiving Fallingwater

When the Kaufmanns visited Taliesin in November of 1934, they discovered an immediate affinity with the Wrights. Wright and E.J. were enough alike to respect and enjoy each other's company; both responded deeply to the natural world. Liliane and Olgivanna shared an interest in the arts. During the visit, they discussed civic projects with Wright, the possibility of Wright's designing a new office for E.J., and arrangements for exhibiting a 12 x 12 foot model of Broadacre City that the apprentices were assembling.

That December, Wright visited Pittsburgh for follow-up discussions of the Kaufmanns' various projects, which now included a country house to replace the old cabin at Bear Run. A vigorous tradition of rustic country houses flourished in the '30s—chalet-like, shingled, log-sided, festooned with branches and antlers. Perhaps that was what the Kaufmanns expected. What they got from Wright was far different, but they rose to the occasion.

Wright Encounters Bear Run

E.J. and Wright drove from Pittsburgh down to Bear Run to inspect the site. In the 1930s, access to Bear Run was much as it is today. The site lies just off a stretch of State Highway 381 between the small villages of Mill Run and Ohiopyle, which is now a center for backpacking and white water rafting. From Highway 381, a private road winds downhill to the northwest to cross the stream at a bridge just above the falls, and then loops up the steep bank beyond. (See color plate III.)

A few hundred feet downstream from the falls and bridge, the southeast bank flattens out to form a small platform, a natural front row seat for viewing the falls above. It was the Kaufmanns' favorite spot, and apparently they assumed it would be the site for the house. Wright inspected the stream breaking over rocks in its forest glen, requested a detailed site plan showing contours, boulders, and large trees, and left for New York to see about arrangements for exhibiting the Broadacre City model.

The falls at the house site before construction.
(Photo courtesy of Western Pennsylvania Conservancy.)

In March of 1935, the completed plan of the area around the falls was sent to Wright in Arizona, where he had moved himself and his entourage for the winter. In the following months, correspondence between Wright and E.J. dealt mainly with financial matters. Nothing much was said about the Bear Run project, other than mention to Kaufmann that a house had taken vague shape in Wright's mind inspired by the music of the stream.

That September, E.J. Kaufmann and a business associate went to Milwaukee for a retailers' conference. Kaufmann called Wright from Milwaukee, saying that he was on his way to Taliesin to look at the drawings for his house.

The 140-Minute Masterpiece

There are different accounts of what happened next. Wright always maintained that one should not put pencil to paper before a building had fully taken shape in one's mind. In any event, there is no firm evidence that one line of Fallingwater had been drawn before Kaufmann called. Edgar Tafel, an apprentice at Taliesin, recounts his memories of what happened in the approximately 140 minutes it took Kaufmann to drive from Milwaukee:

> He [Wright] hung up the phone, briskly emerged from his office, some twelve steps from the drafting room, sat down at the table set with the plot plan, and started to draw. First floor plan. Second floor. Section, elevation. Side sketches of details, talking sotto voce all the while. The design just poured out of him. "Liliane and E.J. will have tea on the balcony… they'll cross the bridge to walk into the woods…" Pencils being used up as fast as we could sharpen them when broken—H's, HB's colored Castell's, again and again being worn down or broken. Erasures, overdrawing, modifying. Flipping sheets back and forth. Then, the bold title across the bottom: "Fallingwater." A house has to have a name…
>
> Just before noon Mr. Kaufmann arrived. As he walked up the outside stone steps, he was greeted graciously by the master. They came straight to the drafting table. "E.J.," said Mr. Wright, "we've been waiting for you." (Tafel, p. 3)

The Kaufmanns were initially surprised by the placement of the house, but, caught by Wright's vision, did not hesitate to proceed. Within a month, they received a more detailed set of drawings. The design of the house changed little from that first conception, cantilevered out over the falls from what seemed an entirely inadequate footprint area.

Almost as an aside to the visual drama of the house, Wright offered a couple of other reasons for its singular placement. If the falls were constantly in view out the windows, the sight would grow mundane over time. Invisible from the house, yet always present, the falls would retain their singular essence.

Also, whenever possible, Wright oriented a building's principal windows to the southeast. Had he placed the house on the more obvious natural platform on the other side of Bear Run, it would have been impossible to have both south-facing windows and a view of the stream. Or perhaps he just wanted no other spectacular views competing with his masterpiece.

The Design of the House

Whatever Wright's reasons for placing the house as he did, Fallingwater demanded both aesthetic and structural innovations.

A view of the house from below the falls.
(Photo by Harold Corsini, courtesy of Western Pennsylvania Conservancy.)

The Scheme

The dominant theme is horizontal layering, expressed by the cantilevered terraces thrusting into space with as little obvious support as a lenticular cloud formation. Wright had been exhorting the contextual appropriateness of horizontal "organic" lines since his Prairie House period. There is no prairie flatness at Bear Run, but the layers of terrace parapets perfectly repeat the shape, scale, and tactile quality of the rock shelves at the falls.

The horizontal concrete layers are balanced by heavy masonry masses at the west and east ends of the house. Structurally, they counterbalance the weight of the extended terraces. At the west, the masonry "tower" provides vertical thrust, as well as providing a continuous stack for mechanical systems. At the east, the masonry walls integrate the flying terraces with the earth.

In spite of the rich textures and detailing, the interior of the house seems subordinate to the spectacular exterior, as dressing rooms exist to serve the drama of the stage. From the enclosing security of the grotto-like spaces on the north side of the house, one emerges into the larger south rooms where low ceilings force vision outward to the bands of windows and their explosion of light and nature.

Approaching the inconspicuous north entry door through massive walls of stone. (Photo by Harold Corsini, courtesy of Western Pennsylvania Conservancy.)

Building Systems at Fallingwater

And then it gets complicated. The small building, with approximately 2,800 enclosed square feet and a slightly lesser area of terrace, employs multiple systems of support and articulation. Edgar Kaufmann junior notes three different systems of cantilevering—extension from an anchorage, counterbalancing, and loaded extension—and then outlines the various support systems.

> *"Another unobvious aspect of the construction is that each floor level has its own support system. The main level is carried on four inconspicuous stub walls rising at the edge of the stream bed; the slab extends far beyond them. The next level is supported from a central square of reinforced-concrete beams, with corners resting on stone masses; from this square the second slab, or tray is cantilevered. The narrow top level is set along the rear edge of the house, bearing down on the whole." (Kaufmann, p. 90)*

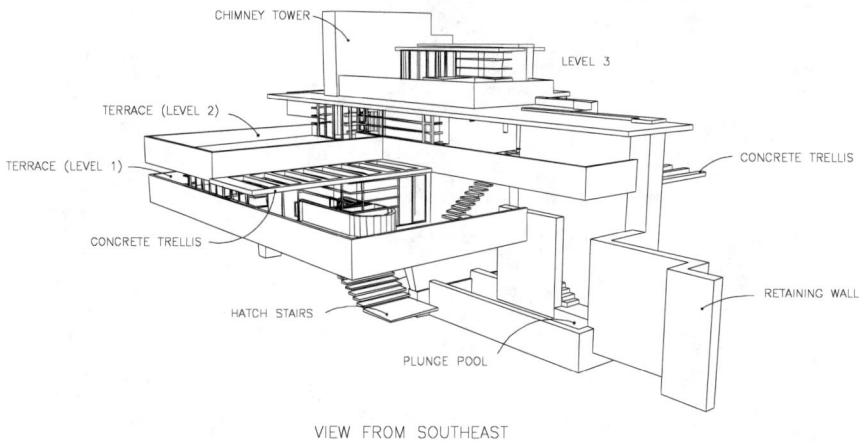

CHIMNEY TOWER

LEVEL 3

TERRACE (LEVEL 2)

TERRACE (LEVEL 1)

CONCRETE TRELLIS

CONCRETE TRELLIS

RETAINING WALL

HATCH STAIRS

PLUNGE POOL

VIEW FROM SOUTHEAST

A line drawing of the house, viewed from the southeast, calls out some of its elements.

Using Computer Analysis

Because of the complexity of the building and its lack of repeating or continuous elements, computer modeling can illustrate aspects of the structure that are difficult to grasp by other means, including site visits. The working chapters of this book describe the use of various tools of separation and selection to analyze a building that stubbornly refuses to be understood by less flexible methods.

Once a three-dimensional model of the house is constructed (no quick task), it can easily be used to separate out related elements, fit mysterious assemblies together, make selected parts visible or invisible, and separate the built structure from its interwoven site. One can pick tools for analysis at will. The incomprehensible tangle shown in the first of the following two illustrations, is a "wireframe" perspective drawing of the entire building. A wireframe drawing, as the name implies, delineates the planes of a building's structure as if all materials were transparent, except for wires applied along each edge.

In the second rendering, all building components have been made invisible except for the tower walls and the three floor slabs. In contrast to the wireframe drawing, this version conceals all edges that would not be visible in an actual view of Fallingwater minus its walls.

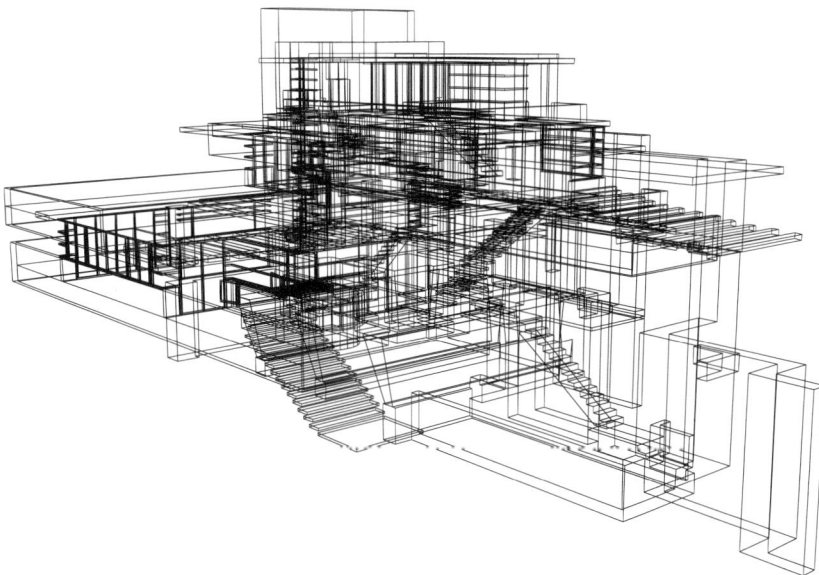

A wireframe of the building's structure drives home its complexity.

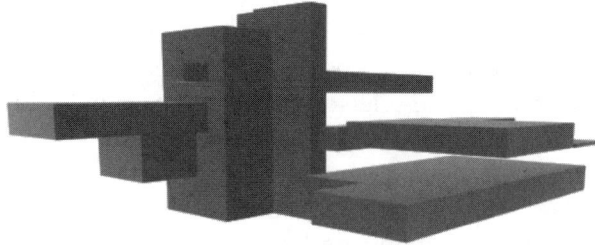

Simplifying the structure by showing only the floor levels
is one of many tools for analysis.

Structural Innovations and Engineering Wars

Though many of Fallingwater's features were foreshadowed in Wright's earlier work, the great cantilevered terraces of the Kaufmanns' house explored unfamiliar building techniques.

The terraces of Fallingwater stretch for approximately 115 feet east and west, and the house extends 67 feet from the north-most wall south to the far extension of parapet over the stream. The stream- and road-bound arrowhead of earth, which actually supports the house, measures only about 40 feet across its broad west end and tapers east to a point approximately 70 feet away. This small patch of ground slopes 10 feet down from the road and contains three massive boulders within the perimeter of the house. A juicy engineering problem.

E.J. Kaufmann hired his own engineers, who did not agree with Wright and *his* engineers. In the spring of 1936, Kaufmann sent the partially completed plans to his consulting engineers, Morris Knowles, in Pittsburgh. In April, their report came back. Since the plans had contained little in the way of dimensions and reinforcing specifications, Morris Knowles could not really comment on the structural stability of the house, but they listed several problems with its siting.

In both the original and a follow-up report they objected, reasonably enough, to placing the house on the edge of the stream bed: the rate of the stream's erosion, stability of the undercut rock shelves at the falls, and the maximum water level during flooding were all unknown. Nor did they approve of using the large boulders *in situ* as part of the foundation. Wright reassured E.J. and assigned two of his associates, William Wesley Peters and Mendel Glickman, to start working on structural calculations for the house itself. The engineering battles would intensify once construction began.

Design Debates and Modifications

Though the overall plan of the house never changed, the Kaufmanns questioned certain features of the house and made many suggestions that were carried out before and during construction.

Going Down to the Water   Several features that first appeared at Fallingwater have become commonplace, but not the stairs that descend from a glassed-in hatch in the main room to hover above the stream below. Understandably, E.J. and Liliane doubted the need for a partially perforated living room floor, or that anyone would use an 8-foot-wide staircase down to the rushing water.

Wright, backed up by Edgar junior, insisted that the staircase was necessary. It completed a transparent shaft of light and movement from the ceiling skylights down through the hatch to the stream, and counter-balanced both the solid mass of the chimney and the flow of water at the falls. Wright prevailed, and the stairs became the culmination of the physical and symbolic connection of stream and house. On a more mundane level, the hatch was an effective source of ventilation in the humid summers.

E.J. Kaufmann wanted a swimming pool, and he advanced ideas for including one until he finally got his wish some years later when the guest wing was built. Bob Mosher, Wright's clerk of the works, was worried about a flight of stairs down to the stream that stopped several feet above water level. The concerns of both men resulted in the inclusion of a small plunge pool adjacent to the shallow stream. It would provide still water, deep enough for early morning dips, though inadequate for E.J.'s more athletic ambitions. Wright assented readily, and the little pool was set into the long retaining wall extending to the east.

The Kaufmanns also requested the outside staircase from the second floor. This feature would allow one to come and go from the pool without dripping through the living room.

The stream stairs and plunge pool.
(Photo by Harold Corsini, courtesy of Western Pennsylvania Conservancy.)

The "Heraldic" Device   On the east side of the second-floor terrace, there is a disconcerting little stone wall with nothing under it (see photo, upper right, between the branches). The cantilevered roof of the terrace, as first built, needed more support. Originally Wright designed a fussy arrangement of small vertical steel straps centered by a painted concrete square with a hole in it. The Kaufmanns thought it too pretentious and unrelated to the rest of the house. Plain steel bars were then tried and eventually discarded in favor of extending the masonry, supported only by the cantilevered terrace floor slab, far enough to support the roof.

The Bridge to the Guest Wing   It was evident from the beginning that the house would need more accommodation for visitors and staff than the single guest room in the main building. The only place to put extra quarters was across the road and up the hill. Wright's original scheme showed an enclosed passageway bridging the drive from the third story of the house to steps leading up the hill to the guest house.

The Kaufmanns objected to their guests having to climb all the way to the third floor, so the passageway was begun on the second floor at the head of the main stairs. This change left an odd nook in the third floor. Since Edgar junior wanted morning light in his bedroom anyway, he used the space as a bedroom and the original bedroom as a study.

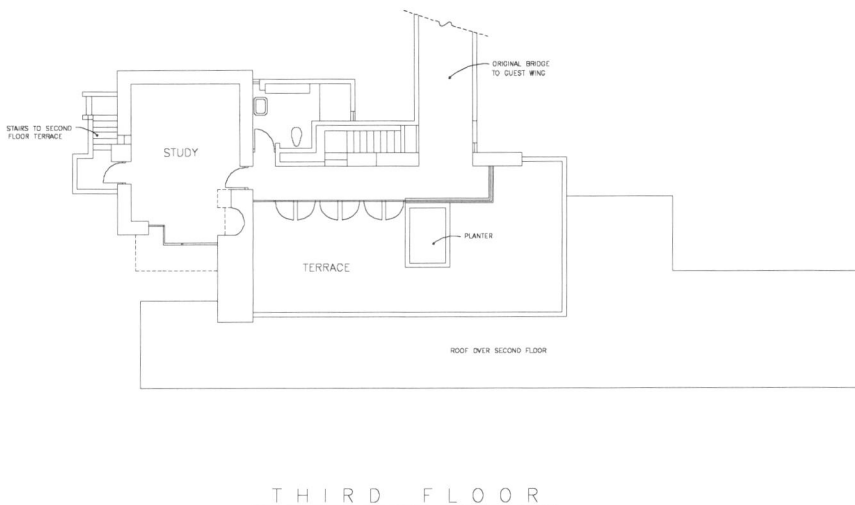

THIRD   FLOOR

In the original design for the house, the passage to the guest wing originated on the third floor. When the third floor access was eliminated, Edgar junior decided to use the alcove that remained for a bedroom.

The Legendary Gold Leaf   Before and during construction, Wright told E.J. Kaufmann that the project would cost more than $35,000 and less than $45,000. By the time Fallingwater was completed, the total bill reached $145,000. This was a daunting amount in an era when the typical house cost between $5,000 and $10,000, but Kaufmann was determined that the house should be fully realized.

The only feature that he vetoed because of cost was Wright's fancy that the exterior concrete surfaces of the house should be covered with gold leaf to blend subtly with the autumn foliage of the glen. (It is possible that Kaufmann was as appalled by the potential garishness of this idea as many later purists have been, but decided to tackle the irascible Wright on financial rather than aesthetic grounds.)

After fighting a holding action for a brushed aluminum compromise, Wright finally gave up and turned his energy to matching paint and stucco colors to "the sere leaves of the rhododendron," even though most rhododendron leaves stay green all year (Hoffmann, p. 61).

Wright may not have been serious—opinions differ—but he had successfully used gold leaf in the mortar joints of earlier houses, and greatly admired the quiet gold backgrounds of certain Japanese screens. Although gold is one of the most difficult materials to simulate in computer rendering, and Wright apparently had a very specific shade of gold in mind, in a fit of morbid imagination we have tried to reproduce the gilded version of Fallingwater (see color plate I.)

Building Fallingwater

Fallingwater was under construction from 1936 until 1939, during the depths of the Depression. Wage scales ran from 25 cents an hour for common laborers to 85 cents an hour for masons, and much of the material came from the site. Even so, the complexity of the work, the innovative techniques, the custom-fabricated components, and the determination of all involved to make no compromises in quality required a staggering amount of effort and money.

Labor and Materials

An old stone quarry only 500 feet from the falls was opened to provide the sandstone used for masonry throughout the building. It was handy, saving both the cost of the material and its transportation. The Fallingwater workers cut the stone to Wright's specifications, and the stones' local origin helped fulfill his insistence on organically integrating the house with the site.

The building itself was constructed entirely by local labor. WPA projects had cut into the local skilled labor pool, and the men available to work at Fallingwater tended to show up according to their own schedules. Wright's on-site representatives were continually irked by what they considered country workmen geared to a country pace (Hoffmann, p. 57).

The masons had to be trained to lay stone to Wright's specifications. He demanded that the masonry pattern simulate the natural layering of the strata in the surrounding area, with courses that varied in thickness and intermittently protruded from the face of the wall. The bridge across the stream was constructed first. It pleased no one and was later torn down and rebuilt. The stonework became more accomplished as work went on, and the masonry of the guest wing was noticeably smoother than that constructed earlier.

Laying the stone to Wright's satisfaction was an
educational experience for local masons.

Except in the baths and kitchen, flagstone from the area covers the floors throughout. Wright made every effort to eliminate the barrier between inside and outside, and he specified that the flagstone be coated with Johnson's Wax® to imitate the sheen of wet river rock.

The Chain of Command

Few building sites are blessed with continuous harmony, but the construction of Fallingwater presented challenges beyond the ordinary. In addition to the inherent difficulty of the project, the work was complicated by the number of people with authority, and at times no one seemed to get along with anyone else.

Wright's Deputies   Though determined to control every detail of the building, Wright made only three recorded visits to the site during construction. When questions and conflicts arose, correspondence (sometimes heated) flew between the architect and client, engineers, representatives, contractor, and apprentices. Wright assigned two of his apprentices, first Bob Mosher and later Edgar Tafel, and then Bob Mosher again, as his clerks of the works and personal representatives.

Both young men were able but inexperienced. They were in the difficult position of having to guess what Wright's answer would be to any question that arose, decide to go ahead with improvisations or wait, settle engineering disputes, and establish their authority over contractors and workmen a generation older than they.

Dombar and Zeller and Thumm and Hall   Abe Dombar, a former Taliesin apprentice, was working at Kaufmann's store when construction began at Fallingwater. He served as the first clerk of the works, but was soon withdrawn by Wright, who refused to pay him a salary because he considered Dombar still an apprentice. For a while, N.J. Zeller, a local masonry contractor, was in sole charge. Zeller tried to start construction, but was hampered by Wright's laggard delivery of detailed plans—a problem that continued throughout the project. The unlucky Zeller disappeared from Fallingwater for good when he was jailed for nonsupport in June (Hoffmann, p. 37).

During construction, E.J. Kaufmann could visit Bear Run only on weekends, so he appointed one of the store's assistant managers, Carl F. Thumm, as his permanent representative at the building site. Thumm performed valuable services, expediting material deliveries and overseeing the construction, but he annoyed Wright and disliked the official contractor, Walter J. Hall.

When construction started at Fallingwater, Hall was working on his own project, an inn near Port Allegheny, Pennsylvania. He had conceived an admiration for Wright years before and was eager for the chance to work on one of Wright's buildings. Perhaps that admiration was what recommended him to Wright, who often used "unholy" and "contractor" as one word. In any event, under trying circumstances, Hall was remarkably faithful to Wright's vision.

Bob Mosher frequently argued with Hall and thought it the height of stupidity when Hall built the construction shed and stored materials at the very edge of the second-floor terrace—the loading point creating the greatest bending moment. However, the engineering tests that went on during construction loaded the terraces even more severely without exceeding their capacities.

Edgar Kaufmann junior made frequent visits and suggestions, sometimes unwelcomed, and engineering controversies continued. The new techniques and garbled communications led to a couple of mistakes that created permanent problems, as we shall see in Chapter 3.

Although slowed by the stew of authorities, growing worry over concrete cracks, and inexperienced labor, work progressed. The shell of the house was largely completed by the end of 1936. By the fall of 1937 enough of the finish work was completed for the Kaufmanns to begin using the house. The guest wing was completed in 1939.

The Test of Time

In spite of problems during construction, the house has held up magnificently—aesthetically, structurally, and as a magnet for the public. After almost 60 years, its sweeping lines are in no way dated; it is a distinct mental shock to imagine automobiles of the 1930s pulling up to a "house of the future."

Whether because of its daring design or because of public curiosity about Wright (which he did everything possible to encourage) or because the nation just needed something splendid to contemplate during the Depression, the secluded weekend retreat became famous before it was finished.

As well as being featured in architectural publications in 1938, Wright and Fallingwater appeared on the January 17, 1938, cover of *Time* magazine, and were given a special exhibition at the Museum of Modern Art. During the Kaufmanns' years there, the house became a place of pilgrimage for leading figures from the architectural and museum worlds and was often filled with personal friends.

Frank Lloyd Wright. The Guggenheim museum is under construction in the background. (Photo courtesy of Western Pennsylvania Conservancy.)

Structural Survival

Cracks in the parapets, which might have forecast structural failure, continued to worry E.J. Kaufmann until his death in 1955. However, the following year, Fallingwater met and passed an extreme test of stability. Edgar junior recounts,

> ...*August, 1956, Bear Run and Fallingwater were both put to an extraordinary test. One weekend afternoon with the usual company in residence, a great tornado hit our area square on. Violent rain and wind whipped in; the run rose rapidly above its banks—one could see it expanding minute by minute. For exterior painting, the house was girt in wooden scaffolding that was hung from parapets on three sides, and gusts of wind shook the gross temporary structure to and fro. The house was being racked. It was terrifying; we were trapped in a house subjected to huge strains no one had ever foreseen. Would it hold up?...*

> *We attempted to loosen nails in the scaffolding to let the lumber be carried away—trying to reduce stress on the building—but the wood, swollen with water, kept a tight grip; the effort was useless. Meanwhile, movable furniture in living room and kitchen was piled up off the floor, for water had risen higher than the terrace parapets... Ankle-deep in water, we looked over an alien lake obliterating the glen and shoving restlessly against glass doors, while the wind howled and rain poured down in wild sheets...*

> *The next morning we awoke to a house thick with sludge. The banks of Bear Run were ravaged, large areas of native rhododendron were torn out, smaller boulders were swept away, trees were down... Two bronze statues, set outdoors near the house, had disappeared, Lipchitz's Mother and Child and a Marini horseman... if a building were in danger of collapse that test would have made it evident; Fallingwater came through structurally unscathed. (Kaufmann, pp. 62–64)*

Edgar Kaufmann junior.
(Photo by Kenneth Love, courtesy of Western Pennsylvania Conservancy.)

The Western Pennsylvania Conservancy

Before E.J. Kaufmann's death, father and son decided that Fallingwater should eventually be a gift to the public. Edgar junior returned to, and watched over, the house throughout the years of his career as a scholar of architectural history, and in 1963 he transferred ownership of the house to the Western Pennsylvania Conservancy.

The Conservancy, with funding from the Kaufmann Foundation, has done much vital maintenance on the house and has opened it to the public. To further protect the Bear Run watershed, the original acreage has been more than doubled. An innovative Visitors' Center designed by Paul Mayen, parking lots, and paths to the house were installed in the 1980s; all accessory and maintenance buildings are visually apart from the house itself.

Summary

Fallingwater is open every day for both brief and extended tours except Monday, from April through mid-November. Tours are available the remainder of the year on Saturdays and Sundays, weather permitting. In 1992, more than 135,000 visitors traveled to this somewhat isolated spot. The house that, according to *New York Times* architecture critic Paul Goldberger, "summed up the 20th century and then thrust it forward still further," has not lost its immediacy.

Before and After Fallingwater

An old design dictum says, "Always Visit the Site First." You really shouldn't ignore it. We visited Fallingwater in May 1993. As with most site visits, this one changed both our sense of the house and our strategies and goals for modeling, rendering, and animating (MRA) it. In describing how the site visit changed our thinking about the house, this chapter discusses factors, limitations, and priorities that affect using modeling, rendering, and animation for a typical architectural project.

Many volumes have been written about Wright, often concentrating on his excessively dramatic life. Before the site visit, we had absorbed the popular theories about Wright: that he embodied functional democratic architecture by designing houses from the inside out, that it was all done by pure inspiration, that his use of strong horizontals was in response to the expanses of the midwestern prairie, and so on. Fallingwater itself seemed an imposing and somewhat forbidding Monument to Great Architecture.

Site Reconnaissance: The House

Seen from the path to the Visitors' Center, the house still matched the image in our heads; there, through the trees, was Fallingwater, just like the photographs. As we drew closer and entered, it changed—in terms of sound, scale, tactile quality, and formality.

Contextualism and the Surrounding Area

We half expected that the house would be surrounded by the sort of "Get your Fallingwater Burgers here" detritus typical of tourist sites. But only a few small signs on the highway announce Fallingwater, hidden in the forest with only the Visitors' Center for company.

The house is utterly symbiotic with its site, but has not the slightest contextual reference to the architecture of the region—foursquare farm houses with pitched roofs and porches and great, swelling three-story barns. Nothing could be more different from the wheeling energy of Fallingwater and its tenuous boundary between house and nature.

Local people display a dignified acceptance that the most famous house in the world is in their neighborhood. Yes, it's real pretty and brings in a lot of business, but let's not get carried away. As a cartoon tacked on the wall of a local cafe says:

> *Frank Lloyd Wright built Fallingwater*
> *Where one would think he hadn't oughter.*

The House and the Stream

Just reading that the falls can't be seen from the house in no way conveys the almost-edgy feeling that something momentous is happening just beyond one's peripheral vision. By pulling the house out over the falls, Wright destroyed the separation between spectators and the view they observed—a convention of observing Nature from the outside that had held sway since the Romantic era.

The house works as a natural event dynamically enmeshed in time. Neil Levine, Professor and Chairman of Fine Arts, Harvard University, makes a subtle and powerful point: "The extraordinary thing about Fallingwater is that it never stops. When one leaves, one expects it to be turned off—but it *can't* be." (*The Friends of Fallingwater Newsletter, Vol.1, #1.* p.5)

Without visiting, one can't get the full sense of the building as the ultimate water house: the unceasing sound of water flowing past and under, water in fountains, mist rising from the stream, water seeping from the cliff face, Lipchitz's half-amphibian water goddess. The omniscience of water has also demanded a constant battle against its effects on some of the finish materials—wood warping or losing its luster, rebar rusting, stucco damaged by efflorescence.

The Elusive Scale

In photographs, the house is almost pompous in its monumentality. When confronted, the house constantly performs tricks of scale, depending on the location of the observer. Watching from the bridge over the stream, it is jolting to see people walk out onto the terraces.

Conditioned by standardized ceiling heights, one unconsciously reads the bearing plates as 8 or 9 feet high and the terrace parapet walls as a standard $3\frac{1}{2}$ feet, but the bearing plates are at 7 feet 1 inch and the parapets only rise to mid-thigh. When people are present for comparison, the house seems to shrink to $\frac{7}{8}$ scale. Seen from the stream below, it grows again, swelling to the imposing bulk of a hydroelectric dam seen from a fish's viewpoint.

Seen against the low bearing plates and parapets, visitors on the terrace seem oversized. (Photo, Sanchez)

From below, the house is, literally, overbearing.
(Photo by Harold Corsini, courtesy of Western Pennsylvania Conservancy.)

The Details

The rich, tactile articulation of the interior surfaces equals in impact the famous drama of the exterior, but the impact of detail is diluted by two-dimensional photographs. The presence of a dynamic and cosmopolitan family lingers in the collection of sculpture, prints, and paintings placed wherever there's room.

This visual feast is not intimidating; the art is of the highest quality, but casual, playful. Much of it is Asian or Latin American, rather than more formal nineteenth-century or aggressive twentieth-century Western works. Four pieces by Mexican sculptor Mardonio Magaña seem the true inhabitants of the house. They come out at night when everyone has left, and go about their business, undecided about letting us reproduce their world.

The children and their dog, sculpted by Mardonio Magaña, play under the stair canopy during the day. (Photo by Lynda Waggoner, courtesy of Western Pennsylvania Conservancy.)

The house is full of unexpected recesses and odd turns; perhaps they were necessary to make everything fit together, but they also give to spaces a childlike, secretive playfulness. Perhaps no one knew exactly how certain details would turn out until they were built, but what could have been unfortunate accidents were turned into further embellishments.

The desktops in the two studies weren't big enough, and the windows were in the way of expanding them. As shown in the following illustration, Wright simply had quarter-circles cut out of the tops, achieving bigger work surfaces and playing a new note on the circle theme that appears throughout the house.

To give more working room, the study desks were extended to the corner mullions and quarter-circles were cut out to allow the casement windows to open. A bust of Edgar Kaufmann junior by Richmond Barthe is on the desk. (Photo by Harold Corsini, courtesy of Western Pennsylvania Conservancy.)

Almost all of the architectural detailing was custom-fabricated: cabinetry, window frames and glazing, metalwork. It was the opposite of the Usonian concept of low-cost housing achieved through the use of prefabricated parts, but it gave Wright the opportunity to give every detail one more twist. The design elements of the house are repeated in ever-decreasing scale, which gives the house a satisfying unity, but promised to complicate the process of reproducing it with a computer model.

The baluster hangers on the east exterior staircase were given a half-circle terminus and painted Cherokee red to pick up the red circle accents throughout the house.

MRA Strategies: The Basic Approach

The following considerations define basic parameters and sequences that should be established before beginning an MRA project. As in any process, the further upstream a decision is made, the greater cumulative effect it will have.

Study Models Versus Presentation Models

The first decision you have to make affects all future work: what *type* of model do you need? The two major categories—study and presentation—have different purposes, and therefore different requirements and different sequences for completing them. The appropriate level of detail varies as greatly as that of traditional model-building, from foamcore board stuck together with straight pins to fully detailed Plexiglas models with surrounding buildings and entourage.

MRA programs are great fun to play with; it's easy to get drawn into days (or weeks) of modeling details, messing around with surfaces and experimenting with animations. If you have time, have at it! It sounds simplistic to say it, but if your time is limited, decide first on the basic requirements and stick to them.

To complicate matters, the categories of design and presentation often overlap. The Fallingwater project combines functions of both types. The project concentrates on study-model aspects, for reasons explained later, but also includes many of the operations typically used for presentation models in order to demonstrate more of the capabilities of 3D Studio.

Study Models   Study models fit into the design process by reducing, refining, and dissecting. The first burst of exploring and expanding is done, and the next step narrows down the number of schemes and makes adjustments to the most successful. Subcategories of study models include massing, interior, lighting, and structural models.

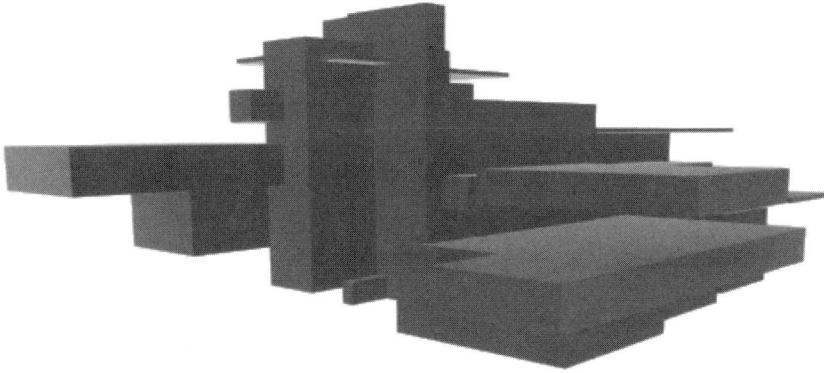

A massing study model. Stripping Fallingwater down to a collection of simplified planes and volumes clarifies the basic geometry.

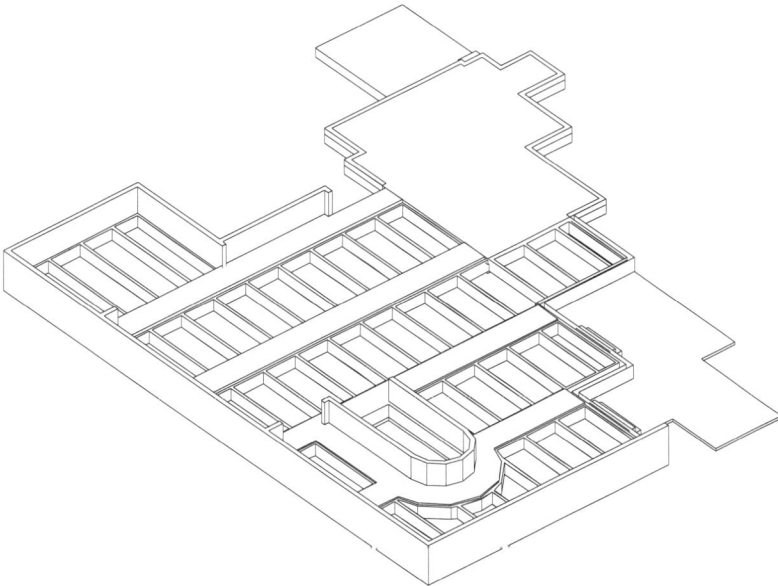

A structural study model. Peeling the "skin" off the first floor reveals the waffle slab construction and its relation to bearing surfaces.

The most effective level of detail for a model depends on its specific purpose. You need take the process no further than is necessary to explore the immediate consideration:

❏ If you need a massing model, a rendering using generic materials and the overall dimensions of the exterior planes will suffice.

❏ If you're investigating specific design options, such as the effect of different wall heights, a wireframe perspective generated from the plan is sufficient.

❏ If you're deciding on surface colors or materials, you can use 3D Studio to render only selection windows or individual objects within a scene.

❏ If you're refining the depth of overhangs, or different layouts for skylights, you can set up a simplified partial model and use simulated sunlight to test different arrangements.

Being drawn too far into details carries three risks. You use up time that invariably will be needed later in the project. Too much detail sometimes obscures the very problem you're trying to solve. Pouring time and effort into a single solution often has the effect of making the designer fall in love with that solution and remain faithful to it ever after, no matter what its faults.

❏ Study Models: Typical Givens

    ❏ Requirements of the client's program

    ❏ Budget, building code, and site constraints

    ❏ What, and how much, of the design is considered finalized (For example, someone has determined that there *will* be a barrel vault lobby, and everything else will just have to fit around it.)

    ❏ Structural and mechanical requirements

❏ Study Models: Typical Options

    ❏ What particular problem do you want to investigate?

    ❏ How many solutions to the problem do you want to explore?

    ❏ Other elements of the building will be affected by how you solve the particular problem you're studying. How many of these peripheral elements do you want to include in the model?

    ❏ How far do you want to take the modeling process before proceeding to design development?

Presentation Models Presentation models are tools for illustrating, explaining, and convincing. To some extent, a presentation model adopts the client's (or potential client's) viewpoint, concentrating on the experience rather than the anatomy of a building.

Creating a presentation model starts by defining its desired effect. The next step is working backward to decide the minimum information necessary to produce that effect. When work starts on the presentation model, the building design—plans, elevations, interior features, materials, and engineering—is often near completion. Subcategories of presentation models include models for client approval, models entered in design competitions, models used by developers to sell space in a proposed project, and as-built models used for historical documentation.

How far to take detailing is a judgment call. It's tempting to make finish work, lighting, materials, and entourage as elaborate as possible to impress the client, but sometimes an overwhelming amount of detail can distract the client from the basic factors that will determine the final decision to go ahead or not.

A view of the living room from a walkthrough animation. The level of detail is medium. Compare with the photographs of the living room in Chapter 3.

❏ Some questions to consider when planning a Presentation Model:

   ❏ What minimum level of realism is necessary?

   ❏ How much time do you have? Have you done a project that's similar enough to give you an accurate time estimate?

   ❏ Does your firm specify a fixed percentage for the cost of a presentation to the cost of design work to the cost of the building project? If so, is it adequate for MRA? Does the budget allotment have to cover other types of presentation?

   ❏ Will the client pay a higher fee for your increased capabilities?

   ❏ What's the competition going to do?

   ❏ Is a computerized presentation required? (This is rare now, but it will become more common.)

   ❏ Can you do it all yourself or do you have adequately experienced staff to help, or should parts of the work be farmed out?

   ❏ In what setting will the presentation be seen? Will you be there to explain and discuss the model? Will you have to bring, and operate, your own hardware to display your model? Will you furnish hard copy along with the computer model?

❏ Presentation Models: Typical Givens

   ❏ Date when the model must be finished

   ❏ Budget allotment

   ❏ The developed design

   ❏ Availability of experienced personnel and equipment

❏ Presentation Models: Typical Options

   ❏ What special features of the design do you want to emphasize?

   ❏ How much of the surrounding area should you include?

   ❏ How elaborate and detailed do you want to make the presentation?

   ❏ How much latitude in matching design specifications is acceptable? This is an ethical and contractual question as well as a technical one. For instance, you might be rendering a marble tile wall covering. Two library textures are close, but one looks better than the actual material, and the other not as good. Which do you use? Be very careful to spell out to the client exactly what is going on.

Realistic Goals

The Really Hot Stuff gets into the computer graphics magazines. Most of these cutting-edge renderings take a lot of time, experience, and equipment. You don't have to start with fully detailed, landscaped, fly-through animations to achieve a competent and cost-effective result. It's better to start with a modest goal and actually get it done than to plan an Old Dutch Master and dissolve into frustration and deadline guilt.

At an A/E/C Systems '93 Seminar, Bob Bennett, Senior Product Manager of Autodesk's Multimedia Division, recommended the following strategies when beginning to use 3D Studio:

❏ Don't try it the first time on a hard deadline. If possible, experiment with an already completed project.

❏ Don't attempt to use multiple new technologies all at once. Pick a skill that you have already mastered, and try to extend your ability in that direction with one new tool at a time.

❏ Draw on local resources. When you start learning a new skill, try to locate knowledgeable experts in your area—colleagues, user groups, schools, or vendors.

Time   An early rule of thumb for estimating MRA time was to make a generous guess of how long you thought it would take, and then multiply by ten. Increasingly powerful hardware and software have speeded up the process greatly, but it is still time-consuming. For individual users the process gets much quicker with subsequent renderings as the operator's experience increases and libraries of reusable or adjustable files are compiled.

The time spent on animations is particularly elastic and depends primarily on getting the most viewing time out of the least amount of modeling and rendering effort. A videotape presentation can be lengthened by pausing, sweeping in one direction and then back, reversing action, and inserting drawings and live video into the animation sequences. Deciding on efficient camera paths before modeling and rendering everything saves great amounts of time.

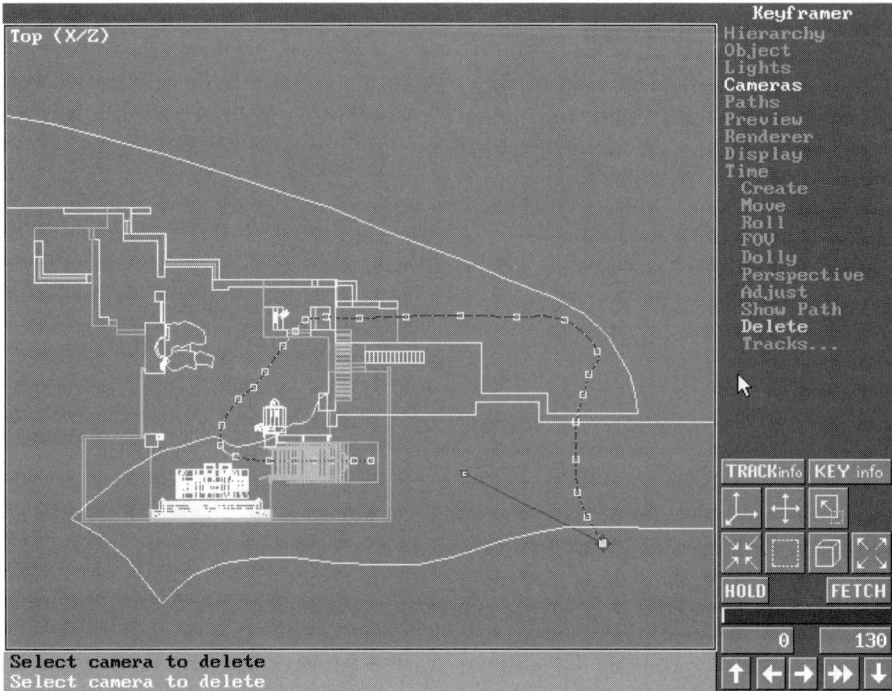

The curving line marks a path for the camera to follow for a walk-through animation. The field of view is limited, thus reducing the area that must be modeled in detail. Animation is discussed in detail in Chapters 6 and 9.

MRA Is an Iterative Process

It's not a good idea to work all the way through one stage of the MRA process before experimenting with the downstream stages. Just as one would not begin designing a building by drawing a finished foundation plan, then a detailed floor plan, and so on, completely finishing the model before investigating rendering and animation requirements is an invitation to trouble.

For the Fallingwater project, we built enough of the model to test material applications, textures, lights, and minimum levels of detail needed; and then went ahead with test animations to get an idea of file sizes, frame intervals, and walk-through paths. This information determined how detailed the entire structural model needed to be, which areas would need further detailing, where modeled furnishings were needed, what textures and materials needed further experimentation, and most importantly, which areas were so impossible to duplicate that they needed to be finessed completely.

Having stressed this point, the organization of this book ignores it in order to avoid skipping back and forth from one operation to another. So, do as we say, not as this book does.

Summary

The physical experience of visiting the house—both alone and as part of a crowd—overwhelmed preconceived theoretical notions and abstract plans. The scope of the house and the vastness of 3D Studio's capabilities combined to force a ruthless weeding out of embellishments that would be great fun but were irrelevant to the essential goals of the project.

Reality will do it every time, and at some point every project goes through a similar focusing and weeding process. So, visit the site, count up the hours available, decide your priorities, and then go to work.

Building the Model

This chapter explores the spaces and structure of Fallingwater and the initial stages of an MRA project. After a brief look at the levels of the house, the major portion of the chapter describes the strategies for building the model in AutoCAD—how to handle files, what to do first, how to do it, and what to leave out on the first modeling pass.

The chapter concludes with two detailed exercises for using 3D Studio. You can use the exercises, in combination with the distribution disk files, to:

❏ Model Fallingwater's three foundation bolsters with 3D Studio.

❏ Import the *.dxf* file of the foundation into 3D Studio and merge it with the *.3ds* bolster file to complete the foundation.

The Levels of the House

Frank Lloyd Wright spoke often and long about the virtues of democratic architecture. In theoretical terms, an architecture suited to the American public rejected formal, hierarchical living spaces and opulent decoration so that free men and women could live as they naturally, organically should (or rather, as Wright thought they should). In practical terms, the theory reinforced Wright's development of the open floor plan—a design mode now so prevalent as to seem inevitable, but drastically new in its time.

The Main Level

The living room at Fallingwater makes masterful use of the open plan. This main room contains approximately 825 square feet, around 30% of the enclosed area, and flows into two large terraces on the southeast and southwest, visually adding another 400 square feet to the only large space in the house.

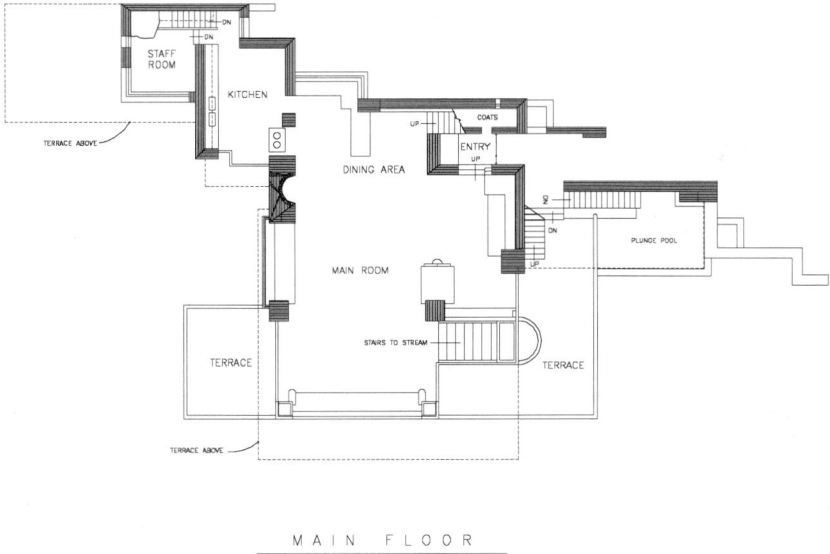

MAIN FLOOR

The main-level floor plan.

The living room space is articulated, clockwise from the entry, into music, study, L-shaped sitting, hearth, and dining areas. The large room is empty in the center, in front of the hearth with its aisle of living rock.

The house was centered on the great boulder that forms the living room hearth. E.J. Kaufmann insisted that the top of the boulder remain in its natural state where it rose through the floor. (Photo by Kenneth Love, courtesy of Western Pennsylvania Conservancy.)

The low room is stretched between rock and light; windows surround the south and stone surround the north. Small support areas—kitchen, staff room, stairs, and entry—adjoin the main area, directing circulation across the dark, north side of the room. Visual circulation is pulled out to the windows wrapping around the south side and to the flanking terraces. The east and west terraces are not connected; Wright doled out carefully the experience of the setting.

The south end of the living room. (Photo by Kenneth Love, courtesy of Western Pennsylvania Conservancy.)

Rock surrounds the dining area at the north end of the main room. At the rear is the main staircase. (Photo courtesy Donald Hoffmann.)

The Foundation Level

Along the north side of the house, 18-inch-thick concrete retaining walls plunge down beside the road to support the back wall and form three small basement rooms. Across the west end of the house, the perimeter foundation wall marches on, engulfing boulders in its path. Above grade, masonry replaces concrete, rising at the east end to form the walls behind the plunge pool. There is no south foundation wall, but a series of piers running to the stream bed.

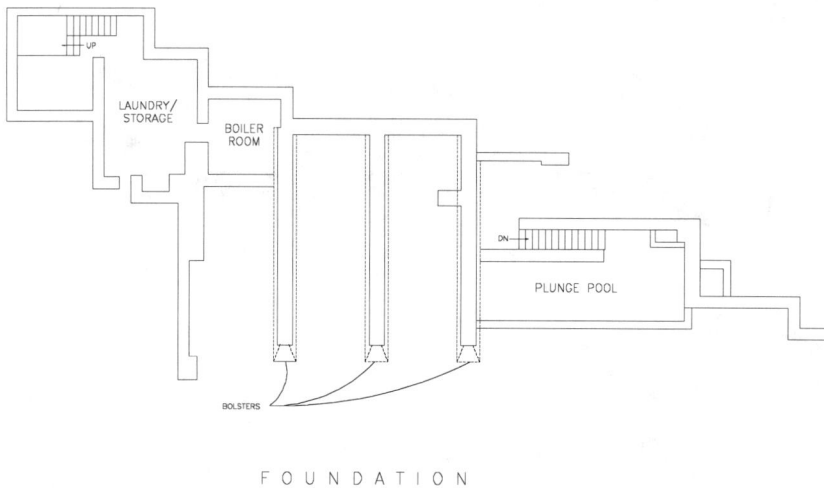

FOUNDATION

The foundation-level floor plan. The three tapered bolsters were poured concrete on masonry footings. They deeply upset the consulting engineers. The three rooms serve as stair landing, laundry and storage, and boiler room.

The Bolsters   The great cantilever of the main floor is carried by the west foundation wall and the three bolsters. The poured concrete bolsters flare out from a base only 15 inches wide to a 3 foot width at the top, and rest on a 2-foot-wide masonry footing. The consulting engineers argued unsuccessfully that the footing should be widened to 3 feet. They also objected to placing the ends of the bolsters directly at the stream side.

The Waffle Slabs   Fallingwater's cantilevered terraces required reinforced concrete. Wright used a waffle slab design with the main 24-inch-square north-south beams supported by the bolsters and the west wall. To support the stairwell opening leading down to the stream, the last beam on the east thickens to 3 feet in width and curves into a half-circle beyond the end of the bolsters.

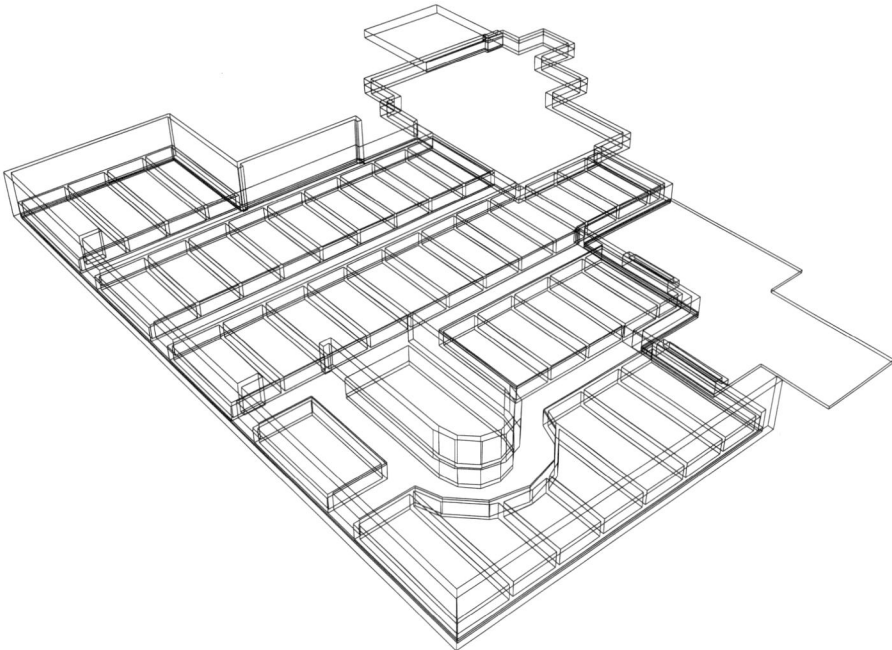

A perspective drawing of the first-floor waffle slab.

The terraces droop a little, like the wings of an airplane at rest. There is no sign that this sag indicates any kind of structural failure, but the deflection has been a source of worry and controversy ever since the house was built. Several theories were advanced for its cause.

The forms for the concrete pour, put together out of 1 x 8s, were absolutely level, producing a slab "straight as a schoolmarm's leg," as Hall expressed it. No one thought to build in any camber to compensate for the normal deflection, with the result that the cantilevered terraces sagged between $1\frac{1}{2}$ and 2 inches when the scaffolding was removed. When the flagstone flooring was installed, the deflection increased another half-inch.

E.J. Kaufmann worried about the 18-foot extent of the cantilever that held the living room and its terraces. The plans supplied by Wright were not overly detailed, and Kaufmann hired Metzger-Richardson, a Pittsburgh firm of engineers and steel suppliers, to furnish more specific structural drawings as well as the steel reinforcing. The engineers specified twice the amount of reinforcing as shown in the original plans, and the steel was placed without consulting Wright (Hoffmann, p. 43).

The 12 extra 1-inch-square steel bars add less than 1 pound per square foot to the weight of the heavy concrete and flagstone structure. Thus, it seems questionable that the weight of the steel caused the sag, but Wright seized on the extra weight as the reason for the deflection, getting so upset that he summoned Bob Mosher back to Wisconsin and sent Edgar Tafel to supervise instead.

Wright maintained that "folding up" the edges of the slab to form the parapet walls would strengthen the structure, as the edges of a shoe box top strengthen the flat rectangle of cardboard (Kaufmann, p. 109). The parapet walls were necessary for the design—Wright would have insisted on them to reflect the shape of the rock ledges—but it is debatable whether the stronger shape was enough to offset the extra weight of the concrete parapets.

The Upper Levels

Wright was often rather cursory about the bedroom zone of a house, preferring to concentrate on the main living areas. In spite of his verbal insistence that a house should be designed from the inside out to reflect the living habits of its owners, at Fallingwater the plan is controlled more by the aesthetics of the exterior than by standard principles of efficient room layout.

The same themes introduced in the living room continue in the upper bedroom levels—terraces fronting each room, rock playing against glass, low ceilings forcing the view outward through banks of windows on the south—but the window scale and grid pattern is subtly adjusted, and the building profile steps back up the hill.

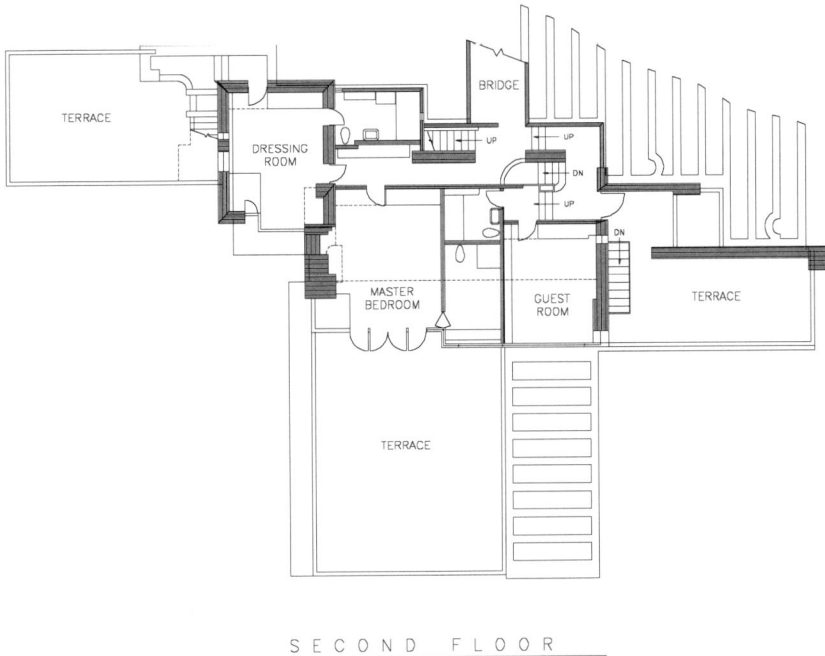

S E C O N D   F L O O R

The second-level floor plan. The trellis grid and passage to the guest wing extend from the upper right across the drive.

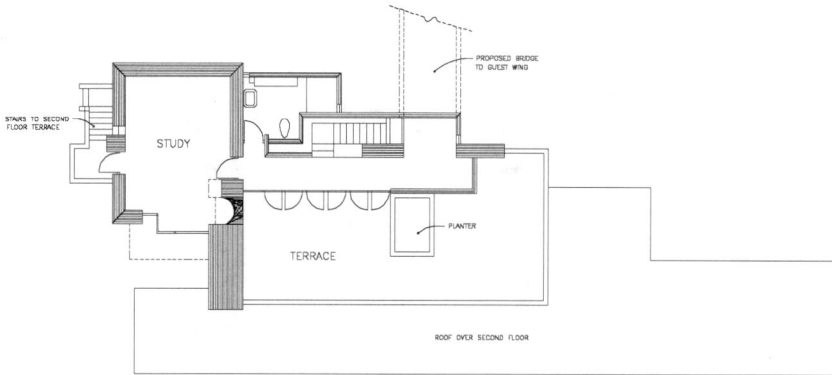

STUDY

PROPOSED BRIDGE
TO GUEST WING

PLANTER

TERRACE

ROOF OVER SECOND FLOOR

T H I R D   F L O O R

The third-level floor plan contains only one actual room, which Edgar Kaufmann junior used for a study, and, of course, a large terrace.

The West Terrace   On the west side of the masonry tower, another terrace extends the sweep of the rising curve of rock ledges and terraces on the south side of the building. E.J. Kaufmann toyed with the concept of using the west terrace for his elusive swimming pool. Wright firmly rejected the idea; even his structural daring wasn't up to accepting the extra load of hundreds of cubic feet of water.

The main support of the 28-foot-long terrace is a single concrete beam 18 inches wide and 3 feet deep. Narrower transverse beams extend from the main beams; three of them are keyed directly into a boulder by the side of the drive.

The west terrace, shown in the foreground, proved a rich source of engineering controversies. (Photo by Thomas A. Heinz, courtesy of Western Pennsylvania Conservancy.)

The Guest Wing Access   At Fallingwater, guests went off to bed through a procession of architectural fireworks. Once beyond the passageway with its tiny sculpture garden and Diego Rivera painting, a visitor exits to a tightly curled stair, which switches back on itself as it climbs the hill. The canopy over the stairway is another structural experiment: it forms linked half-circles; it is "folded" at intervals to raise its clearance to follow the stairs' rise; it is supported on only one side with steel posts. (See color plates II and IX.)

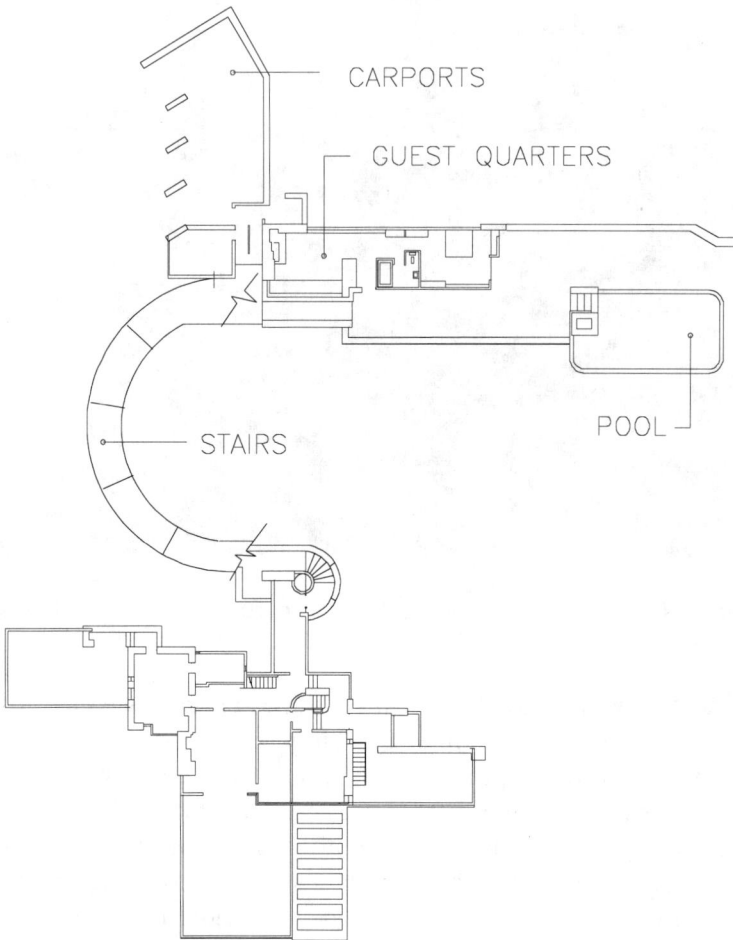

CARPORTS

GUEST QUARTERS

STAIRS

POOL

A plan schematic of the passage, double-curve stairs, and guest wing. The upper floor of the guest wing and carports now serve as offices for the Western Pennsylvania Conservancy.

The trellis over the drive ties into the cliff face and blurs the transition between inside and outside. Half-circles were formed in two of the reinforced trellis beams so that they would curve around existing trees. Beyond and behind the trellis, the second-level passageway leads to steps up to the guest wing. (Photo by Thomas A. Heinz, courtesy of Western Pennsylvania Conservancy.)

The Chimney Tower   The masonry tower that anchors the central and west portions of the building is the only uniform and continuous vertical element in the house. Starting at the basement, its walls enclose a storage area, the small kitchen on the main floor, and two studies on the upper levels. Flues from the four fireplaces rise through the tower's east wall. The three-story window rises without a break, appearing to enclose a continuous vertical space. Floating behind the glazing, the bottom edges of the slab are tapered up to meet the narrow steel window grid.

AutoCAD Modeling for 3D Studio Rendering

AutoCAD and 3D Studio are designed for different jobs. AutoCAD was developed and refined as a general-purpose drafting engine. 3D Studio is intended for uses both more flexible and more specific—everything from modeling little space creatures to animating titles to metamorphosing objects from one shape or material to another. Although 3D Studio can import .*dxf* files from other programs, the ideal setup for a project like this is AutoCAD Release 12 with AME (Advanced Modeling Extension) plus 3D Studio Release 3.

Some of AutoCAD's drawing tools, lacking in 3D Studio, make AutoCAD easier to use when modeling complex rectilinear objects:

❑ AutoCAD's Ortho mode forces lines into horizontal and vertical alignment.

❑ AutoCAD has geometric filters (object snaps) that allow you to latch onto mid-points of lines, centers of arcs and circles, and so forth.

❑ Solid modeling operations are more developed in AutoCAD.

❑ Inquiry commands in AutoCAD are stronger.

Whether you are producing dimensioned construction documents or making a three-dimensional (3D) model, in most cases the first step is making a two-dimensional (2D) floor plan. If the floor plan already exists in AutoCAD (a common situation) there's no point in redrawing it in 3D Studio because you can easily import it.

However, 3D Studio's sophisticated extrusion capabilities perform some architectural modeling operations much more easily than does AutoCAD. We'll look at one in this chapter—modeling the bolsters—and explore others in depth in Chapter 7 when modeling details.

Working with 3D Studio and AutoCAD Files

3D Studio separates the parts of a model into individual "objects" for manipulating and rendering. This separation into objects serves the same purpose as AutoCAD's separation into layers and colors. When importing a .*dxf* file into 3D Studio, you can specify that the model be separated into objects by layers, colors, or entities. Layers is the default and was the importing mode used in this project.

3D Studio normally assigns materials, hides or unhides, and changes model geometry by object. Therefore, as in any rendering program, you need to consider future operations, such as which materials will be applied to which components, when deciding what to put on each layer of the AutoCAD model.

The files for this project have a basic two-tier organization. Each original.*dxf* file consisted of a single floor level of the building: foundation, main level, second level, and so on. Within each file, the components of that floor level were separated into layers by material: all masonry walls on one layer, all concrete walls on one layer, all window casings on one layer, and so on.

The following chart diagrams the steps for bringing a *.dxf* file into 3D Studio, working on it, and rendering it. (If the original modeling is done in 3D Studio, there are additional file types involved that will be discussed in later chapters.)

```
 ①  LAYERS         ②  AUTOCAD        ③  EXPORT FROM      ④  IMPORT TO
                       FILE              AUTOCAD            3D STUDIO

 L1-FLOOR                                 ▷
 L1-MWALL                              L1-COMB.DXF
 L1-CWALL      ▷  L1-COMB.DWG  ─┤                    ▷ L1-COMB.3DS  ─▷
 L1-WINS                               L1-COMB.FLM
 L1-GLAZ                                  ▷


 ⑤  SEPARATE       ⑥  COMBINE        ⑦  OUTPUT
    INTO OBJECTS       TO RENDER         FORMAT

                                                        ▷
                                                    L1-COMB.TIF
          ▷                                         L1-COMB.TGA
 L1-FLOOR                                            L1-COMB.GIF
 L1-MWALL                                               ▷
 L1-CWALL           ▷  L1-COMB.3DS  ─────┤
 L1-WINS                                                ▷
 L1-GLAZ                                             L1-COMB.FLI
          ▷                                         (320 x 200)

     object             or render                   L1-COMB.FLC
     element            by object                   (640 X 480+)
     face               or region                      ▷
     vertex
```

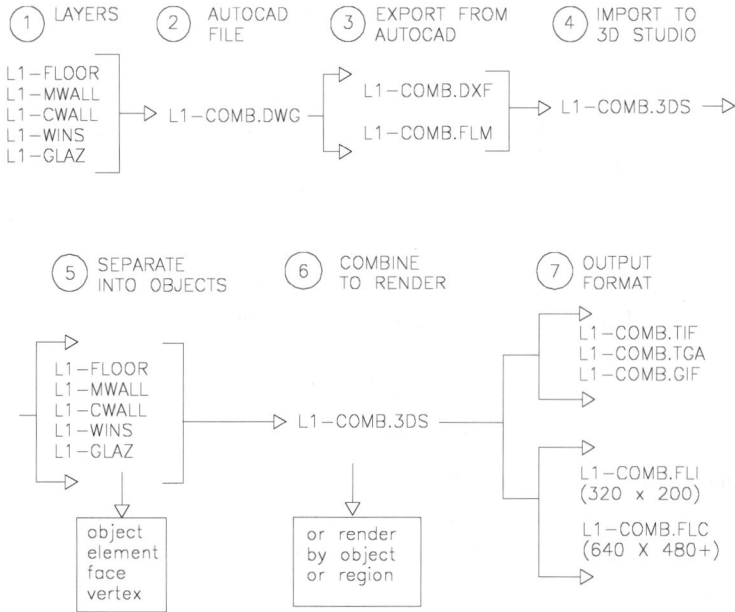

The project file trail.

1. The different components (walls, slab, windows, etc.) of each level of the building are modeled on separate layers.

2. All the layers for level 1 are combined in an AutoCAD *.dwg* file.

3. The file is typically exported from AutoCAD as a *.dxf* file. It can also be exported as a filmroll file, *.flm,* which is about a tenth of the size, but which can only separate the components into objects by colors.

4. 3D Studio assigns a *.3ds* extension to the file the first time it is saved.

5. The *.3ds* file is automatically separated into objects corresponding to the layers. 3D Studio includes commands that can further separate each object into elements, faces, and vertices as needed.

6. When you are ready to render the scene, 3D Studio can render the entire scene or selected objects or the contents of a selection window.

7. The rendering can be output in a variety of file formats. Still shots can be in the default *.gif, .tif, .tga,* or several other bitmap file formats.

Animations will be output as flic files, *.fli* if they are Autodesk Animator files at 320 x 200 resolution. All other flic files use the *.flc* extension, regardless of their resolution.

The second exercise in this chapter takes you through the sequence of importing a *.dxf* file into 3D Studio and combining it accurately with objects modeled in 3D Studio.

What to Leave Out and What to Include

The general concept is not to drown yourself in complexity by attempting to do everything at once. Drown yourself a little bit at a time. This project began with building a simplified model. Then, another pass added the structural "insides" to the floor slabs. Later, architectural detailing was added as needed, depending on the paths and views chosen for renderings.

We limited detail on the first modeling pass by:

❏ Ignoring the interpenetration of building elements with the site, modeling the structure as a self-contained object.

❏ Modeling surface geometry only, leaving out features such as floor structural members and decking.

❏ Assigning each wall a single thickness, disregarding the uneven surface of the stone and minor indentations.

❏ Leaving off the heating/seating, shelving, and other built-in features.

❏ Modeling only the window grids, without the operable casements and glazing.

Building the Model with AutoCAD

This section describes the modeling sequence for the main level of the building and the procedures used. The order of the steps is tailored to modeling Fallingwater—already built, very complicated, and lacking a complete paper trail of design documents. Other projects may require a different sequence of steps.

Whatever the situation, it's a good idea to start with the building component that is most completely documented or developed, and then move on to areas of ever-greater fuzziness, extrapolating missing or conflicting data. When you begin a project, what you consider as *given* has a huge effect on how much grief you may cause yourself.

Establish a Reference Point and Draw the Floor Plan

Young Bob Mosher arrived at Bear Run to oversee the construction of Fallingwater. Looking down the steep slope at the tangle of rhododendrons and boulders, Mosher asked Frank Lloyd Wright where the main floor level would be in relation to the wild and tilted terrain. Wright pointed out a large boulder and told Mosher to climb up on it. After Mosher had scrambled through the bushes and pulled himself up on the rock, Wright told him that the rock would be the datum, or floor level, and left for Wisconsin. (Hoffman, p. 34)

It was much simpler setting up a reference point in AutoCAD. Setting the 0,0 origin at the lower left corner of the drawing space includes the entire building in the positive X and Y drawing quadrant. Because the masonry tower is the only continuous vertical element, the lower left corner of the tower furnished a convenient reference point for each floor level. Dimensions were then scaled from the as-built drawings, starting with exterior wall dimensions.

Create Polylines to Extrude the Walls

Once the 2D floor plan was complete, the masonry walls were begun on a separate layer, using AutoCAD's Endpoint Osnap command to align inner and outer wall lines with the floor plan. During this step, all doors and windows were ignored.

After the wall outlines were done, we determined the distances from the finish floor to the different ceiling heights, using the vertical dimensions cited in various texts and scaling from the as-built sections. The AutoCAD Change command easily extruded the walls to the correct heights.

The floor slabs at Fallingwater rest on, and interrupt, the masonry walls. If the wall layers on the exterior of the model were interrupted by the edges of the slab layers, it would create problems when applying a masonry texture to the walls. To prevent this, once the masonry walls had been extruded to ceiling height, along the perimeter of the building a six-inch wide wall "veneer" was extruded farther, to the height of the finish floor above. This veneer concealed the inset edges of the slab layers, creating an uninterrupted plane consisting entirely of wall layer.

Two different layers were used for masonry and concrete/stucco walls. The only concrete walls on Fallingwater's main level are parapet walls and kneewalls below banks of windows. These walls were poured, along with the floor slab, as turned-up ledges. We included the terrace parapet walls on the slab layer, but assigned the kneewalls under the windows to a separate concrete wall layer.

Model the Staircases

The next step was modeling the five staircases that begin on the main floor. Each has a different width, style, length of run, and enclosure setup.

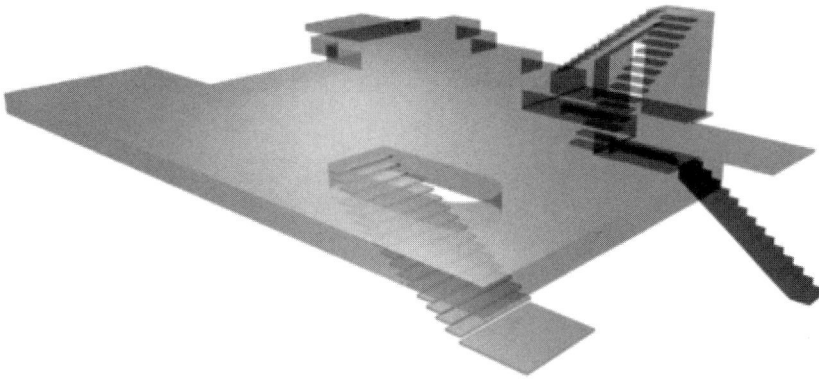

The main-level slab, with its five staircases, rendered in a transparent material.

Insert Door and Window Openings into Wall Volumes

Next, door and window openings were created on the wall layer, within the extruded wall volumes. We used polylines to trace the horizontal dimensions of the openings on the floor plan, snapping to endpoints in order to match the interior and exterior wall lines exactly.

The polyline was moved up the wall to header height (in this particular project, header and ceiling height were often the same) and then extruded down to the height of the sill, leaving a rectangular volume within the volume of the wall. AutoCAD's Solsub solid modeling command subtracted the door/window prism from the wall mass.

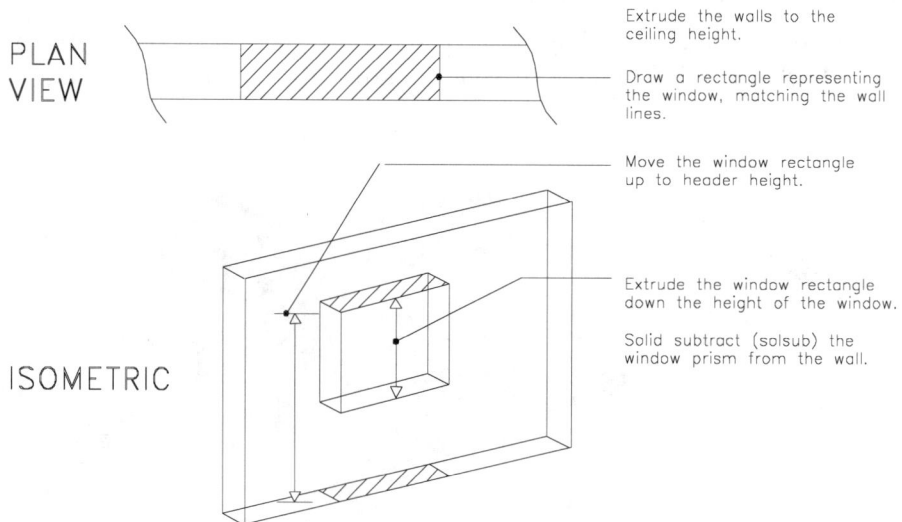

PLAN VIEW

ISOMETRIC

Extrude the walls to the ceiling height.

Draw a rectangle representing the window, matching the wall lines.

Move the window rectangle up to header height.

Extrude the window rectangle down the height of the window.

Solid subtract (solsub) the window prism from the wall.

The door and window volumes were subtracted from the solid wall volume.

Model the Window Grids

The window grids required yet another layer. The muntin pattern changes slightly for each bank of windows and for windows on each level. This different muntin setup for each bank of windows limited the use of copied elements. The window installations have other unusual features: the corner windows have no corner mullions, one window boxes out unsupported from the face of the wall, and glass returns directly into rock at the sides of most windows.

The most flexible method of drawing the window grids was to draw the exterior outline of the grid with a polyline first, offset the profile to the inside, and explode the resulting shape in order to copy the side and bottom muntins for intermediate muntins spaced center to center. Overlapping lines at muntin intersections were removed with the Trim command, and then the whole drawing was changed back into polylines and extruded. The individual panels were subtracted from the overall outline with Solsub. Then the Block command was used to turn the window into a block.

This somewhat complicated process was simpler in the long run, because it allowed the window blocks to be inserted, removed, and combined at will.

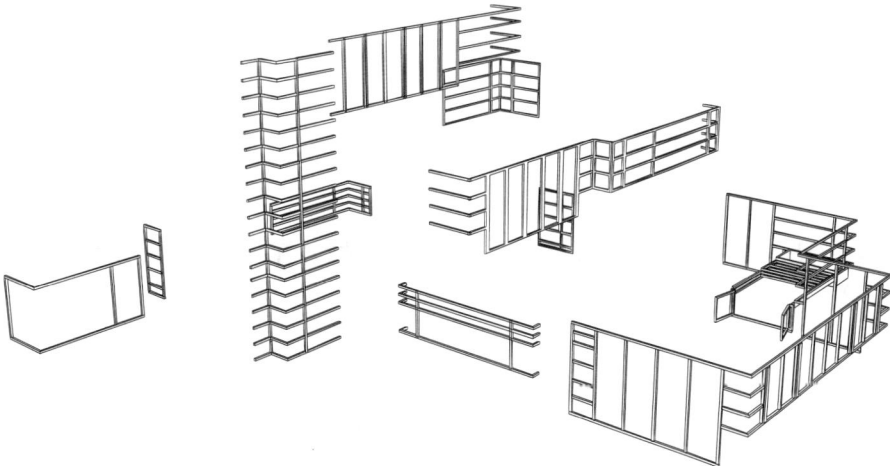

The window layers shown alone.

Using a simple rectangle for the muntin cross-section saved time and greatly reduced the size of the 3D mesh geometry. In the following illustration, the section of rectangular muntin contains 12 vertices, while the section of muntin using the actual shape contains 204 vertices.

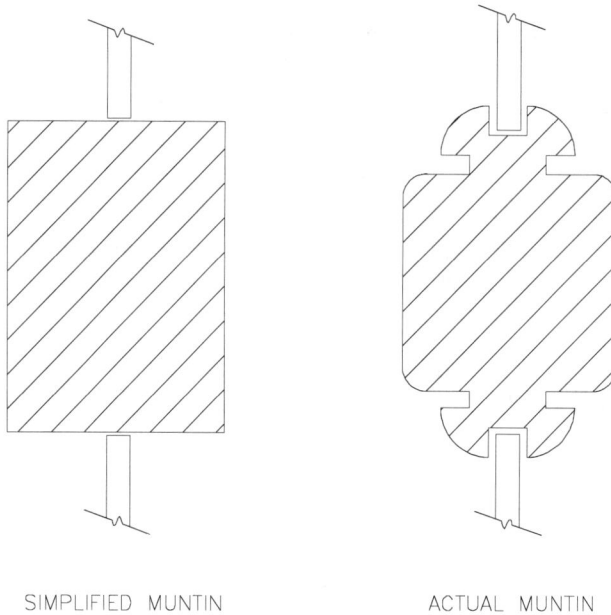

SIMPLIFIED MUNTIN   ACTUAL MUNTIN

A plain rectangular section is adequate for the window muntins in all but the largest scale renderings.

Extrude the 3D Slab Down from the Floor Plan

Finally, the slab was extruded in a two-step process—first down, then up. The floor plan served as a guide to draw a horizontal outline of the slab. The slab outline was offset 6 inches within the building perimeter where masonry walls form the exterior, and snapped to the exterior wall line at the terrace parapets.

The slab outline was positioned vertically at the finish floor level and divided into separate sections for each area of different thickness. Then each area was extruded down separately to meet the level of the walls below. The floor level drops at the entry, so the Move command was used to lower that section before it was extruded.

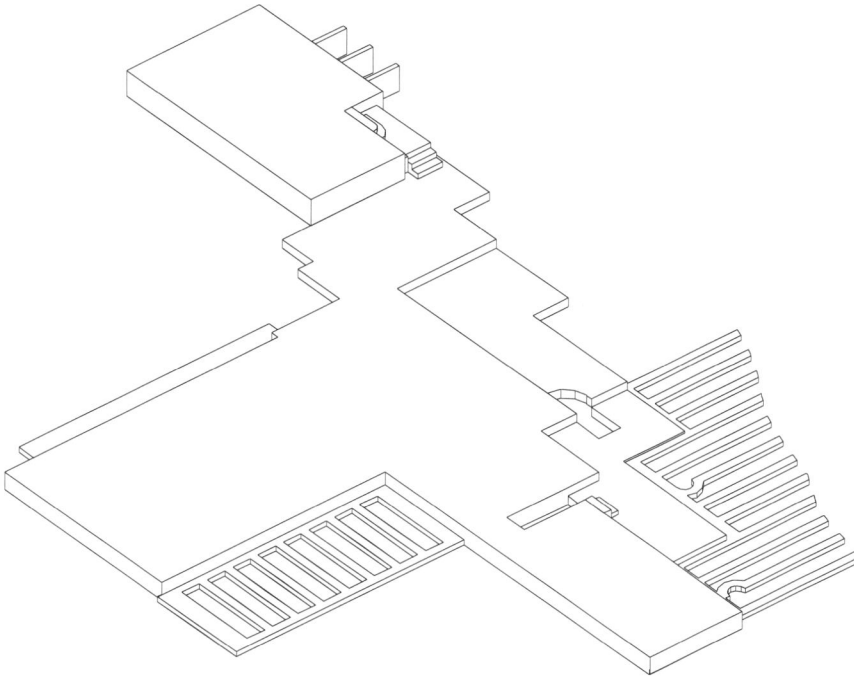

The 2D slab outline was separated into sections, according to thickness. Then each section was extruded separately to its correct overall thickness.

On the flat top of the slab, the outlines of the parapet walls were drawn and extruded up. This completed the model of the slab volume, but included none of the interior configuration that would be needed for a realistic structural model.

Then Go Back and Add the Tricky Stuff

The same sequence was used to model the upper levels: 2D floor plan, walls, window and door openings, window grids, and slab. On some projects you could re-use elements from lower levels, but not on this one, because there are almost no repeats. The second-level floor plan was drawn using the first-level floor plan as a reference.

Once the basic building model was completed, it was necessary to go back to selected areas and add interior detailing, "hidden" structural members, and operable window casings. The slab between the first and second floor is probably the most complicated structural element in the building and is a good example of the further detailing needed once the basic shape has been established.

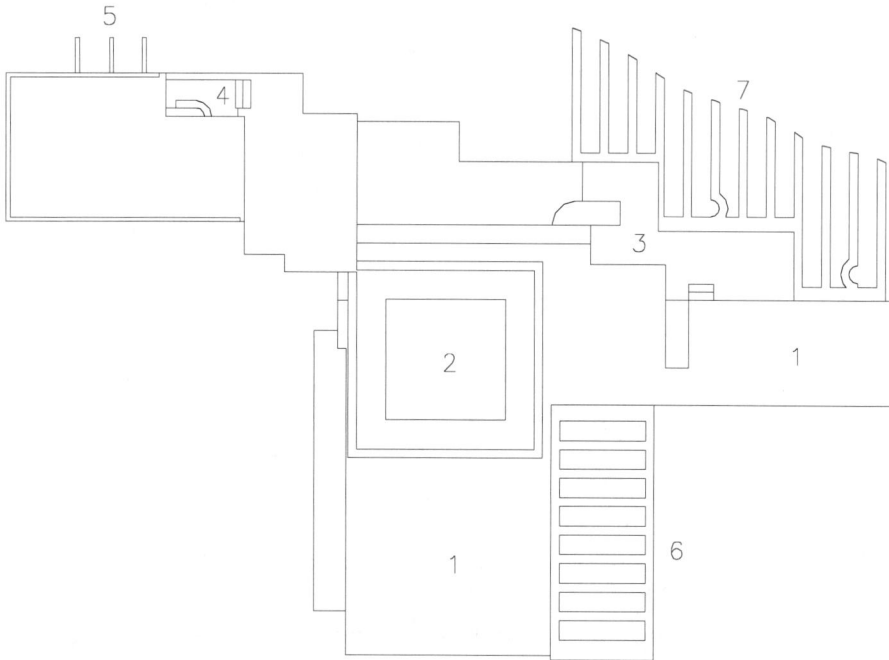

The word "slab" hardly describes the complex configuration of reinforced concrete that separates the first and second floors. The numbers refer to the features described in the text.

The south and east portions of the floor structure consist of a reinforced waffle grid that cantilevers out to form the terraces at the main and guest bedrooms (1). The main north-south beams, hidden by the surface concrete in this drawing, were modeled on a separate layer, as were the smaller east-west joists. The procedure used was similar to the one used for drawing the window grids.

Over the center of the living room, the slab is recessed from below to accommodated the lighting installation (2). The volume of the stepped-up recess was subtracted from the slab volume with the Solsub command.

The floor level drops to form a landing at the top of the main stairs (3), and steps up 3 feet at the northwest corner to form the terrace (4). The Move and Change commands were used to adjust the level and extrude the slab sections. At the west terrace, a massive east-west concrete beam supports crossbeams anchored into a boulder (5).

Two trellis grids extend from the main slab; one covers the hatch area in the living room below (6) and continues past the living room wall line. A prism was drawn within the volume, arrayed, and subtracted with the Solsub command.

The other trellis extends back from the north side of the house (7) to cross over the drive and tie into the cliff face beyond. A single beam was drawn and arrayed. Then a line was drawn to approximate the profile of the cliff face that the beams tie into. The Trim command was used to trim the array of beams at the cliff face. Then arcs were drawn where two beams curve to accommodate trees.

3D Studio Modeling Sequences

The two exercises in this section are very detailed, taking you pick by pick on a brief tour through some of 3D Studio's modules and operations. Later chapters include overviews of 3D Studio concepts, strategies, and capabilities, along with more streamlined exercises to guide you through more complex operations. For now, just follow the bouncing ball as you begin to build and assemble Fallingwater.

You will be using the three modules that handle 3D Studio modeling—the 2D Shaper, the 3D Lofter, and the 3D Editor. The Shaper provides a 2D environment in which you can draw and assemble shapes with a variety of geometric commands (Circle, Quad, N-gon, etc.) or with the Freehand command.

The Lofter then extrudes the shapes into a 3D configuration along a path that controls the object's third dimension. The shapes can be lofted with a continuous cross-section, or with a variety of deformations.

Exercise 1: Modeling the Tapered Bolsters with 3D Studio

Wright's early designs for the bolsters were stepped up and out like a slender upside-down ziggurat. There was a delay in sending plans from Wisconsin to Bear Run, and this version was poured, only to be torn out when a later design arrived. The final design showed a graceful shape flaring continuously up from the base to meet the underside of the slab with a terminating curve—a configuration that Wright likened to the natural expansion of a tree from trunk to branches.

3D Studio can quickly and simply model shapes formed with a double taper. To make the foundation bolster shapes in AutoCAD, you would have to either (1) model a solid prism with the Solext command, first using trigonometry to calculate the taper angle, then lopping off the flat back of the bolster, and finally subtracting an inverted wedge from the front; or (2) make the top and bottom of the bolster, and then use 3D Face to add the side surfaces one by one, and do the same to the intersecting wall behind.

With 3D Studio, you draw rectangles for the top and bottom planes and a line that determines the extrusion height, bring the geometry into the 3D Lofter, and then use the Objects/Make command. That's it.

Setup

First, you'll launch 3D Studio, specify drawing units, and adjust the snap and grid settings.

1. To load 3D Studio, at the C:\ prompt, type **3DS** and press [Enter].

2. From the menu bar choose Program/2D Shaper (or press [F1]) to get into the Shaper module.

3. From the menu bar choose Views/Unit Setup to display the Measurement Unit Selection dialog box.

4. Click on the Architectural button, type **1** in the Denominator: text box, click on the 1 Unit = text box and type **1**, click on the In button and then the OK button.

5. Choose Views/Drawing Aids (or press [Ctrl] + [A]) to set the snap and grid spacing. In the top row of Snap Spacing text boxes, type **1″** in the X-axis text box, then click on the Y: to set the same snap interval in the Y- and Z-axis text boxes. In the Grid Spacing text boxes below, click on the X: text box and type **6″**, and click on the Y: to copy those values. Click on the OK button.

6. Press [S] to toggle on Snap and [G] to toggle on the Grid.

Result: You now have a workspace appropriate for the scale of the drawing.

Draw the Bolster Shapes

Next, you'll draw two rectangles to represent the top and bottom planes of the bolster, and a line, or "path," which will determine the height of the bolster.

1. First, draw the outline of the base of the bolster. Click on the Zoom Window button (second button, bottom row in icon panel) and draw a window around the grid by moving the cursor to the upper left corner of the grid and click, then click on the lower right corner of the grid. From the screen menu choose Create/Quad. Click on a start point near the upper left corner of the grid. As soon as you move the mouse, brackets will appear on the status line at the top of the screen.

2. Move the mouse and then click again when the status line coordinates read

    ```
    [1' 3"    26' 8"]
    ```

3. Next draw a shape for the top of the bolster. The Create/Quad command is still active, so pick another start point for the top rectangle. (The exact placement of the two rectangles in relation to each other doesn't matter.)

4. Move the mouse and click when the status line reads

    ```
    [3' 0"    28' 10"]
    ```

Tip: For a simple modeling operation like this, it is easier to draw a line in the 2D Shaper to function as the path, or extruded dimension, than to adjust the default path in the 3D Lofter.

5. To make the path, choose Create/Line from the screen menu. Click on a point to the right of the rectangles. Move the mouse straight down, generating a line in the Y dimension, until the status line reads

    ```
    [0     -7' 6"]
    ```

6. Click the left mouse button to set the end point, and then click right to cancel the command.

    Tip: 3D Studio has no Ortho command. Keeping the Snap spacing as large as possible helps somewhat when drawing orthogonal lines. Check the status line to see that either the X value is zero for vertical lines, or Y value is zero for horizontal lines, before clicking the end of a line.

7. Choose Shape/Assign from the screen menu and click on the smaller rectangle; the selected rectangle will turn yellow.

Result: There should be one white rectangle, one yellow rectangle, and a short line, on your screen.

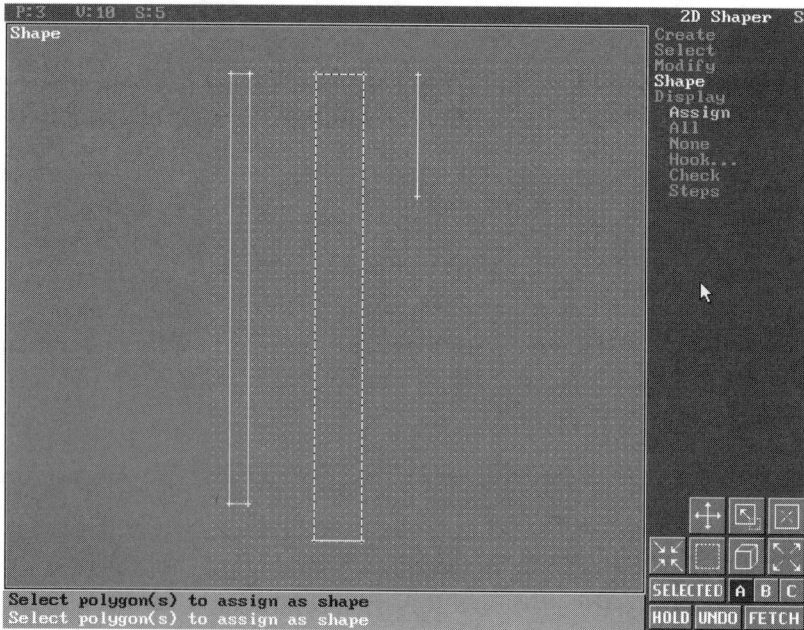

The 2D Shaper screen, showing the bolster rectangles and path.

Bring the Shapes into the 3D Lofter

Now you'll import the rectangles and the path line into the 3D Lofter and assemble them.

1. Choose Program/3D Lofter from the menu bar (or [F2]). Press [S] to toggle on Snap.

2. Choose Shapes/Get/Shaper from the 3D Lofter screen menu. The yellow selected shape (the smaller rectangle) appears in the large Shape viewport.

3. The cross in the Shape viewport marks the position of the path. Choose Shapes/Center to align the rectangle with the path marker.

4. In the lower right corner of the screen, right click on the Zoom Extents icon button to show all geometry in all viewports.

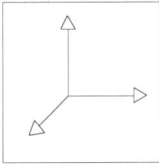

AXIS TRIPOD

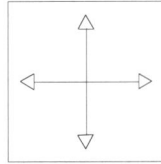

PAN

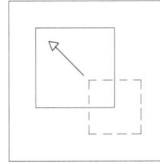

FULL SCREEN
TOGGLE

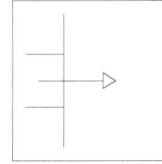

SWITCH VIEWPORTS

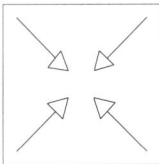

ZOOM IN

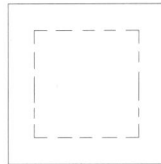

ZOOM WINDOW

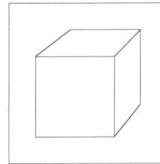

ZOOM EXTENTS

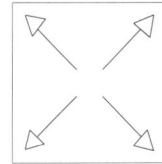

ZOOM OUT

The 3D Lofter icon buttons used to maneuver around the screen.

5. Press [F1] to get back to the Shaper. Click on the smaller rectangle to unassign it, and then click on the path line.

6. Press [F2] to return to the Lofter and choose Path/Get/Shaper. Pick the OK button when the warning box appears. The 7'6" path (shown as a blue line) replaces the default path.

7. Choose Shapes/Pick. In the Top viewport click on the end of the path that doesn't have a white line across it. This operation will place the next shape imported into the Lofter at the opposite end of the path.

8. Return to the Shaper [F1], click on the path line to unassign it, and click on the larger rectangle.

9. Go to the Lofter [F2] and choose Shapes/Get/Shaper to import the larger rectangle.

10. Choose Shapes/Center to align the two rectangles.

Result: Each rectangle is centered on an end of the lofting path.

Adjust and Loft the Shapes

Since the back of each bolster is a flat plane that abuts the retaining wall, you will need to adjust the two rectangles so that they are aligned at one end. Then you'll turn the shapes into a 3D object.

1. On the Lofter screen, pick anywhere inside the Shape viewport to activate it. Press [S] to activate Snap.

2. Choose Shapes/Move and move the cursor into the Shape viewport. Press the [Tab] key until the cursor shows vertical arrows.

3. Click on the rectangle, move the cursor down, and click again when the status line reads

        Offsets: X: 0' 0"   Y: -1' 1"

4. Choose Objects/Make. When the Object Lofting Controls dialog box appears, type **bolster** in the Object Name text box and click on the Create button.

5. From the menu bar, choose Program/3D Editor (or press [F3]) to change modules. Right click on the Zoom Extents icon button.

6. To change the lower right viewport to an isometric User view, choose Views/Viewports from the menu bar to display the Viewport Division dialog box.

7. Select the button labeled User. At the lower left of the dialog box is a rectangle divided into quadrants. Click on the lower right quadrant labeled "N" to replace the "None" viewport with the User viewport. Click on the OK button.

8. Right click Zoom Extents again.

Result: The bolster appears in the four 3D Editor viewports.

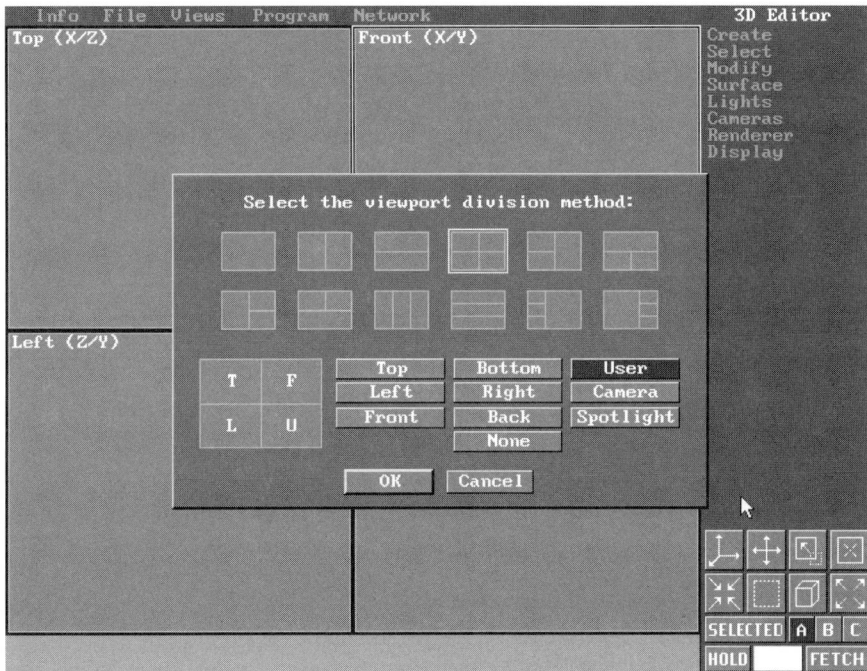

The Viewport Division dialog box. The 12 rectangles at the top display the available viewport configurations. The panel of ten labeled buttons assigns view options. The box with four lettered quadrants shows which view has been assigned to each viewport.

Rotate and Array the Bolsters

At this point, the bolster is balanced on its nose, which would have upset the Fallingwater engineers even more. In this section you'll rotate the bolster to the correct position and copy it.

1. In the 3D Editor module, click in the Left viewport to activate it.

2. Press [A] to turn on Angle Snap and toggle on the Local Axis icon button (top right in the icon panel).

3. Choose Modify/Object/Rotate and click on the bolster. Move the mouse to rotate the bolster and click again when the status line reads

    ```
    Bolster Angle: 90.00 degrees
    ```

4. Right click on the Zoom Extents button.

5. Click within the Top viewport to activate it.

6. Choose Create/Array/Linear, move the cursor back into the Top viewport, and press the Tab key until the cursor shows a right arrow.

7. Click on the bolster. When the Linear Array dialog box appears, type **3** in the Total number in array: text box, click in the Object Spacing text box and type **12′**, and pick the Center-to-Center button. Click on the OK button.

8. Right click Zoom Extents.

9. Choose File/Save from the menu bar, type **bolsters** in the Filename: text box to save your geometry as a mesh file, and pick OK. Make a note of the drive and path for the bolster file.

10. Choose File/Reset and pick Yes to clear the screen.

Result: Congratulations! You just recreated the geometry that made strong men weep in 1936.

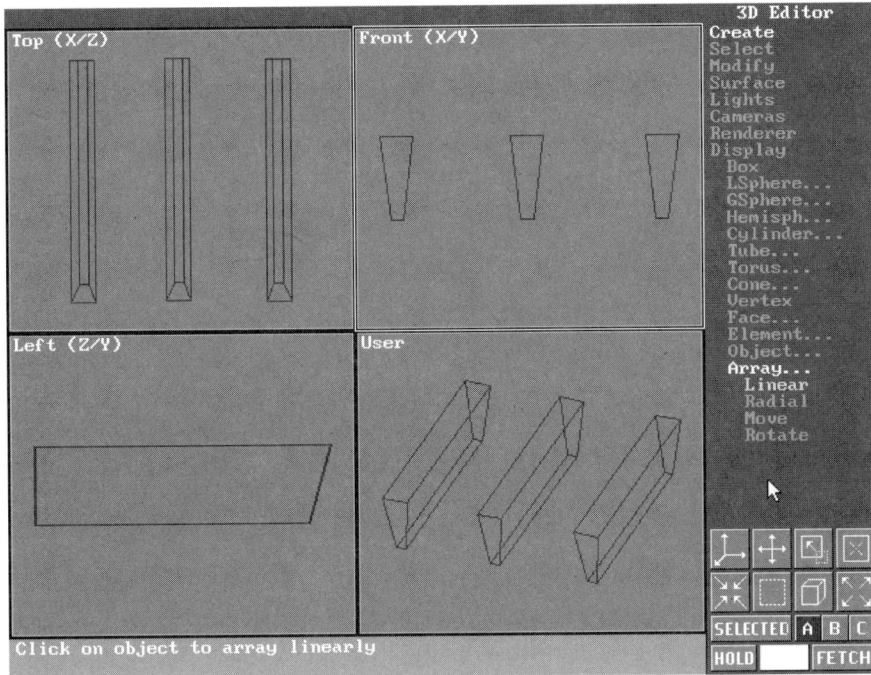

The 3D Editor screen, showing the arrayed bolsters.

Exercise 2: Merging the .3DS Bolsters with the .DXF Foundation

Bob Mosher was neither reckless nor lacking in innovation, so he devised a slot in the bolsters' masonry footings to receive and further anchor the slender bases of the concrete forms. Frank Lloyd Wright was not amused by Mosher's improvisation (Hoffmann, p. 38).

To place the bolsters within the rest of the foundation, we'll go back to the original scheme and simply rest them on top of the footings.

The Fallingwater model was built in pieces, with each level in a different file. As well as making the model more manageable, separating it into levels facilitates combining parts of the model created in different programs. In the following exercise, you will merge the bolsters, saved as a 3D Studio *.3ds* file, with the AutoCAD foundation level, stored as a *.dxf* file.

Load the Foundation File into 3D Studio

For this exercise, you will use a file from the distribution disk that you copied to your hard drive.

1. At the C:\ prompt, type **3DS** to start 3D Studio.

2. Choose File/Load ([Ctrl] + [L]) from the menu bar to display the file selector dialog box.

3. Click on the appropriate drive button, and then click on the *.DXF button to display all .dxf files.

4. Click on the FOUND.DXF file in the scroll box, and then click on the OK button.

5. When the Loading DXF File dialog box appears, click on the OK button to accept the default settings.

6. In a few seconds, the foundation will appear in the 3D Editor viewports. (If the lower right viewport is labeled "No view defined," click on the viewport and press [U], [R], and [Enter] to assign it as a User viewport.)

7. Right click on the Zoom Extents icon button.

Result: The foundation level model appears in the four viewports.

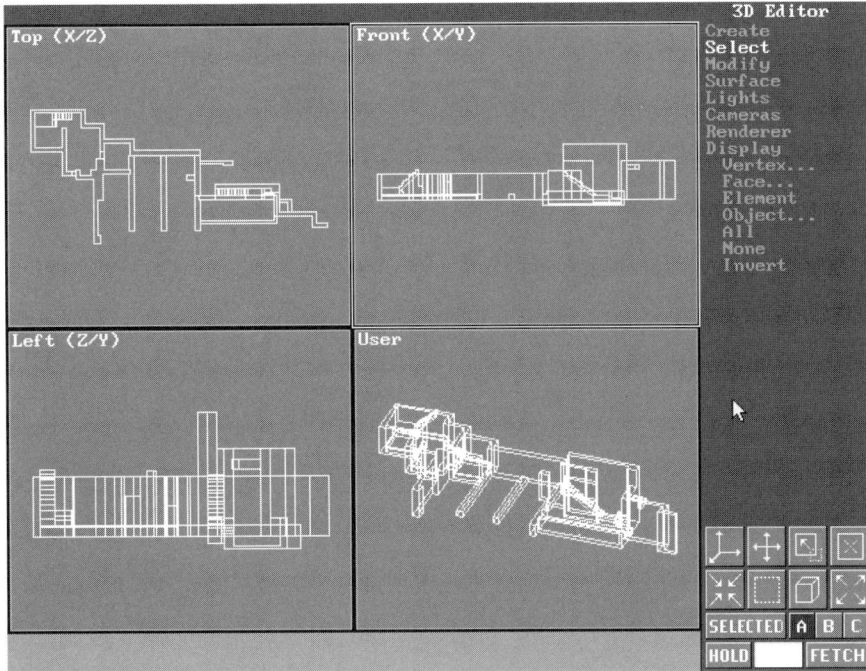

The foundation model loaded into the 3D Editor.

Merge the Files

Next, you'll merge the bolster *.3ds* file with the rest of the foundation model and adjust the drawing units and snap spacing.

1. Choose File/Merge from the menu bar to display the Merge dialog box. Leave the Mesh Objects button on (red) and toggle off the buttons for cameras, lights, and animation. Click OK.

2. When the File Merge dialog box appears, click the *.3DS button, and choose BOLSTERS.3DS from the file scroll box.

3. Yet another dialog box appears. In the Select Objects to Merge dialog box, click on the All button to select all three bolsters. Click OK. The bolsters will appear.

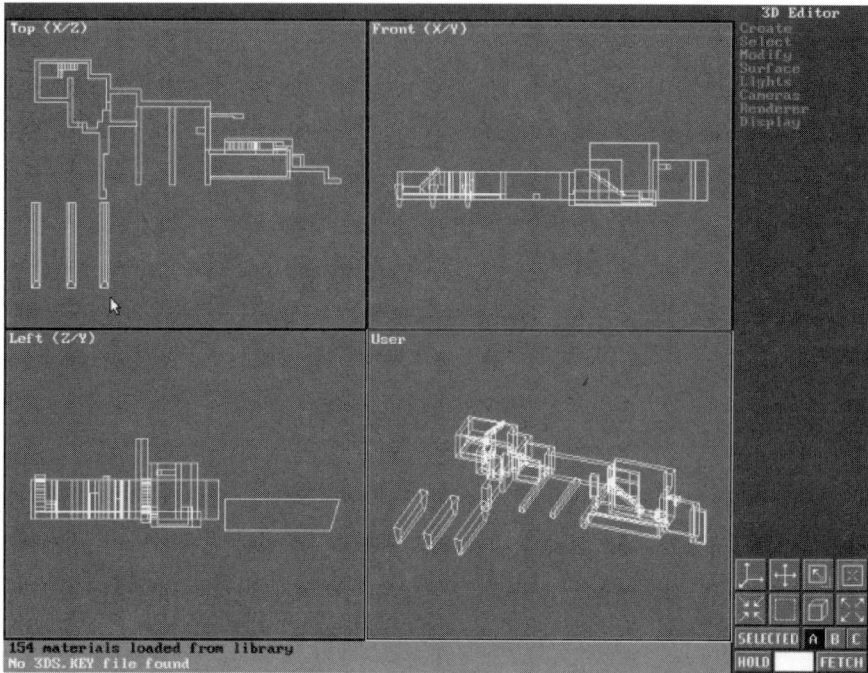

The bolsters appear next to, or superimposed on, the foundation.

4. Now, reset the Units and Snap settings. Press [Ctrl] + [U] to display the Measurement Unit Selection dialog box. Click on the Architectural button, type **1** in the Denominator: text box, click on the In button, and the OK button.

5. Press [Ctrl] + [A] to change the Snap setting. Type **1"** in the X: text box and click on the Y: to copy the setting. Click OK.

Result: Both model components are combined, and drawing settings are restored.

Position the Bolsters

Next, you'll position the bolsters correctly within the AutoCAD foundation model—on top of their three footings and backed up against the rear retaining wall.

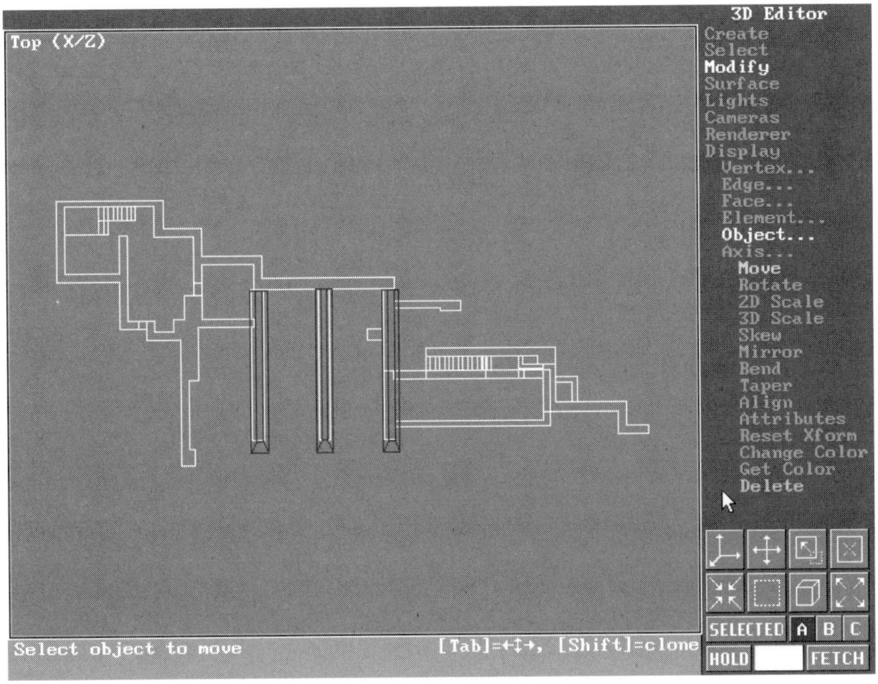
3D Editor
Top (X/Z)
Create
Select
Modify
Surface
Lights
Cameras
Renderer
Display
Vertex...
Edge...
Face...
Element...
Object...
Axis...
Move
Rotate
2D Scale
3D Scale
Skew
Mirror
Bend
Taper
Align
Attributes
Reset Xform
Change Color
Get Color
Delete
SELECTED
A
B
C
HOLD
FETCH
Select object to move
[Tab]=↔↕, [Shift]=clone

The bolsters positioned approximately over the footings.

1. In the 3D Editor, click inside the Top viewport and right click Zoom Extents.
2. Make a selection set of the three bolsters so that they can be moved as a unit. Choose Select/Object/Quad. In the Top viewport, draw a window around the bolsters. They will turn red to indicate their selection.
3. Press [S] to activate Snap. Choose Modify/Object/Move from the screen menu. In the icon panel, click on the Selected button. It will turn red, assigning the bolster selection set as the object to be moved.
4. Use the [Tab] key to toggle the cursor until it shows four directional arrows. Click on the bolsters in the Top viewport.
5. Use the mouse to move the bolsters over the footings.
6. To refine the bolster placement, click on the Zoom Window icon button. Draw a window around just the top end of one of the bolsters.

Choose Modify/Object/Move and click on the Selected button again.
Use the mouse to align the bolsters exactly. Right click Zoom Extents.

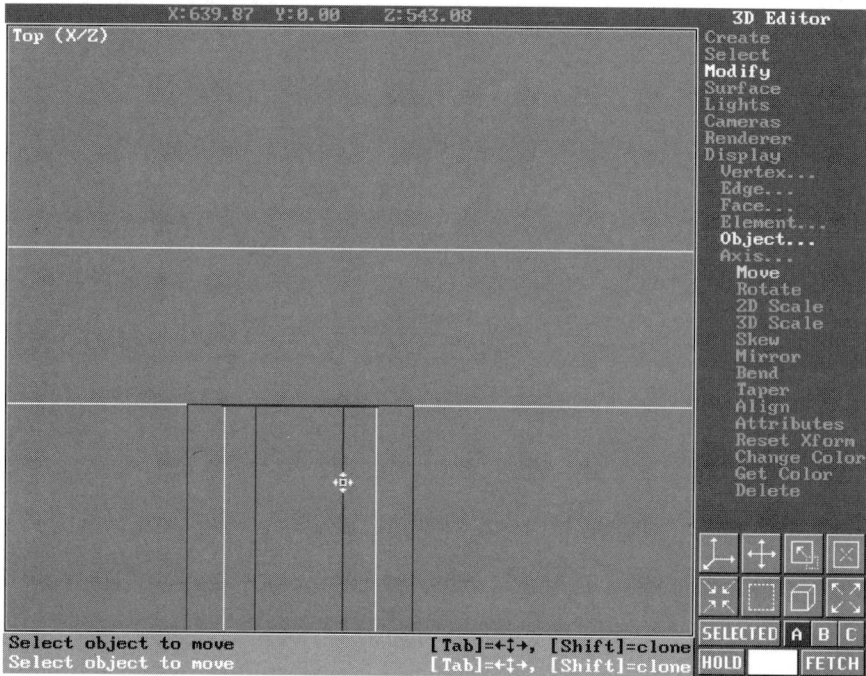

Use the Zoom Window icon to window a small area for fine-tuning the bolster position.

7. The bolsters are correctly positioned in the Top view but still out of
   place in the Front view. To vertically adjust them, first click in the
   Front viewport to activate it.

8. Click on the Zoom Window icon and window the area surrounding
   the bolsters.

9. Choose Modify/Object/Move, toggle on the Selected button, and click
   on the bolsters. Use the [Tab] key to toggle the cursor to vertical
   arrows. Move the bolsters into approximate vertical position with the
   mouse.

10. Click on Zoom Window and window a small area around the base of
    one of the bolsters. Fine-tune the vertical position as you did the
    horizontal position.

11. Choose File/Save and type **found** in the Filename: text box. The *.3ds* extension is added automatically.

Result: The foundation is now completely assembled.

Summary

This chapter has taken you on a brief floor-by-floor tour of Fallingwater, discussed using AutoCAD models with 3D Studio, and described the AutoCAD procedures for making the model of Fallingwater. The exercises demonstrated modeling in 3D Studio and merging a *.dxf* file. While this chapter has concentrated on AutoCAD—the starting point of many architectural rendering projects—the next chapter plunges into 3D Studio proper with an overview of the five modules.

3D Studio Overview

This chapter briefly tours 3D Studio's five modules and describes how they interact. The exercises at the end of the chapter introduce you to some screen controls and rendering operations:

❑ Setting up a default environment

❑ Using Display and Selection controls with the model's combined foundation and main levels

❑ Using the 3D Editor to apply two library materials to the model.

Fallingwater: Mass and Detail

Over the course of his career, Frank Lloyd Wright's work evolved (with occasional backsliding) from a generous use of applied ornament to a reliance on the natural textures of building materials to enrich surfaces. Combined with the Kaufmanns' insistence on informality, Wright's evolution produced a house "decorated" only with its form and building materials. In any case, further ornament would have been superfluous applied to the geometry—a layered weave of rectilinear, pinwheeling shapes diminishing in size toward the top of the building, integrated into the site.

We've mentioned that Fallingwater is a complicated building; one way to understand the structure is by stripping it down to the basic geometry appropriate for a massing model. Even though the exterior derives much of its impact from masonry, the beauty of its sculptural balance comes through clearly if plain unadorned surfaces are used to render. This type of simplification serves any design project well; unless the massing is right, adding snappy details won't help.

This chapter and Chapters 5 and 6 concentrate on Fallingwater as a structural study model. These three chapters constitute a pass through the simpler aspects of 3D Studio. The remaining chapters of the book make another pass to delve into more complex operations and to add photo-realistic detail to the model.

The Five Modules

This section briefly discusses the functions and relationships of the five modules, describes the main command groups, and includes some tips for basic operations. The modules need not be used in any particular order, though some type of model is necessary for applying rendering and animation operations.

Three of the modules—the 2D Lofter, 3D Shaper, and 3D Editor—are collectively known as the Modeler. As demonstrated in the previous chapter, the Shaper and Lofter work together. You can create models independently in the 3D Editor, or use it to refine models created in the Shaper and Lofter. In addition to modeling commands, the 3D Editor contains a full array of rendering tools, used in conjunction with the Materials Editor. The Keyframer controls object movement, movement paths, compositing, and transferring animations to videotape.

Tip: You'll be constantly switching back and forth among modules. Use the function keys [F1] through [F5] to switch, instead of the mouse. The tiny amount of time saved eventually adds up.

3D Studio's menu structure is displayed in both pull-down menus and on-screen menus. Appendix A contains menu maps for the complete program. In addition to pull-down and on-screen menu commands, 3D Studio includes numerous dialog boxes. The maps show a "D" to the right of commands that branch to a dialog box.

The menu bar pull-downs control global operations that apply to all modules except the Materials Editor. These include files, view controls, drawing environment, program switching, networking functions—the housekeeping and systems stuff. The same pull-down menus appear with each module, but different entries are disabled (shown in black), depending on previous operations and which module is in use.

INFO	FILE	VIEWS	PROGRAM	NETWORK
About 3D Studio... !	New N	Redraw '	2D Shaper F1	Slave
Current Status ?	Reset	Redraw All ~	3D Lofter F2	————————
Configure *	Load ^L	————————	3D Editor F3	Configure
System Options	Merge ^M	Viewports ^V	Keyframer F4	Edit Queue
Scene Info	Replace Mesh ^R	Drawing Aids ^A	Materials F5	
Key Assignments	Save ^S	Grid Extents E	DOS Window F10	
Gamma Control	Save Selected	Unit Setup ^U	Text Editor F11	
	————————	————————	PXP Loader F12	
	Load Project ^J	Use Snap S		
	Save Project ^P	Use Grid G		
	Merge Project ^G	Fastview V		
	Archive	Disable D		
	————————	Scroll Lock l		
	File Info	Safe Frame @E		
	Rename	See Backgrnd @G		
	Delete ^D	Adj Backgrnd		
	————————	————————		
	Quit Q	Vertex Snap @V		
		————————		
		Save Current [		
		Restore Saved }		
		Angle Snap A		

The pull-down menus for all modules except the Materials Editor.

Operations specific to each individual module are controlled by individual screen menus and customized icon panels on the right side of each display screen. (Again, the Materials Editor is the exception.) Some branches of the screen menus are similar in different modules, so it's not as intimidating as it looks at first. For instance, the majority of Lights, Cameras, Renderer, and Display commands in the Keyframer module are the same as commands in the 3D Editor.

Tip: Whenever you want on-screen help, hold down the [Alt] key, move the mouse over any dialog box button or command name, and click. A help menu will appear with a brief definition of the item.

The 2D Shaper

As previewed in the last chapter, the basic operation in the 2D Shaper is to draw 2D shapes in 2D space. The Shaper uses spline functions to create polygons, and to generate curves when you manipulate a single polygon, vertex, or segment.

The *3D Studio Reference Manual* lists four things you can do with a shape you have created:

❑ Import it into the 3D Lofter and extrude (or loft) it to create a 3D object.

❑ Import it into the 3D Lofter to use as a path to guide the lofting of another shape.

❑ Import the shape directly into the 3D Editor and use it as a flat shape.

❑ Import it into the Keyframer to use as a path for the animation motion to follow.

The strengths and weaknesses of the Shaper stem from the same feature: you have to think in three dimensions from the start. The shape that you draw establishes the configuration of an object in one plane. This shape is then extruded along a path to generate the third dimension. The path can be deformed, curved, or bent in various ways to control the progressive cross-sections of the original shape—rather like an incredibly advanced lathe.

Thus you need to visualize beforehand which plane of a proposed object will work best as a shape and which dimension is most suitable for a path. For example, consider a simplified version of a building far removed from

Fallingwater—a typical convenience store, with its shoe box shape and tilted, upside-down gable roof. There are two basic ways to model the building's exterior walls: you can start with the floor plan and extrude the wall lines up, with adjustments (as described in the previous chapter); or you can model a slab, then model each wall as a shallow 3D polygon, and tilt the walls into place—rather like assembling a gingerbread house. In either case, the defining plane is the plan view.

The defining plane, or shape that should be drawn in the Shaper and lofted, changes when you get to the shallow, V-shaped roof. Here, you would use the triangular end section as the shape and loft (extrude) it along its length.

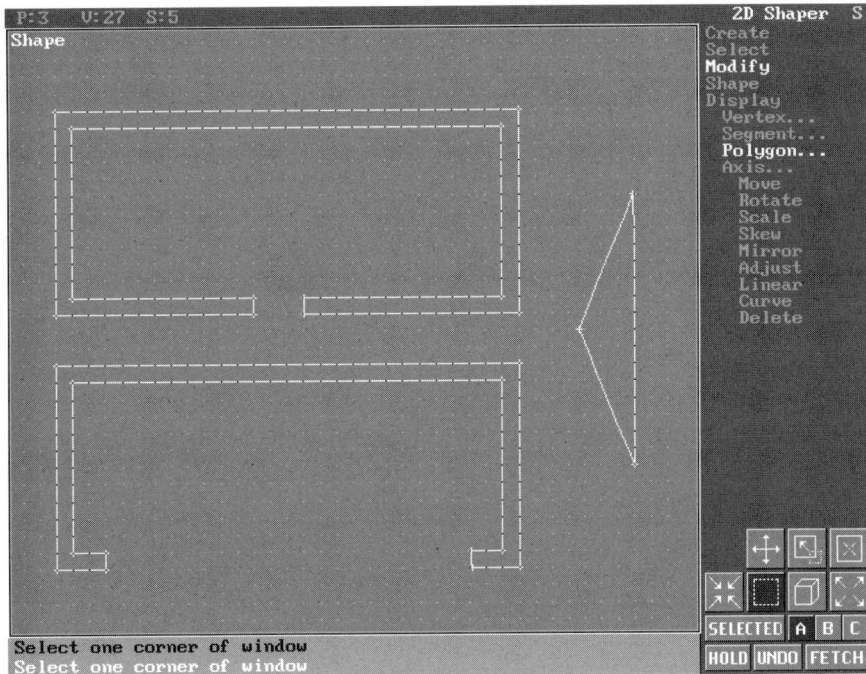

Shaping a convenience store. The two rectangular sections are lofted vertically to form the walls. The triangular section lofts "sideways" to form the roof.

Some compact objects can be shaped and lofted in one operation. However, if an object has various discrete extensions (such as the Lipchitz sculpture in Chapter 7), usually it is necessary to construct the extensions separately.

Shape Components   The *3D Studio Reference Manual* describes shape components as building blocks that go together to create the final shape and goes on to describe the available building blocks:

Vertex. The point where two or more segments meet to form an angle. (You can also insert vertices along the segments of a preexisting shape if you need to break or deform the segments at some place that doesn't have a vertex.)

Segment. The connecting line between two vertices.

Step. A segment divider that enables curve formation. (Steps are the only shape component that is not visible on the Shaper screen.)

Polygon. One or more curved or straight segments. (Regardless of what you learned in Geometry 101, 3D Studio considers any line to be a polygon.)

Shape. One or more polygons that you've assigned as a shape using the Shape/Assign command.

The program is very sensitive to *valid* and *invalid* shapes; it will loft only valid shapes. Even though a line is defined as a polygon, it is an invalid shape. To be valid, a shape must be a closed, non-intersecting polygon. This means no sloppy corners that overlap or don't meet and no kinks that cause a line to cross itself.

Tip: If you seem to have a closed polygon, but it still won't loft, you may have inadvertently added vertices that cause the line to cross itself. Use Shapes/Assign to assign the shape, and then use the Shapes/Check command to check its closure and number of vertices. If the shape is not closed, use the Zoom Window to check areas around corners for extra vertices not visible at normal scale.

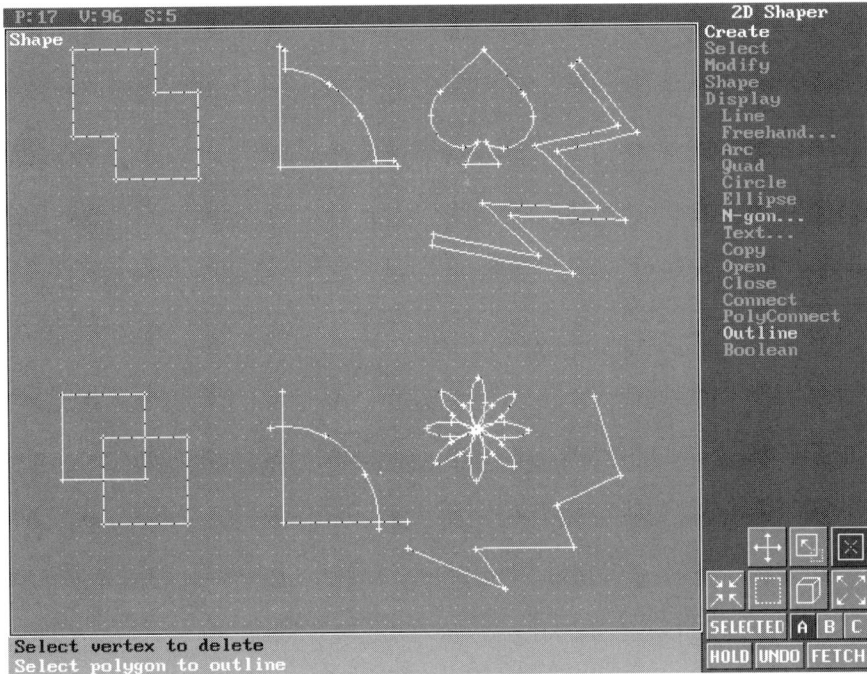

```
P:17  V:96  S:5                                    2D Shaper
Shape                                              Create
                                                   Select
                                                   Modify
                                                   Shape
                                                   Display
                                                     Line
                                                     Freehand...
                                                     Arc
                                                     Quad
                                                     Circle
                                                     Ellipse
                                                     N-gon...
                                                     Text...
                                                     Copy
                                                     Open
                                                     Close
                                                     Connect
                                                     PolyConnect
                                                     Outline
                                                     Boolean





                                                   SELECTED  A  B  C
Select vertex to delete
Select polygon to outline                          HOLD  UNDO  FETCH
```

The illustration shows valid shapes at the top of the screen and invalid shapes below.

Tip: Because it's easy to accidentally insert extra vertices when using the Draw commands, and because only Snap controls the Ortho, use the Polygon commands (Quad, Circle, N-gon, etc.) and then modify them as necessary whenever possible, instead of constructing shapes with individual lines.

2D Shaper Command Groups

Following are the commands in the main branch of the 2D Shaper screen menu.

Create Use the Create commands for drawing polygons, lines, and text; drawing double lines with Outline; joining and separating polygons (Open, Close, Connect, and Polyconnect); and performing Boolean operations. It may take a little experimenting to decide which basic operation is most efficient for a particular purpose. The following illustration depicts various Create commands. The letters were added with Create/Text.

(a) **Line.** Set vertices with left mouse clicks; cancel with a right click.

(b) **Freehand.** Scribble at will with the left button held down. The vertices are inserted automatically.

(c) **Arc.** Set the centerpoint, then the starting and ending point of the arc.

(d) **Quad.** Click the first and opposite corners of a rectangle. Hold down the [Ctrl] key to force a square.

(e) **Circle.** Click once to locate the center and again to set the radius.

(f) **Ellipse.** Click on both ends of the long axis and hold down the mouse button to adjust the short axis.

(g) **N-gon.** Specify the number of sides; then click once to set the center and again to place a vertex.

(h) **Outline.** Click on the shape you want to outline. Then click twice to draw a line that determines the width of the outline. Whether the outline is drawn inside or outside of the polygon depends on where you draw the width line.

(i) The **ellipse** again.

(j) **Open.** Click on a segment to remove it.

(k) **Close.** Click on an open polygon to connect the vertices with a straight line.

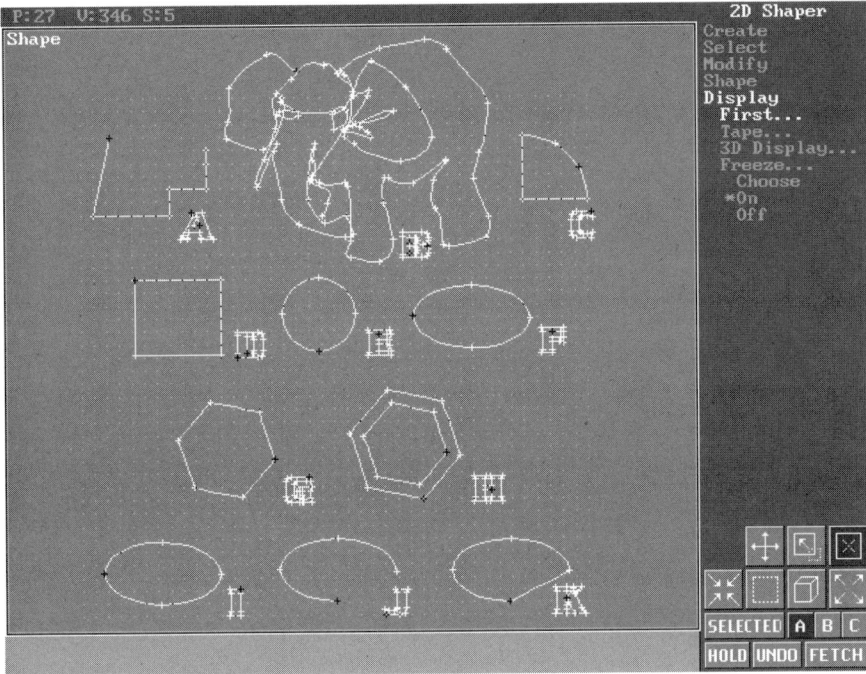

Creating shapes in the 2D Shaper. The black dots mark the first vertices of each shape.

Select   3D Studio provides a standard set of selection tools to use on either polygons or individual vertices. The general sequence is (1) Choose Select/(Vertex or Polygon) and a windowing configuration; (2) Window the appropriate area in the drawing; (3) Pick the command you wish to use on the selected items and then pick the selected button.

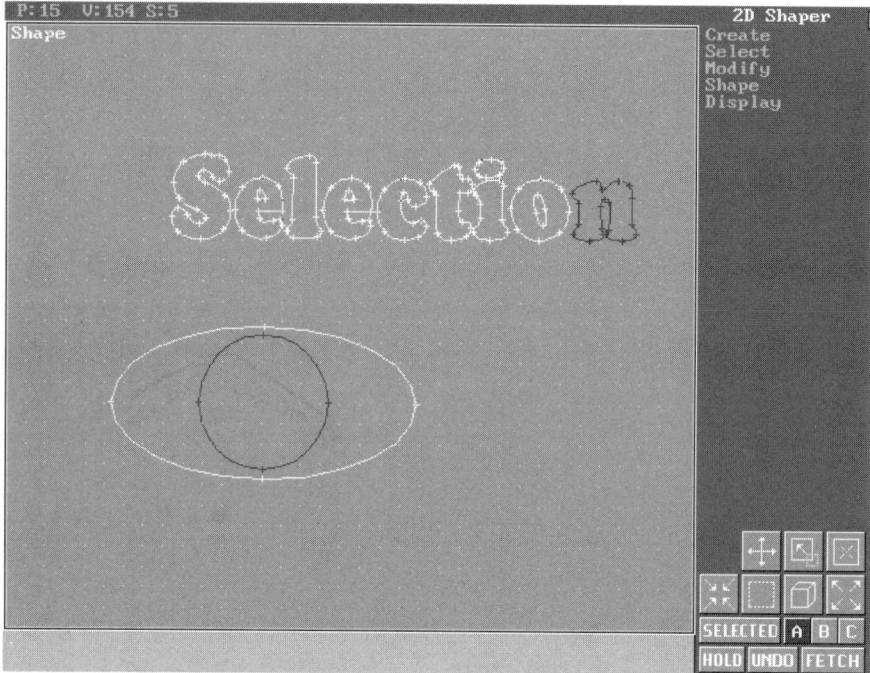

The Select/Polygon/Circle command is used to separate the circle out from the enclosing ellipse. Select/Polygon/Fence is used to draw a fence around the "N."

Modify   The following illustration demonstrates the result of using various Modify commands on a single polygon, a single segment, and a single vertex.

(a) **Modify/Polygon/Move.** The quad is moved into place by clicking on it and moving it with the button held down.

(b) **Modify/Polygon/Rotate.** Press [A] to turn on Angle Snap. Click on the Local Axis icon button (last right in upper row). Click on the quad and rotate it with the mouse, watching the status line to verify the angle of rotation.

(c) **Modify/Polygon/Scale.** Pick the quad and hold down the mouse button to scale the polygon larger or smaller.

(d) **Modify/Polygon/Skew.** Use the [Tab] key to change the cursor arrow to the desired direction of skew. Then pick the quad and hold down the button to determine the amount of skew.

(e) **Modify/Polygon/Curve.** Pick the quad. All segments curve, producing a circle.

(f) **Modify/Segment/Curve.** Use the Curve command on just the side segments. Anytime you want to undo Curve or Adjust operations, you can use the Linear command to straighten the segment again.

(g) **Modify/Segment/Adjust.** Pick the right side segment and adjust the spline.

(h) **Modify/Segment/Refine.** Use Refine to add two vertices to each segment. Then use Curve on each corner segment to add "ears" to the quad.

(i) **Modify/Vertex/Move.** Pick the upper right vertex and re-position with the button held down.

(j) **Modify/Vertex/Skew.** Turn off the Local Axis icon button. Use the [Tab] key to specify horizontal or vertical skew, pick a vertex and position with the button held down.

(k) **Modify/Vertex/Adjust.** Pick a vertex and adjust the spline.

(l) **Modify/Vertex/Curve.** Pick a vertex, and the segments on each side curve.

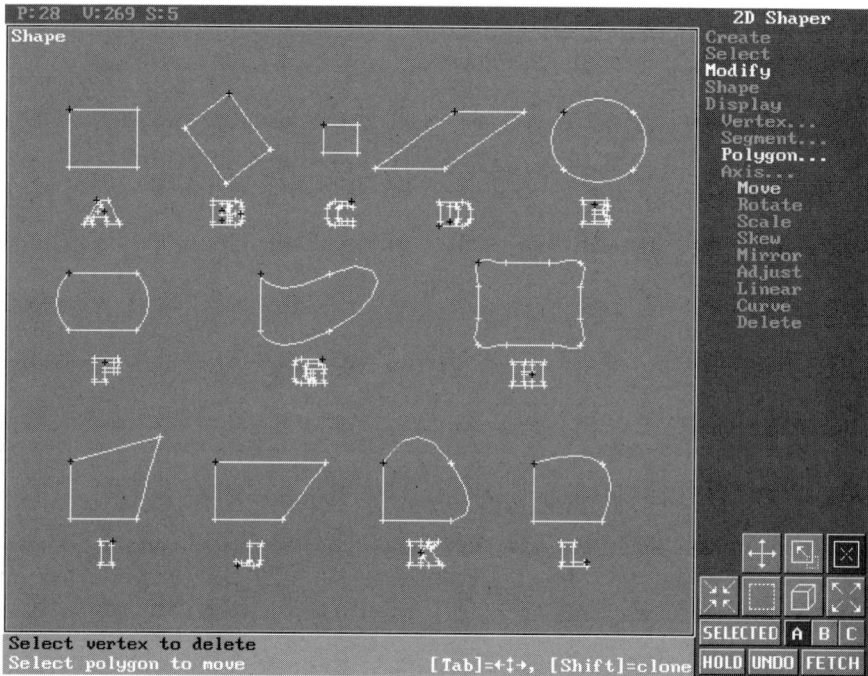

Modifying a Quad.

Tip: To join polygons, the Union function of the Boolean command is usually the easiest method. However, you can also use the Modify/Vertex/Weld command as a vertex snap to ensure that the combined polygon is closed with no stray vertices. If you're joining two open polygons, move the polygons so that the appropriate vertices are close to each other and then weld them. If you're joining closed polygons, first move them into place relative to each other and use the Refine command to insert vertices close to the junction points on each polygon. Then use the Open command to delete the overlapping segments. Finally, weld the adjacent vertices together to close the new, combined polygon.

The Adjust commands are extremely versatile and can be unpredictable when you begin using them. Draw some polygons and experiment at length, read the *Reference Manual* sections, and go through the *3D Studio Tutorial* exercises related to spline adjustments.

Shape   The Shape commands assign shapes for export to the Lofter, manipulate a Hook used to align shapes, and check shapes for validity and number of vertices. The Shape/Steps dialog box sets the number of steps between each vertex of the shape, which controls the smoothness of a curved segment.

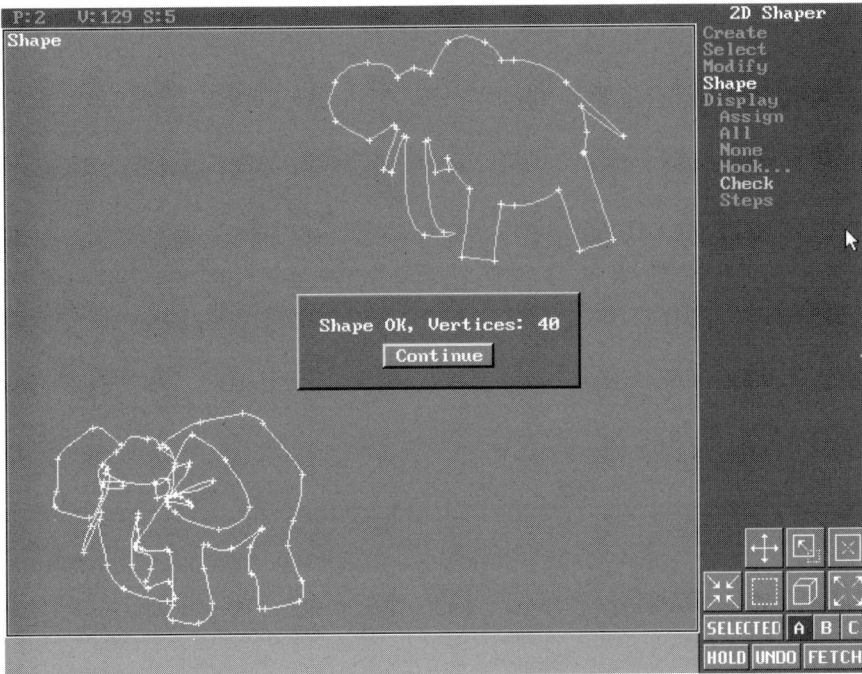

Lofting elephants. The scribbled elephant is an invalid shape because it self-intersects and is not closed. The Shape/Check command has checked, counted vertices, and accepted the Boolean elephant made of polygons—it looks stupid, but it's a closed polygon.

Display   When on, the First command displays a polygon's first vertex as a black dot. First vertices control how a segment can be connected to other polygons. Also, if you are lofting multiple shapes along the same path, each shape must have the same number of vertices, and the first vertices must be aligned along the path axis, or the object will twist along its path to make the first vertices connect.

The Tape command displays 3D Studio's rather limited measuring tool. The 3D Display command serves as a kind of layer control in that it can display a 3D object as a base layer. The Freeze command turns elements off so that they cannot be manipulated.

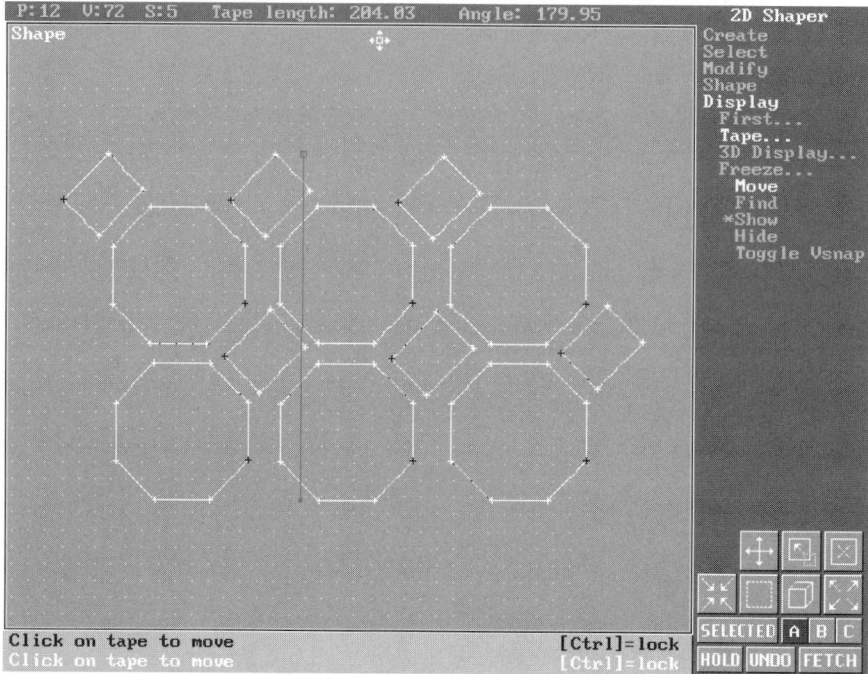

Using the Display commands. The First command is on, displaying first vertices in black. The Tape command is set to Show, displaying the tape, which has been placed to display on the status line the height of the tiling pattern from top to bottom.

The 3D Lofter

Why *lofting?* The term is derived from ancient shipbuilders who would construct a series of lofts, or formwork, to support a ship's hull during construction. Lifting the cross-sections into the lofts was known as *lofting.* It's a very accurate term, because you're not drawing objects in the Shaper; you're drawing cross-sections that serve as formwork to determine the shape of the object.

Lofting, from Simple to Complex   3D Studio lofting operations allow both simple and complex modes of transformation. You can

❏ Loft a single shape along a straight path

❏ Place different shapes at each end of a straight path to transform an object automatically from one shape to the other (as in the bolster exercise in the previous chapter)

❏ Place identical shapes at the ends of the path and rotate one of them so that the first vertices don't line up, causing the lofted shape to twist along its length

❏ Place a series of different shapes at the vertices of a straight lofting path and produce an object whose cross-section changes at every vertex

❏ Loft single or multiple shapes along a path that bends or curves

❏ Loft single or multiple shapes along a path that has been adjusted with the Deform commands so that the object shrinks, swells, twists, teeters, or is beveled along its length

❏ Use the SurfRev command to loft profiles in a circular path to create objects such as goblets, columns, and spindles

❏ Use the Fit command to loft objects with different X and Y cross-sections.

How the Lofter Shows 3D Space   The 3D Lofter uses four default viewports. The large Shape viewport shows the imported shape in the same orientation as the 2D Shaper. Down the left side of the screen are the Top, Front, and User viewports. The Top viewport shows the length of the path, the Front viewport repeats the orientation of the large Shape viewport, and the User viewport shows a perspective view.

Now, if you are Architecturally Empowered, you may automatically visualize in a plan view mode—picturing things from the top view—but drawing space turns 90 degrees when you get into the Lofter. The flat plane of the Shaper, which you may have been thinking of as the top/plan view, becomes the Front plane in the Lofter. This Front X-Y plane/viewport is a head-on view of the shape and looks "straight down the barrel" of the path.

The Top plane/viewport looks down on the top "edge" of the shape and the length of the path stretching back from the shape. Thus you loft shapes from front to back, along the Z axis, and the path exists in the Z dimension. When you bring a shape into the Lofter, it's tilted up on its side. (Remember the bolsters on their noses?)

3D Lofter Command Groups

There are five command groups in the Lofter. Shape imports and manipulates shapes. Path imports and manipulates paths. Deform controls how a shape is transformed along the path. Display controls screen display. Objects creates a 3D mesh and exports it to the 3D Editor.

Shapes   The Shapes commands import shapes into the Lofter and arrange them in relation to the path. You can scale, rotate, or move a shape, but you can't change its basic outline within the Lofter. The Shapes command branch also includes a command for Steps, used to define the number of segments between each cross-section along the path.

Tip: Keep the Step setting as low as possible. The more steps, the more complex the resulting mesh object, the harder to single out individual vertices to modify, and the more rendering time and disk storage needed.

Path   The Path commands control getting and configuring the path which determines the third dimension. You can use the default path in the Lofter or import a path from the Shaper or a disk. Whatever the source, the path can be manipulated extensively once in the Lofter. The vertices along the path are used to place the shapes and locate points of deformation. Vertices can be inserted, deleted, and moved.

The path's configuration (and thus the cross-sections of the object) can be changed with 2D and 3D Scale, Skew, Mirror, Helix, Rotate, and Refine commands. SurfRev generates cylindrical lofts. You can undo path manipulations with the Default Angle, Straighten, and Default Path commands.

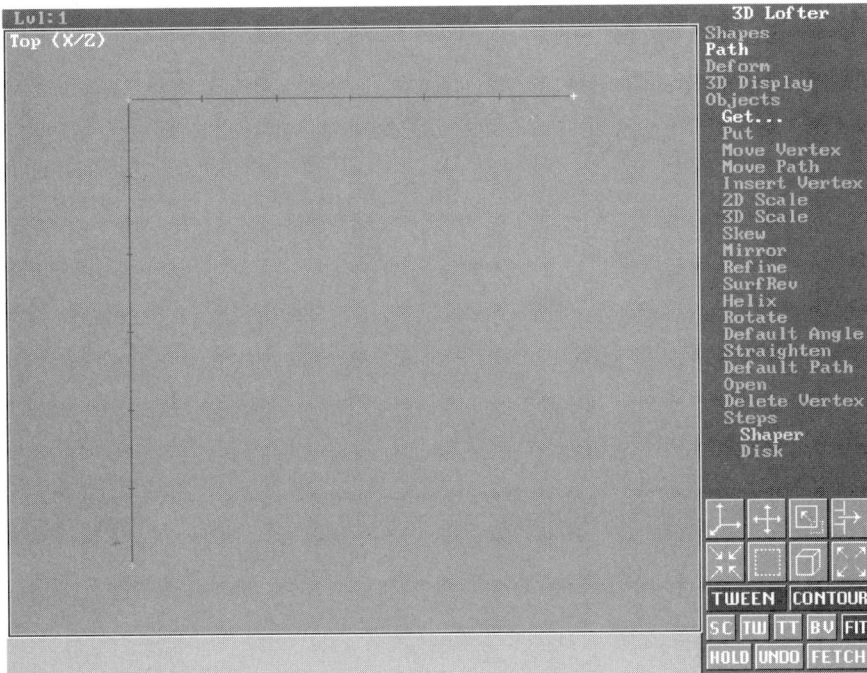

A full-screen view of the Top viewport showing the Path in detail. This path, imported from the Shaper, has a 90-degree angle. It is used to generate the muntin shape shown in Chapter 3 and in the section on Deform in this chapter.

Deform   While the Path commands affect the entire path, the Deform commands can be used to modify a shape based on its relationship to the path, vertex by vertex. The Scale command shrinks or swells the shape along the path. The Twist command rotates a shape around the path, or Z-axis. The Teeter command tilts the shapes in the X-Y plane, in relationship to the path. The Bevel Command acts as a 3D fillet.

Each Deform command calls up a grid to map the degree of deformation along the path. The Deform branch includes a Preview command to check your geometry before you loft the object.

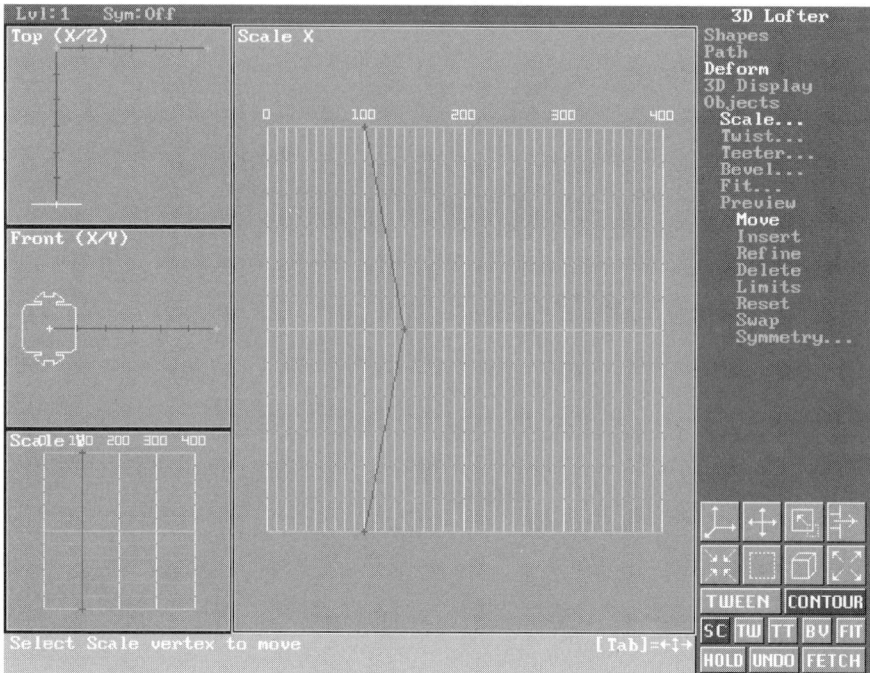

If the muntin shape were lofted as it is in a right angle, the object would "squeeze down" at the angle, because same-size sections would be used at 45 and 90 degrees to the path. (Remember $a^2 + b^2 = c^2$?) Insert superscript 2s for a squared, etc. To counteract the shrinking, the Deform/Scale command is used to insert a vertex at the angle and scale up the section along the X axis.

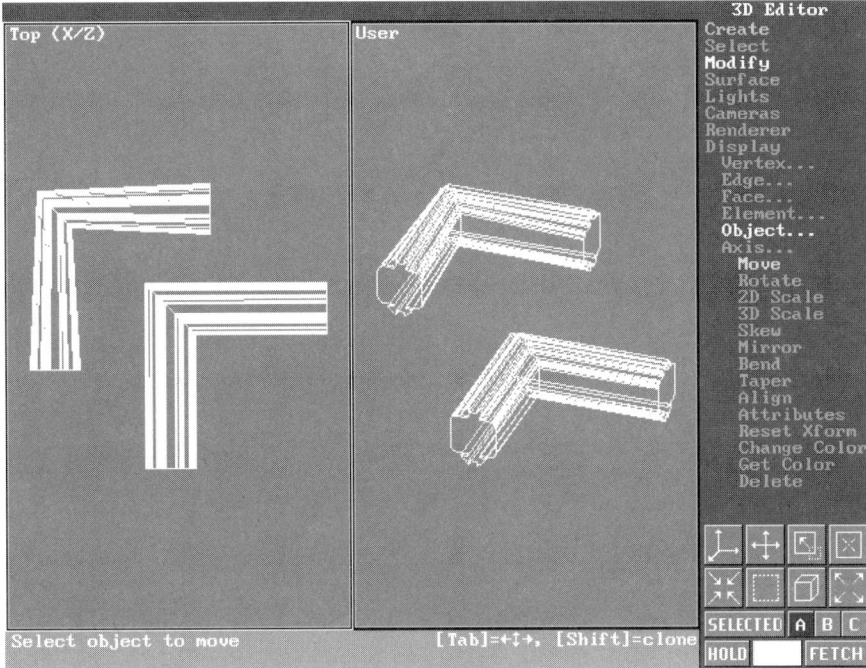

The top muntin is lofted without scaling. The path used for the bottom muntin is scaled up in the X axis at the angle.

The Fit command uses X and Y deformation grids to loft shapes, using different fit shapes for the X and Y axes. The next two illustrations demonstrate the Fit command.

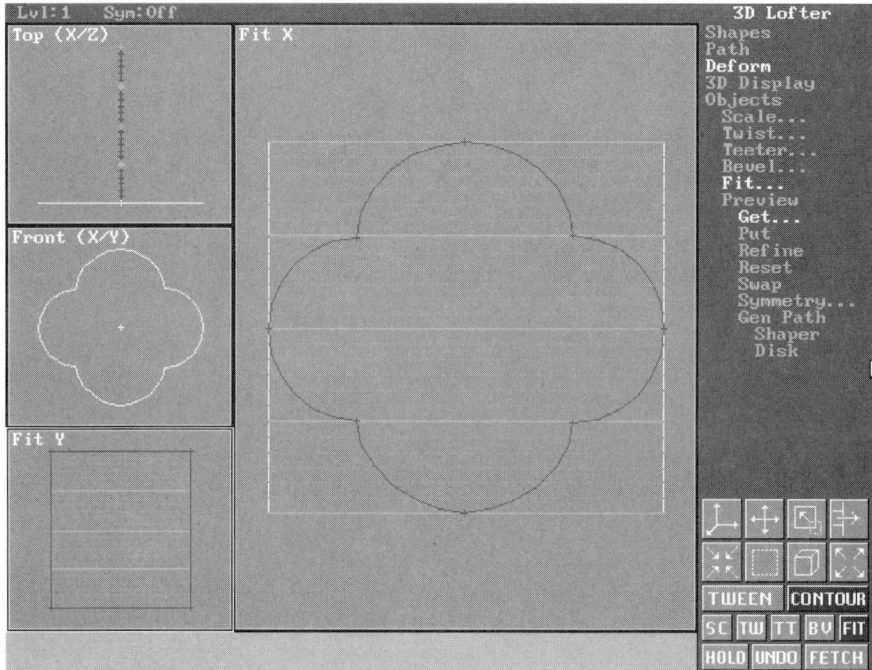

A quatrefoil fit shape is imported to the X grid and a rectangular fit shape of the same height is imported to the Y grid. The actual shape that is lofted is unimportant; the program forces it to the configuration determined by the fit shapes. The 3D mesh object will tween from one fit shape to the other.

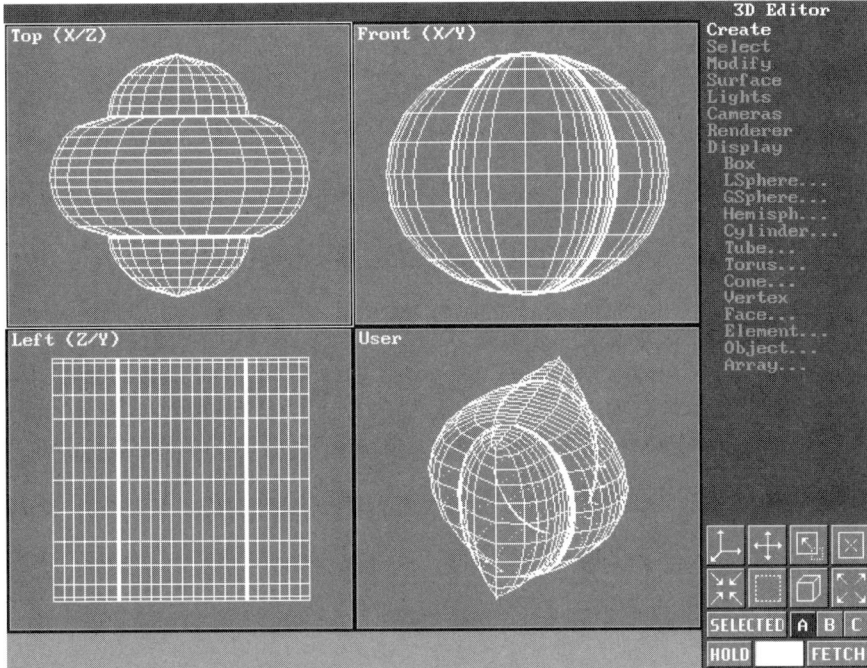

The mesh object generated by using the quatrefoil and rectangular fit shapes. If you live in New Mexico, you will recognize it as a tri-lobular sopapilla.

3D Display   The Display commands are similar to those in the 2D Shaper, applied to all three dimensions in the Lofter.

Objects   The Objects group includes only two commands, Make and Preview. Make computes the 3D geometry you have specified and sends the completed object to the 3D Editor for viewing. The Preview command shows the shape's cross-sections located as specified along the path.

The 3D Editor

The *3D Studio Reference Manual* refers to the 3D Editor as the central module for object and scene creation and lists its capabilities:

❑ Load geometry from a disk in *.3ds, .dxf, .flm.,* or *.asc* formats

❑ Create basic 3D primitives, such as spheres, boxes, and cones.

❑ Create other 3D mesh objects by connecting vertices and building faces, or by using Boolean operations on existing mesh objects.

❑ Arrange 3D mesh objects created in both the 3D Lofter and 3D Editor.

❑ Display, move, and alter the geometry of 3D mesh objects.

❑ Apply materials to the surfaces of 3D mesh objects.

❑ Create, position, and adjust lights and cameras.

❑ Render the resulting scene as viewed from any viewport.

The Parts of a Mesh Object   The first step in many 3D Editor operations is deciding whether you want to apply the operation to a vertex, face, element, or object. So we might as well untangle the graphic component terms now. You've met a couple of them before, but they're back in a new guise.

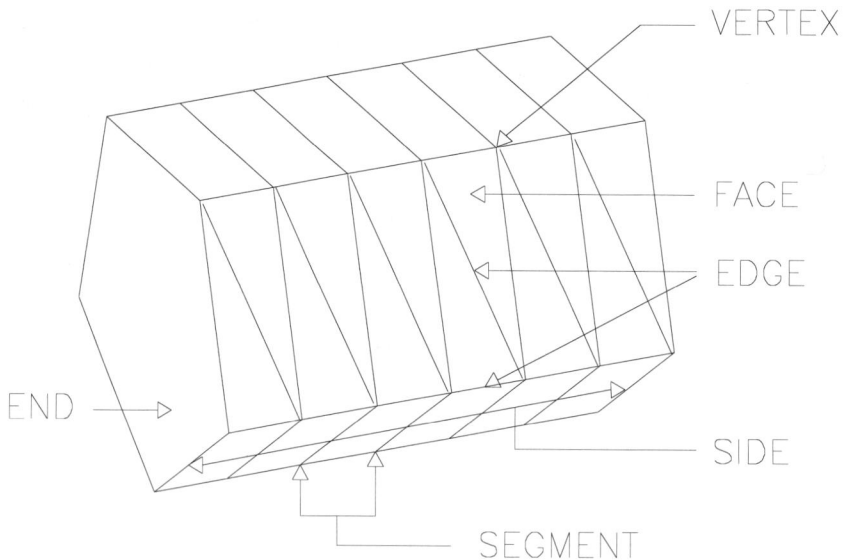

The graphic components of a mesh object.

Vertex. A point in space. Vertices form the structure on which faces are built. When you create a mesh object, faces and vertices are created together, but you can also create vertices independently.

Face. A triangle formed by three vertices—the simplest possible plane. A face is not the same thing as a segment or side.

Edge. A line formed between two vertices of a face. Each face is bounded by three edges, though contiguous faces share a single edge. Edges are not visible if the faces they separate are coplanar.

End. The end of a mesh object, such as the circles at the ends of a cylinder or truncated cone.

Sides. The flat surfaces that run from one end of the mesh object to the other.

Segment. The portion of an object between two of its cross-sections.

Object. A collection of one or more vertices forming a net-like appearance; hence, the term *mesh object*.

Element. One of two or more individual mesh objects grouped together into one larger object.

3D Editor Command Groups

3D Editor commands fall into two major groups. (1) The Create, Select, Modify, and Display commands are primarily concerned with modeling. (2) Lights, Cameras, Surfaces, and Renderer commands deal principally with rendering operations.

Create The commands in this group create 3D mesh primitives and vertices. The primitives can be either smooth or faceted with any number of faces. Individual faces, elements, and objects can be arrayed, copied, tessellated, detached, exploded, or subjected to Boolean operations.

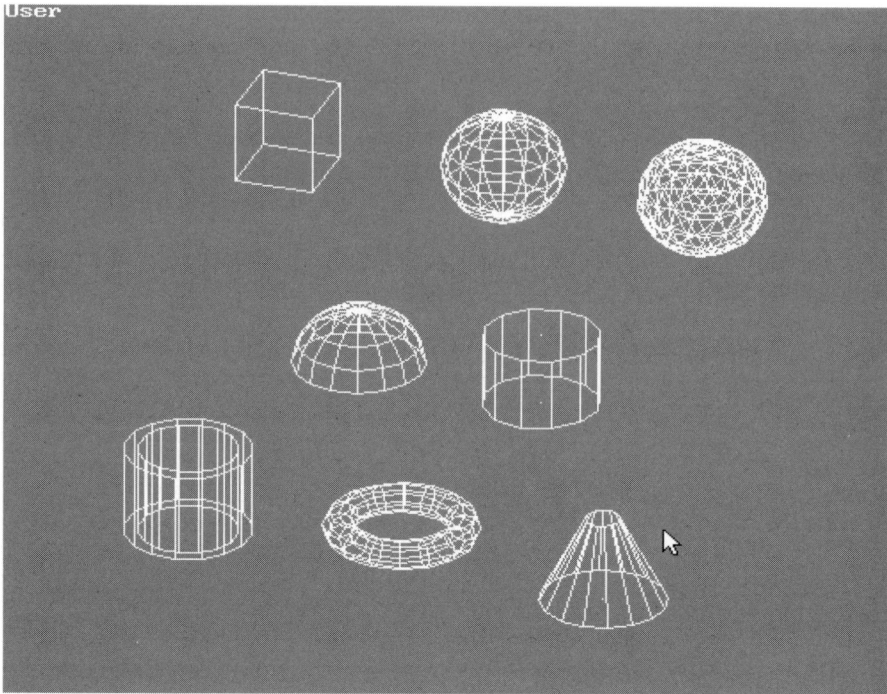

3D Editor primitives. Top row: Box, Lsphere (latitude/longitude), Gsphere (geodesic).
Second row: Hemisphere, Cylinder. Bottom row: Tube, Torus, Cone.

Select   The 3D Editor selection tools are similar to those in the 2D Shaper, with the addition that you can select by vertex, face, element, or object. The second exercise at the end of this chapter explores the use of selection tools.

Modify   This group includes a powerful set of commands to further adjust the 3D primitives and modify 3D shapes that have been lofted. The first branch of the Modify commands specifies whether you want to work on a vertex, edge, face, element, object, or axis.

The component you choose to manipulate can be moved, rotated, scaled in two or three dimensions, skewed, mirrored, bent, tapered, aligned, or welded to another component. The following illustration shows various modifications of a cylinder.

Top row: The cylinder on the left has been 2D-scaled in the top viewport. By scaling in only one plane, you can change the proportions of an object—in this case, increasing the X-Z plane scale, or diameter, and leaving the Y dimension intact, which makes the object squatter. The middle cylinder has been 3D-scaled, which increases its size proportionally. The cylinder on the right has been skewed to the right. Use the [Tab] key to choose the direction of the skew.

Bottom row: The cylinder on the left has been bent, and the one on the right has been tapered. Pick the Local Axis button before using Taper operations.

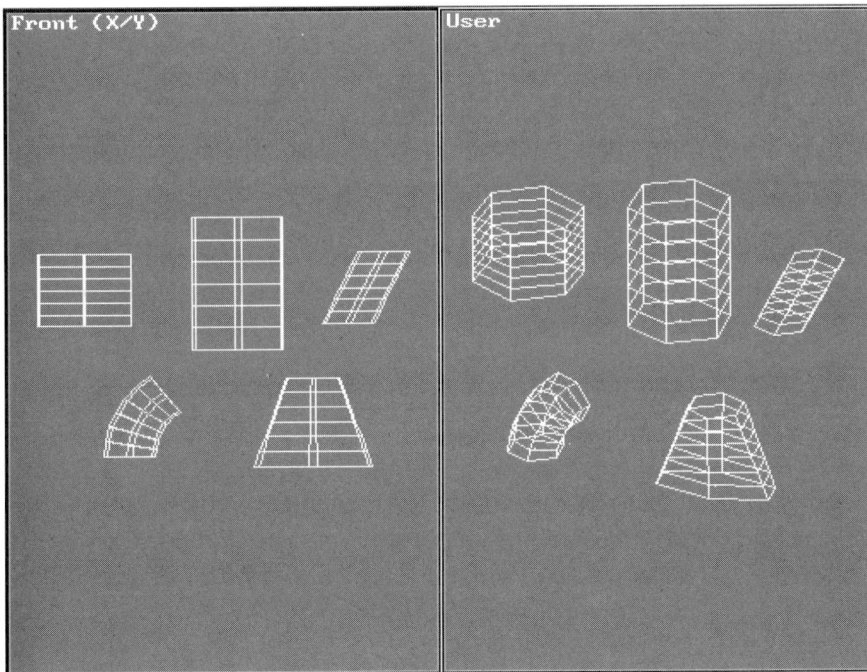

Modifying a cylinder as a complete object. Further changes can be made to individual faces, edges, or vertices.

Understanding which directional arrow to use and which area of the object to select for specific skew, bend, and taper operations can take a little practice. For example, refer to both the 2D Lofter and 3D Editor sections on these commands in the 3D Studio documentation.

Surface The group of surface commands, in combination with the Lights and Cameras commands and the Materials Editor, takes care of everything that most rendering programs accomplish.

In the Surface group, the Material subset controls the application of materials by face, element, and object. The Smoothing subset controls whether the rendering process delineates or smoothes over non-coplanar edges. Surface normals can be flipped at will with the Normals commands. A surface normal is a vector perpendicular to a plane surface. For successful rendering, surface normals should project outward from a object's planar surfaces. The Mapping subset controls the application of texture, bump, reflection, and opacity maps.

Lights and Cameras The Lights commands control the three types of light: Ambient, Spot, and Omni. You can create, move, adjust color and intensity, place highlights in a specific spot, and specify Spotlight Hotspot and Falloff. With the Cameras commands, you can create and control single or multiple cameras. The exercises in this chapter take you through a simple setup for lights, camera, and rendering, and Chapter 5 discusses these operations in detail.

Renderer The Renderer branch includes several commands for specifying which portion of a scene to render. In addition, the Renderer/Setup command branches to a series of dialog boxes that control Atmosphere, Background, Configuration, Options, Shadows, and cubic mapping. The Renderer/View commands allow you to display picture files, flic animations, the last image rendered, and to save a rendering to a specified file.

Display The Display branch expands the standard Display commands by adding Geometry commands, which control whether the mesh object is shown in full detail, in a variety of partially hidden modes, or simplified to a collection of "boxes" to speed up redraws. The second exercise in this chapter concentrates on Display functions.

The Materials Editor

The Materials Editor is your workshop for obtaining, refining, and creating surface characteristics. In some ways, it is the most standalone of the five modules, because its functions don't involve any change in object geometry or location. However, the final effect of a rendered surface depends on interactions of the specified material with lights, atmosphere, and cameras, which are controlled in the 3D Editor.

If you are using an existing library material (as in the last exercise in this chapter), you don't need to get into the Materials Editor. You do need to use the Materials Editor if you want to

❏ See what a material looks like before you use it

❏ Alter the properties of the material in any way

❏ Create a new material

The Materials Editor Pull-Down Menus   The menu bar for the
Materials Editor displays pull-down menus for Library, Material, and Options. The Appendix A menu maps include these menus.

The Library menu includes commands for loading, merging, creating, and deleting libraries of materials. 3D Studio ships with three libraries: the 3DS.MLI library, which contains 154 materials; the TUTORIAL.MLI library, which contains materials used in the tutorial; and the ACADCLR.MLI library of the 256 standard colors that match AutoCAD colors. Appendix B describes library contents in detail.

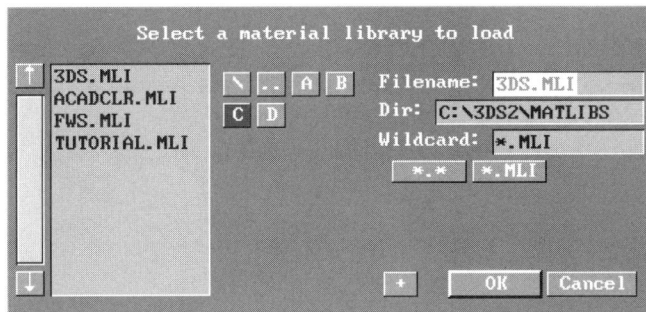

```
                 Select a material library to load
↑   3DS.MLI          \  ..  A  B   Filename: 3DS.MLI
    ACADCLR.MLI       C  D        Dir: C:\3DS2\MATLIBS
    FWS.MLI                        Wildcard: *.MLI
    TUTORIAL.MLI                     *.*   *.MLI


↓                               +     OK    Cancel
```

The Load Library command displays a list of the available libraries.

The Material menu contains commands for moving materials to and from libraries and for moving materials back and forth to the current scene in the 3D Editor. The Material commands control traffic for individual materials, as the Library commands do for groups of materials. If you do

not assign a material to an object before rendering, 3D Studio will assign
a default, shiny white material.

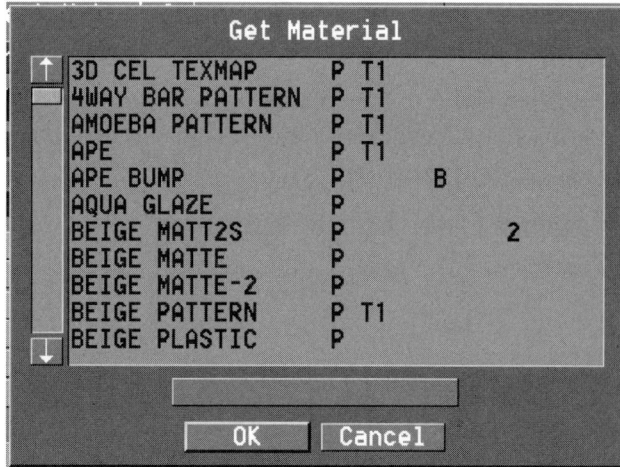

```
                          Get Material
 ┌┬┐ 3D CEL TEXMAP      P  T1
 │ │ 4WAY BAR PATTERN   P  T1
 │ │ AMOEBA PATTERN     P  T1
 │ │ APE                P  T1
 │ │ APE BUMP           P         B
 │ │ AQUA GLAZE         P
 │ │ BEIGE MATT2S       P              2
 │ │ BEIGE MATTE        P
 │ │ BEIGE MATTE-2      P
 │ │ BEIGE PATTERN      P  T1
 └┴┘ BEIGE PLASTIC      P

          [         OK        ]  [  Cancel  ]
```

The Get Material command calls up a list of the materials in the current library. The
letters to the right of the material names indicate mapping features.

The Options menu controls anti-aliasing and back lighting in the sample
windows of the Materials Editor screen. You can also use its commands
to view the last image and check images for transparency levels and illegal
video colors.

The Materials Editor Screen   Rather than displaying viewports
and a screen menu, the Materials Editor screen resembles a giant dialog
box with color (see the following illustration).

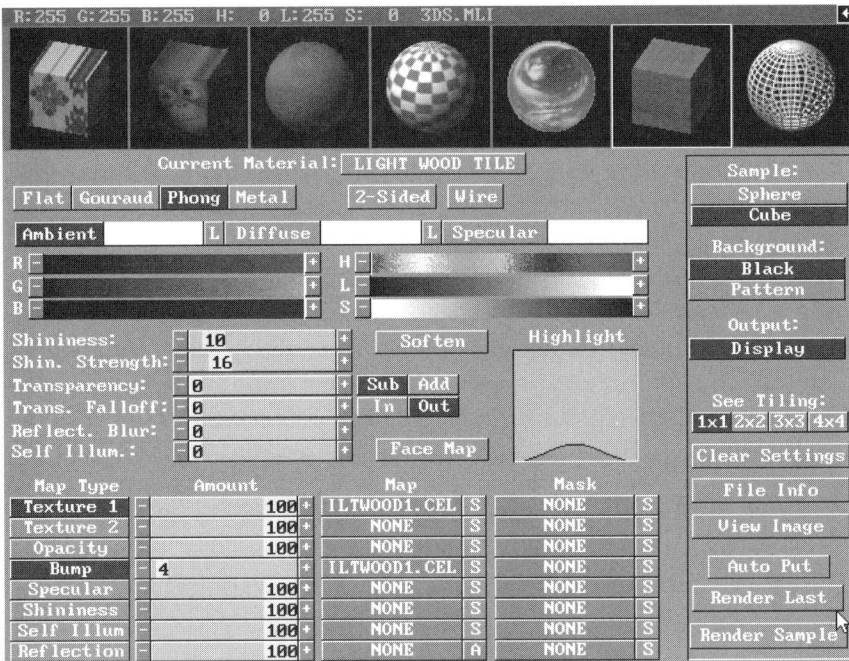

The Materials Editor screen.

The main portion of the screen contains tools for adjusting material properties. From the top down, they are

❏ The status bar, which displays settings for RGB and HLS color models, and the name of the current library

❏ Seven sample windows, which display test renderings of the current material

❏ A text box listing Current Material

❏ Buttons for choosing the shading limit—Flat, Gouraud, Phong, or Metal

❏ Special attribute buttons to apply 2-Sided or Wireframe properties to the current material

❏ Boxes that display swatches of the material's Ambient, Diffuse, and Specular color settings

❏ Slide bars to adjust RGB and HLS color settings

❏ Six slide bars and four buttons to control material properties—shininess, transparency, reflection blur, and self illumination.

❏ To the right of the material property controls are Soften and Face Map buttons, and a dynamic Highlight Graph.

❏ Eight slide bar sets for controlling the available types of mapping.

The control panel, which runs down the right side of the screen, includes buttons for controlling various display options, specifying output format, tiling repetitions, and performing operations related to editing materials.

Color   The color controls in the Materials Editor determine the color of all non mapped materials. Rather than assigning a color to uniformly cover an object, 3D Studio refines the color to more accurately simulate the effects of light in three types of lighting conditions. The buttons and associated color swatches specify separate colors for the following areas of each object:

❏ Ambient color is that which appears on an object where it is not in direct light.

❏ Diffuse color is the color of a matte, or non shiny, object in direct light.

❏ Specular color is the color of a highlight on a shiny object. Specular reflection colors differ for metallic and nonmetallic objects. If you are using Metal as the Shading Limit (see description of same), the Specular button does not appear.

Tip: This three-way color assignment mode increases your ability to simulate realistic color, but it also triples your opportunities for messing up. When you begin using 3D Studio, you can lock the Ambient controls to the Diffuse controls by toggling on the L button between them. Thus, you only have to manage two color definitions, without much loss of realism.

3D Studio provides controls for using both RGB (red, green, blue) and HLS (hue, luminance, saturation) colorspaces. If you are familiar with mixing traditional pigment colors, HLS may be easier and more intuitive for you to use. The Hue slider determines the material's basic spectral color—red, orange, yellow, etc. The Luminance slider controls the lightness and darkness of the color. The Saturation slider controls the purity of the color, or amount of gray mixed into the spectral hue.

Tip: Go easy on Saturation. The temptation is to set Saturation too high, resulting in eye-cracking Day-Glo™ colors throughout the scene.

The RGB colorspace more accurately reflects the way a computer actually produces color by mixing colored light instead of pigment. However, RGB systems have a couple of characteristics that are upsetting to those more familiar with mixing pigments.

When you increase the number and amount of colors in a pigment mixture, it usually gets darker; when you increase the amount, or intensity, of the components in a mixture of colored light, the mixture gets brighter, because the total amount of light is increased. Also, because the primary colors of light are red, green, and blue, rather than red, yellow, and blue, mixing red and green light together produces yellow light, instead of the muddy gray of mixed red and green pigment.

The RGB and HLS controls interact. That is, moving the RGB sliders will automatically move the HLS sliders to settings that produce the same color, and vice versa.

Tip: If you've used the RGB controls to get the hue you want, but it's too light or dark, you can use the Luminance slider to adjust the intensity without wrecking your Hue setting. Ditto for Saturation.

Shading Limits   3D Studio provides four shading limits or modes. In increasing order of rendering time and realism they are Flat, Gouraud, Phong, and Metal. In a single rendering, you can assign different shading limits to different objects.

Flat shading applies a single color to each facet of an object, depending on the angle of the facet in relationship to light sources. It is the fastest mode and can be used for objects without curved surfaces.

Gouraud shading interpolates color for each face of an object based on the colors of the three vertices. It is slower than flat shading, but provides a smooth, non faceted appearance.

Phong shading is still slower and more realistic. It assigns a color to each pixel of the rendering, interpolating from the surface normals of each vertex. If an object is bump-mapped, or receives cast shadows, it is necessary to use Phong shading for these effects to work.

Metal shading creates a metallic effect by mixing ambient and diffuse colors into the color of the specular highlight. It also increases the contrast of the highlight and will calculate additional highlights from glancing light.

Material Properties and Mapping   Material properties and mapping move you to a higher level of complexity. Rather than explore them in this overview, we'll save them for Chapters 7 and 8, where they will be discussed in conjunction with actual exercises.

The Keyframer

Once you have created geometry in the 3D Editor, you can use the Keyframer to animate any part of a scene, including lights and cameras. The *3D Studio Reference Manual* explains the origin of the keyframing concept:

> *Depending on the quality you want, one minute of animation requires between 720 and 1,800 separate still images. Creating images by hand is a big job. That's where keyframing comes in.*
>
> *Most of the frames in an animation are routine, incremental changes from the previous frame directed toward some predefined goal. Early animation studios quickly realized they could increase the productivity of their master artists by having them draw only the important frames, called keyframes. Assistants could then figure out the frames that were required in between the keyframes. These frames were (and still area) called tweens.*
>
> *The Keyframer is your 3D Studio animation assistant. As the animator, you create the keyframes that record the beginning and end of each transformation of a scene. Then the Keyframer calculates the tweens.*

Still Shots Versus Slide Shows Versus Animations

Which procedure you want depends on what you're interested in. If the content of a particular view is the important feature, a series of still shots shown in a predetermined sequence—a slide show—is quickest and better suited to studying detail. If the movement itself is what you're after, or the physical sensation of moving through a building, then you need to use animations.

The Track Info Dialog Box   The Track Info dialog box is comparable to a highly detailed story board; it determines the overall sequence of the animation. After first specifying the total number of frames over which the action will occur, you can use the Track Info grid to place keys along the sequence of the animation to establish the frame position of scene elements at their desired ending states.

Each scene component—mesh objects, lights, cameras, and targets—has its own Track Info dialog box. Within each component's dialog box, there are individual tracks for Position, Rotate, Scale, Morph, and Hide, and a combined track.

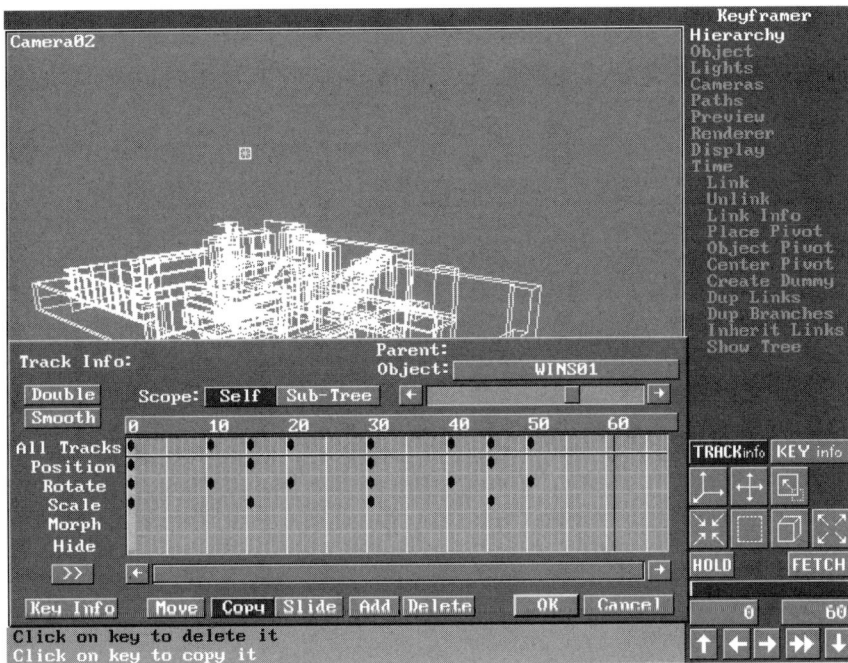

The Track Info dialog box controls the frame-by-frame sequence of the animation. The black dots within the grid locate the keyframes for various motion states.

The Key Info Dialog Box   The Key Info dialog box fine-tunes the motion of elements in individual keyframes. Different options are displayed, depending on which scene component is selected—mesh, light, camera.

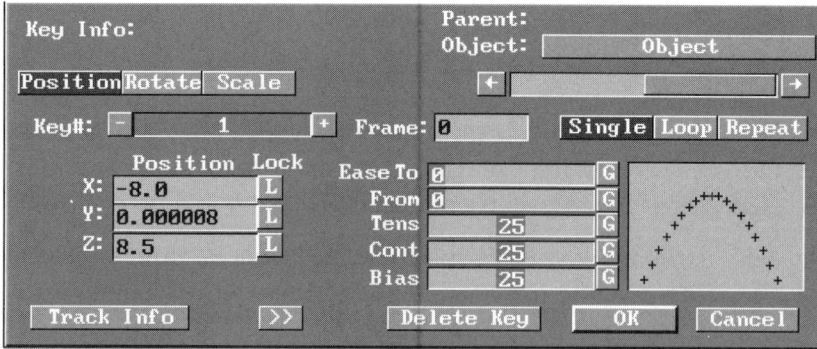

Key Info:				Parent: Object:			Object	

The Key Info dialog box controls elements in an individual frame. The controls in this illustration are for a mesh object.

Keyframer Command Groups

Several command branches in the Keyframer are similar to those in the 3D Editor, but have additional commands that control operations over a span of time and tie them into the sequence established in the Track and Key Info dialog boxes.

Hierarchy Commands in this branch control the movement of parts of a model in relation to each other. To produce animations, object parts are linked together in a specific hierarchy, so that when one part moves, the action is carried through in various ways to subordinate parts.

The human body is a good analogy for hierarchical linkage. The fingers are linked to, and subordinate to, the hand; the hand is subordinate to the arm; the arm to the torso. In 3D Studio, the subordinate part is referred to as *the child,* the controlling part as *the parent.* Just as the parent arm controls the child hand, the action of the parent model part controls the action of the child model part.

The Hierarchy commands establish both the hierarchy of the linkages and duplicate linkages through multiple parts. Other commands in the Hierarchy branch control the placement of movement pivots—the point of connection between two parts, which is the originating point of movement or rotation.

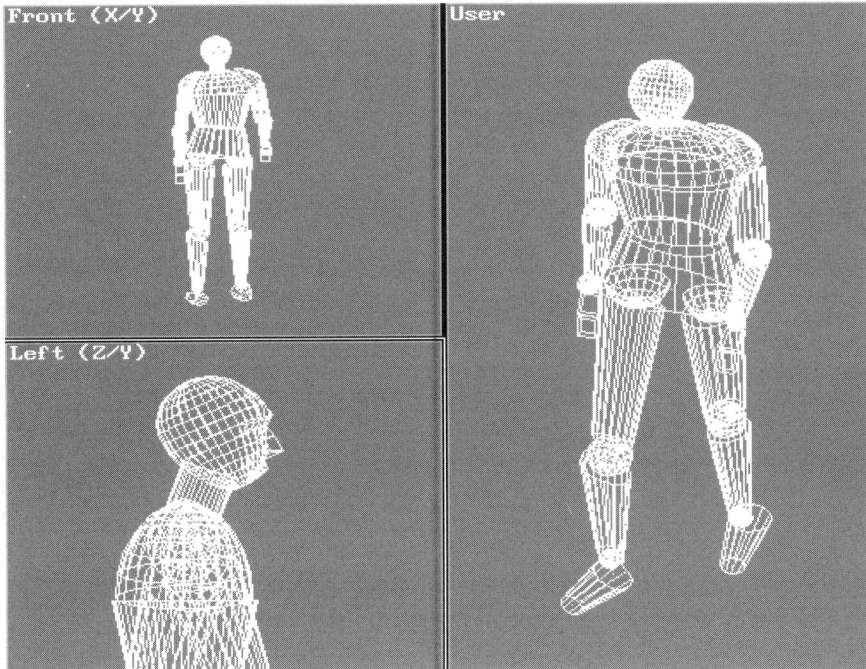

The first step in animating HulkMan is to locate pivot points in the ball joints, and then to establish hierarchical linkages: parent chest to child shoulder, upper arm, forearm, hand, and so on.

Object   The commands in the Object branch allow you to transform an object from keyframe to keyframe by scaling, squashing, moving, or morphing it. Once established, the motion sequence can be looped or set to repeat over and over.

Lights, Cameras, Display, and Renderer   The commands in these branches are similar to the ones in the 3D Editor. The Lights and Cameras groups have additional commands for Tracks, which allow you to set up sequences and loop (or repeat) them, copy, or reverse the action. The Renderer group includes a branch of commands for linking with a videotape recorder.

Paths   The Paths commands control getting, hiding, and following paths, and moving, adding, and deleting keys. This branch also includes controls for video Tension, Continuity, and Bias.

Preview   The Preview commands allow you to make, play, and save quick previews of the animation, and to adjust the speed at which the animation runs.

Time   The Time commands allow you to move to a specified frame, change the total number of frames, define an active segment, and change the time scale (speed up or slow down) for the active segment.

Exercise 1: Setting up a Project Specific Work Environment

Plans drawn by Frank Lloyd Wright were rarely defaced by unsightly strings of dimensions. Instead, he drew the floor plan upon a background grid of squares (typically 4 feet by 4 feet), or other regular geometrical shapes. This unit system often frustrated workmen used to more conventional methods of dimensioning. At Fallingwater, space is organized by a scheme of bays roughly 12 feet square, overlaid by a 3-foot grid. Vertical dimensions are generated from a 17-inch unit. (Hoffman, p. 45)

Whether following Wright's plans or using computer modeling, continually adjusting Units and Grids (or Snaps and Viewports) is tiresome, so in this exercise you'll set up a default environment tailored to the Fallingwater model and save it as a project file. You can call up the file whenever you want to work on the entire model.

The project file is like an empty photo studio ready for a subject. You can create customized project files for any frequently used environments. You can load the project file at the beginning of a session and create geometry within its environment. Alternately, you can create the geometry first, and then merge the geometry and project files. The 3D Studio documentation covers many other settings that you can incorporate into a project file to automatically set up specific conditions.

Setup Units and Drawing Aids

In this section, you'll launch 3D Studio and, once more, define the settings we've already encountered.

1. At the C:\ prompt, type **3DS** and press [Enter].

2. Press [Ctrl] + [U] to display the Measurement Unit Selection dialog box.

3. Pick the Architectural button, type **1** in the Unit text box, and pick the In button.

4. Type **16** in the Denominator text box and pick the OK button.

5. Press [Ctrl] + [A] to display the Drawing Aids dialog box.

6. Type **1″** in the Snap Setting X: text box and click on Y: to copy the setting to the Y and Z text boxes.

7. Type **6″** in the Grid Spacing X: text box and click on the Y: to copy the value. Leave the Grid Extents settings at their default values. Click OK.

Result: When you save these settings to a project file, they can be loaded automatically.

Setup a Default Omni Light

A 3D Studio omni light functions as a point in 3D space that radiates light evenly in all directions. In this section you'll create one omni light to serve as a default lighting setup.

1. Press [F3] to get into the 3D Editor, if necessary.

2. Choose Lights/Omni/Create.

3. To locate the light in 3D space, type:

> **-80 [Enter]**
> **100 [Enter]**
> **-120 [Enter]**

4. The Light Definition dialog box appears. Click on the Create button to accept the defaults.

5. Right click Zoom Extents.

Result: The light appears in the viewports as a yellow star.

Tip: Generally, lights and cameras are located in relation to the model more easily using the mouse. However, for these exercises it's easier to type coordinates to replicate a specific position. When working on a project, make a note of location coordinates in case you need to move something back to the same position later.

Setup a Default Camera

In this section, you'll set up a default camera by specifying locations for both the camera and its target.

1. Choose Cameras/Create.

2. Type in the coordinates for the camera:

>   **130 [Enter]**
>   **20   [Enter]**
>   **-40 [Enter]**

3. Type in the target coordinates:

>   **65 [Enter]**
>   **0   [Enter]**
>   **30 [Enter]**

4. The Camera Definition dialog box appears. In the Stock Lenses group of buttons, pick the 35mm button, and pick the Create button.

5. Right click Zoom Extents.

Result: The camera appears in the viewports as a blue circle connected to the target—a small square.

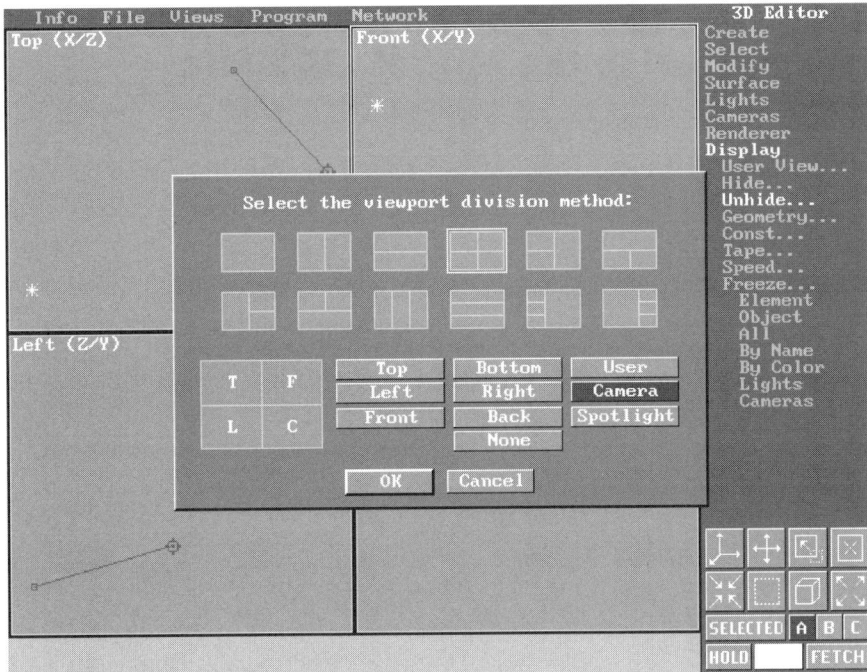

The 3D Editor screen, with light, camera, and Viewports dialog box.

Setup Default Viewports

Now that you've created a camera, you can specify the lower right 3D Editor viewport as a Camera viewport.

1.   Press [Ctrl] + [V] to display the Viewports dialog box.

2.   From the ten view name buttons, choose Camera, then click on the lower right quadrant of the viewport configuration diagram. Click on OK.

Result: The 3D Editor will appear with a Camera viewport.

Save the .3DS Scene as a Project File, and Merge it with the Model .3DS File

The *.prj* file can be used like a *.3ds* file.

1. To save the settings, choose File/Save Project from the menu bar. Type a filename (for example, **Fwater**) in the filename text box; the *.prj* extension is added automatically. Make a note of the drive and directory to which the file is saved. Click OK.

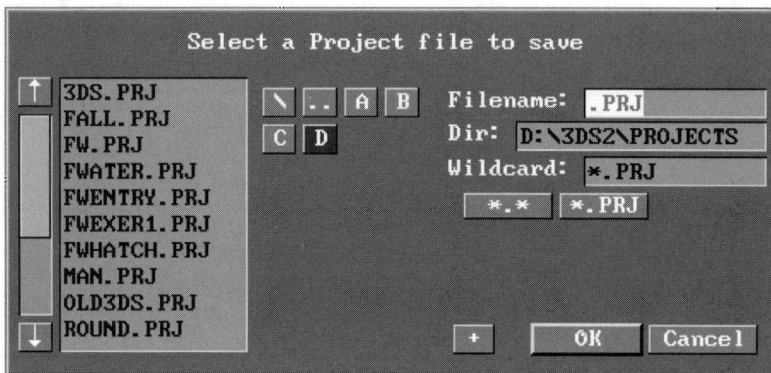

The File/Save Project dialog box.

2. Choose File/Reset from the menu bar to clear the screen, and pick Yes in the message box.

3. To use the settings, choose File/Load Project from the menu bar. Get to the correct drive and directory and choose FWATER.PRJ from the scroll box. Click Yes.

4. To load the foundation model into the project file environment, choose File/Merge from the menu bar. In the Merge dialog box, toggle off everything except Mesh Objects. Click OK.

5. In the Merge a 3DS, DXF, or FLM File dialog box, pick the correct drive button, if necessary, and click on the FOUND.3DS file. Click OK.

6. When the Select Object to Merge dialog box appears, click on the All button and the OK button. The foundation will appear in the 3D Editor viewports. Right click Zoom Extents.

7. Now you'll merge the main level 3DS file with the foundation level. Pick File/Merge. Toggle off all buttons in the Merge dialog box except Mesh Objects.

8. From the Merge a 3DS, DXF, or FLM File dialog box, press the correct drive button, pick the LVL-1.3DS file in the scroll box, click the All Button, and click OK.

9. To save the combined file, choose File/Save and type **FND-LVL1** in the filename text box and click OK.

Result: The first two levels and the project file settings are combined in a single file. Since the two levels were created with the same coordinates, they should be aligned properly.

Exercise 2: Getting the Big Picture with Display Controls

Throughout this book emphasis is placed on the distinction between mass and detail and on a basic principle: don't drown yourself in detail unnecessary for the job at hand. It overloads both you and your computer.

Combining just two levels of Fallingwater creates a model that is confusing in full wireframe display and that requires a noticeable redraw time. Since we will be working with the entire model in many of the subsequent exercises, this exercise will take you through some Display controls that are useful in manipulating a large model.

There are many more Display options than those demonstrated here, which were chosen because they are particularly useful for simplifying the screen image. The following exercise looks at display controls that affect the whole screen, a single viewport, and individual parts of the model.

Use Fastdraw and Box Display in All Viewports

Redraw speed is a function of the complexity of the model and the speed of your hardware. 3D Studio provides several Display commands to minimize redraw time and simplify the visual display.

1. If you stopped after the last exercise, load 3D Studio and the FND-LVL1.3DS file.

2. Choose Display/Hide/Lights and Display/Hide/Cameras, and then right click Zoom Extents.

3. Hold down the [Shift] key and tap the [Tilde] key. Notice the time the system takes to redraw the model.

4. Choose Display/Speed/Set Fast. The speed display default is 10. Use the slider bar to change it to 4 and click OK.

5. Choose Display/Speed/Fastdraw to turn on the fast display; hold down the [Shift] key and tap the [Tilde] key to verify the increase in redraw speed.

6. Click on Display/Speed/Fulldraw to return to the fully detailed model.

7. To *really* speed up and simplify, click on Display/Geometry/Box (or hold down the [Alt] key and press the [B] key). The model is redrawn as a collection of "bounding boxes." This display mode is adequate if you don't need to examine model details.

8. Hold down the [Alt] key and press [B] to return to full detail.

Result: Setting the Fastdraw speed to 4 displays only one in every four faces of the model. Using Box display simplifies the model further. Holding down the [Shift] key and pressing the [Tilde] key redraws the screen.

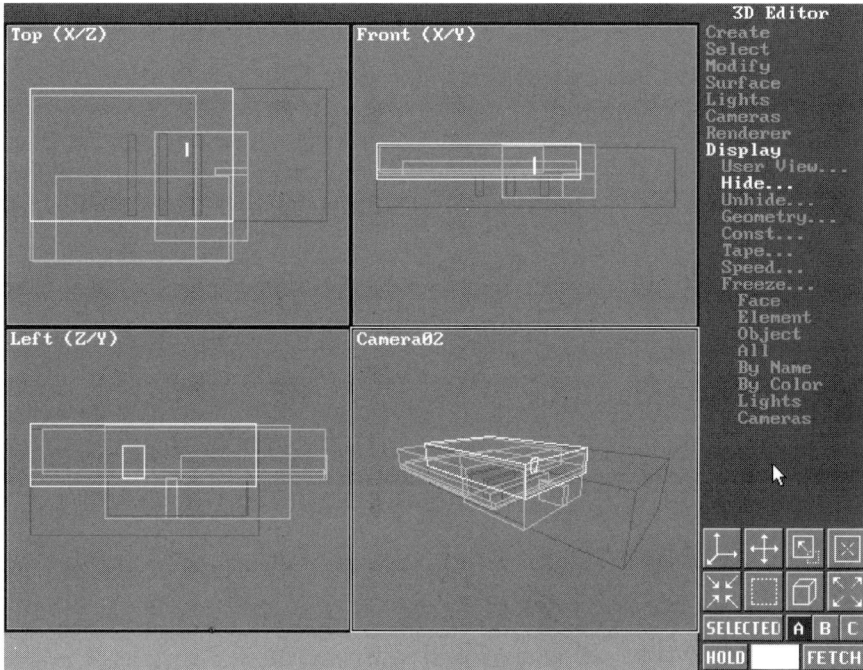

The Box display mode shown in all viewports.

Control Display in Individual Viewports

You can set individual viewports to Fastdraw if you don't need them for detailed display, or eliminate them from the screen display altogether.

1. Click on any viewport to make it active. Press the [V] key to toggle on Fastdraw for the active viewport.

2. To provide the largest possible display area for the model, click on the Single Port icon button (second from the right in the top row of the icon panel.) You can switch views in the single port by pressing a single letter representing the view—[T] for top, [L] for left, and so on.

3. Click on the Single Port button again to return to four viewports and press [V] to toggle off Fastdraw.

Result: You can control the display mode in individual viewports.

Use Display Controls on Individual Objects

At the next lower level, you can hide or assign Fastdraw to selected parts of the model.

1. Choose Select/Object/By Name. To select all the windows in Falling-water, in the scroll box click on the objects that include "WINS" as part of the name. Click OK.

2. Click on Display/Speed/Object and then click the Selected button in the icon panel. Click in any viewport. The model's windows are redrawn in Fastdraw mode.

3. To hide part of the model, choose Display/Hide/By Name. In the scroll box, click on the object "Found," and then click OK. The foundation level is no longer displayed. It is still in memory, but cannot be affected by the editing commands.

4. Click on Display/Unhide/All to restore the foundation to the screen. Press [Q] and then [Y] to quit without saving, and restore the default Display settings.

Result: After a series of Display manipulations, the full screen is returned to Fulldraw mode.

Exercise 3: Putting a Skin on Fallingwater

All the metalwork at Fallingwater is painted Cherokee red—a vibrant, slightly rusty color that Wright enshrined as symbolic of fire, of blood...of Life. Not only did he apply the color to buildings and furnishings, all his vehicles were painted Cherokee red. (Tafel, p.179)

This exercise assigns "generic" materials to Fallingwater—Beige Matte to serve for stucco and masonry and Red Matte to stand in for the Cherokee red window frames. Since you set up a light and camera in this chapter's first exercise, you'll have all you need to render the model. Doing a simple preliminary rendering is a good way to check the model for missing faces and edges, hidden line removal, and so on.

Assign Materials to the Model

In this section, you will assign a beige material to all objects and then replace the beige with red on the window frames. This application method is quicker than singly selecting every object except the windows for the beige material.

Load the FND-LVL1.3DS file as described previously.

1. From the 3D Editor screen menu, choose Surface/Material/Choose to display the Material selector scroll box.

2. Scroll down until BEIGE MATTE appears, and click on it. Click OK.

3. Choose Surface/Material/Assign/By Name and click on the All button. Click OK. When the message box appears, click OK.

4. Click on Surface/Material/Choose again. Hold down the [Alt] key and tap the [R] key to go directly to the listings starting with that letter.

5. Click on the RED MATTE listing and click OK.

6. Choose Surface/Material/Assign/By Name again. From the scroll box, choose all objects that include "WINS" in their name. Click OK twice. Choose File/Save to save the materials. Check that FND-LVL1.3DS appears in the filename textbox, and click OK twice.

Result: The red material is assigned to the window frames, and the beige material to everything else.

```
                    Material Selector
    ↑  3D CEL TEXMAP       P  T1
       4WAY BAR PATTERN    P  T1
       AMOEBA PATTERN      P  T1
       APE                 P  T1
       APE BUMP            P       B
       AQUA GLAZE          P
       BEIGE MATT2S        P              2
       BEIGE MATTE         P
       BEIGE MATTE-2       P
    ↓  BEIGE PATTERN       P  T1

       Current Material:   BEIGE MATTE
                       Default

       Current Library:    3DS
                  OK       Cancel
```

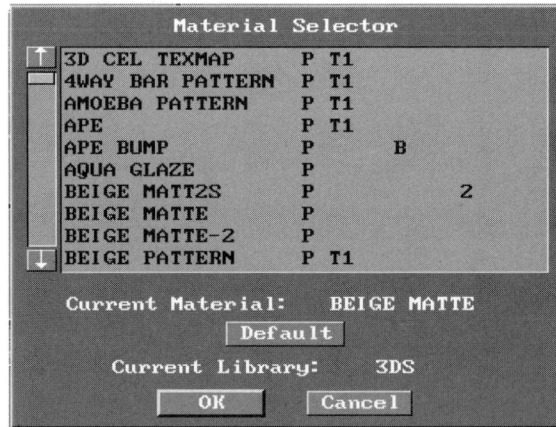

The Material Selector dialog box.

Render the Scene

Now you'll check some rendering settings and render the scene.

1. From the screen menu choose Renderer/Render View. Click twice on the lower right Camera viewport.

2. When the Render Still Image dialog box appears, toggle on the Phong button.

3. Check to make sure the following Configure settings are displayed:

    ```
    File Type = GIF
    Resolution = 640 x 480 x 1.0
    ```

4. If you wish to render the scene to disk as well as to the screen, click on the Disk button in the Output group. When the dialog box appears, type **FND-LVL1** in the text box and click OK. Make a note of the drive and path.

5. Click the Render button. In a few minutes the rendering will appear. Press the [Esc] key to return to the interface screen.

Result: You just created your first 3D Studio rendering.

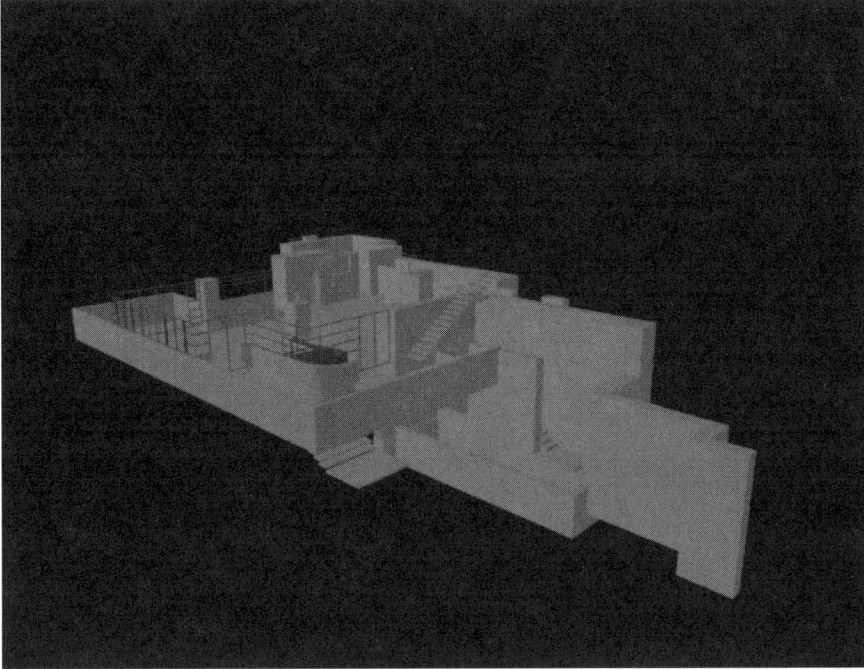

The preliminary rendering of the two lower levels

Summary

This chapter has picked a single, simplistic path through a huge amount of material about a complicated program applied to a complicated model. The next chapter returns to Lights, Cameras, and Rendering operations to explore in detail, and to render Fallingwater with a variety of lighting setups.

Lights, Cameras, and Rendering

Frank Lloyd Wright designed the lighting at Fallingwater, as he did for most of his buildings. Also typically, he derived the lighting design from the same underlying geometry that generated the building—to further articulate the design of the house. And he had a wonderful, malleable new invention to play with—fluorescent lights.

After a look at 3D Studio's basic lighting, camera, and rendering operations, the exercises at the end of this chapter take you through defining lights and cameras and rendering still shots of:

❑ The building exterior in daylight.

❑ The building interior in daylight.

❑ The exterior at night.

❑ The interior at night, simulating light from light fixtures.

Wright's Lighting at Fallingwater

Lest rebellious clients scatter inappropriate lighting around their houses, Wright designed built-in lighting installations wherever possible. In the mid-30s fluorescent lights began to be manufactured in sizes appropriate for residences, and Wright used them in concealed arrangements throughout the house. In the bedrooms, lights were installed over closets to reflect from the ceiling, and in the living room, fluorescent tubes were placed behind the back of built-in seating.

The hidden light sources emphasized interior volumes in ways impossible for traditional, hanging ceiling fixtures. Although the normal hue of the fluorescents was chilly, many of the valance arrangements placed lights close to walls and ceilings, tinting the visible light as it reflected off the warm-colored stucco.

Incandescent installations at Fallingwater were also innovative. In the ceilings of the third-floor hallway and in the skylights of the corridor to the guest wing, Wright recessed bulbs behind translucent glass. In the hallways and stairwells, wall-mounted bulbs were covered by hemispherical sconces of frosted glass, secured with wooded cleats. The south side of the house was flooded with light from the banks of windows, but the darker north and east sides of the building were punctuated only by a few tall and narrow casement windows.

The Living Room Ceiling

The grid of slender, walnut strips recessed into the central portion of the living room ceiling reflects Wright's long-standing admiration for Japanese design. His original concept called for incandescent bulbs behind rice-paper shields. However, the bulbs would have protruded too far from the ceiling and scorched the covering. Wright replaced the bulbs with shallower fluorescent tubes and used unbleached muslin for the screens, which gives a warm, diffuse light. (Kaufmann, p. 121)

The installation takes risks with scale. The living room ceiling at the windows is only 7′1″ high. It steps up a foot at the center of the room, still leaving the spectacular 14′0″ by 13′9″ grid close overhead. Any sense of hovering oppressiveness is offset by the powerful pull of the view beyond the wall of windows. The recess for the light grid was formed into the concrete during construction. It steps up twice, repeating the double step-up that runs around the central part of the room, articulating the structural system.

An elongated panel of similar design runs behind the concrete ceiling beam that separates the central, empty space from the dining area, echoing the light from high windows on the north side. The two ceiling panels and the fluorescents behind the seating, which wash light up across the windows, were the only original lighting in the large room.

The Trellis Lights

Small exterior lights with translucent glazing are recessed two by two into the end of each trellis bay. Their Cherokee red steel frames are shaped like irregular pentagons. Pentagons appear nowhere else in the building. Whether avoiding squares and circles as too obvious, elaborating the bottom of a square, or transforming a five-pointed star, Wright imparted an airy sparkle to the building's exterior with the pentagonal trellis lights.

The house today has same lighting system as in the 1930s. According to Edgar Kaufmann junior, extensive exterior lighting was tried and soon abandoned; it destroyed the delicate melding of house and setting. The house at night floats in the glen, illuminated only by the tiny trellis lights and the bands of windows.

Two lights were inserted at the end of each trellis bay.
(Photo by Harold Corsini, courtesy of Western Pennsylvania Conservancy.)

The Table Lamps

Wright originally designed elaborate floor lamps for the living room—tall, flaring standards made of parchment, Cherokee red metal, and walnut. The lamps in these early drawings are handsome but are more suited to a hotel lobby. The Kaufmanns thought them far too solemn and stately.

Returning to the inspiration of his beloved square, Wright designed a clever, somewhat rickety-looking table lamp to be used throughout the house. A long rectangular walnut box with two sides removed tops a slender cast iron shaft and base. The inside of the box is painted with aluminum to increase the reflection from a fluorescent tube.

The table lamp in its horizontal incarnation.
(Photo by Thomas A. Heinz, courtesy of Western Pennsylvania Conservancy.)

3D Studio Cameras

The basic theory of cameras is simple: place a camera at the point from which you wish to view the scene, and place the target at the point toward which you wish to look. As you manipulate the camera and target with the mouse, the Camera viewport displays Box geometry that concurrently tracks the model in the position that the rendering will record.

Using multiple cameras is easier than moving a single camera if you're experimenting, because you can test views, adjust views, and get back to previous views without repositioning the camera. When creating animations, you can tween from one key camera position to another.

Tip: A wireframe of a building model is often a confusing tangle of lines. You can use the Display/Geometry/Backface command to reduce the visible complexity of the 3D mesh sufficiently to see what you're doing.

Viewports

The 3D Editor's default viewports are Top, Front, Left, and No View Defined (which is usually replaced by the isometric User viewport). These are generally the most efficient to use while creating geometry because there are some modifications you can perform on the isometric wireframe in the User viewport. Once you have created a camera, change the User viewport to a Camera viewport so that you can see the camera shot.

When you start a session, a camera may exist but be hidden; it will become visible as soon as the Cameras command branch is chosen. You can use Zoom Extents to expand the viewports to contain the Camera and Target symbols.

Tip: If you are using multiple cameras, you can assign up to four viewports as Camera viewports for the individual cameras. Pick a viewport and then press [C] to display a scroll list of the cameras. Pick a camera to assign to the viewport.

Manipulating the Camera and Target

For still shots and slide shows, the available camera commands are Create, Adjust, Move, Roll, FOV (field of view), Dolly, Perspective, Ranges, and Delete. Picking Create or Adjust displays a dialog box for reciprocally specifying FOV and lens, degree of roll, and whether the camera cone is visible.

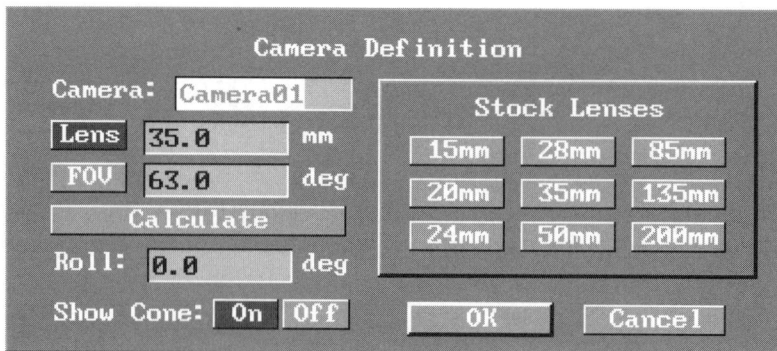

The Camera Definition dialog box, which appears when
you choose Cameras/Create or Cameras/Adjust.

The procedures for creating, moving, and deleting cameras are self-explanatory with the aid of the command line. The Ranges command specifies the area that will be affected by atmospheric effects, discussed later in conjunction with rendering.

Roll and Dolly

Once you have found the correct angle for the view you want, Roll and Dolly are useful for refining the view. The Dolly command moves the camera closer or farther from the model along the line from the camera to the target.

Roll rotates the camera around the axis formed by an imaginary line stretched between camera and target, thus tilting the X-Y plane. Remember: it's the camera and not the scene that is rotating; if you rotate the camera clockwise, the scene appears to rotate counterclockwise.

Perspective, FOV, and Lens Setting

Dramatic close-up views of buildings, particularly those with deep surface indentations, often produce extreme perspective distortions. You can "fudge" or accentuate them at will in a manual rendering; with a computer, you can use the Lens/FOV and Perspective commands to control perspective distortion.

3D Studio Lens settings mimic the effect of actual camera lenses. To wildly simplify, the smaller the lens, the wider the field of view. The wider the field of view, the smaller the model appears to be in relation to the area covered by the view. For instance, a 35mm lens displays a 63-degree field of view, and a 200mm lens displays a 12-degree field of view. Lens settings between 45mm and 55mm approximate the normal field of view of the human eye.

The following renderings demonstrate (1) balancing camera distance and FOV to control perspective distortion and (2) the size of the model relative to the frame.

A view with the camera at middle distance, with a 35mm lens, shows little perspective distortion, but the building is too small in relation to the viewing plane.

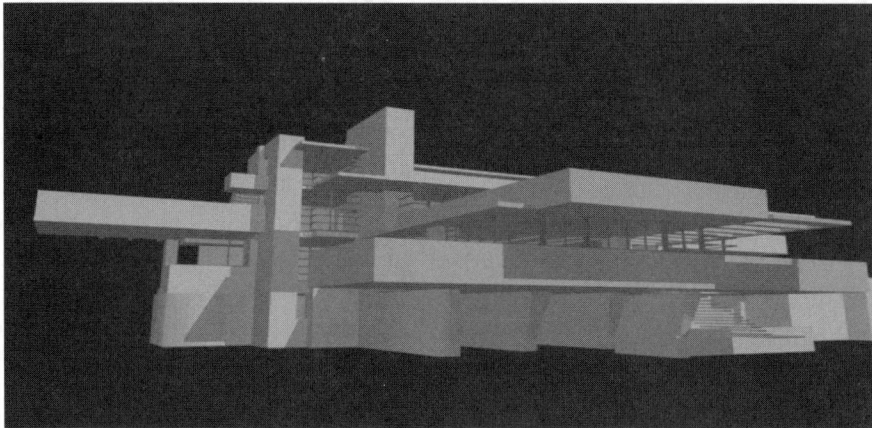

Dollying the camera closer, with the same 35mm lens setting, increases the building's size, but accentuates the perspective distortion, partially blocking the view of the upper levels.

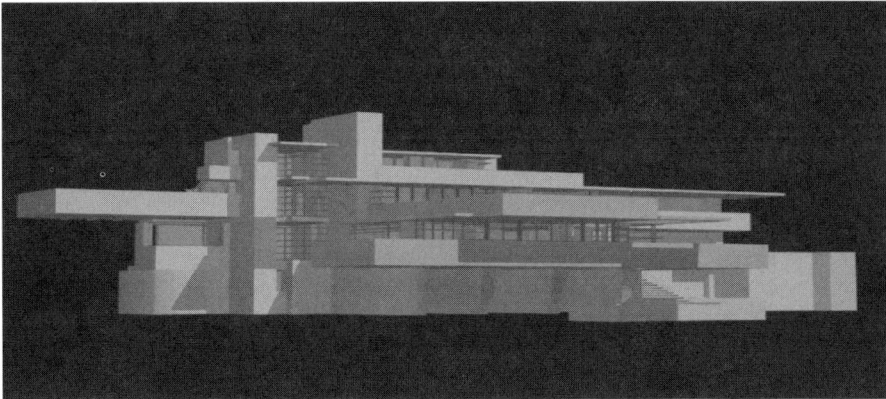

Keeping the camera at the middle distance but changing the lens to 85mm (decreasing the field of view) yields a larger building with little perspective distortion.

The effects of changing lens FOV and camera position can be modified further by using the Perspective command, which fixes the position and size of the camera view plane while automatically adjusting the FOV as the camera is dollied.

Tip: When you're deciding which angle and distance to use for rendering a building, consider the way the building will actually be sited. Will it be built in an urban setting, hemmed in by other buildings on either side and across the street, so that it is usually seen from a low, close-up point, or will the area around it be open enough that the characteristic view will be from a distance?

3D Studio Lighting

3D Studio provides three types of light: ambient, omni, and spotlight. Each rendered scene contains one ambient light setting, and can include as many individual omni lights and spotlights as you wish. As you create individual lights, 3D Studio automatically assigns them sequential file names—*light01, light02, light03, etc.* It's a good idea to assign new descriptive names to lights because a long numerical sequence on the light list doesn't help much for remembering each light's function. Ditto for naming cameras and model objects.

Once you have created a light, the light settings and placement are saved along with all the objects in the scene as soon as you save the scene. As demonstrated in the previous chapter, you can transport mesh objects into and out of an "empty studio" that contains a lighting setup. When creating animations, each light has its own Track and Key Info dialog boxes, so that you can move it as you would a mesh object.

Working with Lights

The following list provides basic tips for using lights.

❑ Don't start creating lights until you have an idea of what the view will be.

❑ Keep in mind the total brightness of the scene. The more lights, the less bright each should be.

❑ Turn shadows off to speed up preliminary renderings.

❑ Use omni lights when possible. They're "less expensive" in terms of computing time than are spotlights. Save the spotlights for emphasizing limited areas, casting shadows, and creating specific shapes of light.

❑ In general, use neutral white light for exteriors. Save the colored lights for special effects, after you've assigned materials.

❑ Use as few lights as possible. Fewer lights reduce rendering time, file size, and shadow confusion. As shown in the following illustrations, too many lights casting too many shadows in too many directions confuse the clarity of the 3D geometry.

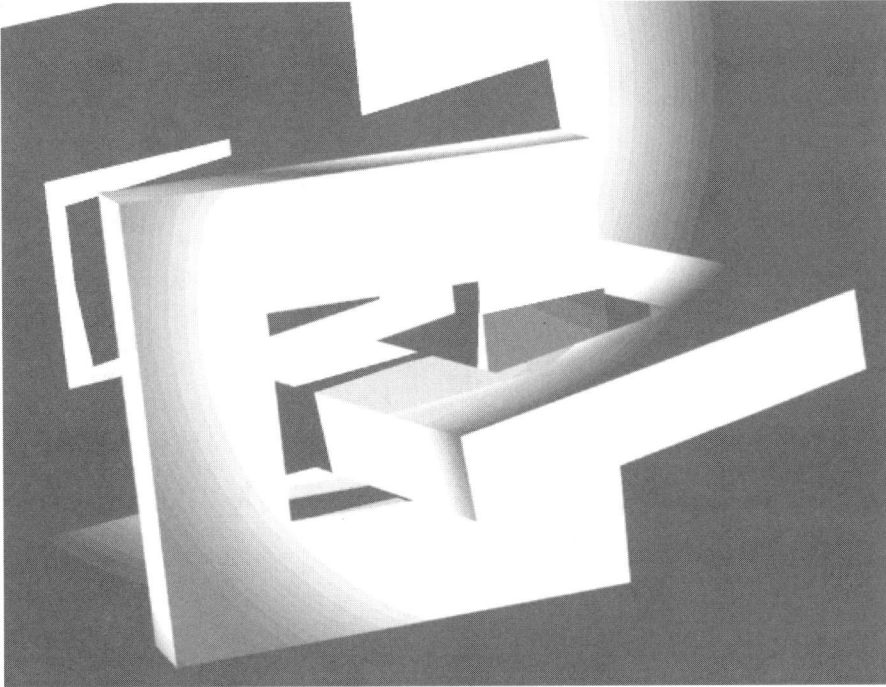

All objects in this scene are assigned the same material so that the geometry is visually defined only by light. Lighting the scene with three spotlights destroys intensity differentiation in planes and creates shadows that are too confused to give the eye clear and simple depth cues.

The same scene from the same angle, rendered with one spotlight and an omni fill light.

Ambient Light

Ambient light has no origin or location, and it does not cast shadows. It simulates a general level of background illumination produced by light from a hidden source repeatedly bouncing off objects and atmosphere—a sort of "white noise" of lighting. The default settings for ambient light (77, 77, 77) are suitable for most jobs.

The amount of ambient light in a scene affects contrast; the less ambient light, the sharper the contrast. (Without any ambient light, surfaces not otherwise lit would be dead black, resembling photos of the surface of the moon.) The following pictures are exaggerated illustrations of the relationship of ambient and spotlight luminance (intensity) settings and resulting contrast.

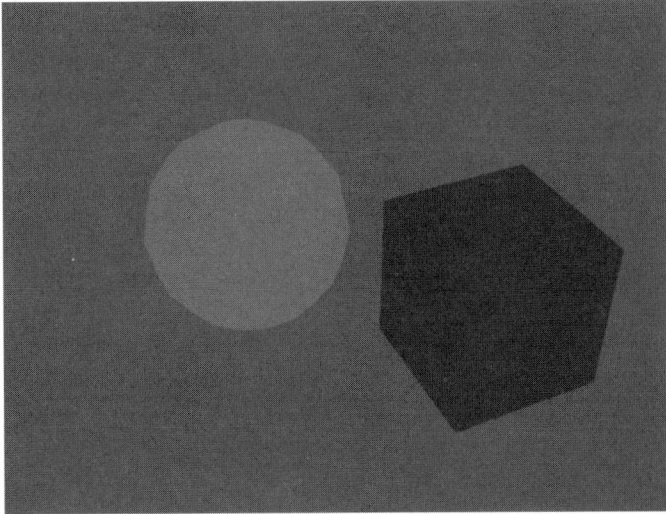

A blue cube and faceted white sphere on a light red background, with ambient light only. The ambient luminance setting is 80.

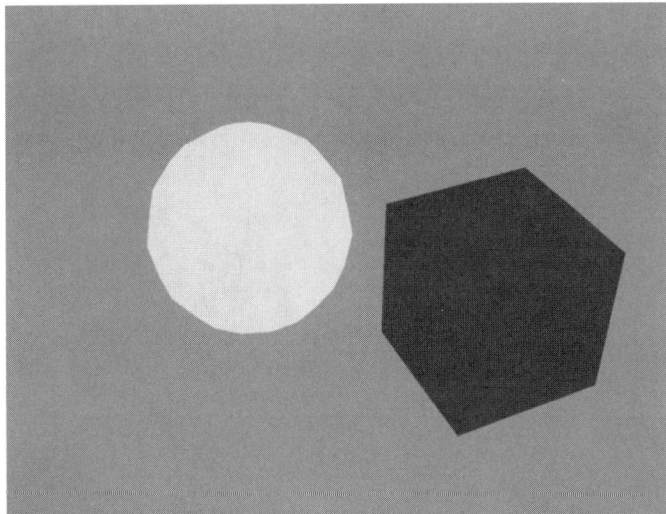

Ambient light only, boosted to 255. There's plenty of light, but no more shape definition than blue and white cutouts stuck on a red felt board.

Adding a single spotlight to cast ray-traced shadows. Setting ambient at a low 50 and a spotlight to 255 yields enough definition of surfaces for 3D depth cueing and sharp shadow contrast.

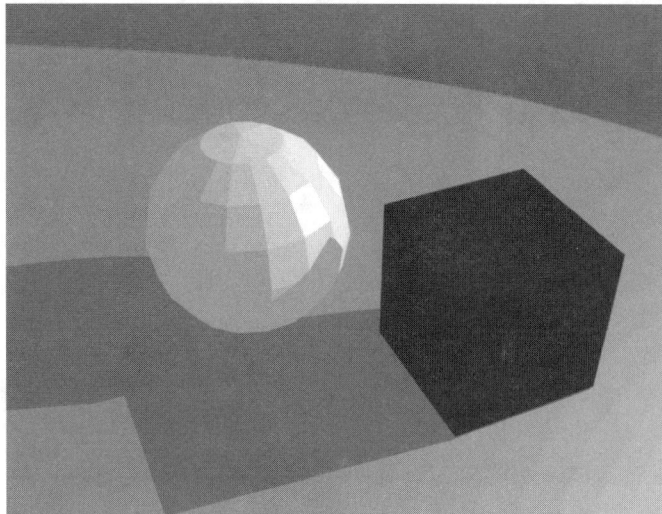

Upping the ambient setting to 150 and reducing the spotlight to 150 reduces the contrast of both the shadows and the modeling of the faceted sphere.

Omni Lights

Omni lights are point lights that radiate equally in all directions and cast no shadows. For a "generic" lighting setup, the *3D Studio Reference Manual* recommends using ambient light set at 70, a dominant omni light set at 200, and a secondary omni light set at 100.

Omni lights can be turned on and off without losing their settings and placement. If a scene requires a large number of them, you can clone a single light by holding down the [Shift] key, picking the light, and placing its clone.

Range and Attenuation   Omni lights normally maintain the same intensity out to the limits of a scene. If you want the omni light to attenuate, or fade out with distance, use the Ranges command to place two concentric circles around the light. The smaller circle sets the distance at which the light begins to fade out, and the larger one sets the distance at which the light fades completely. Once you have specified the ranges, toggle on the Attenuation button in the Light Definition dialog box.

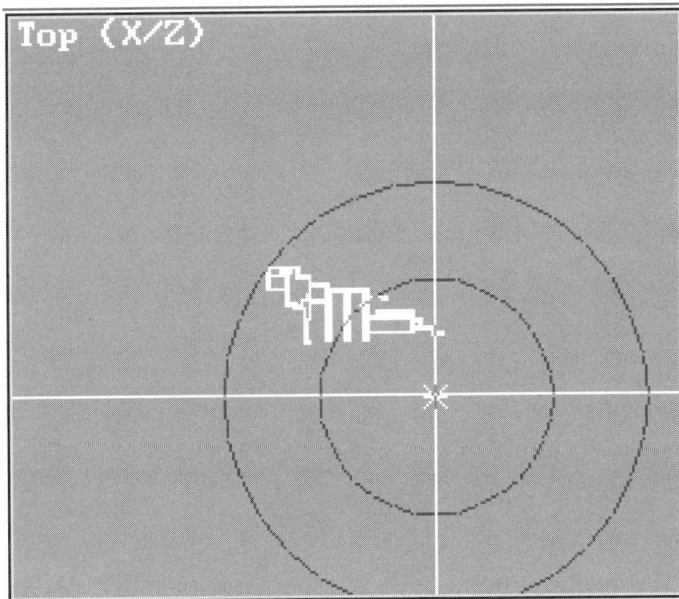

The screen shows near and far ranges set with the Lights/Omni/ Ranges command. The cursor is centered over the omni light.

Special Uses for Omni Lights   You can also use omni lights to "remove" light from a scene. Mesh objects selected with the Exclude button on the Light Definition dialog box will not receive any omni light.

The value entered in the Multiplier text box boosts or reduces light. The default is 1. If used with a white light, a positive setting of 2 will double the intensity of the light. Using negative Multiplier values causes a light to cast a dark area of an intensity in proportion to the setting. For instance, a negative setting of -1 causes a white light set at 255 to cast a black area. Negative values used with colored lights change the light to its complementary color.

Rather than fiddling endlessly with a light, trying to get it to cast a highlight in a particular place, you can use the Place Hilite command to locate a highlight exactly where you want it. The light will move automatically to the correct position to produce the highlight.

Omni lights do not cast shadows, and they will shine through objects. Thus, they can be used as a sort of "x-ray light." Place an omni light behind an object, and it will light the planes of the object facing the camera. The nearer the surface normals of a plane approach the direction of the light source, the more light the plane will receive. The first exercise in this chapter uses omni lights in this manner.

Spotlights

The capabilities of spotlights include those of omni lights—Exclude, Multiplier, Attenuate, Place Hilite, Color, and Intensity—and add others:

❏ Shadow casting

❏ Falloff and Hotspot adjustments

❏ Target placement

❏ Rectangular or Circular projection cones

❏ Dolly and Roll (as with a camera)

❏ Visible cone geometry

❏ Projector (projects a bitmap; similar to a slide or movie projector)

As with cameras, to create a spotlight, first you must place the light and then its target.

The "Shape" of the Light   **Falloff** and **Hotspot** adjust the angle of the light's cone, and thus the size of the area illuminated by the light. The two commands place concentric circles, sized between 1 and 160 degrees, around the light's target. The Hotspot circle defines the area of full illumination. The Falloff circle, which must be at least 1 degree bigger, sets the perimeter at which the light fades to zero. If Hotspot and Falloff are almost the same size, the edge of the illuminated area is sharp. If Falloff is appreciably larger, the edge of the area is soft.

As Falloff and Hotspot set the "width" of the light cone, **Range** and **Attenuation** affect the "length" of the beam's full intensity. **Lights/Spot/Ranges** creates two concentric circles around the light (not around the target, as with Falloff and Hotspot.)

The inner circle sets the distance at which the light begins to fade from the full intensity set in the Light Definition dialog box. The outer circle sets the distance at which the light has faded to zero. If the Attenuation button is on, the spotlight conforms to the Ranges set; if off, the light shines to the limits of the scene.

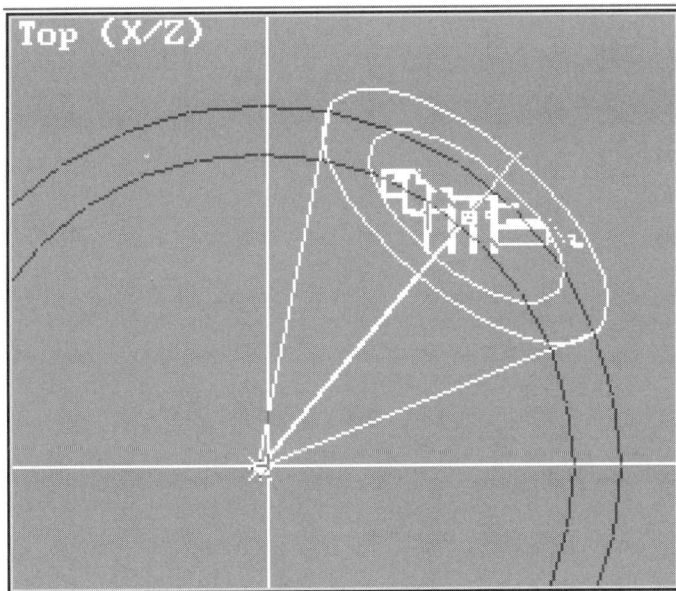

Show Cone displays the Falloff and Hotspot cones, originating at the spotlight and circling the target. The Ranges command places two concentric circles around the spotlight.

Tip: If a spotlight is pointed at a backdrop, but the circle doesn't show against the plane of the backdrop, check to see if Attenuation is on with Ranges set too close for the light to reach the backdrop.

The **Rectangle** and **Circle** buttons on the Light Definition dialog box define the shape of the light's beam. If the light is a rectangle, you can adjust its length and width with the Lights/Spot/Aspect command. Roll will rotate a rectangular light around the line from light to target, similar to the camera Roll command.

Toggling on Show Cone displays the shape of the light's extents in the 3D Editor. To fine-tune light placement, you can assign one of the viewports as a Spotlight viewport, which displays the view straight down the cone of the selected spotlight.

Tip: Show Cone has nothing to do with placing a visible cone of light in the rendering, as in the following illustration. If you want to include a visible spotlight cone in the rendering, you can model a cone of translucent glass and fit it around the displayed cone of the spotlight. Turn Shininess to zero to avoid glassy reflections, and turn Transparency to 80 so that the cone shows faintly. Use the Add button so that the cone will appear lighter than the background.

The dancer and the stage are lit with a bright spotlight overhead (with glass cone) and four less-intense footlights.

Shadows   3D Studio provides controls located in four places that determine whether shadows are cast and, if so, what kind. It's a little confusing at first, so here are the main points:

❏ The **material** assigned to an object can receive shadows or not. To show cast shadows, the material must have a Phong or Metal shading limit.

❏ Each **object** can receive or generate cast shadows, depending on the settings in the Object Attributes dialog box, accessed with the Modify/Object/Attributes Command.

❏ Each **spotlight** can cast shadows or not. If it casts shadows, they can be either ray-traced or bitmapped. (See the Renderer section.)

❏ The Render Still Image dialog box can turn shadows On or Off **globally**. If Off, there are no shadows. If On, you can further specify whether each spotlight casts shadows, whether objects cast or receive shadows, or whether a material receives cast shadows. The following diagram traces the route for creating shadows.

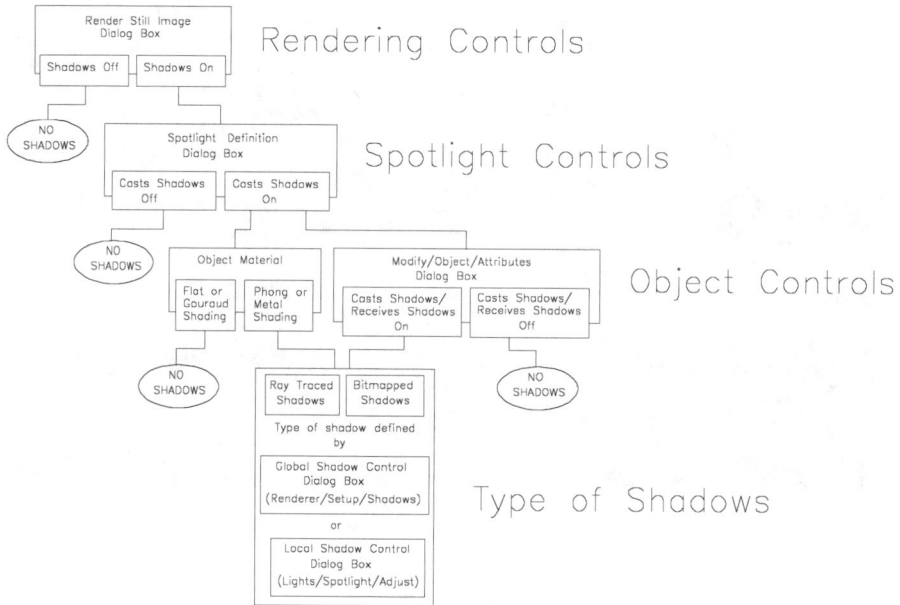

```
┌─────────────────────────┐
│   Render Still Image     │       Rendering Controls
│      Dialog Box          │
│ ┌──────────┐ ┌─────────┐ │
│ │Shadows Off│ │Shadows On│ │
│ └──────────┘ └─────────┘ │
└─────────────────────────┘

   ( NO
   SHADOWS )
          ┌─────────────────────────┐
          │   Spotlight Definition   │   Spotlight Controls
          │      Dialog Box          │
          │ ┌──────────┐ ┌─────────┐ │
          │ │Casts Shadows│ │Casts Shadows│ │
          │ │    Off     │ │    On    │ │
          │ └──────────┘ └─────────┘ │
          └─────────────────────────┘

             ( NO
             SHADOWS )

          ┌───────────────┐  ┌──────────────────────┐
          │ Object Material │  │ Modify/Object/Attributes│   Object Controls
          │                │  │      Dialog Box        │
          │ ┌────┐ ┌─────┐ │  │ ┌──────────┐ ┌────────┐│
          │ │Flat or│ │Phong or│ │  │ │Casts Shadows/│ │Casts Shadows/││
          │ │Gouraud│ │Metal │ │  │ │Receives Shadows│ │Receives Shadows││
          │ │Shading│ │Shading│ │  │ │    On      │ │   Off   ││
          │ └────┘ └─────┘ │  │ └──────────┘ └────────┘│
          └───────────────┘  └──────────────────────┘

            ( NO                              ( NO
            SHADOWS )                         SHADOWS )

          ┌──────────┐ ┌─────────┐
          │Ray Traced │ │Bitmapped │
          │ Shadows   │ │ Shadows  │
          └──────────┘ └─────────┘
          Type of shadow defined
                  by
          ┌─────────────────────┐
          │ Global Shadow Control│
          │     Dialog Box       │
          │(Renderer/Setup/Shadows)│   Type of Shadows
          └─────────────────────┘
                  or
          ┌─────────────────────┐
          │ Local Shadow Control │
          │     Dialog Box       │
          │(Lights/Spotlight/Adjust)│
          └─────────────────────┘
```

The Shadow Tree.

Using Colored Lights

Fluorescent, incandescent, sodium, and other types of colored light can be closely matched by adjusting the color definition of the lights in a scene. For bluish fluorescent lights, you can set RGB to 180, 205, and 255. For incandescent light, use RGB settings of around 250, 210, and 150. Sodium lights can be pumped up to a shade of orange by using RGB settings of 255, 170, and 110. You should render the scene first, though, with white neutral light; you may not need colored lights.

When using a spotlight for the sun, 250, 220, and 150 are typical RGB settings for a sunny day; 110, 125, and 145 for a cloudy one. (Positioning the sun to match specific times and locations is discussed in detail in Chapter 6.) If you're rendering a dawn or sunset scene, you can adjust sun color toward the red end of the spectrum, and if you're creating a science fiction world with multiple and rainbow suns, you can really have fun.

Colored lights can be used in conjunction with atmospheric effects. Background and Atmosphere controls are located in the Renderer menu branch, discussed in the next section.

3D Studio Rendering

In one sense, once you're ready to render a still shot, the work's all done. But there are many parameters that affect the final product—and still some surprises.

Five of the seven Renderer commands specify which area of a scene you wish to render. The various options are explained in detail in the documentation:

❏ **Render View** renders the scene in any viewport.

❏ **Render Region** renders the contents of a selection window drawn in the active viewport. The rendering is at the same relative size and position on the screen as the window is in the viewport.

❏ **Render Blowup** renders a selection window but enlarges it to fill the screen.

❏ **Render Object** renders any selected object in the scene, plus a portion of the surrounding area.

❏ **Render Last** repeats the last rendering done, from the same viewport.

The two other commands in the Renderer group are Setup and View. The View command allows you to call up and view previously rendered images, either still shots or animations. The next section discusses the commands in the Setup branch.

Renderer Setup

The Setup branch of the Renderer menu contains controls for Atmosphere, Background, Configure, Options, Shadows, and Make .CUB. The commands in this branch range from basic, intuitive, and easy to use to quite subtle and complex. We'll take up the basic ones in this chapter.

Atmosphere   The three atmosphere options can include Fog in a scene, darken the scene as it recedes from the camera (Distance Cue), or create Layered Fog that "disperses" as it rises from the ground plane. Only one effect can be used at a time. To use Fog and Distance Cueing (which is basically black fog), you must render the Camera viewport. Layered Fog can be rendered from any viewport.

The placement of Fog and Distance Cueing effects is set by the Cameras/Ranges command; the inner circle sets the beginning of the fog or darkening, and the outer circle sets the extent of its maximum effect. Anything beyond the outer circle is dimmed to the Far percentage.

The percentages of fog or darkening are set in the respective dialog boxes that appear when each option is chosen. The Fog Definition dialog box also contains sliders for defining the color of the fog. Each dialog box includes a Background button. If the button is toggled on, the background displays as a solid wall of the defined fog color (or black for Distance Cue). If the button is off, the background is unaffected by the atmospheric settings.

Tip: Traditional landscape paintings employ atmospheric perspective to lend depth to scenes by progressively lightening objects, such as mountains in the far distance. You can reproduce this effect by setting a camera range extending from the mid-to-far distance and defining a barely blue-colored fog from zero to approximately 25%.

The following illustrations show the same geometry rendered with different Lighting, Atmosphere, Shadow, and Background settings. For the sunny day, the sun spotlight is set to RGB values 255, 216, and 125, and the shadows are ray-traced. (The umbrella, palm trees, and rubber ducky are stolen from the collection of mesh objects that ships with 3D Studio—a rich source for quick geometry.)

The foggy beach scene has spotlight RGB values of 108, 122, and 144, and the shadows are bitmapped. Fog is set to 153, 168, and 179 RGB, with Near Range setting of 20% and a Far Range of 100%.

A simple scene of a sunny day.

The fog rolls in.

Layered fog is placed in a scene by using the world coordinates of the model. Typically, the X-Z plane is the base, or plane from which the fog extends upward. Fog color and density are set in the Layered Fog Definition dialog box, as is the direction of dispersal (toward the top or toward the bottom).

Tip: If you're doing renderings of certain prominent cities, you can use a grayish brown layered fog to render smog!

Background   Four types of background are available: None, Solid Color, Bitmap, and three-color Gradient. Choosing None leaves the background black. Choosing Solid Color displays a dialog box with color sliders for defining the color. Choosing Bitmap displays a file selector for calling up a bitmap file; the file must be located in a directory specified by one of the map paths in the Program Configuration dialog box (see *Reference Manual*, Chapter 3).

The Gradient background is a wonderful tool for setting up multicolored backgrounds with minimum hassle. Choosing Gradient displays a dialog box used to define three horizontal bands of background color. You define the color and width of each band, and the program smoothly *dithers* (blends the color) between them. The sunny beach scene shown above uses a gradient background of three shades of blue to realistically lighten the sky toward the horizon.

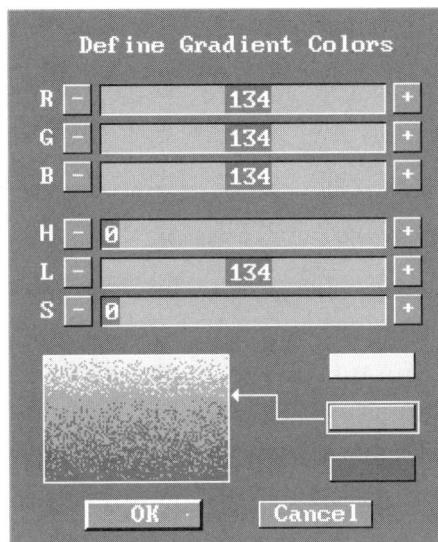

The Gradient background dialog box.

Configure   The Render/Setup/Configure command displays the Device Configuration dialog box, which contains branching controls to specify rendering output: type of file, whether the file is compressed, the display device, the driver, resolution, and aspect ratio. The correct settings depend on the hardware you have, and later use of the rendering.

As well as preparing presentation renderings, rendering is useful at earlier stages of a project for checking geometry, materials, lighting, and view angles. The following settings can be used for preliminary test renderings and presentation renderings.

For quick test renderings:

❏ Use Renderer/Setup/Configure to set resolution to 320 x 200.

❏ Use Renderer/Render Region or Renderer/Render Object instead of rendering an entire viewport.

❏ Use Renderer/Setup/Atmosphere to turn off any atmospheric effects.

❏ In the Render Still Image dialog box, use the following settings:

    ❏ Shading Limit at Flat or Gouraud

    ❏ Anti-aliasing Off

❏ Shadows Off

❏ Mapping Off

❏ Auto-Reflect Off

❏ Force 2-Sided Off

❏ Background set to Tile

For presentation renderings:

❏ Use Renderer/Setup/Configure to set resolution to 640 x 480 or higher.

❏ Use Renderer/Render View.

❏ Use Renderer/Setup/Atmosphere to specify and enable any atmospheric effects.

❏ In the Render Still Image dialog box, use the following settings:

❏ Shading Limit at Phong or Metal, depending on scene contents

❏ Anti-aliasing On

❏ Shadows On, and Ray Traced or Mapped shadows specified in the Renderer/Setup/Shadows dialog box

❏ Mapping On, with necessary maps and mapping coordinates assigned

❏ Auto-Reflect On if automatic reflection maps are used

❏ Force 2-Sided On if a scene contains objects with visible "inside" surfaces, or if an imported *.dxf* file has inconsistent surface normals that leave "holes"

❏ Hidden Geometry set to Show if automatic reflection maps are positioned to reflect hidden geometry

❏ Background set to Rescale if needed to adjust the scale of a bitmapped background

Options, Shadows, and Make .CUB   Most of the Renderer/ Setup/Options commands deal with operations pertaining to animations and video post processing, and are beyond the scope of this book. The Shadows dialog box sets the shadow definitions globally, as mentioned in the previous discussion of shadows. The Make .CUB commands involve creating a six-sided cubic reflection map, or cubic environment map.

The Render Still Image Dialog Box

This dialog box appears as soon as you select a viewport to render. It contains controls for specifying certain rendering parameters, as well as information from the Configure and Options dialog boxes.

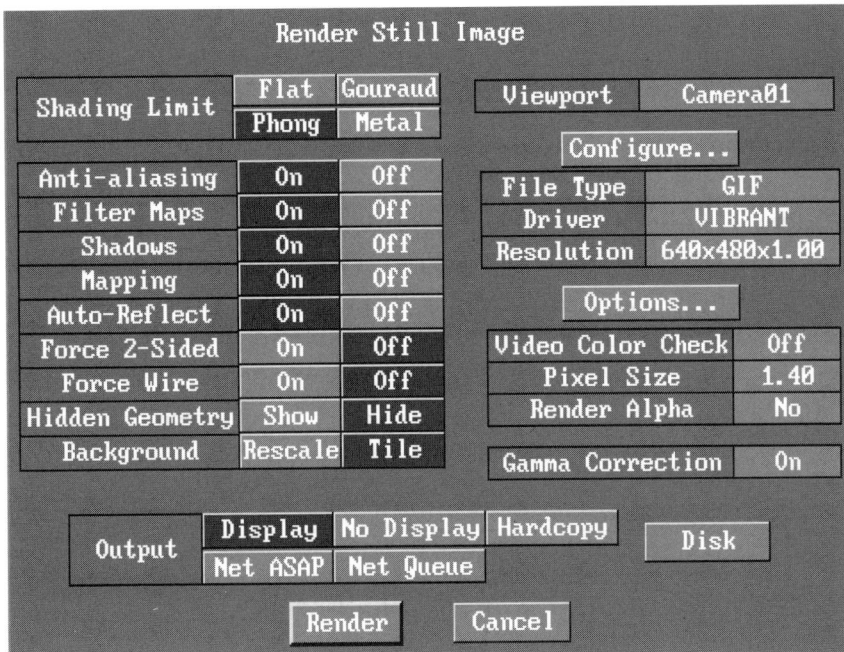

```
                        Render Still Image

                      ┌──────┬────────┐
Shading Limit         │ Flat │Gouraud │    Viewport    │  Camera01
                      ├──────┼────────┤  ┌─────────────┴──────────┐
                      │Phong │ Metal  │        Configure...
                                          ┌────────────┬──────────┐
Anti-aliasing         │  On  │  Off   │   File Type    │    GIF
Filter Maps           │  On  │  Off   │     Driver     │  VIBRANT
Shadows               │  On  │  Off   │   Resolution   │640x480x1.00
Mapping               │  On  │  Off   │
Auto-Reflect          │  On  │  Off   │        Options...
Force 2-Sided         │  On  │  Off   │ Video Color Check │    Off
Force Wire            │  On  │  Off   │    Pixel Size     │   1.40
Hidden Geometry       │ Show │  Hide  │    Render Alpha   │    No
Background            │Rescale│ Tile  │
                                          Gamma Correction │    On

            ┌─────────┬───────────┬──────────┐
Output      │ Display │No Display │ Hardcopy │     Disk
            ├─────────┼───────────┴──────────┤
            │ Net ASAP│ Net Queue │

                  Render        Cancel
```

The Render Still Image dialog box.

At the upper left of the dialog box is a set of buttons for specifying shading limit. Phong is the default and is the necessary setting for several features such as Shadows or Texture Mapping.

The set of nine toggle buttons below activate or disable various operations. If you're creating a test rendering, you can turn many of them off to save time:

❏ **Anti-aliasing** can be turned off to speed up rendering time for preliminaries. Otherwise leave it on to eliminate jagged diagonal or circular lines.

❏ **Filter Maps** controls the filtering of mapped materials. Leave it turned on for now.

❏ **Shadows** controls whether cast shadows are rendered.

❑ **Mapping** controls whether material mapping information is employed or ignored.

❑ **Auto-Reflect** either renders or ignores automatic reflection maps.

❑ **Force 2-Sided** renders both sides of a face when turned on. This takes more time but may be necessary if you're rendering an object (such as a bucket) that shows an inside surface. Otherwise, the interior surface of the bucket will render in the background color. An better solution is to assign a two-sided material to the object.

❑ **Force Wire**, toggled on, renders all objects in a scene as if they had been assigned a wireframe material.

❑ **Hidden Geometry** should be set to Hide unless you want portions of the scene not visible to the camera to show.

❑ **Background** controls whether a bitmapped background is rescaled to fit the size of the scene background or repeated (or rendered in part) to fill up the necessary area. Tiling is quicker.

On the right side of the screen, the top two boxes display the viewport to be rendered. Selecting either the Configure or Options button takes you to each corresponding dialog box. The information shown below each button cannot be changed from the Render Still Image dialog box.

The Gamma Correction box toggles on that function, which controls the proper display of values in the middle of the intensity range. Using gamma compensates for variances in individual display devices. Gamma correction should be calibrated and left on when 3D Studio is installed. The *3D Studio Reference Manual* and *Installation Guide* discuss gamma features in detail.

The Rendering in Progress Dialog Box

This dialog box appears while the scene is being rendered. You can't do anything with it—just check your settings and watch the red line at the top move across, tracking the percentage of the scene done.

Rendering in progress...

Shading Limit	Phong		3DS File	FWBEACH.3DS
			Viewport	Camera01
Anti-aliasing	On		Output File	
Filter Maps	On		Objects	10
Shadows	On		Faces	5884
Mapping	On		Lights	1: 1M 0R
Auto-Reflect	On			
Motion-Blur	On		Resolution	640x480x1.00
Force 2-Sided		Off	Palette	Low
Force Wire		Off	Pixel Size	1.40
Hidden Geometry		Hide	Video Color Check	Off
Background		Tile	Render Alpha	No
Atmosphere	None		Render Fields	Off
			Gamma Correction	On

Last Frame Time: --:--:--
(Press [Esc] to cancel rendering)
(Press [Space] to toggle to rendering screen)

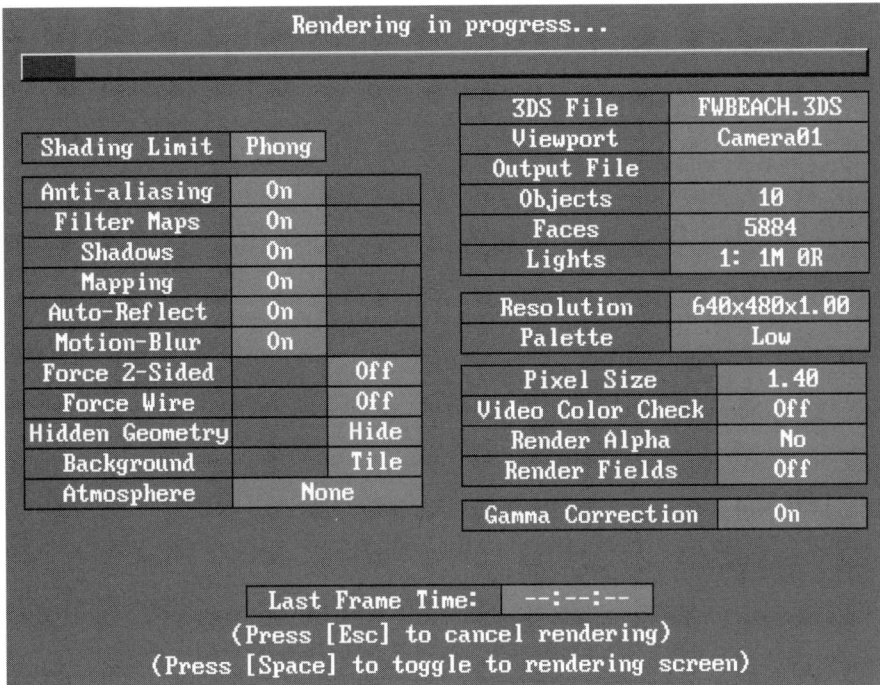

The Rendering in Progress dialog box.

If you want to watch the scene being rendered, use the spacebar to toggle back and forth between the display screen and the dialog box. Single screen rendering is faster when the Rendering in Progress dialog box is displayed. However, watching the rendered image can often tip you off quickly that the scene needs adjustment, and you can abort the rendering by pressing the [Esc] key.

When the image is rendered to a VGA display using an RCPADI driver, or to a 256-color display, the image is initially displayed using either a default palette or the last palette used. Then the program recalculates the palette and redraws the image. Some of the initial color images are strange and quite wonderful, rivaling the better Abstract Expressionists. You can experiment with using a screen-grab program to capture these images. Wait until the rendering screen display has almost reached the bottom of the screen, and initiate the screen-grab (pressing [Shift] + [Print Scrn] in Pizazz Plus®.)

Exercise 1: The Front Door by Day

Edgar Kaufmann junior advanced a theory that Fallingwater has no exterior "elevations" as such. Wright's sense of visual dynamics, of the energy generated by diagonals, produced a building meant to be seen from an angle—from corner views which emphasize the thrusts and recesses of the building's profile. (Kaufmann, pp. 172–178)

Truly, there are no "head-on" views of the four sides which give even an approximate idea of Fallingwater's geometry. Thus, with traditional front, right, left, and rear elevations irrelevant, this exercise recreates that remaining classic of architectural delineation—The Front Entrance.

The view is primarily lit by sun shining between stone masses on the south side of the entry loggia. In this exercise you will load a file containing a spotlight "sun," a camera aimed at the front door, and the upper levels of the model. Next, you'll merge the two lower levels from the previous chapter's project file. Then you'll add two more lights to duplicate realistically the light on a winter morning and render the scene.

Launch 3D Studio and Load the Upper Levels File

The two upper levels are already combined, and materials have been applied to them.

1. Type **3DS** to launch the program.

2. Choose File/Load from the menu bar. Check that the Wildcard text box displays *.3DS. Pick the appropriate drive button on the File Selector dialog box, and choose LVLS2-3.3DS from the scroll box. Click Yes. The two upper levels with light and camera will appear in a single viewport.

3. Move the cursor over the camera or target to look at the X, Y, and Z coordinates on the status line, which define the camera's location.

4. Choose Cameras/Adjust from the screen menu and click on the blue camera icon to display the Camera Definition dialog box. This camera

has been named "log-cam," short for loggia camera. Toggle on the Show Cone button so that the camera's field-of-view cone is displayed on the screen. Pick OK.

5. Press the Zoom Extents button to display the sun spotlight. Note that it is positioned approximately 10x the model's long dimension in order to generate seemingly parallel rays.

6. Draw a zoom window around the building model to get back to the original view. Click on the Full Screen icon button to change to four viewports.

Result: The upper-level geometry is loaded along with a light and camera. The light is placed at an altitude angle of $5\frac{1}{2}$ degrees above the horizon and at an azimuth angle of 37 degrees south of east to simulate the position of the sun at 8:00 AM, December 21, in Bear Run, Pennsylvania. (Chapter 6 discusses locating the sun in detail.)

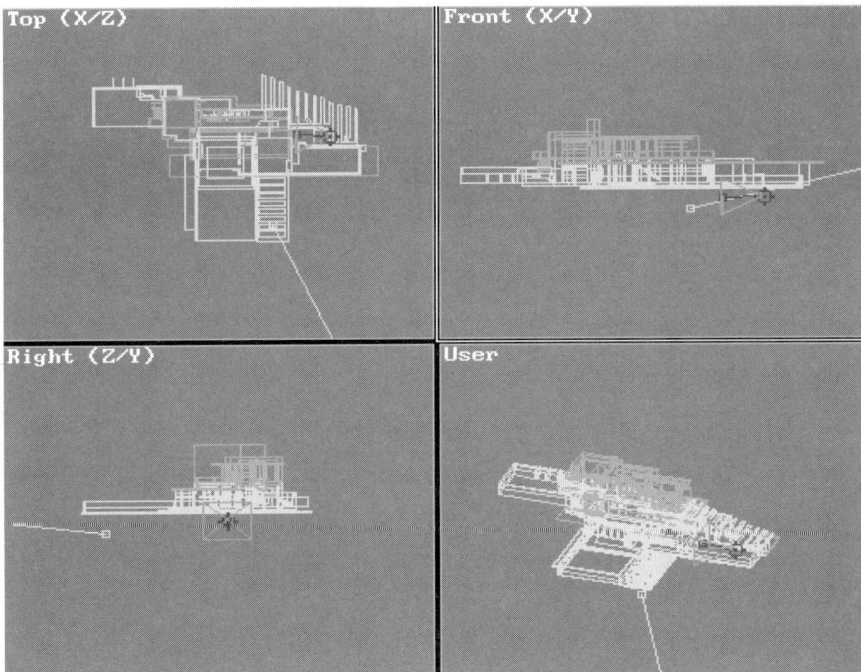

The upper-level geometry with spotlight and camera.

Merge the Lower Levels and Render a Preliminary View

In this section you will merge the geometry from the previous chapter and render the scene with only one light.

1. Choose File/Merge, toggle off everything in the Merge dialog box except Mesh Objects, and click OK.

2. In the Merge a 3DS, DXF, or FLM File dialog box, choose FND-LVL1.3DS from the scroll box and click OK. When the Select Object to Merge dialog box appears, click on the All button and OK.

3. Choose Views/Viewports and change the User viewport to a camera viewport.

4. Choose Renderer/Setup/Shadows, and toggle on the Ray Trace button if necessary.

5. Choose Renderer/Render View. Click on the Camera viewport once to activate it and again to assign it as the rendered view.

6. On the Render Still Image dialog box, check to make sure that Shading Limit is set to Phong, Shadows are On, and Resolution is set to 320 x 200. Click on the Render button.

Result: The rendered image is still too dark, but the patches of "sunlight" are correctly placed for the day of the year and time of day.

The loggia rendering with a single spotlight.

Add Secondary Lights

In reality, light enters the loggia from four sides, creating complex reflections. Although the sun is positioned correctly, the scene requires additional lighting to simulate the overall lightness of daytime. The goal is to illuminate the scene with as few individual lights as possible.

In the following section, you will add an omni light beyond the north (right) side of the loggia to simulate the reflected sunlight that shines through an opening in the wall. This omni light also shines less intensely through the model's walls, creating the effect of the reflected sunlight bouncing around within the loggia.

Then you will create a non–shadow-casting spotlight positioned close to the camera and pointed at the front door. The purpose of this light is to brighten shadows cast by the sun spotlight and simulate the light coming in from the end of the loggia. (Spotlights are easier to control for this purpose than are omni lights.)

1. Click in the Top viewport to activate it. Press [Ctrl-U] and toggle on the Architectural button.

2. Choose Lights/Omni/Create. Type in the following X, Y, and Z coordinates to place the light. Be sure to include the inch and foot symbols.

    69′ [Enter]

    5′ 6″ [Enter]

    49′ [Enter]

3. The Light Definition dialog box appears showing default settings. Type in the name **logomni** and move the Luminance slider until the setting is at 175. Click the Create button to accept the settings.

4. Choose Lights/Spot/Create and type in the following light location coordinates:

    79′ [Enter]

    5′ [Enter]

    36′ [Enter]

5. Type the target location coordinates:

    68′ 6″ [Enter]

    6′ 7″ [Enter]

    43′ [Enter]

6. The Spotlight Definition dialog box appears showing default settings. Type in the name **logspot** and move the Luminance slider to 135. Set Hotspot angle to 105 and Falloff angle to 106. Toggle on the Show Cone button to display the light's geometry, and click OK. Choose Renderer/Setup/Configure and set resolution to 640 x 480.

7. Choose File/Save Project, type in **fwentry** and pick OK to save the completed scene file.

Tip: Saving a file as a Project rather than simply using File/Save or File/Save As guarantees that interface settings, viewport status, and unit settings will be saved along with the scene.

8. Choose Renderer/Render View and specify the Camera viewport to render. Click the Render button when the Render Still Image dialog box appears.

Result: The addition of two subordinate lights provides a closer simulation of the complex, indirect lighting within the loggia.

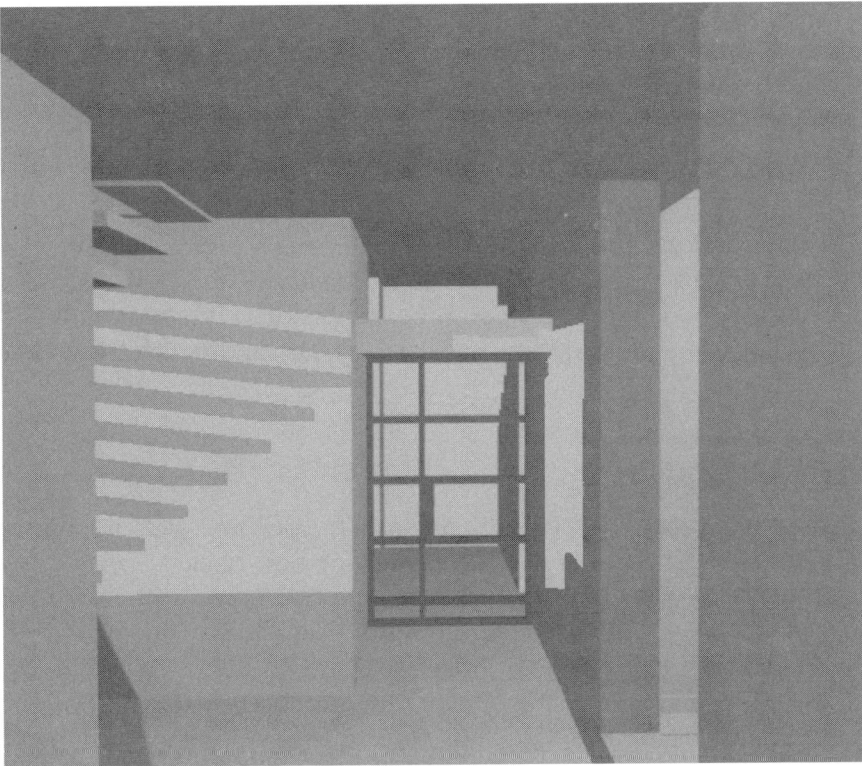

The loggia with three lights.

Exercise 2: Lighting the Hatch

Fallingwater's unique design has overshadowed its contribution as a precursor of solar houses. The flood of sunlight through the banks of south-facing windows created some of the same problems faced decades later by its energy-efficient descendants. The more delicate paintings had to be moved far back from the windows, leaving the sunlit areas populated by ceramics and by sculptures of glass and stone less likely to fade in the strong light.

For this exercise, the view is from the center of the living room toward the hatch and out to the east terrace. The hatch itself is glazed with three custom sliding panels across the top that telescope back to give access to the stairs. They are shown half-open in this view. The front of the hatch consists of double casement windows, open toward the room. In this shot, the glass has not been added yet.

In addition, this exercise will use a blue background to simulate a daytime sky. Actually, this is deceptive; outside the windows, the view consists of trees and rhododendrons covering the steep side of the glen, but we'll get to that later. Illusion, after all, is the heart and soul of computer rendering.

Create the Sun

You'll be using the FWENTRY.PRJ file from the previous exercise, turning off the current lights and camera and creating new ones.

1. Activate the Top viewport and right click Zoom Extents to display all the lights.

2. Choose Lights/Spot/Adjust and pick the sun spotlight. On the Spotlight Definition dialog box, toggle off the Show Cone button, pick the Off button to disable the light, and pick OK. The light icon will turn black and the cone will disappear.

3. Pick the fill-in spot and do the same; then choose Lights/Omni/Adjust and turn off the omni light.

4. The new sun will be located to simulate the light at 10:00 AM, December 22. Choose Lights/Spot/Create and type the following X, Y, and Z coordinates for the camera:

   -77′ [Enter]

   354′ [Enter]

   -896′ [Enter]

5. Type the coordinates for the target:

   49′ [Enter]

   0   [Enter]

   42′ [Enter]

6. In the Spotlight Definition dialog box, type **Hatchsun** for the light name. Set Luminance at 180. Then pick the Multiplier text box and type in a value of **3**, which will triple the intensity.

7. Type **13** in the Hotspot text box and **14** in the Falloff text box to specify the angle of the light cone.

8. Toggle on the Overshoot button and the Show Cone button.

9. Toggle on the Cast Shadows button and pick Create.

10. Choose Renderer/Setup/Shadows and toggle on the Ray Trace button.

Result: The sun has an effective intensity of 540, a narrow cone of concentrated light, and casts ray-traced shadows. Using the Overshoot function creates a light that combines the effects of spot and omni lights. The principle light is cast in a spotlight cone, but the spotlight also radiates a less intense light in all directions, as does an omni light.

```
                  Spotlight Definition
             Light Name: hatchsun

      R  -  [          180          ]  +
      G  -  [          180          ]  +          [        ]
      B  -  [          180          ]  +          [        ]
                                                  [        ]
      H  -  [0                       ]  +          [        ]
      L  -  [          180          ]  +          [        ]
      S  -  [0                       ]  +          [        ]

   Hotspot: 13      Falloff: 14      Roll: 0.0
              Multiplier: 3
                  [  On  ] [  Off  ]
   [ Cast Shadows ] [ Show Cone ] [ Attenuate ] [ Exclude ]
      [  Adjust  ]
      Type:      [ Rectangle ] [ Projector ]
      Global     [  Circle  ] [          ] [ Overshoot ]
                 [ Create ] [ Cancel ]
```

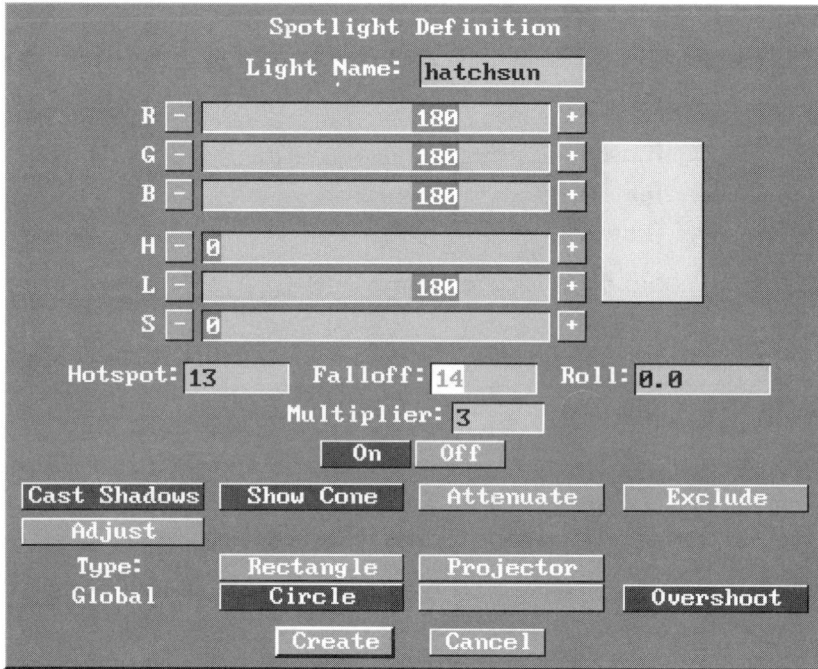

The new settings in the Spotlight Definition dialog box.

Setup a New Camera and Background

In this section, you'll change the black background to light blue and place the camera.

1. Choose Renderer/Setup/Background. On the Background Method dialog box, toggle on the Solid Color button, and click on the swatch beside it.

2. The Define Solid Color dialog box will appear. Adjust the sliders to the following values:

    > R = 170
    > G = 200
    > B = 255

    The sample color swatch will turn light blue. Pick OK twice.

3. Choose Cameras/Create and type the following camera coordinates:

I. A rendering of Fallingwater with a gold material applied to the surfaces that are, in reality, stucco.

Color Plates I-XI
Falling Water in 3D Studio by Laura Sanchez and Alex Sanchez.

ONWORD
PRESS

11. The north end of the passageway over the drive. The goddess, boulders, and the inside-outside moss garden provide a rich transition to the exterior spiralling stairs. (Photo by Thomas Heinz, courtesy the Western Pennsylvania Conservancy.)

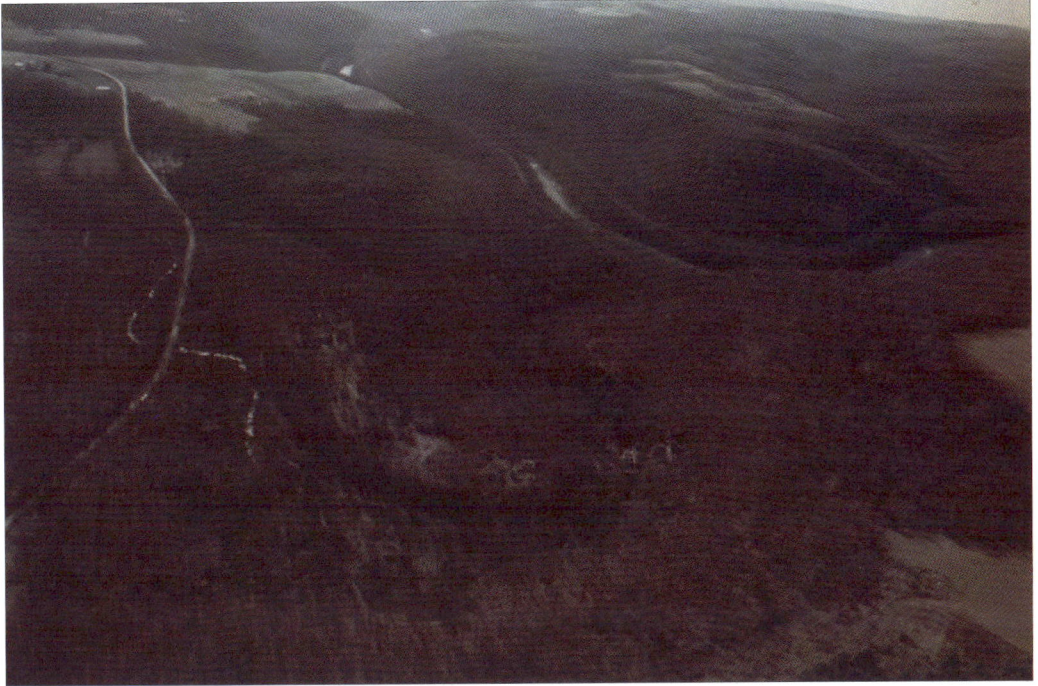

III. An aerial view of the immediate area. On the far left is Highway 381, crossed by the glinting loop of Bear Run, which empties into the larger Youghiogheny River at the upper right. In the lower center of the picture, the X-shaped building on the left is the Visitors' Center and Fallingwater is to the right. (Photo by Thomas Heinz, courtesy the Western Pennsylvania Conservancy.)

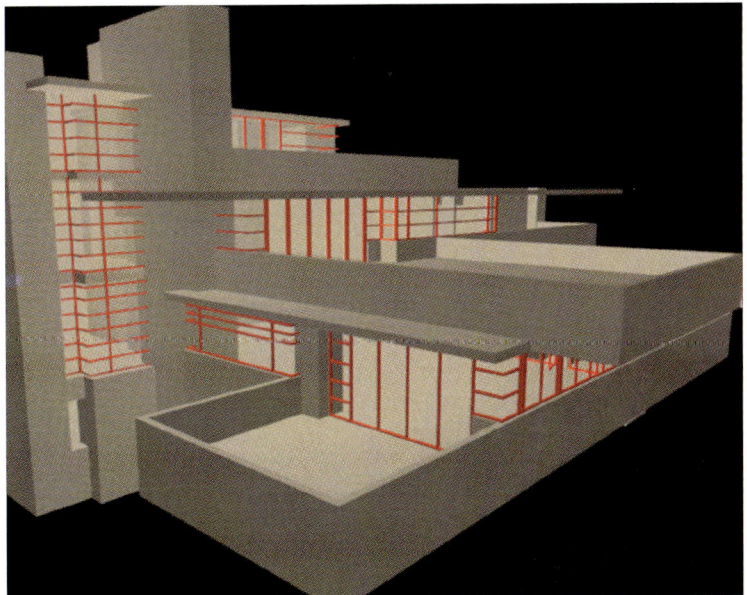

IV. A rendering of Fallingwater at night, floating in space and lit with six omni lights, from Exercise 3, Chapter 5.

V. A rendering of Wright's barrel chair, from Exercise 2, Chapter 7.

VI. The modeled Lipchitz in place on the plunge pool wall, from Exercise 3, Chapter 7.

VII. The final rendering of the hatch area with materials applied, from Exercises 1 and 2, Chapter 8.

VIII. An exterior view of Fallingwater.

IX. A view of the building complex from the east shows the main house at lower left, the passageway and trellis over the drive, and the half-circle stairs spiralling up to the guest wing. (Photo by Thomas Heinz, courtesy the Western Pennsylvania Conservancy.)

X. A frame from the walkthrough exercise in Chapter 9.

XI. The modeled and textured furniture in the south end of the living room.

> **38′** **[Enter]**
> **4′4″** **[Enter]**
> **27′4″** **[Enter]**

4. Now type the target coordinates:

> **54′** **[Enter]**
> **4′1″** **[Enter]**
> **14′3″** **[Enter]**

5. In the Camera Definition dialog box, type **Htch-cam** in the name text box, select a 35mm lens, toggle on the Show Cone button, and pick Create.

6. Activate the lower right viewport and press [C]. When the Camera Selector dialog box appears, pick Htch-cam from the scroll list and pick OK.

Result: The background will be blue, and the Camera viewport shows the new view, chosen to illustrate the hatch geometry and show patterns of sunlight on the floor.

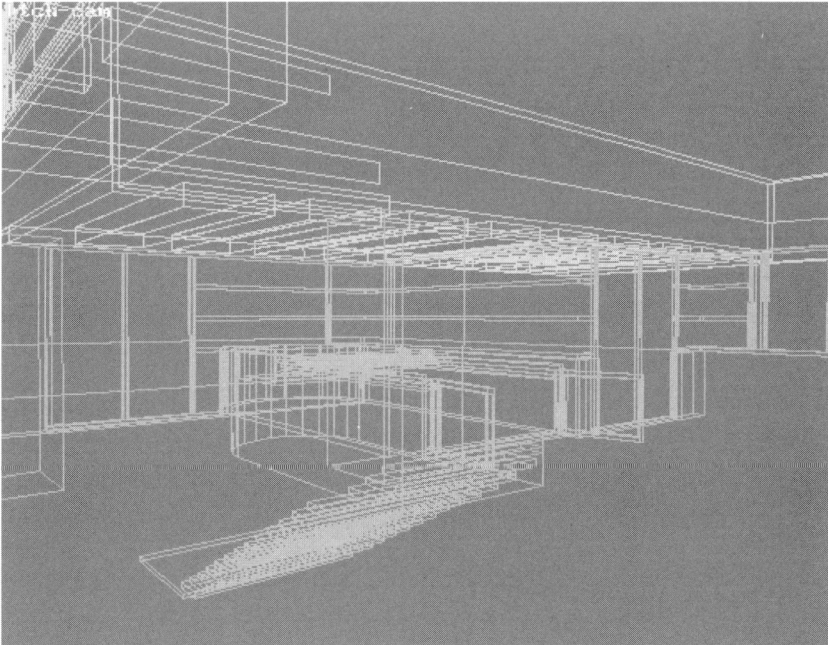

A full screen display of the new camera view.

Add a Fill-In Spotlight

This section adds a less intense spotlight with a broader cone to simulate the reflected light in the living room.

1. Choose Lights/Spot/Create and type in the following light coordinates:

    > **38′**   [Enter]
    > **4′11″** [Enter]
    > **28′**   [Enter]

2. Type in the target coordinates:

    > **57′5″**   [Enter]
    > **5′3″**   [Enter]
    > **11′10″** [Enter]

3. In the Spotlight Definition dialog box, type in **Hatchfil** for the light's name and set the Luminance slider to 180.

4. Set Hotspot to 107 and Falloff to 108. Check that the Multiplier value is set to the default of 1. Toggle off the Casts Shadows button and toggle on Show Cone. Pick the Create button.

Result: The fill spotlight placed close to the camera will lighten the visible surfaces to simulate reflected light.

Render the View

1. Choose File/Save Project to save the new setup. This will overwrite the settings from the previous exercise. If you wish to save both scenes, type **fwhatch** in the Filename text box.

2. Choose Renderer/Render View. Click the Camera viewport to activate it, and click again to designate it as the viewport to render.

3. If you wish to save the rendered view, toggle on the Disk button and then pick the Render button. The rendering will be displayed on the screen and also be saved to disk.

4. If you're saving the rendering to disk, type **fwhatch** in the Filename text box in the File Selector dialog box. The file will be saved in the default GIF format.

Result: The rendering shows the hatch with patches of morning sunlight across the floor.

The hatch rendering.

Exercise 3: It was a Dark and Siteless Night. . .

Fallingwater was to be a place where human beings lived intimately with nature. So intimately that Wright resisted even the use of screens on the doors and windows until he was defeated by the abundant insect population at Bear Run. As for window coverings, they were banished completely except for blinds in the guest room. The house is secluded in its glorious glen, and at night, light shines unimpeded from the window-walls.

The following exercise takes you from inserting omni lights into the building to simulate the lighting at night, through defining a position for the camera downstream from the house. Ambient light is left at its default setting, which produces enough non directional light to define the exterior surfaces of the building, along with the amount of omni light that penetrates the solid walls.

Place the Camera and Adjust the Background

In this section, you'll place the camera just southwest of the house and replace the black background.

1. Choose Cameras/Create and type in the following camera coordinates:

    -5'   [Enter]
    15'9" [Enter]
    -18'   [Enter]

2. Type in the target coordinates:

    40' [Enter]
    5' [Enter]
    26' [Enter]

    When the Camera Definition dialog box appears, type **Nite-cam** in the name text box, select a 35mm lens, and toggle on Show Cone.

3. Activate the Camera viewport and press [C]. Pick Nite-cam from the Camera Selector scroll list and pick OK. The Camera viewport displays the new view.

4. Choose Renderer/Setup/Background. In the Background dialog box, pick the Solid Color button and the swatch beside it. In the Define Solid Color dialog box, move the Luminance slider to zero to specify a black background.

Place Omni Lights in Rooms

The interior "light fixtures" are as far as possible from the exterior walls so they won't create hotspots through the walls.

1. Activate the Top viewport and pick the Full Screen icon button to display a single viewport. Zoom in on the house.

2. To turn off the current lights, choose Lights/Spot/Adjust, pick each of the spotlights in turn, toggle off Show Cone, and pick the Off button. Choose Display/Hide/Cameras to further clean up screen clutter.

3. To place three omni lights in the south rooms, choose Lights/Omni/Create and type in the following coordinates. The dialog box appears when you have entered all three coordinates for each light. Adjust each Luminance slider to 100 and type a name in the light name text box.

> **35′**   **[Enter]**
> **6′**   **[Enter]**
> **23′**   **[Enter]**
> **Light Name: Livgomni**
> **39′**   **[Enter]**
> **14′6″** **[Enter]**
> **32′**   **[Enter]**
> **Light Name: Mbromni**
> **35′**   **[Enter]**
> **23′**   **[Enter]**
> **46′**   **[Enter]**
> **Light Name: Topomni**

4. Pick the Full Screen icon button to toggle back to four viewports. Activate the Front viewport and assign it as the Full Screen view. The following three lights are all in the "tower," stacked vertically. Enter the coordinates, set Luminance to 100 for each light, and type in the names.

> **22′**   **[Enter]**
> **6′**   **[Enter]**
> **49′**   **[Enter]**
> **Light Name: Twr1omni**
> **22′**   **[Enter]**
> **14′6″** **[Enter]**

49'   [Enter[

Light Name: Twr2omni

22'   [Enter]

23'   [Enter]

49'   [Enter]

Light Name: Twr3omni

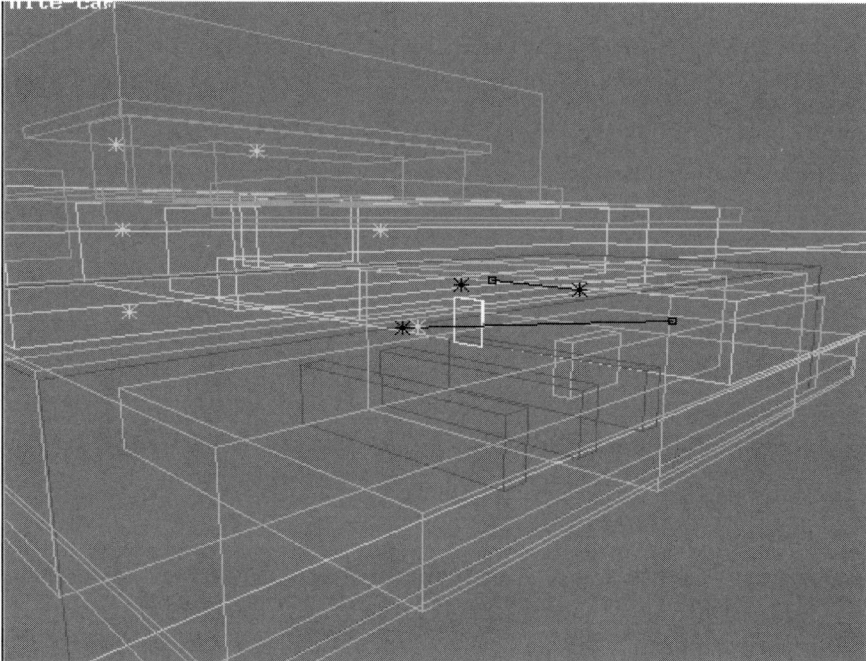

The model displayed using Box geometry, which simplifies it sufficiently to see the omni lights.

5. Change back to four viewports. Choose File/Save Project and save the scene with the name **fwnight** (if you wish to save each rendering separately).

6. Choose Renderer/Render View and click on the Camera viewport. On the Render Still Image dialog box, click the Render button.

Result: The night scene is rendered, lit by the minimum "light budget"—six omni lights. Plate IV in the color section presents the finished rendering.

Exercise 4: The Living Room at Night

The rendering for this exercise shows a hemispherical indentation next to the hearth. The indentation was carefully laid up in the masonry to form a niche for the wine kettle, a sphere nearly 2 feet across made from ⅜-inch cast iron, equipped with a spigot, and painted Cherokee red. The kettle is hung on a cantilevered support which allows it to be swung in over the hearth.

Wright intended the kettle to be used for heating wine over the fire, an activity that would wonderfully symbolize the communal, sacramental nature of the hearth. Unfortunately, the one time it was tried, the fire quickly blackened the bottom of the kettle but was slow to heat the large quantity of wine. The wine was finally heated up over the kitchen stove and then poured into the kettle. But the kettle *looks* grand.

Since the room's lighting is concealed by built-in features, this exercise imports a file containing the central ceiling grid. After placing the camera so that it points across the room to the southwest, you'll insert lights in the ceiling grid and use an auxiliary spotlight to bring up the room's light levels.

The ceiling grid was drawn with modified Quads in the 2D Shaper. The different thicknesses of the wood strips required separate lofts, after which the parts were assembled in the 3D Editor with the Attach command. The muslin screening is actually a 3D Studio self-illuminating material.

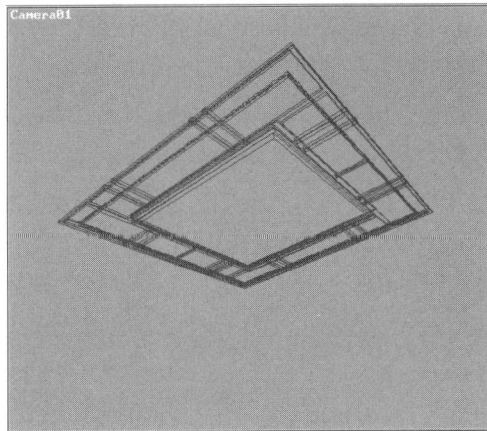

The ceiling grid geometry.

Turn Off Unnecessary Scene Components

First, you'll turn off the previous lights and the unseen levels of the model to speed up display and rendering operations.

1. Activate the Front viewport and pick the Full Screen icon to assign it as the single viewport. Choose Lights/Omni/Adjust and click on an omni light. Turn the light Off when its Light Definition dialog box appears.

2. Using the same command, turn off the other five omni lights.

3. Choose Display/Hide/By Name. A dialog box will appear with a scroll list containing the objects in the scene. Click on the following items:

   ```
   All three bolsters
   FOUND
   All object names beginning with L2 except L2-FLOOR
   All object names beginning with L3
   ```

   Click OK and right click Zoom Extents.

Result: Only the geometry needed to enclose the living room is displayed.

Import the Ceiling Grid and Position the Camera

The grid geometry is already located at its proper coordinates, so you'll merge it directly into place. Then you'll place a camera near the entry, aimed diagonally across the room.

1. Choose File/Merge. In the Merge dialog box, toggle off everything except Mesh Objects and click OK.

2. In the Merge a 3DS, DXF, or FLM File dialog box, click on the correct drive button for your distribution disk. Click on the CLG-GRID.3DS file in the scroll list, and click OK.

3. In the Select Object to Merge dialog box, click on the All button and click OK.

4. Choose Cameras/Create and type in the following camera coordinates:

52′   [Enter]

3′   [Enter]

35′   [Enter]

5. Type in the target coordinates:

40′   [Enter]

5′   [Enter]

25′10″ [Enter]

6. When the Camera Definition dialog box appears, type in the name **Ceil-cam,** and select a 35mm lens. Toggle on Show Cone if you wish to display the camera's field of view.

7. Click within the Camera viewport and press [C]. Choose Ceil-cam from the Camera Selector scroll list.

Result: The Camera viewport shows the new view with ceiling grid.

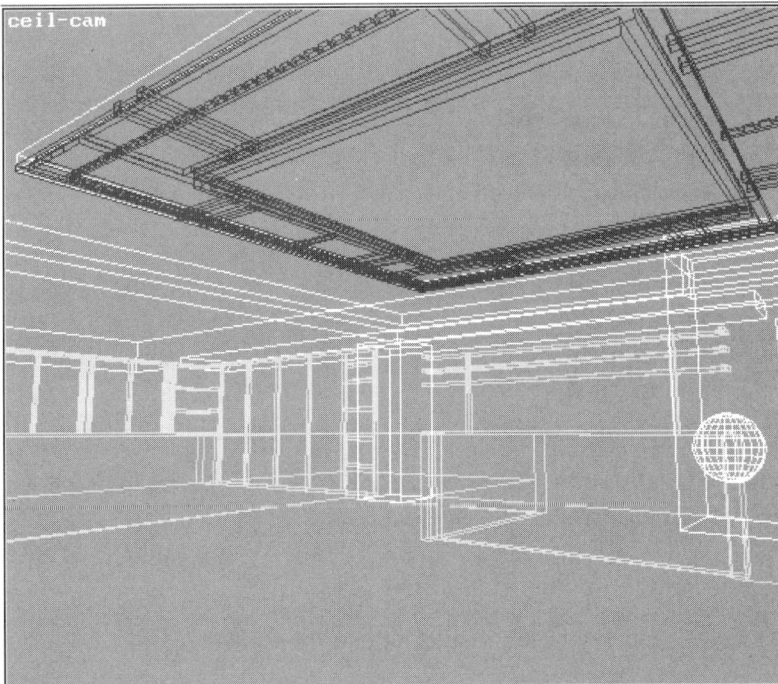

The new view.

Add Lights and Render

To mimic the actual combination of light spilling over the edge of the screen and light shining through the screen, the omni lights are placed behind a self-illuminating material. An auxiliary spotlight is added to boost light levels so that it is not necessary to turn the omni lights so high that they create bright circles on the grid screen. The Exclude button is used to differentiate the planes of the floor and walls.

1. Choose Lights/Omni/Create and type in the following sets of coordinates. In the Light Definition dialog box, use the Luminance slider to assign each omni light an intensity of 180, and then type in each light's name.

> **40′   [Enter]**
> **8′4″ [Enter]**
> **23′9″ [Enter]**
> **Light Name: Grid1**
> **44′6″ [Enter]**
> **8′4″ [Enter]**
> **28′8″ [Enter]**
> **Light Name: Grid2**
> **40′   [Enter]**
> **8′4″ [Enter]**
> **33′2″ [Enter]**
> **Light Name: Grid3**
> **35′   [Enter]**
> **8′4″ [Enter]**
> **28′8″ [Enter]**
> **Light Name: Grid4**

2. Choose Lights/Omni/Adjust and click on Grid1. In the dialog box click on the Exclude button, a scroll list will appear; click on the object L1-FLOOR and click on OK twice. Follow this same procedure to exclude the floor from omni light Grid2.

3. Choose Lights/Spot/Create and type in the following light coordinates:

          40′   **[Enter]**
          1″   **[Enter]**
          28′7″ **[Enter]**

4. Type in the following target coordinates:

          40′   **[Enter]**
          7′   **[Enter]**
          28′7″ **[Enter]**

5. In the Spotlight Definition dialog box, type in the light name **Gridspot**, a Hotspot setting of 140, and a Falloff setting of 141. Move the Luminance slider to 180.

6. Toggle off the Overshoot button and toggle on the Show Cone button. Toggle on the Rectangle button to change the light cone's shape to match the rectangular ceiling grid. Pick Create.

7. Choose File/Save Project from the menu bar and type in the name **fwceilng** (if you wish to save the scene as a separate file).

8. Choose Renderer/Render View and choose the Camera viewport to render. Pick the Render button in the Render Still Image dialog box.

Result: The living room is rendered with some of its lights on.

The living room at night.

Summary

The light and camera information and exercises in this chapter only nibble at the edges of the available setups. A good way to study other setups is to load the *.3ds* files listed in the 3D Editor, study the settings, and then render them to see the effects. Then try some from the World Creating Kit (a CD-ROM shipped with 3D Studio) to sample more elaborate configurations. In the next chapter we'll proceed from rendering single views to sequences of views for slide shows and animations.

Fallingwater in Motion

Now you have all the pieces in simplified form—model, materials, lights, and cameras—to explore animation.

3D Studio's animation capabilities stretch all the way to the feature film level. However, this chapter focuses on basic operations using single, consistent transformations. The exercises are simple, but they cover most basic architectural presentation techniques, giving you a quick start at producing effective real-world animations.

❏ Rotating the building model 360 degrees

❏ Morphing the skin of the building to a transparent material to show structural members

❏ Animating the sun to show shadow patterns throughout a day

In addition, this chapter includes descriptions of methods for creating section graphics and for establishing sun paths. Chapter 9 expands your animation tool kit with instructions for walkthroughs.

The Spaceship Fallingwater

In this chapter Fallingwater is still divorced from its site. Floating in space, the "outrigger" features that are camouflaged in a site visit or photographs are emphasized: stream stairs, entry wing, terraces, and the relationship between void and solid.

If placing a 3D model in space is revealing, animating the model is even more effective. It's difficult to grasp the relationship between different views of an intricate structure when looking at a series of still images.

North, South?

Inside, Outside?

The continuity of motion possible with animation, which shows each view in context with previous and subsequent views, orients a viewer as nothing else can.

The depth of 3D Studio's Keyframer options is necessary for animating complex sequences such as the subtleties of human movement, but it's overkill for most architectural work. For architectural presentations the most useful animation tools are walkarounds and walkthroughs, animations designed to reveal structural features, and daylighting sequences.

Preview Animations

3D Studio's Keyframer Preview commands create low-resolution, flat-shaded, non–anti-aliased preliminary animations. Always make a preview animation before investing the computing time necessary for full renderings of every frame. The preview will reveal any problems with the geometry itself, perspective distortion, overall light levels, reversed surface normals, jumpy motion, overall speed, or choice of paths. Often the preview alone is adequate for a study model.

Previews can be made using either object face or edge line display, a combination of the two, or bounding boxes. The object face mode displays surfaces as default white.

This object face preview shows something strange going on with the surface normals of the main-level floor slab at the tower.

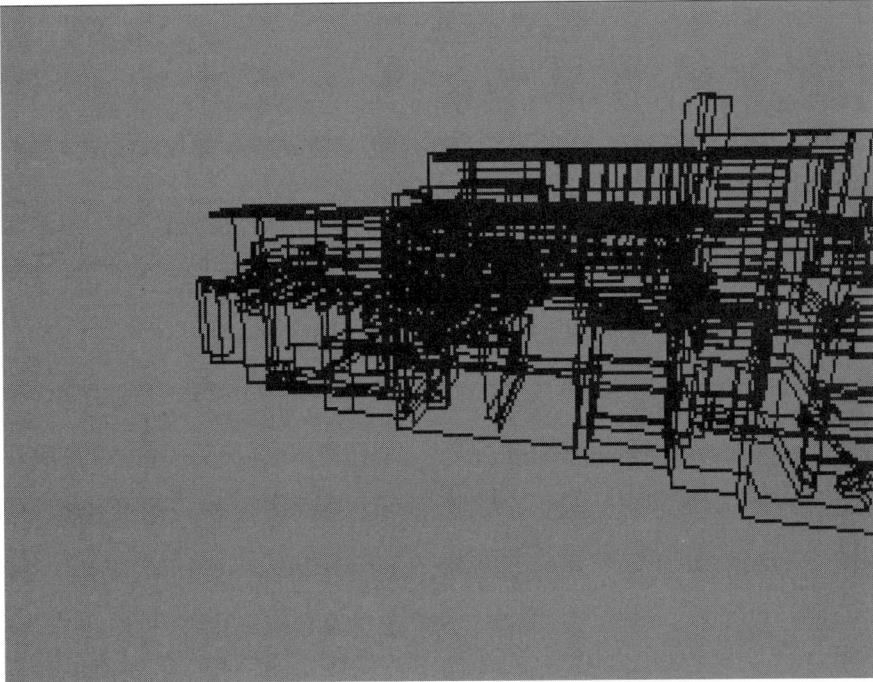

This edge line preview shows the rotating model moving out of the frame at one point in the animation.

Disk Space and Rendering Time

Depending on your system, you may need to consider the amount of disk space that a fully rendered animation will require. The relatively simple 30-frame 360-degree view of Fallingwater in the first exercise is assigned a black background and two material colors. It requires about 250 Kb for the preview animation, and 1 Mb for the fully rendered animation at 640 x 480 resolution.

You can minimize rendering time and disk space by:

❏ Using low resolution

❏ Limiting the number of colors

❏ Avoiding bitmaps on preliminary renderings

❏ Keeping lights (particularly shadow casting spotlights) to a minimum

❏ Avoiding transparent or reflective materials

❏ Rendering every other frame

❏ Using AutoCAD surface rather than solid modeling

When your animation is ready to render, setting up a batch rendering process frees you from sitting at the computer waiting for one frame after another to render. The *3D Studio Advanced User Guide* includes instructions for setting up batch renderings from the DOS prompt line.

The Transformation Commands

After you have added materials, lights, and a camera to your scene in the 3D Editor, switching to the Keyframer imports the scene. The 3D Editor scene becomes the first frame of the animation and is assigned keys at frame 0. Any necessary hierarchical links and pivots are then assigned to the various objects, and the total number of frames is set.

The next step is to move forward to another keyframe and adjust the scene objects to the state you want by using the various transformations in the following list. The program generates the in-between frames. The first two chapter exercises set keys only at the first and last frames, letting 3D Studio do most of the work.

The *3D Studio Reference Manual* lists the following transformations available for different scene components:

❏ **Mesh Objects**

  ❏ Position (including movement along a path)

  ❏ Rotation

  ❏ Scale (including squash, a special form of scale)

  ❏ Morphing (metamorphosis from one object's shape or material to another)

  ❏ Hide (turns on and off the display of the object in the scene)

❏ **Ambient Light**

   ❏ Color

❏ **Omni Lights**

   ❏ Position (including movement along a path)

   ❏ Color

❏ **Spotlights**

   ❏ Spotlight position (including movement along a path)

   ❏ Target position (including movement along a path)

   ❏ Color

   ❏ Hotspot

   ❏ Falloff

   ❏ Roll

❏ **Cameras**

   ❏ Camera position (including dollying toward or away from the target and movement along a custom-designed path)

   ❏ Target position (including movement along a path)

   ❏ Roll

   ❏ Field of view

Hierarchical Links

When a scene is brought into the Keyframer, hierarchical linking commands can be used to connect objects so that movement is transferred from parent objects to child objects. The effects of the assigned transformations always flow down the hierarchy tree, never up. Motion assigned to a child object does not affect the parent object, while the motion assigned a parent object is transferred to the child object, and can be refined, layered, and extended in various complex ways.

Hierarchy/Link (used in exercise 1) creates a simple link between parent and child that replicates movement as if the objects were one. Hierarchy/Unlink removes the connection. Objects that are linked must remain so throughout the animation. When moving the linked objects, the movement can be limited to specific axes by using the Key Info position locks or the Hierarchy/Link Info command.

Exercise 1: Rotating Fallingwater

The integration of Fallingwater with its site perplexed even those who built the house, and the official site plan wasn't much help. One hot night after a long day's work, Bob Mosher decided to refresh himself with a swim. In the darkness, he dove off a rock into a site-plan-certified pool of water. Unfortunately, the water was not where it was supposed to be, and Mosher couldn't move his neck for three days.

"How could he do that?" Wright asked.

"Bob looked at the plot plan," [Edgar] Tafel answered, "saw where it said water, and dove in." The master was not amused (Hoffmann, p. 39).

You can create a 360-degree animation by either rotating the building or moving the camera around it. The most straightforward way is to rotate the building, which is simple when the building is not connected to the site. This exercise links the upper floors to the foundation and assigns rotation to the foundation.

Load the Model File and Create Lights and Camera

1. Choose File/Load from the menu bar. Click on the correct drive button. Pick the ASSEMB.3DS file from the scroll list and pick OK.

2. Choose Views/Unit Setup and specify Architectural units with a Denominator of **1**. Pick the lower right viewport and press [U] to change to a User viewport.

3. In the 3D Editor, choose Lights/Omni/Create. Type in X,Y,Z coordinates and light names, and adjust the luminance settings for the following omni lights:

    > **130′ [Enter]**
    > **43′ [Enter]**
    > **11′ [Enter]**
    > **omni-01, Luminance = 125**

130′ [Enter]
43′ [Enter]
11′ [Enter]
omni-01, Luminance = 125

28′ [Enter]
43′ [Enter]
-52′ [Enter]
omni-02, Luminance = 130

49′ [Enter]
43′ [Enter]
26′ [Enter]
omni-03, Luminance = 75

93′ [Enter]
43′ [Enter]
104′ [Enter]
omni-4, Luminance = 100

4. Right click Zoom Extents. Choose Cameras/Create, type in the following coordinates and name, and select the lens.

Camera location:
149′ [Enter]
41′ [Enter]
-82′ [Enter]
Target location:
58′ [Enter]
0   [Enter]
32′ [Enter]
round-cam, Lens = 35mm

5. Click on the lower right viewport and press [C] to change to a Camera viewport.

Result: The omnis will light the side of the house facing the camera, which is set up for a mid-distance view.

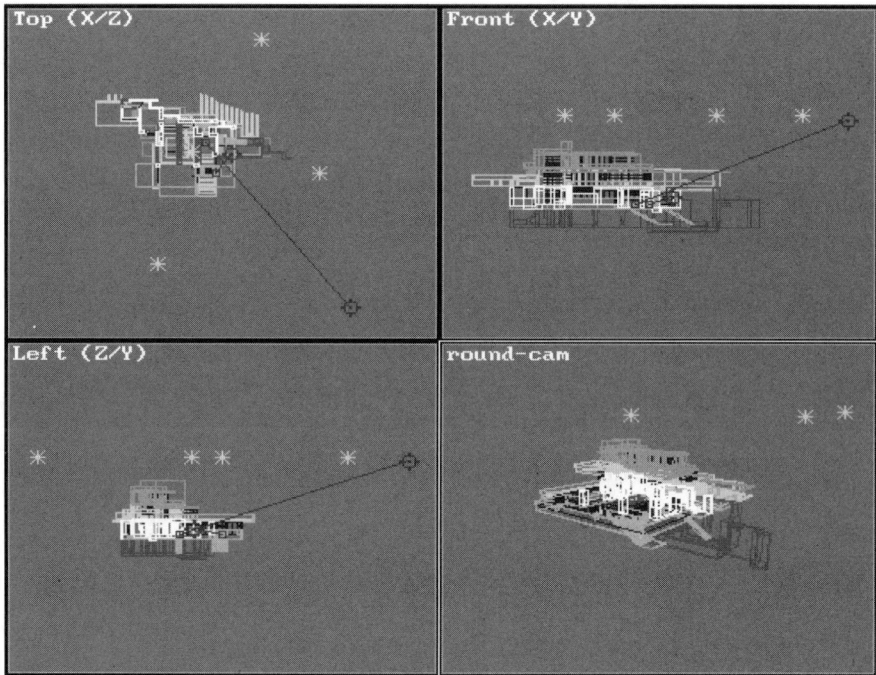

The building model with lights and camera.

Go to the Keyframer and Link the Mesh Objects

In this section, you'll link the upper floors of the house to the foundation, so that when the foundation rotates, the entire building will move, rather than generate a horrible grinding noise as Fallingwater shears apart.

1. Press [F4] to get to the Keyframer. Click on the lower right viewport and press [C]. Right click Zoom Extents.

2. Choose Hierarchy/Link and press the [H] key to display the Select Child Objects dialog box.

3. Click on the All button to select everything, and then click on the following objects to deselect them:

```
FOUND
OMNI-01 through OMNI-04
ROUND-CAM and ROUND-CAM target
```

4.   Click on OK. The command line will read:

    ```
    Child objects selected— now click on parent
    ```

5.   Press [H] and click on parent object FOUND.

Result: The foundation is now the parent of all the upper level children.

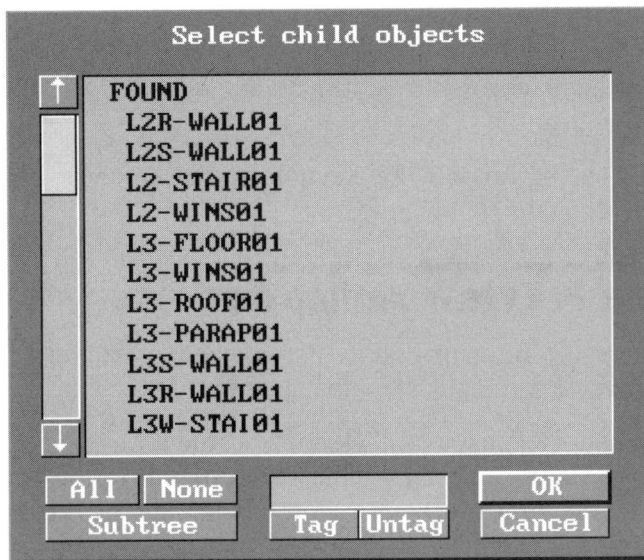

The dialog box will display the parent object flush left, with
succeeding generations of child objects indented.

Rotate the Foundation and the Linked Mesh Objects

The rotation will be limited to the Y axis, specified on the status line.

1.   Click on the Top viewport. Move the cursor down to the command
     line to display the frame slider. Click on the right end of the frame
     slider to position on frame 30.

2.   Press [A] to toggle on Angle Snap, and choose Object/Rotate. Press [H] to display the scroll list, and click on FOUND and OK. (Since FOUND is the parent object, it will now be at the top of the list.)

3.   Press [Tab] twice to specify rotation around the Y axis; The status line should read:

    `"FOUND" Axis: Y  Angle: 0.00 degrees`

4.   Move the mouse to the right to rotate the foundation a full 360 degrees, displayed on the status line, and click the left mouse button.

5.   To view the animation in wireframe, click on the Camera viewport. Click on the Play icon button (the double right arrows). Press [Esc] to stop the animation.

Result: By setting up only one keyframe, you can create an animation of the model rotating 360 degrees.

Create a Preview Animation

Now you'll view your animation in more detail by creating a flat-shaded object face preview and adjusting the speed.

1.   Choose Preview/Make and click on the Camera viewport. In the Make Preview dialog box, click on the Faces button in the Draw group. Click on the Preview button. After a minute or so the Preview animation will play.

2.   Adjust the speed of the animation by using the arrow keys:

    ❏ The left arrow slows the playback.

    ❏ The right arrow speeds up the playback.

    ❏ The up arrow specifies a playback speed of 20 frames per second.

    ❏ The down arrow pauses the animation. In pause mode, the right and left arrows advance the animation one frame at a time. Press the down arrow again to return to full animation.

    ❏ The [Esc] key to returns you to the interface.

Result: The object face preview provides a quick way to check for problems with overall light levels, badly framed objects, reversed surface normals, or incorrect motion.

Create a 640 x 480 Animation

In this section, you'll create the presentation animation and save it to disk.

1. Choose Renderer/Setup/Configure and check that resolution is set to 640 x 480.

2. Choose Renderer/Setup/Background. In the Background Method dialog box, toggle on the Solid Color button and pick OK.

3. Choose Renderer/Render View and click on the Camera viewport.

4. In the Render Animation dialog box, check that Shading Limit is set to Phong. In the Frame group, click on the All button. In the Output group, click on both the Display and the Disk button, and click on the Render button. Type filename, **fwrotate**, for the rendering in the dialog box.

Result: After a while (how long depends on your system), you will have a *.flc* extension file which you can view using the Renderer/View/Flic option. The arrow keys will control the playback as they did with the Preview animation.

A frame from the rendered animation.

Tip: When you're preparing to save a rendering to a floppy disk, it's easy to check disk space without leaving 3D Studio. Choose Program/DOS Window, go to the correct drive, and type **dir** to display the current disk contents. Typing **exit** gets you back to the 3D Studio interface.

Bad News and Good News Concerning Sections

As well as being vital to construction documents, building sections are useful in study and presentation contexts to illustrate tricky structural or spacial features. Once you've cut a section, there are many things you can do with it—hiding and revealing elements, animating portions, zooming in on details, changing (morphing) materials and colors selectively, turning corners, or exploding the elements of the section. The bad news is, it's a little difficult to cut the section in the first place.

Cutting Sections

Since 3D Studio does so many things superbly, it seems unfair to focus on something it's not designed to do, but the program has problems cutting sections in complex objects. Several approaches are mentioned below; each has limited use, and they all have drawbacks. However, 3D Studio does have a great technique for revealing hidden components, illustrated in the next exercise—morphing components to a transparent material.

1. Cut the Section in AutoCAD If you've created a 3D model in AutoCAD, you can use the Solcut command to slice a section in the desired location and import the model section into 3D Studio as a *.dxf* file. As with any other *.dxf* import, how the layers are set up in AutoCAD determines the model's separation into objects in 3D Studio.

2. Extrude or Loft a 2D Section Depending on how the components are arranged in layers, parts of a 2D AutoCAD section can be assigned different thicknesses. The components can be extruded in AutoCAD with the Change command, the drawing can be imported into the 2D Shaper and lofted object by object, or components can be assigned different thicknesses with the 3D Editor Create/Face/Extrude command. This method is not very efficient if the drawing is complex or if its shapes are invalid for lofting.

3. Remove a Wall   A section can be created by removing the end wall of a 3D model to reveal floor, wall, and ceiling profiles. The effectiveness of this approach depends on the amount of detail with which the components of the model have been created, the method used to construct the model, and the design of the building.

4. Use Boolean Subtraction   3D Studio's Boolean Subtraction is potentially the cleanest technique for cutting sections, but unfortunately it usually crashes when you attempt to chop something as complex as a building model. Problems arise when one object has many more faces than the other, and tessellating a flat cutting surface won't help.

Using a cylinder with numerous sides and segments as a cutting tool increases your chances of a successful Boolean Subtraction, but you can't get a flat surface cut, and the complexity is still quite limited.

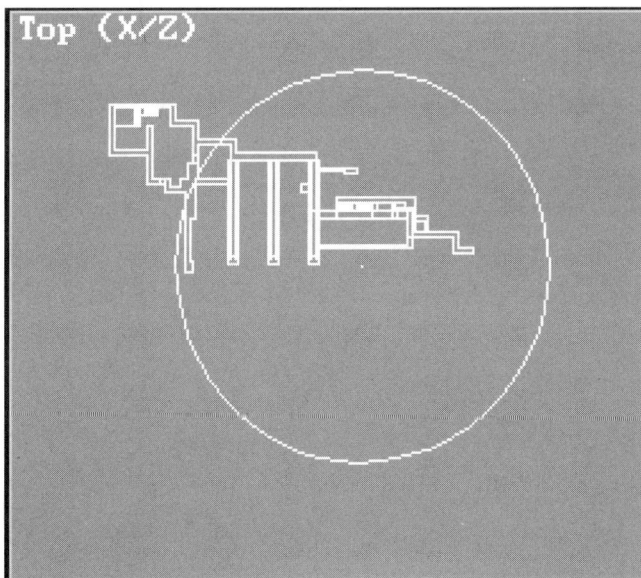

Placing a 70-sided 30-segment cylinder to cut a section through Fallingwater's foundation.

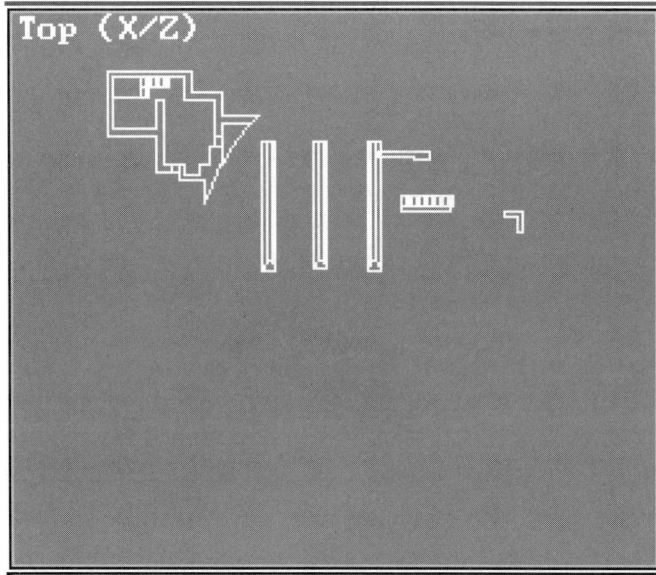

The cylinder succeeded in cutting a simple section through two walls, leaving various elements behind.

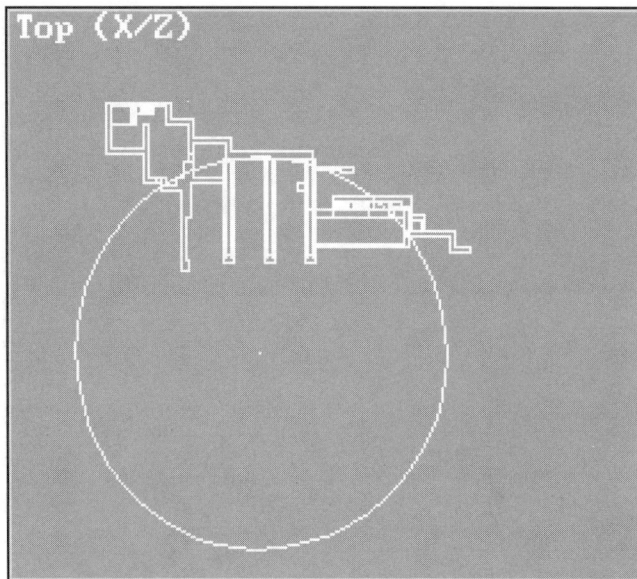

Boolean Subtraction failed when the cylinder was placed to cut a more complex section.

5. Use the Z-Clip-Near Setting   The Z-Clip-Near value (3D Editor, Renderer/Setup/Options) specifies the distance of the near clipping plane from the camera. Its default setting is 1, which specifies that everything in the camera view will be in the rendering except for the area within one unit of the camera's lens. Objects on the camera side of the clipping plane disappear. Since the Z-Clip-Near plane is adjustable, it can be moved far enough away from the camera to intersect the model.

This seems like a perfect tool to cut sections, but as the documentation states, "This can sometimes lead to unexpected results." When the clipping plane cuts through the model, it does not "skin over" the ends of the sectioned objects. Thus, components intersected by the clipping plane appear open and hollow, like the main- and second-level floors in the next illustration. Using Force 2-Sided assigns the object material to the inside of the component, but doesn't close the end.

Also, the clipping plane is always perpendicular to the camera's line of site, which eliminates all but head-on views of sectioned building components.

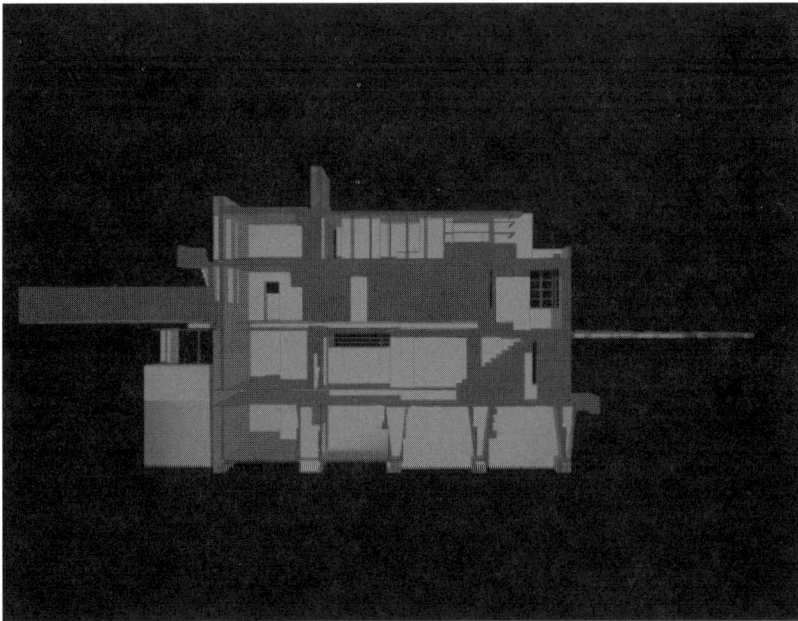

The camera's line of sight is perpendicular to Fallingwater's south wall, with the clipping plane placed near the north wall. Walls close to the clipping plane are dark, and slabs appear hollow.

Morphing Materials to Create Sections

Now for the good news. One of the most sophisticated, expensive, difficult, and effective traditional methods of technical illustration is simple in 3D Studio: the phantom view. The traditional phantom section is usually a perspective color rendering showing the outer layers of a building's structure carefully airbrushed to simulate a transparent material that reveals the layers within.

Transparency is easy to achieve in 3D Studio with a simple material assignment. Morphing from a solid material to a transparent one effectively illustrates the relation between a building's skin and what it contains.

When using transparent materials, pay attention to the Add and Sub buttons to the right of the Transparency slider. The Add button adds the color of the material to the background. Since the sum of material luminance is greater, the material appears brighter than the background— the more layers of transparent material, the brighter. The Sub button subtracts the material color from the background, thus making layers of transparent material progressively darker.

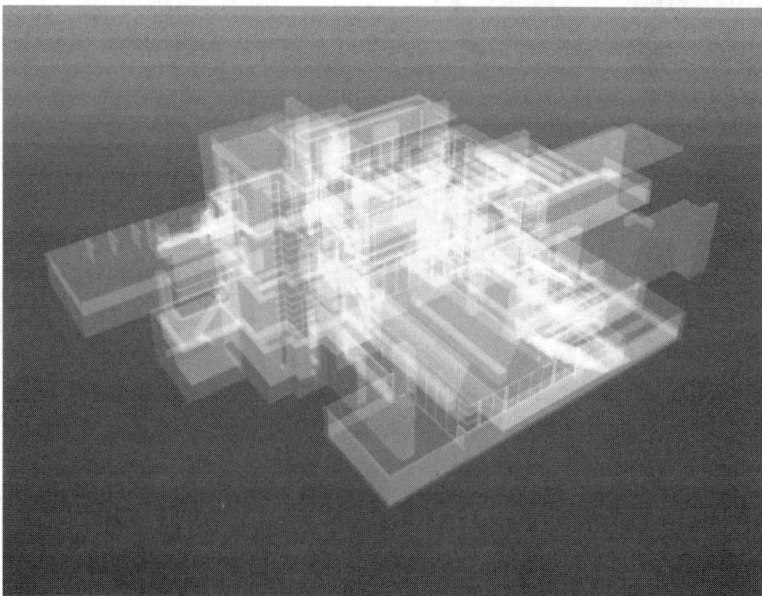

Fallingwater rendered in a transparent material against a gradient background, with the Add button on.

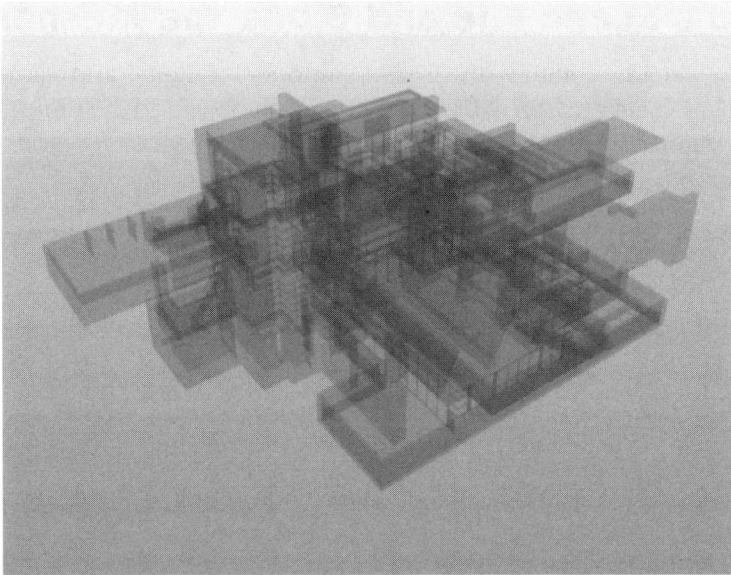

The same view, using the Sub button and a lighter background.

Exercise 2: The Phantom Floor Slab

The finish floor to finish floor height at Fallingwater is over nine feet, but the waffle slabs are so thick that the net ceiling height is only 6′ 4″ in some areas. Such low ceilings were typical of Wright's work; myth has it that he adjusted proportions to his own 5′ 8½″ height. When William Wesley Peters, a long-time associate who towered well over six feet, entered a room, Wright would say, "Wes, sit down—you're ruining the scale of my architecture!" (Hoffmann, p. 38)

This exercise creates a phantom view of Fallingwater's first-floor waffle slab. Instead of cutting sections in the traditional manner, the animation reveals the beams and joists in a series of frames showing the surface material morphing from opaque to 75% transparency.

Load a Scene File and Clone the Meshes

The file already contains the slab components, lights, and camera. To morph an object's material, first copy the mesh objects in the same location as the original objects and then assign a transparent version of the original material to the duplicate objects.

1. Choose File/Load. Press the correct drive button and choose L1-MORPH.3DS from the scroll list.

2. Choose Select/Object/By Name. In the scroll box, pick L1-PARAP and L1-FLOOR, and then pick the OK button. The floor and parapet, which will be cloned to create transparent doubles, will turn red.

3. Choose Create/Object/Copy and click the Selected button.

4. Move to the Top viewport. Left click twice without moving the mouse. (The first click duplicates the selected items and the second click places them in the same location.)

5. In the Copy Objects To dialog box, pick the Multiple button. The Name for New Object dialog box will appear with the cloned objects' default names. Click the Create button to accept the L1-PARAP01 and L1-FLOOR01 names. Choose Select/None to clear the selection set.

Result: The parapet and floor clones are superimposed on the originals.

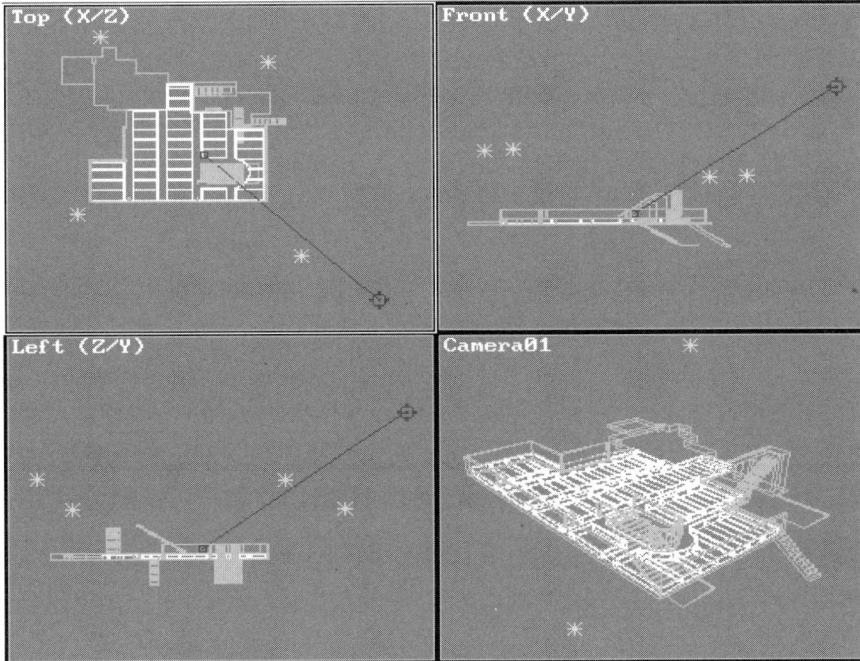

The floor assembly.

Assign a Translucent Material to the Cloned Objects

The original parapet and slab have already been assigned a stucco material. In this section you'll create a transparent material and assign it to the parapet and slab clones. The beams and joists are assigned a white material, which will be visible through the transparent material.

1. Press [F5] to switch to the Materials Editor. From the menu bar choose Material/Get Material.

2. In the Get Material scroll box, click on BEIGE MATTE and the OK button.

3. In the column of Material Property Controls, move the Transparency slider to 75.

4. Choose Material/Put Material from the menu bar. Type in **beige trans** and click OK.

5. Press [F3] to get back to the 3D Editor. Pick Surface/Material/Choose, pick BEIGE TRANS from the Material Selector scroll list, and pick the OK button. (The P beside the material name indicates Phong shading and the X indicates that the material has a transparency setting assigned.)

6. Choose Surface/Material/Assign/By Name to call up a scroll list of object names. Click on L1-FLOOR01 and L1-PARAP01, and then pick the OK buttons on the scroll list and message box.

Result: The parapet and floor clones are assigned a transparent material.

Switch to the Keyframer and Setup a Morph Keyframe

In this section you will morph the beige matte material to the beige translucent material.

1. Press [F4] to switch to the Keyframer.

2. Move the cursor to the command line area at the bottom of the screen to display the frame slider bar. Click on the right end of the frame slider to move to frame 30. Click on the Hold button in the icon panel. (The Fetch button gets you back to the saved frame buffer at this point.)

3. Choose Object/Morph/Assign and press the [H] key. In the Click on Object by Name scroll box, pick L1-FLOOR and OK. In the Select Morph Object dialog box, pick L1-FLOOR01 and OK.

4. Repeat the process, picking L1-PARAP from the Click on Object by Name scroll box, and L1-PARAP01 from the Select Morph Object dialog box.

5. To define the morph as a material transformation, choose Objects/Morph/Options and press the [H] key.

6. In the Click on Object by Name scroll box, pick L1-FLOOR and OK. In the Morph Options dialog box, toggle on the Morph Material button. Press the [H] key again and repeat the process for the parapet.

Result: The slab and parapet material morph keys are complete and you are ready to make an animation.

The Select Morph Object dialog box specifies which paired objects will receive the morph transformation.

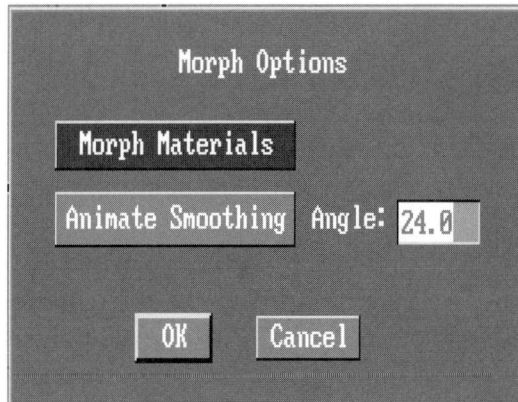

The Morph Options dialog box specifies whether material or smoothing groups will be morphed.

Render the End Frame to Check the Material Morph, and then Render a 15-Frame Animation at 640 x 480

Since the Preview option doesn't show material morphs, you'll render the last frame to check the morphing operation.

1. Choose Renderer/Setup/Configure. In the dialog box, click on the 320 x 200 button, and then click OK.

2. Choose Renderer/Render View and click on the Camera viewport. In the Render Animation dialog box, click on the Single button and the Render button. Click on the OK button in the Render to Screen Only? message box. The last frame rendering will show the slab and parapets in a translucent material.

3. Press the [Esc] key to get back to the interface. Choose Renderer/Setup/Configure and click on the 640 x 480 button to set the image resolution.

4. Choose Renderer/Render View and click on the Camera viewport.

5. In the dialog box, click on the All button in the Frame group. Click on the Every Nth Frame text box and type in **2** to render every other frame. Click on the Render button.

Result: The 15-frame animation shows the parapet and slab fading from an opaque material to a translucent material, exposing the internal structural components.

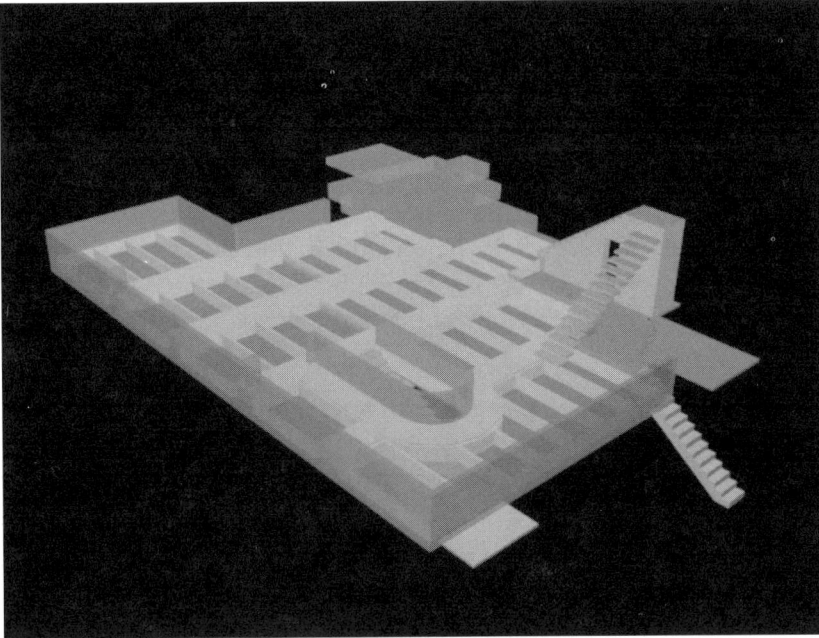

The last frame with transparent slab and parapet.

Creating a Sun

Architects use solar shading studies to examine the way the sun interacts with building geometry—the play of sunlight and shadow across the surface, the effectiveness of shading overhangs, and how deeply sunlight penetrates the building's interior. These studies are particularly useful for buildings with large glazed areas. The appearance of a building can be strongly affected by self-shading; if the shading is controlled, it can be a predictable part of the building design.

Sun angles vary by hour, season, location, and building orientation. In the past, heliodons (mechanical sun simulators) and scaled building models were used to study this interaction. Today, you can do it with a computer either by using 3D Studio with the process described in the next section or by purchasing a separate IPAS sunlight routine designed to augment 3D Studio. Two companies that sell such routines are The Pyros Partnership, Inc., 1201 Dove Street, Suite 550, Newport Beach, CA 92660,

714/833-0334, and Schreiber Instruments, Inc., 400 Happy Canyon Rd., Denver, CO 80237, 303/759-1024.

Making a Sun Path

Shading studies are based on moving a spotlight along a path that replicates the sun's course during a day. The spotlight target is centered on the building, and the light is placed far enough away so that the shadows appear to be cast by parallel rays. Raytraced rather than bitmapped shadows are used to simulate the crisp, hard-edged shadows cast by full sunlight.

The following procedure creates an arrangement of five elongated quads fanning out from a central point, with their far ends marking five hourly sun positions used by the Keyframer to approximate the sun's daily path. (The last exercise imports a sun path for you.)

This process is a bit clumsy, and has a margin of error of 3- or 4-degrees. However, if most of your work is in the same geographical area, a set of three sun paths for December, March (March and September have the same angles), and June will take care of most of your needs. The example below is for May 21 at 36 degrees north latitude.

1. Use a map to find the latitude of your building's location.

2. Decide on the month you want to depict, and look up the sun's altitude (angular distance up from the horizon) and azimuth (horizontal, or bearing, angle) positions for that month and your latitude. Most references give positions for early morning, 10:00 AM, noon, 2:00 PM, and late afternoon. Both *Architectural Graphic Standards* and *Time-Saver Standards* include sun angle data. Sun angle data can also be found in an ephemeris or in many books on solar construction.

3. The next step is to translate altitude and azimuth values into 3D Studio coordinates. For this you need some sticks to use as hour lines. (You can call them "altitude-azimuth insolation vectorizors" to impress clients.)

4. Specify Architectural units with a Denominator of **1**. Go to the 3D Editor and choose Create/Box. Click on the Front viewport. Draw a

box 2 inches by 2 inches by 300 feet. Name the stick **HLINE-6AM** and right click Zoom Extents.

5. In the Top viewport the stick is vertical, pointing due north and south. Use Modify/Axis/Show and Modify/Axis/Place to position the global axis at the top, or north end, of the stick, and turn off the Local Axis button. In the Top viewport, use Create/Object/Copy to make two more sticks, naming them **HLINE-10AM** and **HLINE-NOON.** Move them off to the side for now. Right click Zoom Extents.

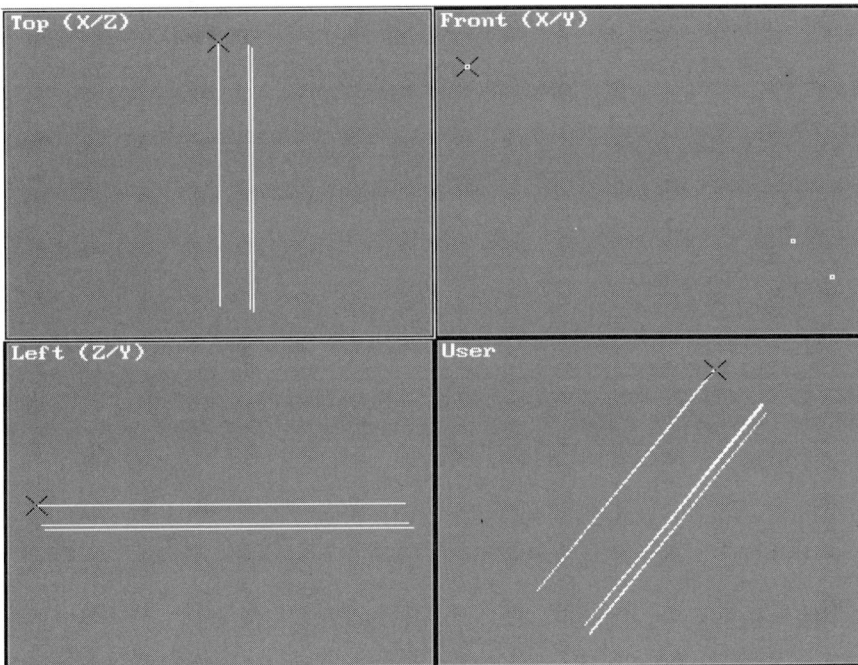

Stick 1 and the global axis in place, with sticks 2 and 3 off to the side.

6. In the Left viewport, use Modify/Object/Rotate to rotate the right (or south) end of stick 1 up 12 degrees, the angular altitude value for 6:00 AM. In the Top viewport, rotate stick 1 to 107 degrees, the bearing angle for 6:00 AM. Right click Zoom Extents.

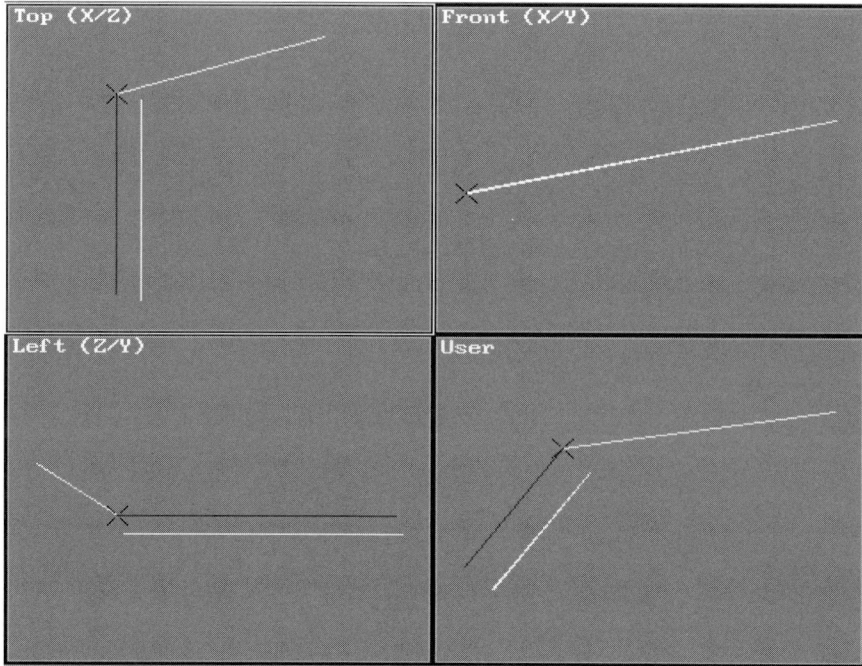

Stick 1 (white) has been rotated into place for the 6:00 AM sun angle, and stick 2 (black) has been placed with its north end at the global axis, ready to position for the 10:00 AM sun angle.

7. In the Front and Left viewports, move stick 2 so that its north end is in the same location as stick 1's north end. Zoom in to the Axis area if necessary. In the Left viewport, rotate stick 2 up 60 degrees for the 10:00 AM altitude. In the Top viewport, rotate stick 2 to 67 degrees, the bearing angle for 10:00 AM.

8. Move stick 3, HLINE-NOON, into place with its north end at the global axis. In the Left viewport, rotate stick 3 up to 74 degrees, the altitude angle for noon. stick 3 will remain in place in the Top viewport, pointing straight south for the noon bearing angle.

9. The afternoon sun positions are mirror copies of the morning ones, so you can duplicate the 6:00 AM and 10:00 AM sticks to establish the 2:00 PM and 6:00 PM sun positions. Choose Select/Object/Single and click on stick 1. Choose Modify/Object/Mirror and toggle to a horizontal cursor. Pick the Selected button, hold down the [Shift] key and

pick the selected stick to make a mirrored copy. Name the stick **HLINE-6PM**. Choose Select/None to clear the selection set, and repeat the operation, copying the second stick, and naming it **HLINE-2PM**.

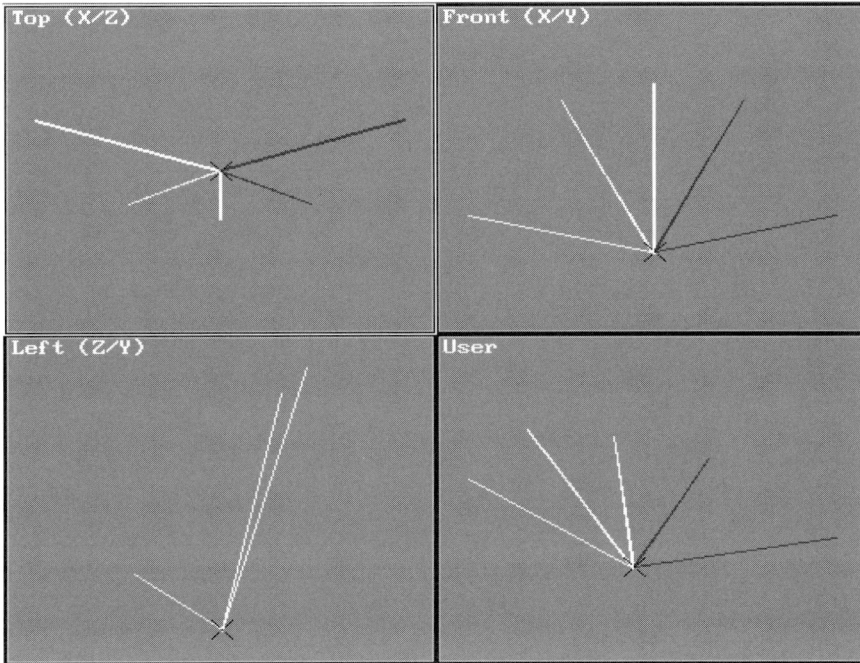

A mirrored copy of sticks 1 and 2.

10. Zoom in on the sticks' convergence point to check that all five "north" ends are in the same location.

11. Load your building model file. Use Select/Object/Quad to make a selection set of all five sticks.

12. Using all viewports, move your sun path so that the converging ends are centered within the building. Relocate the global axis at the connected ends of the sticks.

13. Using the site data for your building, in the Top viewport rotate the sun path so that the center (HLINE-NOON) stick points directly south from your building.

14. The following exercise picks up from here, using 1,000 foot hour line sticks to position a sun spotlight.

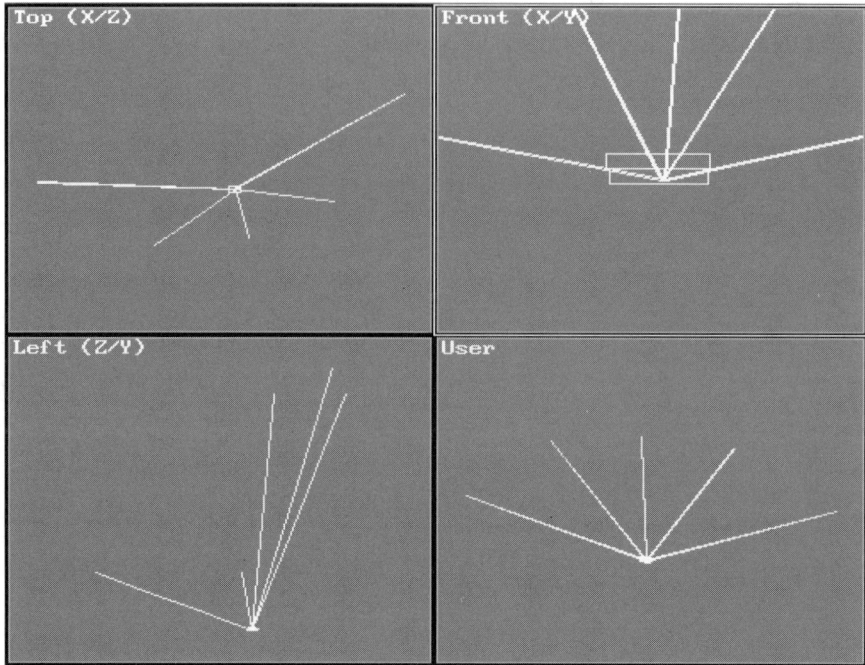

The completed array of hour lines, positioned on a "building." Since the building faces 15 degrees west of south, the hour lines are rotated 15 degrees counterclockwise to compensate.

Tip: If your building is large, you may need to dolly the spotlight farther away from the building and adjust the Hotspot and Falloff angles. The Lights/Spot/Dolly command preserves the existing sun position vectors.

Exercise 3: A Day at Fallingwater

Fallingwater was a refuge from urban life, where the Kaufmanns could be immersed in nature twelve months a year and twenty-four hours a day. "...for a long time the elder Kaufmann entertained what he called his 'bird cage idea' for screened sleeping on the terraces of the new house...he had a drawing made for a mobile steel-framed sleeping chamber—a scheme he abandoned only after a Pittsburgh manufacturer advised him in September of 1937 that it could not make the contraption" (Hoffmann, p. 77).

The following exercise takes you through a summer day at Fallingwater, but skips erecting a sleeping cage on the terrace.

Load the Model File and Merge a File Containing HLINES for June 22, a Camera, and Three Omni Lights

The file's omni lights modulate the light levels, preventing the sun shadows from being unnaturally dark.

1. Launch 3D Studio. Choose File/Load, pick the correct drive button and pick the ASSEMB.3DS file. Pick OK.

2. Choose File/Merge, leave all buttons in the Merge dialog box toggled to red, and pick OK.

3. In the Merge 3DS, DXF, or FLM file dialog box, pick the JUN-SUN40.3DS file (sun angles for June 22 at 40 degrees latitude.)

4. In the Select Objects to Merge dialog box, click on the All button and pick OK. Right click Zoom Extents.

Result: The screen displays three omni lights, a fill spotlight, a camera, and five hour lines. The red line is the noon sun position, the yellow lines are 10:00 AM and 2:00 PM, and the blue lines are 6:00 AM and PM. The array of lines is rotated to the left to compensate for the 39 degrees east of south deviation of the structure.

Create and Position a Sun Spotlight

In this section you'll place a spotlight at the end of the 6:00 AM line with its target at the lines' convergence.

1. Choose Display/Hide/By Name. In the scroll list, pick all the items starting with HLINE, except HLINE-6AM, and click OK.

2. Click in the Top viewport, right click Zoom Extents, and choose Lights/Spot/Create. Place the spotlight at the line's outer end, and the target at the house. (You'll fine-tune the position later.)

3. In the Spotlight dialog box, type in the name **sun**, set Luminance to 255, Hotspot to 9, Falloff to 10, and the Multiplier value to 2.

4. Toggle on Casts Shadows and pick the Adjust button below it. In the Local Shadow Control dialog box, toggle on the Ray Trace button and pick OK.

5. Toggle on the Show Cone button and the Overshoot button, and pick Create.

6. Choose Lights/Spot/Move. In the Front or Left viewport align the spotlight with the hour line. Zoom in on each end of the line in turn, and precisely position the light and its target.

7. Use Views/Viewports to change from a User to a Camera viewport for terr-cam.

Result: The sun is aligned for 6:00 AM, and the camera is positioned to track shadows across Fallingwater's east terrace.

Create Keyframes for the Other Sun Positions

In this section, you'll move the sun to the ends of the other hour lines in sequence, hiding the lines as you go so that the animation won't show a big stick whipping across the sky.

1. Press [F4] to go to the Keyframer. Use Views/Viewports to switch from a User to a Camera viewport, and right click Zoom Extents.

2. Pick the Total Number of Frames box in the icon panel. In the dialog box, set the number to 12 and pick OK.

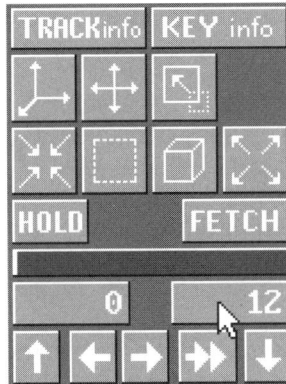

The cursor is pointing to the Total
Number of Frames box.

3. You'll use a frame interval of one frame for each hour, setting keys in
    the frames that correspond to the hour lines. In the following
    illustration, the bar is divided into the total number of frames (actually,
    there is a total of 13 frames, but the first one is zero). The numbers
    above the frames are the corresponding hours of daylight, with circles
    around the keyframes.

The bar contains the frame numbers, with the hours above.

4. Move the cursor to the prompt area to display the frame slider. Click
    on the slider and drag it to frame 4.

5. Choose Display/Unhide/All, and then choose Display/Hide/By Name.
    In the scroll box click on all the HLINE items except HLINE-10AM.

6. Choose Lights/Spot/Move. Leaving the target where it is, move the
    sun spotlight to the end of the 10:00 hour line, zooming in if necessary.
    Choose Display/Hide/By Name and pick HLINE-10PM.

7. Drag the frame slider to frame 6. Unhide everything, and then hide
    all the locator lines except HLINE-NOON. Move the spotlight to the
    end of the line, and use Display/Hide/By Name to hide the noon line.

8. Drag the frame slider to frame 8. Using the same Hide and Unhide process, move the sun to the end of the 2:00 PM hour line and hide the line.

9. Drag the frame slider to frame 12 and place the spotlight at the end of the 6:00 PM hour line.

10. Add a little red to the color of the setting sun. Choose Lights/Spot/Adjust, pick the spotlight, and set the RGB sliders to 255, 175, and 160. Pick OK.

11. Pick the Track Info button in the icon panel and pick the spotlight. So that the sun's color change will be limited to the end of the day, you need to copy the frame 0 color key to frame 10. Click on the Copy button. In the Color track pick the key at frame 0, release the mouse button, and then use the mouse to drag the key to frame 10. Click the OK button.

Result: You've established five sun location keys. The keyframer will create the tween frames.

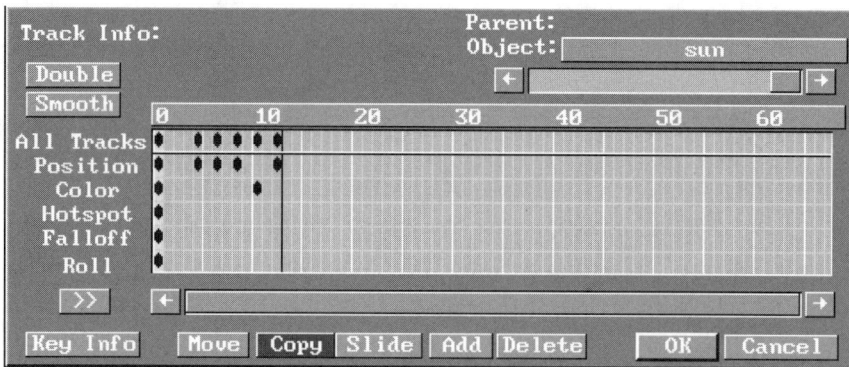

The Track Info dialog box for the sun spotlight. The color key at frame 0 has been copied to frame 10.

Create the Animation

First you'll create a Preview animation, which will show a brightness variation, and then a rendered animation at a low resolution.

1. Choose Preview/Make and click on the Camera viewport. Check that the Faces button is on in the Draw group and that the All button is on in the Frames group. Click Preview.

2. In a minute, your preview will display. Use the arrow keys to adjust the speed.

3. To render the animation, first pick Renderer/Setup/Configure. In the dialog box, pick the 320 x 200 button and pick OK.

4. Choose Renderer/Setup/Background and toggle on the Bitmap button to specify a background included on the file you loaded. Click on TREES.GIF.

5. Pick Renderer/Render View and the Camera viewport. In the dialog box pick All in the Frames group and then the Render button. Depending on your equipment, it may take more than an hour to render the whole animation.

Result: The sun moves across the sky, changing the shadow patterns of the trellis and windows.

The noon frame at a resolution of 640 x 480. The background is a bitmap taken from a video of trees at Fallingwater.

Summary

Even though buildings don't go hopping through space, the options for animated architectural images are numerous: buildings assembling themselves floor by floor, components dissolving or exploding, different areas of usage changing color in turn, structural members deflecting to their calculated limits, landscapes growing, panels gliding, and so on. Chapter 9 discusses walkthroughs, and the 3D Studio documentation offers almost limitless animation tools.

Modeling
Details with 3D
Studio

With this chapter, the focus changes from studying a structure to reproducing a human environment. Aside from walls of books and works of art, most of Fallingwater's furnishings were designed for the house. The line blurs between the architecture and what it contains. And due to Frank Lloyd Wright's genius for dissolving boundaries, the line also blurs between indoors and outdoors.

After a brief look at Wright's use of detail, the bulk of this chapter is devoted to some comments on modeling and three extensive exercises. The exercises use basic modeling commands, in combination to create objects from Fallingwater:

❏ Modeling the table lamp and combining it with imported geometry

❏ Modeling Wright's barrel chair

❏ Modeling the basic form of the Lipchitz sculpture with the Fit command and 3D primitives

The final exercise is more a description of a method than a pick-by-pick exercise, but follow along and see what you come up with. Although materials and textures are discussed in Chapter 8, instructions will be given now for applying materials to the models created in this chapter.

Wright and Details

Wright must have agreed with Mies van der Rohe's comment, "God is in the details," since he concerned himself with so many of them. In addition to lighting fixtures, for many of his houses Wright designed stained glass patterns, textile patterns, and furniture. In fact, myths abound about Wright rearranging, if not throwing out, the personal furnishings of clients in favor of furniture he had designed to extend a building's architectural themes.

A Forerunner of Self-Similarity

Had Wright lived long enough to encounter fractal theory, he might have been thought to be its inventor. He customarily used the elements of a building design to generate patterns for details and furnishings. The microstructures in his buildings mirror the macrostructures.

In *Frank Lloyd Wright: Between Principle and Form,* Paul Laseau and James Tice explore Wright's methods of generating form from underlying patterns and themes. As a child, Wright was given a set of Froebel Gifts— learning toys designed by educator Friedrich Froebel for the purpose of inculcating principles of natural form in children. Sets of wooden blocks, cardboard geometric shapes, sheets of gridded paper, and materials for weaving encouraged a child to manipulate forms in both two- and three-dimensional space. The Froebel Gifts were one of the few influences that Wright acknowledged.

> *Moreover, the Froebel influence extends even deeper, beyond design output, to his [Wright's] processes of design and visualization. The underlying organizational patterns, such as the "unit system" or grid, seem to be forever present, regardless of the geometry or composition employed in a particular design. Looking to Wright's building plans, we can also see the influence of the Froebel weaving exercises in the complex integration of space and structure as a unified fabric. These methods of design helped inform every scale of his work right down to the furniture, tile, and textile designs (Laseau and Tice, pp. 16-17).*

At Fallingwater, the same three-dimensional grid scheme controls both building and details—vertical members supporting cantilevered horizontal elements, punctuated with half-circles.

In the living room, high cantilevered metal shelves curve out from the west window, run across the kitchen entrance and dining room, and return to the masonry in half-circle shapes that echo the wine kettle and the stream stairs parapet. At windows, the horizontal muntins extend beyond the verticals to turn corners with no apparent support. The bookshelves pick up the same cantilevered form.

At the splendid main bedroom fireplace, the division of space implied by more linear grid arrangements becomes solid. Four large stones cantilever out from the stepped-back masonry to form shelves and a mantel, with a smaller replay of the motif at the topmost niche.

The rugged fireplace cantilevers play against the Madonna's delicate Gothic sway.
(Photo courtesy of Donald Hoffmann.)

Dissolving the Building Skin

If you instruct 3D Studio to display Fallingwater in box mode, the program blithely draws bounding boxes around the far extents of the structure. The actual change between inside and outside is not so easily marked.

The window design, which reinforces the controlling cantilever scheme, also undermines any rigid separation between house and site. The glass returns directly into stone, which dissolves the corners of the house and makes the glass seem to disappear. The integration is audio as well as visual; an open window brings the sound of the falls into the room.

The window glass was set directly into a cut in the masonry, a detail that emphasized the continuity of the stone surface inside and outside the room. (Photo by Lynda Waggoner, courtesy of Western Pennsylvania Conservancy.)

The rock intrusions into the house are the ultimate expression of the interpenetration of house and site—the boulder that erupts through the floor to form the hearth is the psychological fulcrum of the building. A staff room off the kitchen was added later, and its exterior wall engulfs another boulder, which also serves as an anchor for the west terrace.

At Edgar Kaufmann junior's suggestion, the bathroom floors and walls were finished with cork to provide a more reassuring surface than flagstone and masonry for vulnerable bare skin. Everywhere else, the waxed flagstone floor imitates the sheen of wet river rock, and the flagstones were chosen and placed so that individual stones seemed to continue under the thresholds between house and terrace.

A rainy night. The waxed flagstone in the main bedroom is differentiated from the wet flagstone on the terrace only by a threshold. (Photo by Thomas Heinz, courtesy of Western Pennsylvania Conservancy.)

Sculptures are placed to emphasize the volumes of the building and the flow of space from inside to out. A Richmond Barthe statue of actress Rose McClendon serves as a pivot at the point where the half-circle stairs reverse their sweep on the way to the guest room. The Bodhisattva stares in from the living room terrace, just in case you're not impressed with the view. And the Lipchitz *Mother and Child* focuses the east end of the house for the arriving visitor.

The Bodhisattva's presence penetrates through the living room to the opposite terrace, creating an axis that ignores the building's walls. (Photo by Thomas Heinz, courtesy of Western Pennsylvania Conservancy.)

Modeling Shortcuts

Making a presentation model usually demands modeling a building's entire structure; when it comes to architectural detailing and entourage, picking and choosing is necessary. Luckily, it's unnecessary to model the entire contents of an area; visual perception does a lot of the work for you. The eye automatically fills in details if clues are given.

Views, Paths, and Cone of Vision

First decide which views you want to use for still shots, or which paths you want to follow for walkthroughs. These areas usually include the building's front entrance and principal living areas, a single instance of repetitive areas, or areas showing some unusual feature. Using a path with a more or less straight route and a narrow cone of vision frustrates human curiosity, but greatly cuts down on modeling time.

For instance, the path used for the walkthrough in Chapter 9 proceeds up to the front door, makes a sharp left turn in the entry, moves toward the hatch stairs, and then descends the stream stairs. This route demands only that the south end of the living room be furnished.

Focus on the Most Important Objects

Once you have defined the view or path, you know which areas will be visible. The next step is to decide which objects to model within these areas. There are two categories of good modeling choices.

❏ Objects that dominate the view in some way:

   ❏ Objects that are necessary to define or separate spaces within a room

   ❏ Objects that are located in an architectural focal point, such as a bay window or articulated end wall

   ❏ Objects that have a strong, dominant color

   ❏ Objects emphasized by lighting, if you're simulating the lighting of the space

❑ Objects that pay off well for the amount of time they require:

   ❑ Objects with a simple, geometric form

   ❑ Repeated objects

   ❑ Flat rectangular objects, such as paintings or bookcase fronts, that can be easily texture-mapped

   ❑ Objects that can be made from preexisting mesh files, either your own or those from a library

Using Mesh Libraries

3D Studio ships with both a collection of 3DS files and the World Creating Kit on a CD-ROM. The World Creating Kit includes hundreds of meshes for individual objects ranging from a ketchup bottle to the Sydney Opera House. There are many plant, vehicle, and architectural components included, as well as texture maps, animations, bitmaps for use as background images, and complete scenes.

The World Creating Kit includes an Acuris, Inc mesh designated as "Frank Lloyd Wright table." Unfortunately for this project, its genesis is from a completely different architectural geometry.

You can modify World Creating Kit files by adjusting, adding, or subtracting geometry, just as if you had created them yourself. You can both assign new materials and maps to the imported meshes and borrow textures from them. The first exercise in this chapter imports World Creating Kit geometry from a file on your distribution disk.

Creating Shapes and Objects

A couple of questions to keep in mind when beginning to model: what geometry should you start with, and which module should you use.

Addition Versus Subtraction

A cabinet maker creates a chair or table by assembling smaller pieces of wood. A sculptor creates a marble statue by removing volumes from a large chunk of stone. The first process is additive; the second, subtractive.

3D Studio modeling can be as much a subtractive process as an additive one. Just as it's easier to assemble shapes from quads, circles, and N-gons than to draw them with individual lines, it's most efficient to begin with the largest possible component when working in three dimensions.

The lamp modeling exercise in this chapter is primarily an additive one. Individual pieces are created and then assembled. The chair exercise combines additive and subtractive processes. The frame of the chair begins as a modified, lofted arc. Then Boolean operations are used to subtract volumes from the basic shape, which is more efficient than trying to assemble the whole thing piece by piece.

Creating Geometry in the 2D Shaper

There are a couple of instances in which the Shaper approach is more direct. If the form of an object is dominated by a particular profile, drawing the 2D shape and lofting it is more efficient than starting with 3D primitives—particularly when the object's edge is filleted, rounded, or cutout.

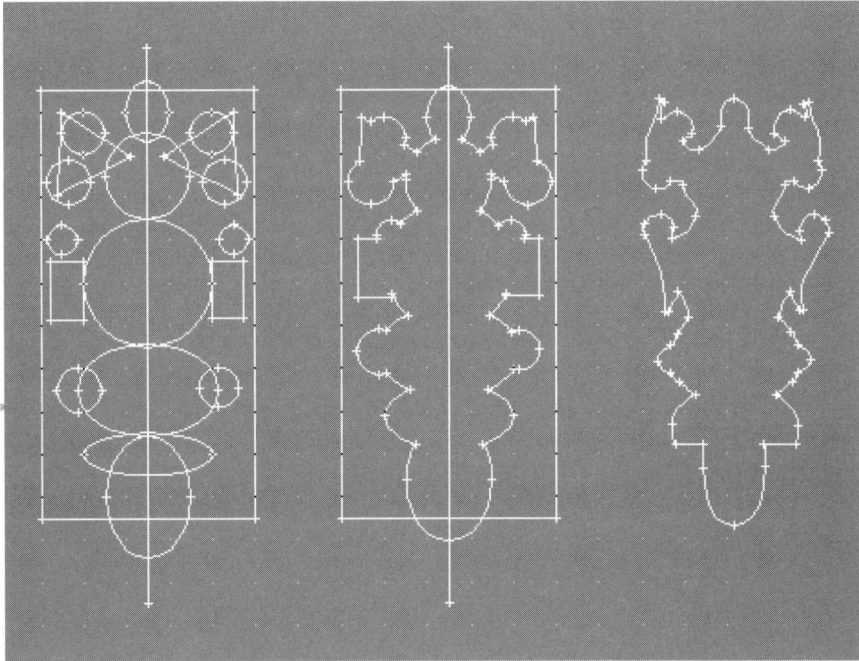

Creating a section with a complex edge is relatively easy in the Shaper. The shape was drawn to outline the backs of the Italian provincial dining room chairs at Fallingwater.

Complex profiles can be lofted with a curved, circular, or deformed path to produce a staggeringly complicated object. The second exercise in this chapter lofts a "bent" profile with rounded edge along a curved path.

Tip: The direction in which you draw path lines in the Shaper determines which view of the objects will appear in which 3D Editor viewport. For instance, if you draw vertical path lines, the ends of the lofted objects will be in the Top viewport; if you draw horizontal path lines, the ends of the lofted objects will be in the Left or Right viewports.

If an object is based on a rectilinear volume that will require further modification, it's usually better to begin in the Shaper with a lofted quad, so that you have more vertices to manipulate, rather than try to add vertices to a box created in the 3D Editor.

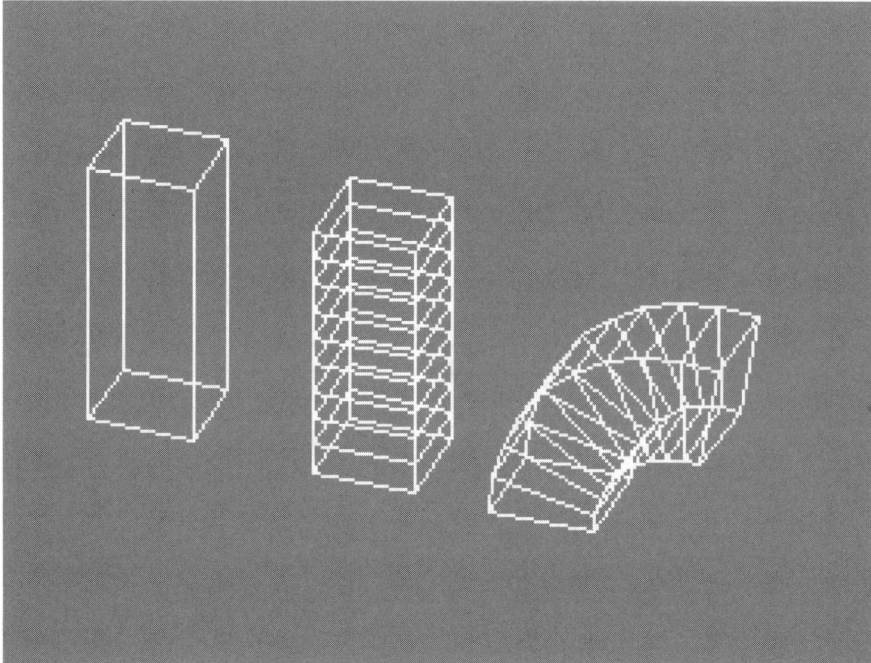

The box on the left was created in the 3D Editor and has no intermediate divisions. The center box was created in the Shaper and Lofter, with eight steps specified. On the right, it has been modified with the Bend command, impossible for the original 3D Editor box.

Exercise 1: Modeling the Table Lamp and Inserting Library Fluorescents

The basic design of Wright's table lamp was a long wooden box with two of the long sides removed. Throughout Fallingwater, the lamp appears in different configurations—long, short, vertical, horizontal. (See photo on page 135.)

In this exercise, you'll use the 2D Shaper to model the geometry for the horizontal lamp, assemble it in the 3D Editor, and insert lights, cameras, and fluorescent tubes from a World Creating Kit scene—a useful shortcut. We've included the fluorescent lamp file on the distribution disk in case you don't have a CD-ROM drive.

Draw Shapes and Paths in the Shaper

In this section, you'll draw quads and use them for the lamp shapes. Because of the small scale of the lamp components, decimal units are used.

1. Choose Views/Unit Setup. Leave the Decimal button toggled on and type **10** in the Denominator text box.

2. Choose Views/Drawing Aids. Set Snap spacing to .2, Grid spacing to 1, and Grid Extents Start to 0 and Grid Extents End to 22. Set Angle Snap to 5. In the 2D Shaper press [S] and [G] to toggle on Snap and Grid

3. Choose Create/Quad. Hold down the [Ctrl] key to force the quad into a square, and draw a quad 2.80 x 2.80 for the ends of the lamp casing. Draw three more squares with side dimensions of 0.60, 2.20, and 3.40 for the stem and base. Draw on paper a sketch of the squares and their corresponding sizes.

4. Now create a right-angle shape for the long casing. Draw a 3.00 x 3.00 quad. Pick Create/Copy and then pick the quad to make a copy, carefully moving it to the right and down so that the status line Offset reads:

    ```
    X: 0.40  Y:-0.40
    ```

5. Pick the Hold button. (Always pick the Hold button before using Boolean commands.) Choose Create/Boolean and pick the upper left square First, and then the lower right square. In the 2D Boolean Operation dialog box, toggle on the Subtraction button and pick OK.

6. You'll need five paths to loft the shapes. Choose Create/Line to draw a series of vertical lines, starting at the top. The lines are 0.20 inches long for the casing ends, 0.40 for one base quad, 0.60 for the other base quad, 5.00 for the stem, and 22.00 for the casing. Add the lines and their lengths to your paper sketch.

Result: The screen should show four squares, one right-angle shape, and five path lines.

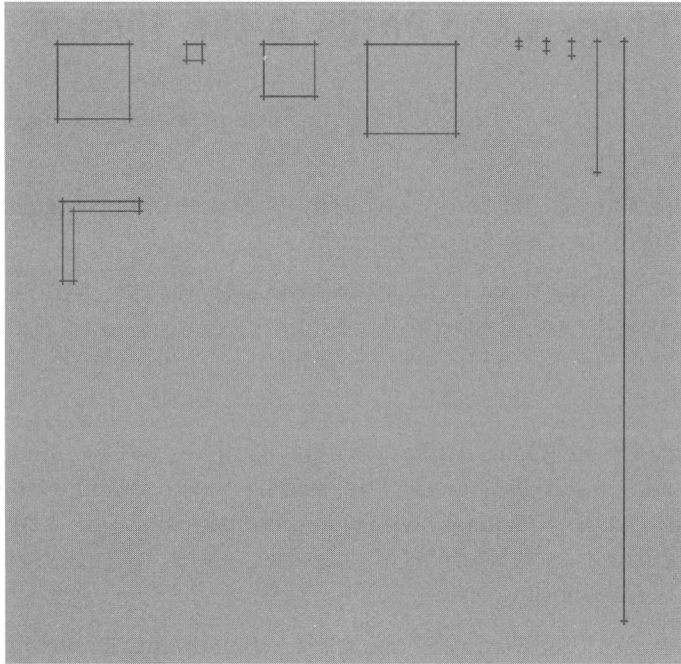

The shapes and paths for the table lamp.

Loft the Shapes

You'll be moving back and forth from the Shaper to the Lofter, assigning and unassigning shapes and paths one at a time.

Tip: Be aware that when very small polygons are assigned, it's difficult to see whether they are yellow or white, so zoom in on the three short lines if you need to.

1. Choose Shape/Assign and pick the right-angled casing shape. Change to the 3D Lofter and choose Shapes/Get/Shaper to import the casing. Pick Shapes/Center to center it.

2. Return to the Shaper, unassign the casing and assign the 22-inch path line. In the Lofter, use Path/Get/Shaper to import the path. Pick Objects/Make to create the casing, naming it "casing." In the dialog box, the Tween button should be off, and the Contour button should be on.

3. Use the same procedure to loft the remaining shapes:

   ❏ Loft the 2.80 quad using the 0.20 path, naming it "end."

   ❏ Loft the 0.60 quad using the 5.00 path, naming it "stem."

   ❏ Loft the 2.20 quad using the 0.40 path, naming it "base1."

   ❏ Loft the 3.40 quad using the 0.60 path, naming it "base2."

4. Press [F3] to get to the 3D Editor and right click Zoom Extents. Use Views/Viewports to assign the lower right viewport as the User viewport.

5. Choose Modify/Object/Move to move the casing and end to one side, away from the stem and base pieces.

Result: The objects are in the 3D Editor, with the bases and stem in one group and the casing and end in another.

Assemble the Stem and Base Pieces, and Slant One End of the Stem

1. Toggle the Front viewport to full screen and choose Modify/Object/Move. Pick the smaller base square and align its upper left corner with the upper left corner of the larger base square—the overlapped lines will turn black. Turn on Snap and toggle to a free move cursor. Move the smaller square to the right and down until the status line reads:

   ```
   Offset X: 0.60    Y: -0.60
   ```

2. Turn Snap off and center the 0.60 stem square within the two base quads.

3. Change to a full-screen Top viewport to stack the bases and stem as shown in the following illustration. Using the vertical cursor, move the stem until its base is flush with the top of the smaller base quad. Then move the large base quad until its top is flush with the bottom of the smaller base.

4. Pick Create/Object/Attach and pick each base in turn to make them a single object, and then pick the base and the stem to attach it.

5. Zoom in to the top of the stem, choose Select/Vertex/Quad, and draw a window around the upper right corner of the stem, as shown in the illustration. Still using the vertical cursor, choose Modify/Vertex/Move and pick the Selected button.

6. Pick the upper right corner of the stem and move the vertices down until the status line reads:

   ```
   Offset Z:-0.60
   ```

   (Toggle off Snap if you need to.) Choose Select/None to clear the selection set. Right click Zoom Extents and toggle back to four viewports.

7. Press [A] to toggle on Angle Snap, and toggle on the Local Axis button. Choose Modify/Object/Rotate and pick the stem in the Left viewport. Rotate the stem clockwise -90 degrees to set it upright.

Result: The base is assembled and ready to fit to the casing.

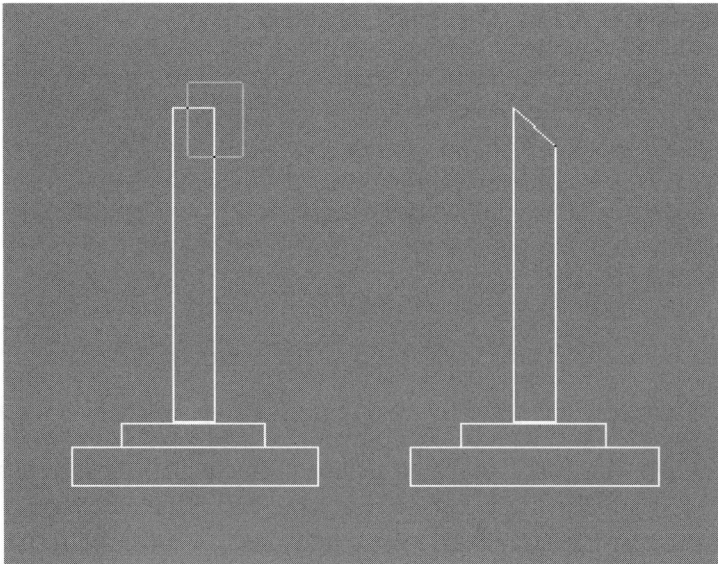

The assembled base and stem, showing the stem before
and after adjusting the vertices.

Edit a Material and Assign It to the Base

The base of the table lamp is made from cast iron painted dark brown. The library material nearest to the color of the lamp base reflects too little light to show the planes of the base in a rendering. In this section you'll edit the material.

1. Press [F5] to get to the Materials Editor. Choose Material/Get Material from the menu bar.

2. In the Get Material dialog box, scroll down and pick DARK BROWN MATTE and OK. DARK BROWN MATTE is the right hue, but it needs some editing to reflect light properly in your rendering.

3. Click on the Diffuse button. On the status line, the Luminance setting is shown as L:15. Pick the Luminance slider and move it to the right so that the status line reads L:30. Pick the Saturation slider and move the indicator to the left to change Saturation from S:233 to S:100.

4. Now pick the Specular button. Move the Luminance slider to change the value to L:50.

5. In the column of sliders below the color controls, move Shininess to 10 and Shin Strength to 15. Pick the Render Sample button in the lower right corner to see the changed material.

6. Now you need to save the new material. Pick Material/Put Material on the menu bar. In the dialog box, type **darkbrownmatte2** and pick OK.

7. Choose Library/Save Library from the menu bar. Pick the 3DS.MLI library from the scroll list and pick OK.

8. Press [F3] to get back to the 3D Editor. Pick Surface/Material/Choose. In the Material Selector dialog box, scroll down and pick the DARK-BROWNMATTE2 material and OK.

9. Choose Surface/Material/Assign/Object and pick the assembled stem and base.

Result: The edited material will reflect enough light for the planes of the base to show up.

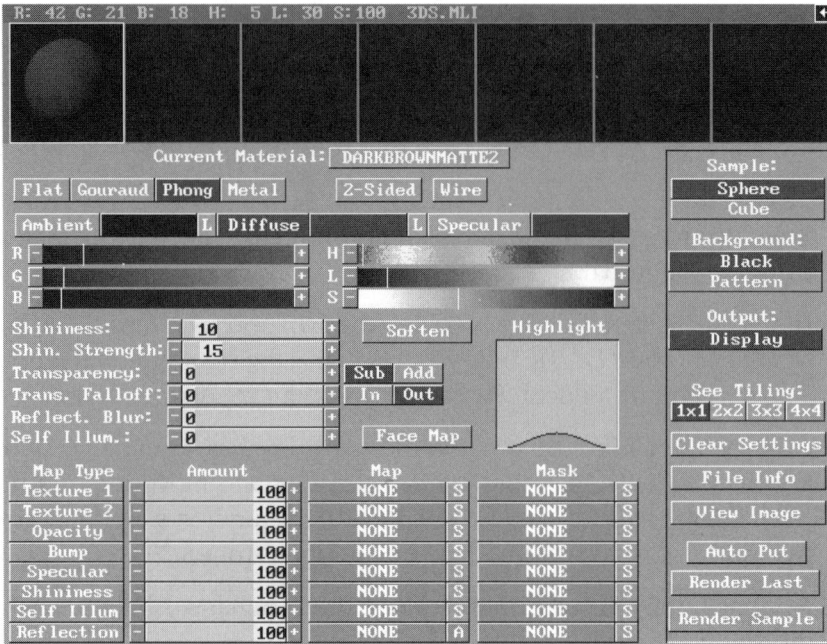

The Materials Editor after the settings have been adjusted.

Assign Mapping Coordinates and Texture to the Casing Pieces

In this section, you'll apply planar mapping coordinates to the casing end and cylindrical mapping coordinates to the casing. Then you'll apply a wood grain texture to the two pieces.

1. Change to four viewports. Choose Surface/Mapping/Type/Planar and click in the Front viewport. Then pick Surface/Mapping/Adjust/Find and OK on the Rescale Map Icon to Viewport message box. A yellow rectangle then appears on the screen.

2. In the same Adjust branch of commands, use the Move command to move the mapping square over the end piece, and use Scale to size it slightly larger than the end piece.

3. Choose Surface/Mapping/Apply Obj. and pick the end piece and OK on the message box.

4. Choose Surface/Mapping/Type/Cylindrical. A ring of yellow dots appears in the Top viewport, and two lines with a short line between them appears in the Front and Left viewports. (Zoom out if you need to, to get the full mapping icon on your screen.)

5. The short center line of the map icon marks the top of the texture map. In this particular map, the wood grain runs sideways. Since the grain of the wood should run the length of the casing, the short top line should be perpendicular to the length of the casing, as shown in the next illustration. In the Top viewport, use the Scale and Move commands to fit the diameter of the mapping cylinder around the length of the casing.

6. In the Left viewport, toggle the cursor to vertical arrows and use the Scale command to make the cylinder slightly longer than the casing's thickness.

7. Choose Surface/Mapping/Apply Obj. and click on the casing.

8. Pick Surface/Material/Choose. Hold down the [Alt] key and press [W] to get to the wood materials. Pick WOOD–DARK ASH and OK.

9. Choose Surface/Material/Assign/Object and pick the casing and the end.

Result: The casing and end piece are assigned a texture and mapped so that the wood grain will run in the proper direction.

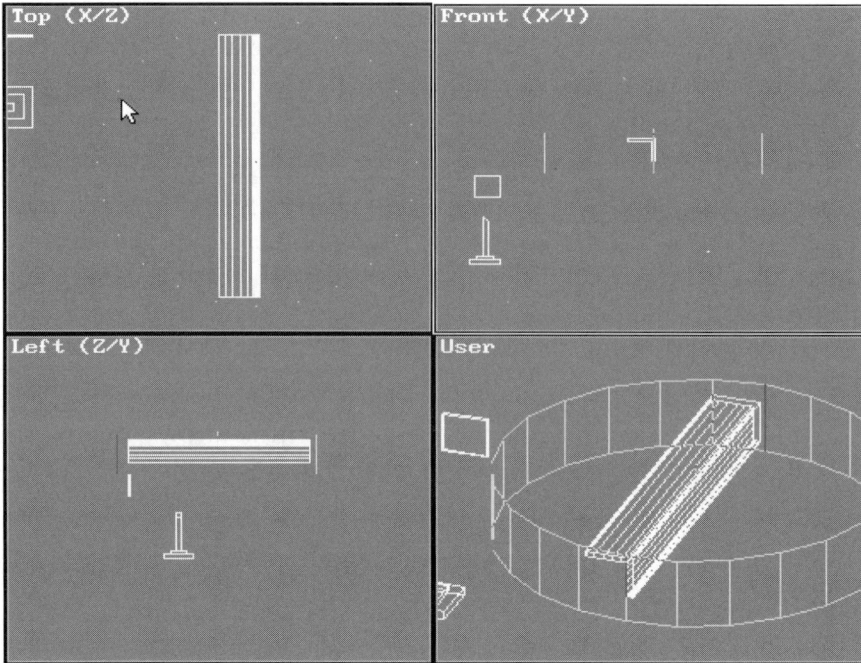

The cylindrical map positioned correctly to apply mapping coordinates to the casing.

Assemble the Casing and Add It to the Stem

As you assemble the casing, use Views/Redraw (for the active viewport) and Views/Redraw All (for all viewports) to retrieve lines temporarily lost when manipulating overlapping objects.

1. Toggle the Top viewport to full screen. Choose Create/Object/Copy and pick the casing end piece to make a copy for the other end.

2. Use Modify/Object/Move to fit each end piece into the casing, aligned flush with the end of the casing. Zoom in to be more accurate. (See the following illustration.)

3. Switch to the Front viewport; zoom in and fit each end piece into the right-angled casing so that the upper right corner is flush with the inside corner of the casing. Switch back to the Top viewport and use Create/Object/Attach to attach each end piece to the casing.

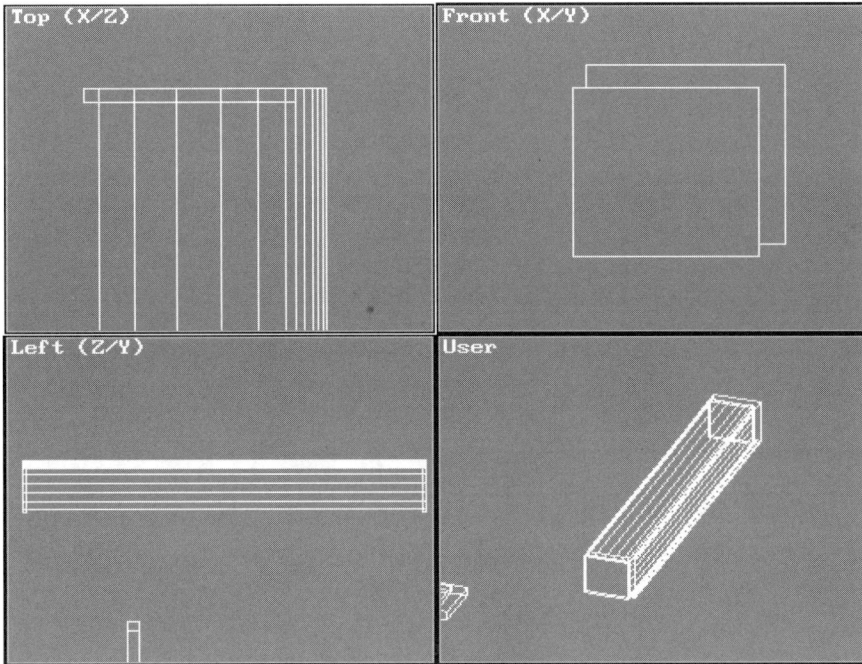

The end pieces, fitted into the casing.

4. Toggle on Angle Snap and the Local Axis button. Choose Modify/Object/Rotate and use the Front viewport to rotate the casing 45 degrees counterclockwise into its proper position.

5. Using Top, Front, and Left viewports, move the stem into position with the casing, as shown in the next illustration. Choose Create/Object/Attach to join the two.

Result: The base and stem are assembled and mapped.

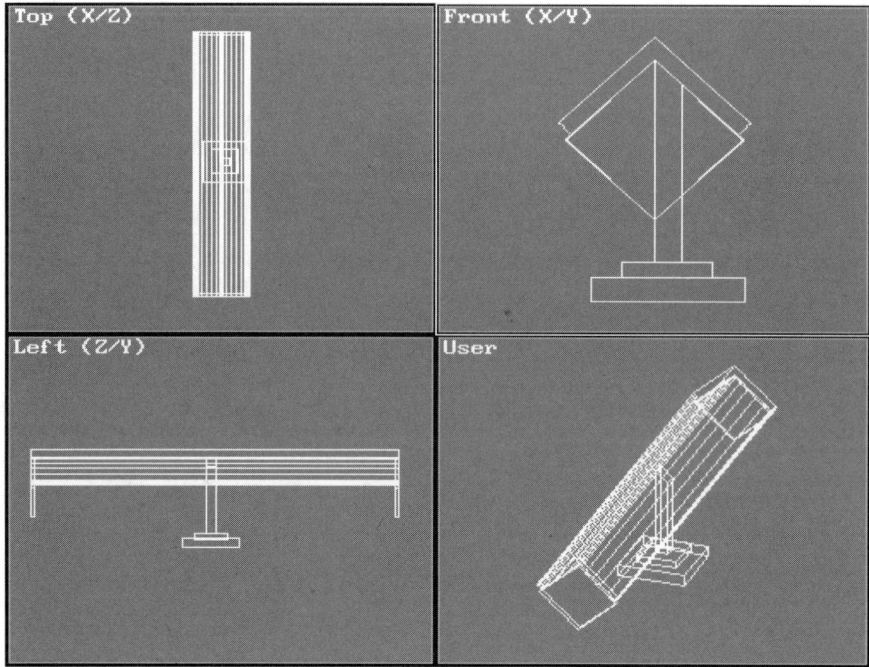

The casing and base, aligned and attached.

Merge a .3DS File of a Fluorescent Light with the Table Lamp Geometry

You'll borrow lights, camera, and fluorescent tubes which have been assigned a self-illuminating material from 3D Studio.

1. Pick File/Save and save the lamp geometry as **flwslamp**. Pick File/Merge, turn off the Animation button in the Merge dialog box, and pick OK.

2. Pick the file LIGHT_FL.3DS from the scroll list.

3. In the Select Objects to Merge dialog box, pick the All button and OK.

4. Right click Zoom Extents. Your lamp is the tiny white dot; the two scenes are at very different scales. Use Modify/Object/Move to drag your lamp very close to the 3DS light fixture.

5. Choose Display/Hide/Lights and Display/Hide/Cameras to turn off the lights and camera for now. Right click Zoom Extents again.

6. You need to get rid of all the 3DS geometry except the two fluorescent tubes and their end pieces. Toggle the Left viewport to full screen and pick the Hold button.

7. Choose Modify/Element/Delete. Pick one of the angled flanges of the 3DS lamp casing. Now pick the vertical rod above the tubes. Choose Views/Redraw to redraw the screen. There are two rods, so you'll need to pick the rod again.

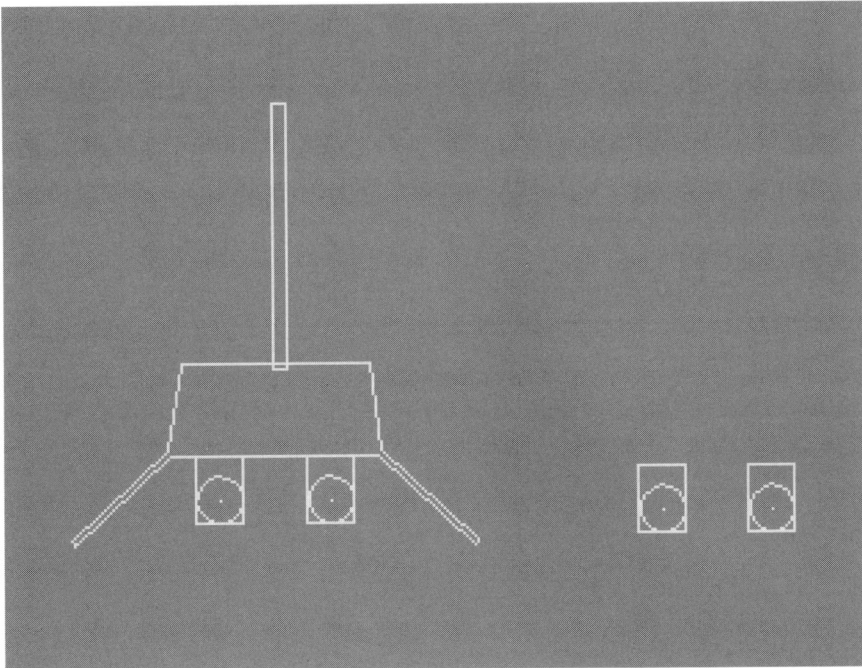

The 3DS light geometry, before and after the unnecessary elements have been removed.

8. Switch to the Top viewport and choose Modify/Objects/3D Scale. Pick the fluorescent tubes and scale them down to 30%. (The status line displays the percentage.)

9. Choose Modify/Objects/Rotate and turn the tubes 90 degrees so that they're aligned with the casing.

10. At this point the tubes and their end pieces are all one object. You need to separate one tube from another, and re-attach the end pieces to the separated tube. Choose Create/Element/Detach and pick the left tube and its two end pieces. Choose Modify/Object/Move and move the right tube to check that it's detached from the left tube elements.

11. Choose Create/Object/Attach. Pick the left tube and one of its end pieces, and then pick the tube again and the other end piece.

12. The fluorescents are still too big, but had you scaled them down any farther with 3D Scale, they would have been too narrow. Pick Modify/Object/2D Scale. Toggle the cursor to vertical arrows. Pick each tube and scale it down to 40%, or just long enough to fit into one end of the FLW lamp casing.

13. Use Top, Front, and Left viewports to move the tubes into proper position, as shown in the illustration. Use Create/Object/Attach to join the tubes and casing.

Result: The table lamp is completely assembled.

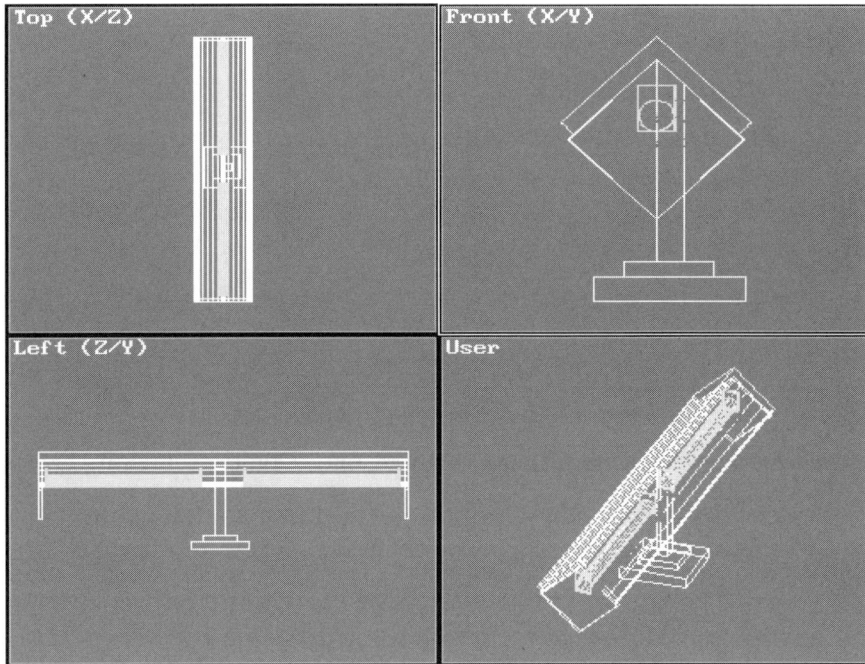

The fluorescents placed in the lamp.

Add an Omni Light and Adjust the Imported Lights and Camera

To resemble a lighted lamp, the brightest light should be within the lamp, with only enough illumination from other lights to show the lamp geometry.

1. Pick Lights/Omni/Create and place an omni light close to the lamp casing. In the dialog box, name it **lampomni**, set Luminance at 255, and pick OK.

2. Choose Lights/Omni/Move. Zoom in and use the Top and Front viewports to locate the omni light inside the casing, as shown in the following illustration.

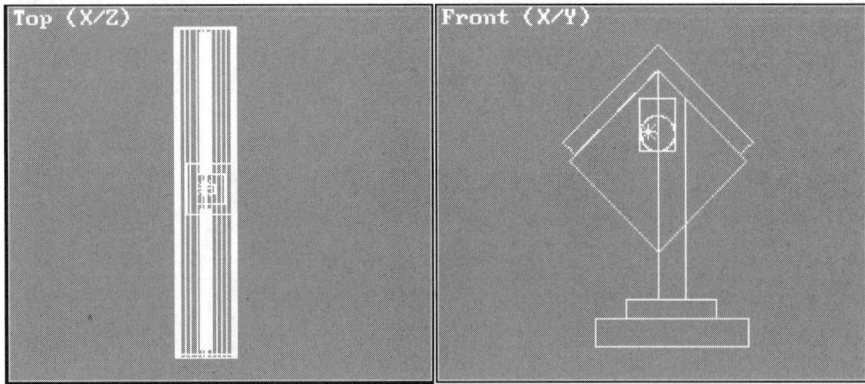

The omni light positioned inside the casing.

3. Choose Display/Unhide/Lights and Display/Unhide/Cameras.

4. Choose Views/Viewports from the menu bar and change the lower right viewport to a Camera viewport. Right click Zoom Extents.

5. First you'll make some gross adjustments in light and camera location, and then you'll fine-tune the positions. Activate the Top viewport and choose Cameras/Move. Pick the camera and move it very close to the lamp. Pick the target and place it at the lamp. Use the Left viewport to vertically position the target at the lamp, and the camera at approximately the same height as the lamp.

6. Choose Lights/Omni/Move and move each omni light close to the lamp in the Top and Left viewports. Right click Zoom Extents. Now that all the scene components are close enough for you to see what you're doing, you can fine-tune the light and camera position.

7. Choose Lights/Omni/Adjust and pick one of the imported omni lights. In the dialog box, turn Luminance down to 125 and pick OK. Pick the other imported omni light and also turn it down to 125.

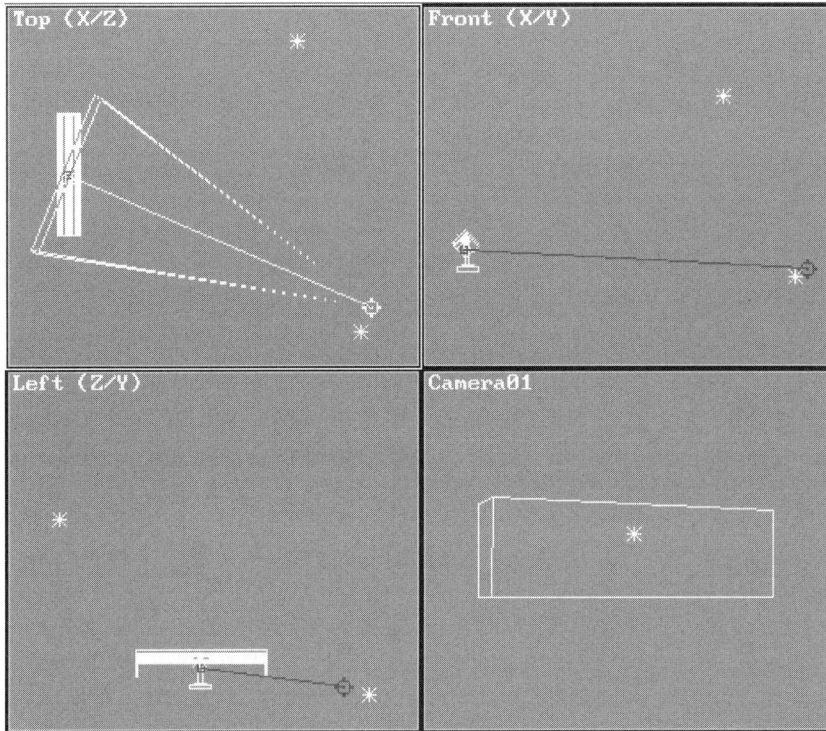

The lights and camera in proper position. (The Camera viewport is in box display mode because the camera FOV command is active to show the field of view.)

8. Choose Cameras/Move. In the Top viewport, move the camera so that it is in front of the light and slightly to the left, positioned about three casing-lengths from the lamp. Pick the target and center it on the lamp.

9. Move to the Left viewport and toggle the cursor to vertical. Center the target on the lamp. Move the camera so that it is level with the lamp's base. (A low point of view will show the fluorescent tubes below the edge of the casing in the rendering.) Right click Zoom Extents.

10. Choose Cameras/FOV and adjust the field of view until it is slightly larger than the lamp in the Camera viewport.

11. Choose Lights/Omni/Move to move one of the omni lights next to the camera in the Top and Left viewports. Position the other omni light as shown in the Top and Front viewports.

12. Choose Renderer/Render View and pick the Camera viewport. Pick the Render button in the Render Still Image dialog box.

Result: The rendered lamp seems to be lit by the fluorescent tubes.

The rendered table lamp.

Manipulating Multiple Components

Single objects and shapes often must be copied, combined, separated, or used as a starting point for other components. Save yourself some time by giving thought to the most efficient point at which to reproduce or combine the component:

❑ Do everything possible to a single component—scaling, tapering, adjusting, rotating—before replicating it.

❑ Don't combine components up-front if they will need to be separated later for other operations, such as applying mapping coordinates.

The following section discusses things to keep in mind when using 3D Studio's powerful replicating and manipulating commands.

Outlining

The 2D Shaper Outline command creates an offset shape at a specified distance from the original shape. The command works differently depending on whether the original shape is a closed or open polygon.

If the original polygon is closed, it makes no difference where you draw the offset distance line; two new polygons will be drawn, spaced equally to either side of the original polygon position, as if it had served as a centerline. If the original polygon is open, a single offset polygon will be drawn on the same side of the original polygon that the length line was drawn. The original polygon will remain in the same position, and the program will draw lines to close the two ends of the double line.

Copying and Mirroring

Copy and Mirror commands are available in both the Shaper and Editor. The displacement of the copied or mirrored component can be limited to vertical or horizontal by using the appropriate cursor, which is handy if you're trying to maintain the same horizontal or vertical position. Using a selection window on multiple components maintains the same spatial relation in the copy as in the original.

Multiple copies of either a shape or an object can be made by holding down the [Shift] key when using the Copy commands. To make a mirrored copy of a component in one step, hold down the [Shift] key and pick Modify/Polygon/Mirror.

In the 3D Editor, faces, elements, and objects can be copied. However, when you copy a face or element, the copy itself becomes an object. If you use Select/Object to copy a selection set of objects, a dialog box appears that allows you to specify whether the copied set will be a single object composed of elements or a collection of individual objects.

Arraying

The 3D Editor Create/Array command produces either linear or radial arrays. When creating a radial array, keep two things in mind:

❏ Turn off the Local Axis button before you use the Radial array command. If you don't, your arrayed objects will pivot around the local axis of the original object. Use the Modify/Axis/Place command to locate the global axis at the point that will be the center of the array.

❏ After you specify the number of objects to be included in the array, you must decide which is the more important placement factor: the distance in degrees, center-to-center, between each arrayed object, or the total length of the arc that will be covered by the array. Activate either the Degrees or the Arc Length button, enter the value, and then pick the Calculate button to bring the other value into compliance. Don't mess with the other button.

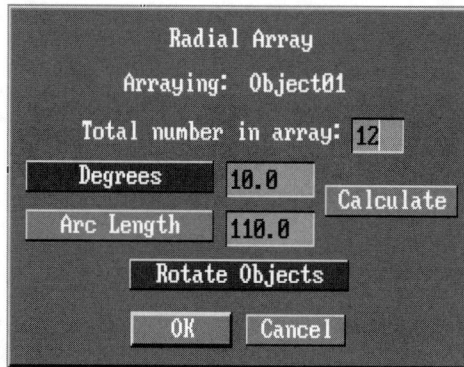

The Radial array dialog box. The Degrees button specifies the distance between each object. The Arc Length button specifies the total degrees of arc covered by the arrayed objects.

Suppose you want to turn your arrayed objects into a single object. There are two ways to do this, depending on how the array is integrated with the rest of the model:

❏ Choose Create/Object/Attach and pick the objects one by one, adding them to a set, as done in the following exercise.

❑ Use Select/Object/Quad to select the whole array, and copy the selection set. In the dialog box, specify that the copied objects be turned into a single object. Then delete the selection set of the original array.

Boolean Operations

Boolean operations—Union, Subtraction, and Intersection—combine two overlapping shapes or objects. The *3D Studio Reference Manual* discusses Boolean operations in detail, both 2D operations in the Shaper and 3D operations in the Editor.

Always pick the Hold button before you begin, and be careful which shape you select first. The first shape selected is altered but retained. The second shape selected is deleted from memory. This doesn't necessarily affect the geometry when using Union or Intersection (although it affects any materials applied to the components), but the order of shape selection is critical when using Subtraction.

Working Around Coincident Vertices   In the 2D Shaper, Boolean operations won't work on two polygons that are overlapped so that a vertex on one polygon occupies the same space as a vertex on the other polygon. All you'll get is a message box saying "Coincident vertices. Continue." To combine the two polygons, they must be placed in such a way that no vertices are coincident or overlapping. This often requires extra steps to produce the shape you want. The first two exercises in this chapter use Boolean workarounds to avoid the coincident vertices problem.

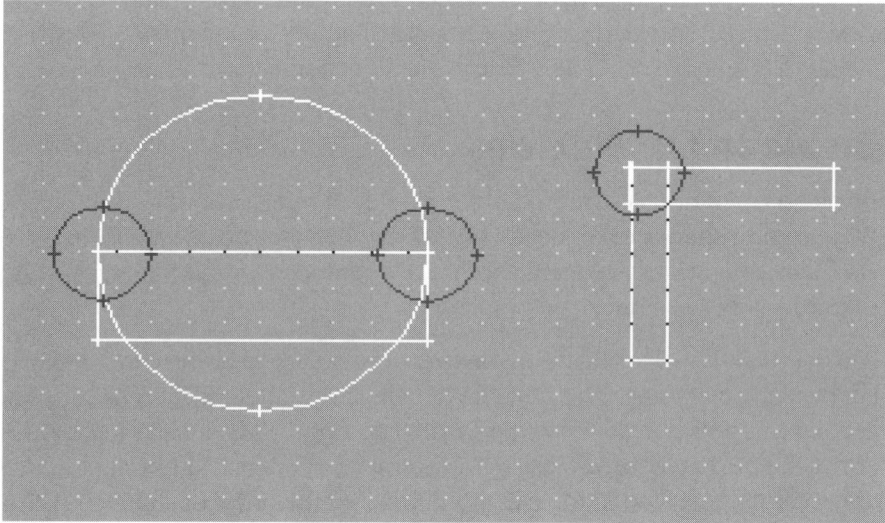

Neither of these "obvious solutions" for Boolean Union will work to create the right-angled casing of the lamp and the seat of the chair. In each case, the circled vertices in the two polygons overlap.

Exercise 2: Modeling Wright's Chair

Wright despised chairs. He considered the human body in a sitting position to be awkward and unnatural—far inferior to a graceful reclining pose—but given the inflexible determination of Americans to sit, he countered as best he could by designing seating for his houses.

For Fallingwater's dining area, he suggested a barrel chair he had designed, but its circular base would not rest smoothly on the flagstone floor, and Liliane Kaufmann insisted on using some three-legged Italian provincial chairs. The graceful barrel chair was banished to the guest room.

Wright's barrel chair at the guest room desk. Note the shape of the seat, the slatted back, the curved upper back, and open sides. The exercise will model the chair, apply textures, and render it. (By Harold Corsini, courtesy of Western Pennsylvania Conservancy.)

Draw the Seat of the Chair

Since Boolean operations won't work on polygons with coincident vertices, drawing the seat demands a workaround using two Boolean operations.

1. Choose Views/Unit Setup and specify Architectural units and a Denominator of **4**.

2. Choose Views/Drawing Aids and set Snap Spacing to 1", Grid Spacing to 2", and Grid Extents at 0 and 60".

3. In the 2D Shaper, choose Shape/Steps and specify 7 steps. Toggle on Snap and Grid.

4. Use Create/Circle to draw a 9" radius circle, moving the mouse horizontally so that both of the circle's side vertices fall on a snap point.

5. Choose Create/Quad and draw a quad 20" by 5". Use Modify/Polygon/Move to place the quad so that its upper horizontal segment overlaps the circle's side vertices, as shown in the following illustration. Pick the Hold button.

6. Choose Create/Boolean and pick first the circle and then the quad. In the 2D Boolean Operation dialog box, make sure that the Union button and the Weld Polygons button are toggled on, and pick OK.

7. Choose Create/Quad again. Zoom in on the polygon. With Snap on, position the cursor so that the right crosshair is tangent to the top vertex of the circle, and the bottom crosshair is tangent to the left vertex of the circle (where it intersects the top of the quad.) Hold down the [Ctrl] button to force a square and draw an 18" square around the circle, as shown in the following illustration.

8. Pick the Hold button and choose Create/Boolean. Pick the circle and then the square. The dialog box will appear in a few moments; toggle on the Intersection button.

9. Choose Shape/Assign and pick the seat polygon, and then pick Shape/Check to verify that there are eight vertices.

Result: The seat shape is created using a circle, rectangle, and square with Boolean Union and Intersection.

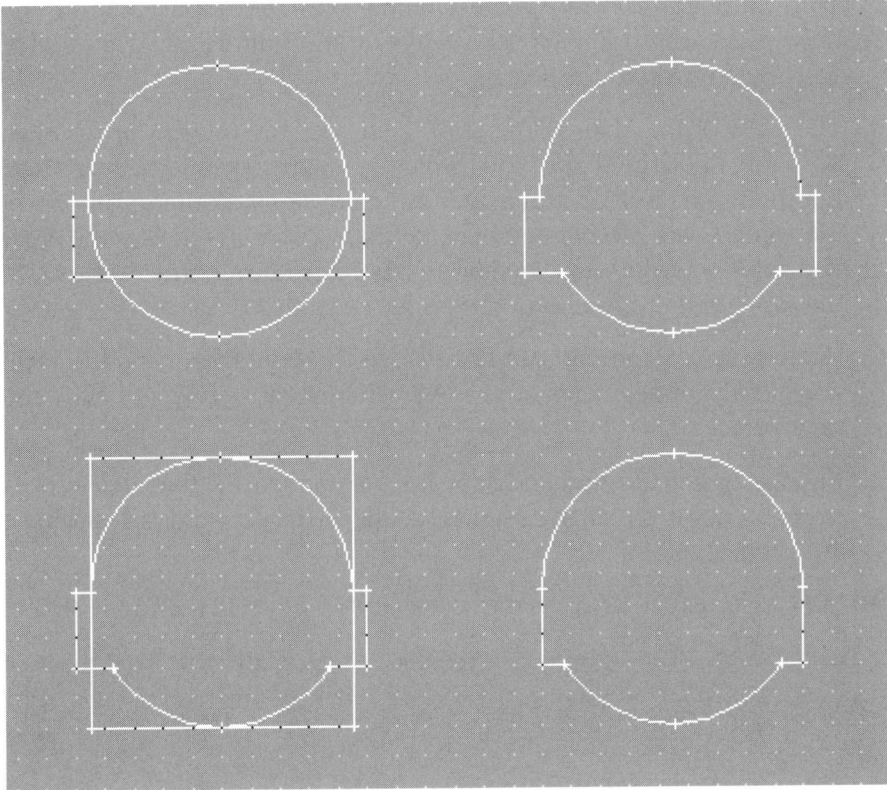

Drawing the seat shape. Upper left: the circle and quad positioned correctly. Upper right: after using Boolean Union. Lower left: the 18″ square positioned correctly. Lower right: after using Boolean Intersection.

Draw the Chair Frame

In this section, you'll use the Outline command to generate a curved shape that will form the frame of the chair.

Tip: Using Architectural inch units with a denominator of four displays the quarter-inches as 1, 2, and 3 on the status line. For example, one foot, four and a quarter inches is displayed as 1′ 4″1.

1. Zoom out and use Create/Copy to duplicate the seat shape off to one side.

2. Turn off Snap. Choose Create/Outline, pick the duplicate seat, and draw a ¾" length line (width: 0′ 0″3 on the status line.) The outline will appear around the seat.

3. The ends of the chair frame stop flush with the corners of the seat. To create the same shape, you'll edit the outline to get rid of everything but the top half-circle and its vertical extensions. Zoom in on one of the corners. Use Modify/Segment/Refine to place a vertex on the outer vertical line at the same height as the inner line's corner vertex. Do the same to the other corner. (See the next illustration.)

4. Using Modify/Segment/Delete, remove the bottom curves, the horizontal straight segments, and the small vertical segments below the new vertices.

5. Choose Create/Connect and draw lines to connect the two end vertices at each end of the arcs. Assign and Check the shape; it should have 10 vertices.

Result: The screen displays the seat shape and the curved frame shape.

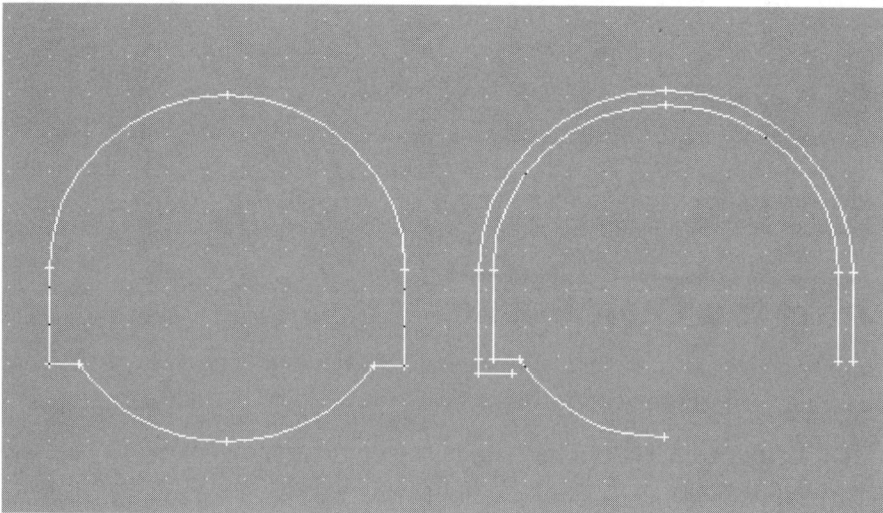

Two vertices have been added to provide ends to the frame, which will be flush with the corners of the seat shape. The other segments are being removed.

Use Boolean Subtraction to Modify the Shapes

In this section you'll make two shapes that will be used to subtract the open sides of the frame. Then you'll create a curved centerline that will be used as a lofting path for the upper back of the chair.

1. Make a copy of the frame with Create/Copy.

2. Use Create/Quad to draw a quad 5″ wide and 10″ high, off to one side. Choose Modify/Vertex/Move and toggle the cursor to vertical arrows. Pick the upper left vertex of the quad and move the vertex down $3\frac{1}{2}$″.

3. Use Modify/Polygon/Move with a free move cursor to position the quad so that its right side is about one inch outside of the frame and its base is aligned with the end of the frame. Toggle to a vertical cursor and move the quad up $1\frac{1}{2}$″. (See the following illustration, right side of the lower right figure.)

4. Toggle to a horizontal cursor. Choose Modify/Polygon/Mirror, hold down the [Shift] key, and pick the quad to make a mirrored copy. Move the quad into position overlapping the left side of the frame.

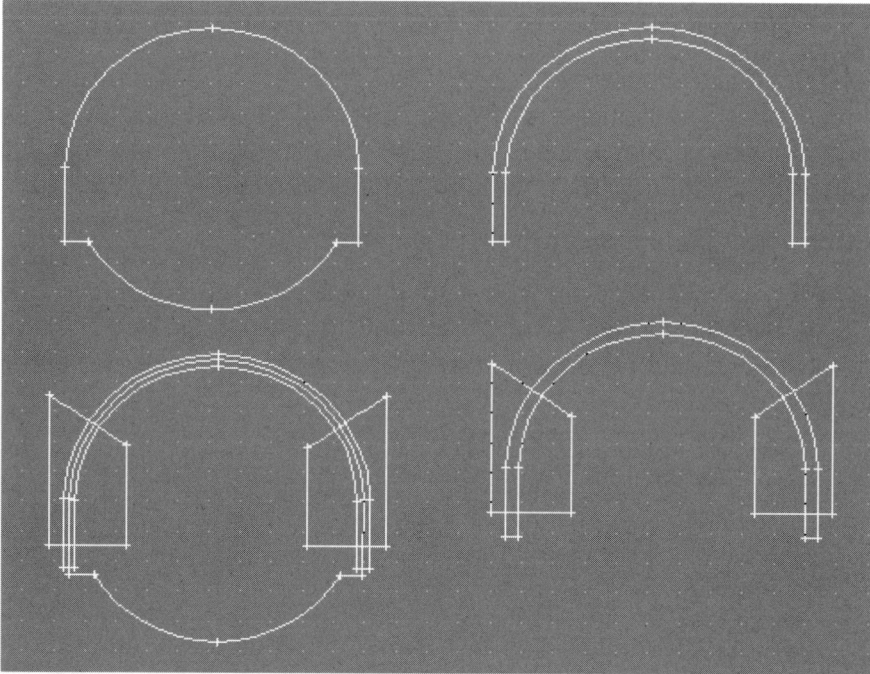

The shapes before using Boolean subtraction. On the lower right, the quads are in place to chop holes out of the frame. On the lower left, the seat shape is in position to form a centerline.

5. Choose Select/Polygon/Quad and draw a selection window around the frame with the overlapped quads. Choose Create/Copy, pick the Selected button, and make a copy of the quads and frame. Choose Select/None to clear the selection set.

6. Use Create/Copy to make a copy of the seat shape, and move it over the copied frame with quads.

7. Zoom in on the combo and carefully position the seat so that its upper portion forms a centerline between the edges of the frame arc. In the next step, the quads will be used to add two vertices to the centerline so that it can be trimmed to the correct length.

8. Click on the Hold button and choose Create/Boolean. Pick the seat/centerline First, and then pick one of the quads. In the Boolean dialog box, toggle on the Subtraction button and pick OK. Now pick

the centerline again, then pick the other quad, and pick OK in the dialog box. The resulting figure is on the left in the next illustration.

9. Use Modify/Segment/Delete to delete all the segments of the figure except the centerline arc that is left between the quad shapes.

10. Delete the frame from the superimposed frame and quads—it just served to properly locate the quads in relation to each other.

Result: On the screen you should have a seat shape, a frame, a curved centerline, and two quads with angled tops.

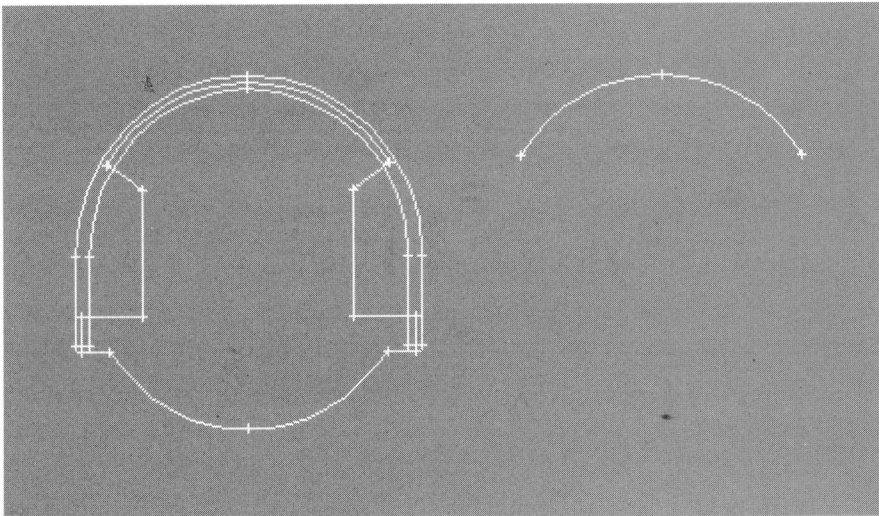

The shape on the left will be displayed after using Boolean Subtraction. Remove all segments but the top of the curved centerline to produce the shape on the right.

Draw the Profile of the Upper Chair Back

In this section you'll draw a cross section of the upper back of the chair. It will be lofted using the arc centerline, creating a curved, beveled top.

1. Draw a quad $\frac{3}{4}''$ wide and 8″ high. Zoom in, choose Modify/Segment/Curve, and pick the horizontal top segment of the quad.

2. Use Modify/Segment/Refine to place vertices on each side of the quad about an inch below the top vertices. (See the following illustration.) Click on the Hold button.

3. Choose Modify/Vertex/Skew and toggle the cursor to horizontal arrows. Pick the right top vertex. Move it slightly to create a flare to the right at the top of the shape. Pick the left top vertex and move it until the curve of each side of the shape is approximately the same. If you're not satisfied with your first try, pick the Fetch button to restore the shape, and try again.

Result: The profile should have a bend at the top and should end in a rounded edge.

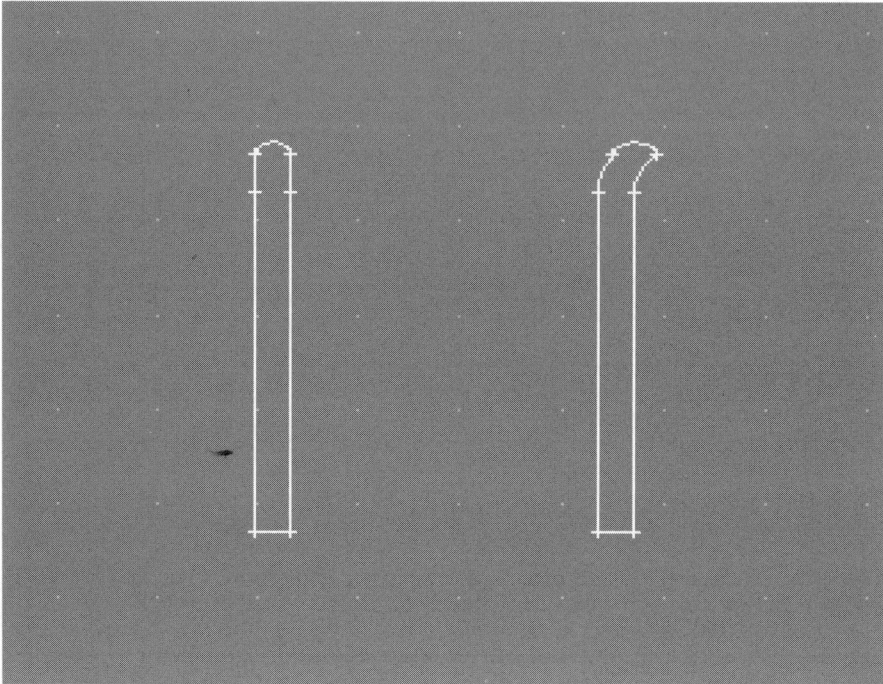

The upper frame profile before and after using Modify/Vertex/Skew.

Draw the Paths and Loft

You'll need three more lofting paths for the shapes on the screen.

1. Press [S] to toggle on Snap and choose Create/Line. Starting at the top, draw vertical lines 1", 2' 1", and 1' 9" long.

2. Assign the seat shape and press [F2] to get to the 3D Lofter. Use Shapes/Get/Shaper to import the seat shape, and use Shapes/Center to center it. Return to the Shaper, unassign the seat shape, and assign the 1″ path line.

3. In the Lofter, import the path with Path/Get/Shaper and use Objects/Make to loft the seat, naming it "seat" in the Object Lofting Controls dialog box. The Tween button should be off, and the Contour button should be on.

4. Using the same procedure:

    ❏ Loft the frame using the 2′ 1″ path and name it "frame."

    ❏ Loft both quads at the same time, using the 1′ 9″ path, and name them "holes."

5. Assign the upper back profile, bring it into the Lofter, and center it. The top of the quad should bend to the right.

6. The center mark will be slightly off. Choose Shapes/Move and pick the Shape viewport. Use a horizontal cursor to move the profile shape slightly to the right so that the center mark is equidistant between the two sides.

7. Assign the centerline arc and bring it into the Lofter with Path/Get/Shaper.

8. Check the side viewports to make sure that the top of the profile bends toward the outside of the curve. If it bends inward instead, choose Path/Mirror, click in the Top viewport, toggle to a vertical cursor, and click on the path.

9. Choose Objects/Make to loft the shape. In the dialog box, type in the name **upback**, toggle on the Tween button, and pick OK.

10. Go to the 3D Editor and right click Zoom Extents. Use Views/Viewports to assign the lower right viewport as the User viewport.

Result: There is a collection of 3D shapes in the Editor, ready for further manipulation.

Subtract the Side Volumes from the Frame

In this section, you'll use the lofted quads to cut holes in the sides of the chair frame.

1.   First, use Modify/Object/Move to move all the objects away from each other so that you can see what you're doing.

2.   Click in the Front viewport and use the Full Screen button to assign it as the only viewport.

3.   Move the quads over the frame into the same position that you used to create them—centered side to side, and 1½″ above the ends of the frame arc. (See the following illustration.)

4.   Select the Top viewport as the single viewport and toggle to a vertical cursor.

5.   Move the quads over the frame until the "left-over" frame area is twice as wide at the top as at the bottom. Switch back to four viewports.

6.   Click on the Hold button. Choose Create/Object/Boolean. In the Front viewport, click first on the frame and then on one of the quads. Check that the Subtraction button is on in the dialog box.

Result: The chair frame now has open sides. Sometimes Boolean operations don't work. If this one didn't, click on the Fetch button to restore the geometry, move the quads very slightly up or down, and try again.

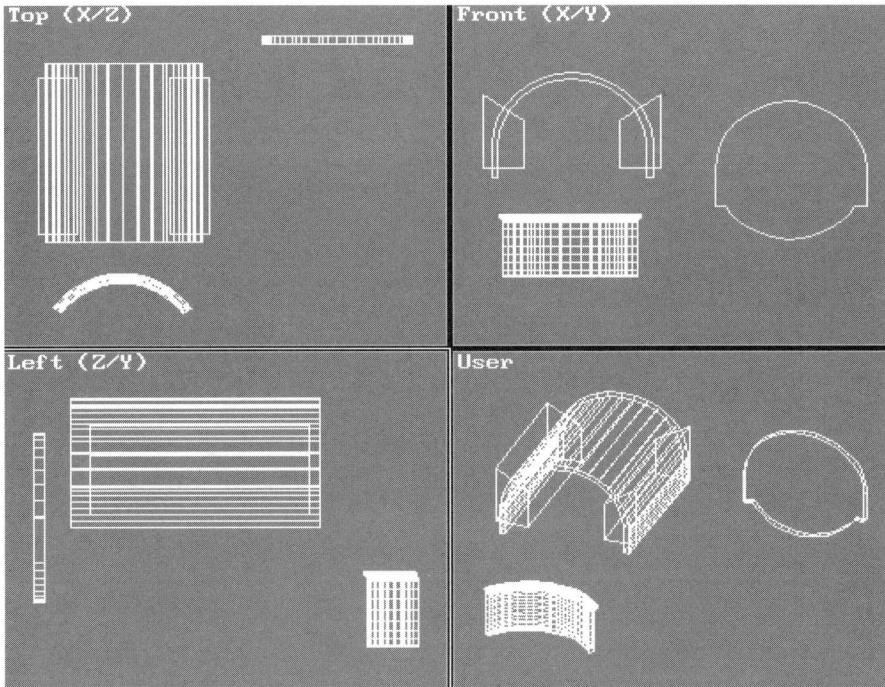

The quads moved into place over the chair frame, ready to cut holes.

Subtract the Volumes Between the Chair's Slats

In this section, you'll create an object, use Radial Array to duplicate it, and use it to subtract the spaces between the slats at the back of the chair frame.

1. Toggle the Front viewport to full screen. Choose Create/Box and draw a box ¾″ by 3″. When the command line asks for a length, draw a line 1′ 9″ long. Name the box **slot**.

2. Zoom in on the box, choose Modify/Object/Taper, and toggle the cursor to a down arrow. Toggle on the Local Axis button. Pick the top edge of the box. Move the mouse to taper in the bottom of the box to 75%.

3. Choose Modify/Axis/Show and then Modify/Axis/Place. Position the cursor to locate the global axis in the center of the frame—vertical crosshair at top center of the arc and horizontal crosshairs where the arc turns straight.

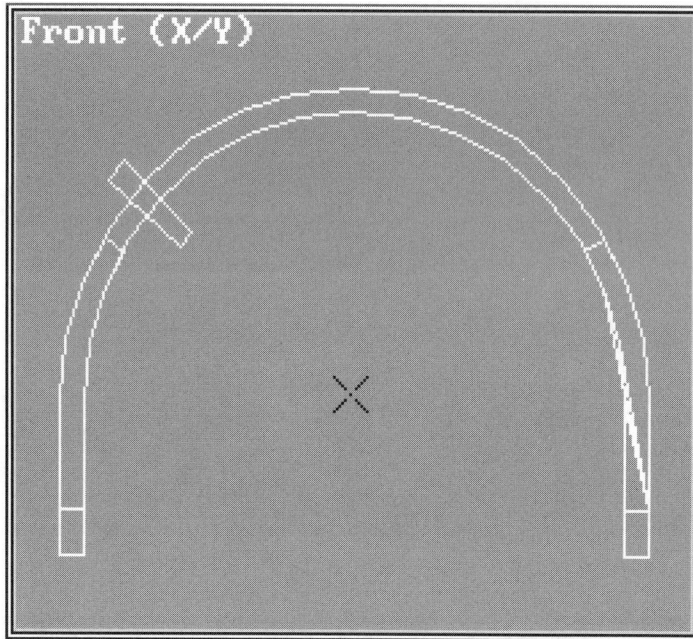

The global axis in place and the tapered box positioned over the frame arc.

4. Use Modify/Object/Move and Modify/Object/Rotate to position the box over the frame, as shown in the illustration. The box should be about 1½″ from the side cutout section, with its tapered end pointed toward the center axis.

5. Toggle off the Local Axis button and click on the Hold button.

6. Choose Create/Array/Radial and click on the box. In the Radial Array dialog box, type **12** in the Total Number in Array text box. Click on the Degrees button and then on its text box. Type in **9.4** to specify the number of degrees between each arrayed box. Pick the Calculate button to adjust the Arc Length setting to the Degrees setting, and pick OK.

7. Now attach all the boxes to make them into a single object. Choose Create/Object/Attach. Pick the box on the far right and then pick the box

next to it; the two are now a single object. Pick the two linked boxes and then pick the next box to the left; it becomes part of the object. Continue adding boxes to the combined set until all are included.

8. If you need to, choose Modify/Object/Move and adjust the array of quads until it is centered in the back, solid section of the frame. Switch to four viewports and right click Zoom Extents.

9. Activate the Left viewport. Using a horizontal cursor, move the array of boxes until it is positioned correctly—aligned flush with the Boolean cutouts. Pick the Hold Button.

10. Choose Create/Object/Boolean. In the Front viewport, pick the frame first and then the arrayed boxes. Use the Subtraction operation.

Result: The chair frame now has two large openings and twelve narrow slots, to match the original.

Attach the Upper Back to the Frame and Assign Mapping Coordinates to Frame and Seat

In this section, you'll assemble the frame and assign mapping coordinates and textures. The seat is still kept separate from the frame because separate mapping techniques will be used on the two objects.

1. Press [A] to toggle on Angle Snap, and toggle on the Local Axis button.

2. Choose Modify/Object/Rotate. In the Left viewport, click on the upper back and rotate it clockwise to -90 degrees.

3. Toggle the Front viewport to full screen and turn off Angle Snap. Move the upper back over the frame and zoom in. Using Object Move and Rotate commands, center the upper back over the top portion of the frame, with inner arcs matching, as shown in the following illustration. (You may need to turn off the Local Axis button.)

4. Toggle the Left viewport to full screen and use the horizontal cursor to move the upper back to the frame. Zoom in and use a vertical cursor to exactly align the two back planes.

5. Choose Create/Object/Attach. Pick the upper back and then the frame to attach the two as one object.

6. Choose Surface/Normals/Object Unify and pick the frame to make sure all the surface normals are pointed outward.

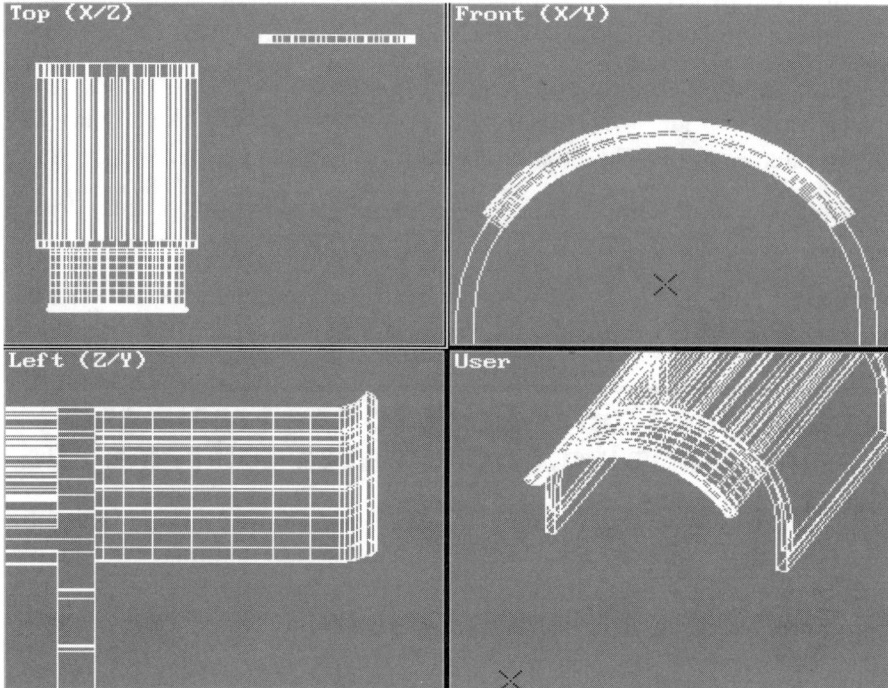

The upper back in place, ready to attach to the frame.

7. Right click Zoom Extents. Toggle on Angle Snap and the Local Axis button and choose Modify/Object/Rotate. In the Left viewport, pick the chair and rotate it to an upright position.

8. Choose Surface/Mapping/Type/Cylindrical. Then choose Surface/Mapping/Adjust/Find and pick Yes on the Rescale Map to Fit dialog box. Yellow lines in a cylindrical arrangement appear on the screen.

9. Use the Adjust commands Move and Scale with a free move cursor to position the yellow-line cylinder so that it just encloses the cylinder of the frame. Toggle to a vertical cursor. In the Left viewport, use the Scale command to size the cylinder so that the yellow lines extend just past the top and bottom of the chair.

10. Choose Surface/Mapping/Apply Obj. and click on the chair frame.

11. In the Left viewport, rotate the seat counterclockwise 90 degrees. Choose Surface/Mapping/Type/Planar. A square with yellow and green sides will appear.

12. Choose Surface/Mapping/Adjust. Using Move and Scale, move the square over the seat shape and scale it down until it is just larger than the seat. Choose Surface/Mapping/Apply Obj. and click on the seat shape.

13. Pick Surface/Material/Choose. When the Material Selector appears, hold down the [Alt] key and press [W] to get to wood textures. Scroll down and pick WOOD-TEAK and OK.

14. Choose Surface/Materials/Assign/Object. Pick the frame and the seat.

Result: The frame and seat will receive a wood texture when rendered.

Assemble the Chair, Taper It, and Add a Cushion

1. Toggle the Top viewport to Full Screen. Choose Modify/Object/Move and a free move cursor. Move the seat into the frame. Choose Modify/Object/2D Scale and scale the seat down to 96.5%. Zoom in and fit the seat exactly into the frame.

2. Toggle to all four screens and right click Zoom Extents. In the Left viewport, use a vertical cursor to move the seat until it is approximately half way between the top and bottom of the chair frame. Choose Create/Object/Attach and pick the seat and then the frame. Pick the Hold button and toggle on the Local Axis button.

3. Choose Modify/Object/Taper and toggle the cursor to an up arrow. In the Front viewport, pick the chair and move the cursor to flare out the top to 120%.

4. Perform the same operation in the Left viewport, tapering the top of the chair out 120%.

5. Choose Create/Hemisphere/Values. In the Set Hemisphere Segments dialog box, set the segment number to 24.

6. Choose Create/Hemisphere/Smoothed and pick the center of the chair seat in the Top viewport. Draw a hemisphere with a radius of 3" and name it "cushion."

7. Choose Modify/Object/2D Scale and a free move cursor. Still in the Top viewport, scale up the cushion until it appears as it does in the following illustration.

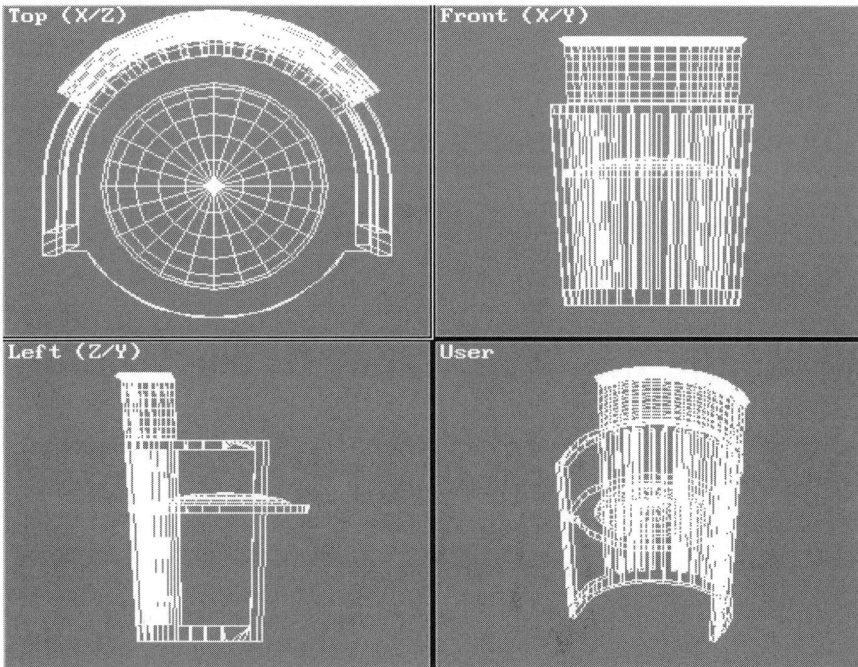

The cushion 2D Scaled in the Top viewport and squashed in the Left viewport.

8. In the Left viewport, toggle to a vertical cursor. Choose Modify/Object/2D Scale and squash the pillow down further until it looks like the one in the illustration. Use Modify/Object/Move to move the cushion to rest on the seat.

9. Pick Surface/Materials/Choose, hold down [Alt], press [R], and pick RED MATTE in the Material Selector box.

10. Choose Surface/Material/Assign/Object and pick the cushion to assign it a red fabric. Pick File/Save and save the scene as **fwschair**.

Result: The chair is completely assembled and ready to render.

Setup Lights and Camera, and Render

This section will finish up the chair. See color plate V in the color section to view the finished results.

1. Right click Zoom Extents and then right click three times on the Zoom Out button. Choose Cameras/Create. In the Top viewport, place a camera in the lower left corner of the viewport, similar to the position in the following illustration. Locate the target at the chair.

2. Use Views/Viewports to change the User viewport to a Camera viewport.

3. Use the Left viewport to move the camera up 2 or 3 feet above the top of the chair, and position the target on the cushion. Pick Cameras/FOV to adjust the field around the chair.

4. Choose Lights/Omni/Create to place an omni light close to the camera. Set the Luminance slider to 210.

5. Choose Lights/Spot/Create. In the Top viewport, place a spotlight to the right front of the chair, with its target at the chair. Set the spotlight Luminance at 255 and toggle on Casts Shadows. Use the Left and Front viewports to move the spotlight up even with the camera.

6. Choose Renderer/Render View and select the Camera viewport.

Result: This exercise has used the Boolean, Taper, Scale, and Array commands—some of the most useful in modeling objects.

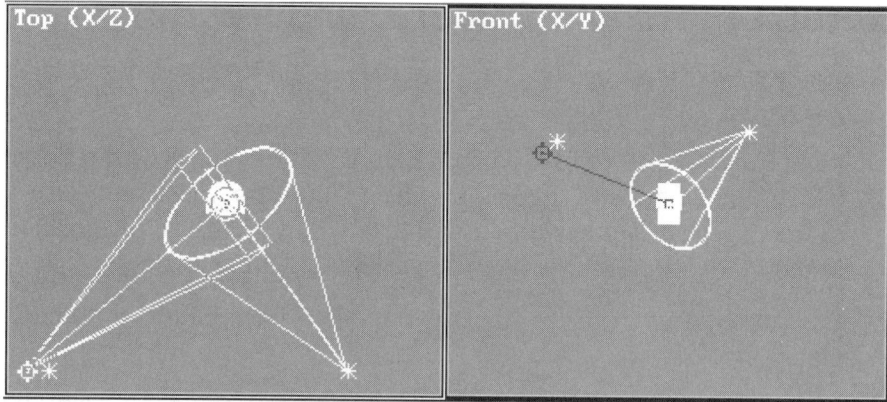

The lights and camera setup in the Top and Front viewports.

Modifying Shapes and Objects

The Move, Rotate, and Scale commands are the workhorses of modification operations. Move and Rotate do their necessary but limited jobs with little fuss, but 2D and 3D Scale are extremely versatile.

2D and 3D Object Scaling

As demonstrated in the previous exercises, the scaling commands are as useful for changing the proportions of objects as they are for making objects larger or smaller. The effect of scaling depends on four factors:

❏ **2D or 3D, Combined with Specific Viewport:** In the 3D Editor, either two or three dimensions can be scaled. Using 3D Scale with the free move cursor increases or decreases the dimensions of the object globally, keeping the same proportions. Using 2D Scale increases or decreases the object only in the plane of the viewport used, as demonstrated when scaling the cushion in the previous exercise.

❏ **Cursor Arrows:** A free move cursor modifies the component in all viewport directions equally. Vertical or horizontal cursors limit the modification to the direction of the arrows.

❏ **Local Axis Button:** If the Local Axis button is on, the component is scaled in relation to its own axis, expanding or shrinking from its centerpoint in the direction specified by the cursor arrow setting. If the Local Axis button is off, the scaled object moves toward or away from the global axis.

Using the various parameters in combination allows an enormous range of transformations. Keep an eye on the status line to track the percentage of scaling. If multiple objects need to be scaled the same amount, include them all in a selection set to simplify scaling them to the same percentage.

Don't Forget the Local Axis Button

Rotating, tapering, and skewing are also affected by whether the Local Axis button is on or off. In the following illustration, the left cylinder of each pair in the upper row is rotated, tapered, and skewed with the local axis *on*. The left cylinders of the lower pairs are rotated, tapered, and skewed the same amount with the local axis *off*, which modifies the cylinder in relation to the global axis placed in the center of the screen.

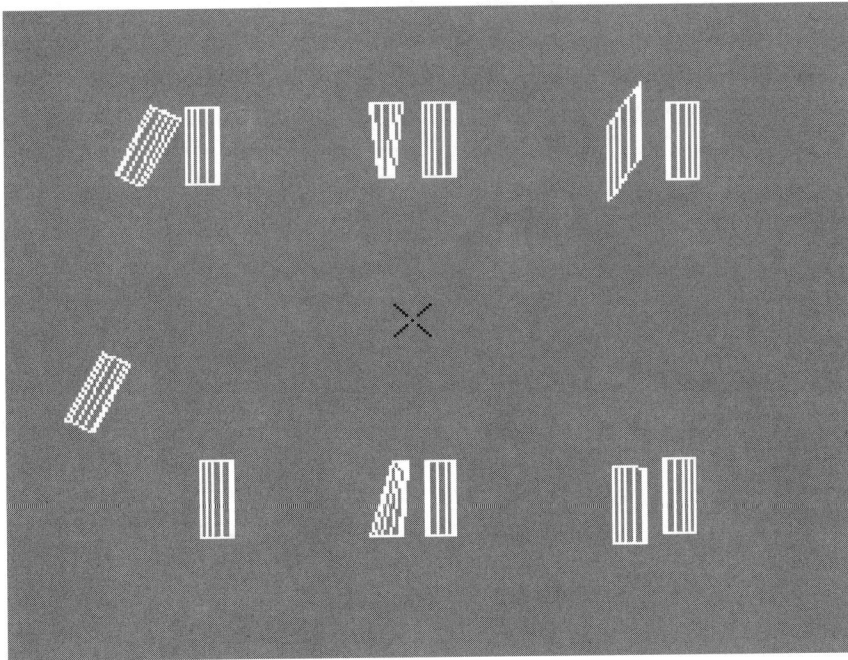

The upper row is modified with the Local Axis button on. The lower row uses the global axis.

Manipulating Selection Sets of Vertices

Once the basic volumes of a model are created, commands for modifying faces and vertices offer many techniques for adding more detail. One of the most versatile techniques is the use of selection sets to modify vertices. The following exercise uses selection sets to bend and angle the arms of the Lipchitz sculpture.

The exercise only goes through creating the basic volumes, but you can experiment further with adding detail to the torso. In the next illustration, grooves are being added between the lower belly and legs by selecting a quad of vertices on one side, moving the set out from the body, pulling the adjacent stationary vertices in, using the Top viewport to rotate the selected vertices forward, and then moving the vertices back into place.

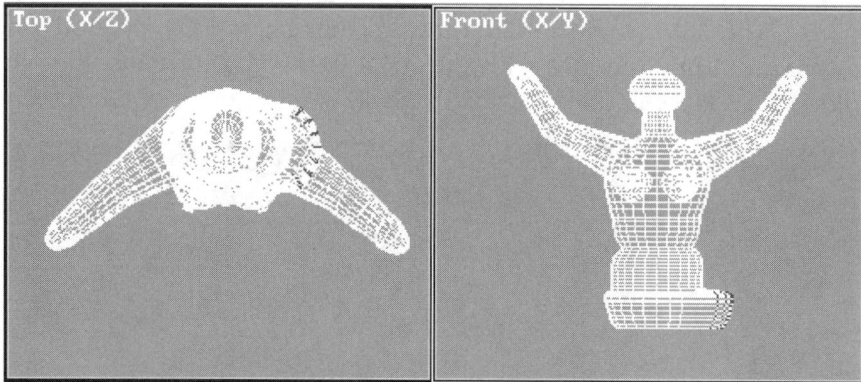

The Top and Front viewports. The selected quad of vertices at the bottom of the figure has been moved away from the body, ready to rotate before being moved back into place.

A common problem is inadvertently picking up vertices on the far side of a model when you want to modify only one side. To avoid this, you can (1) use Select/Face/Quad to enclose the unneeded portion of the model, (2) then use Display/Hide/Face to remove the selected portion from the screen, (3) select the vertices you wish to manipulate, and (4) choose one of the Modify/Vertex commands and pick the Selected button. This selection procedure limits your modifications to the portion of the model displayed.

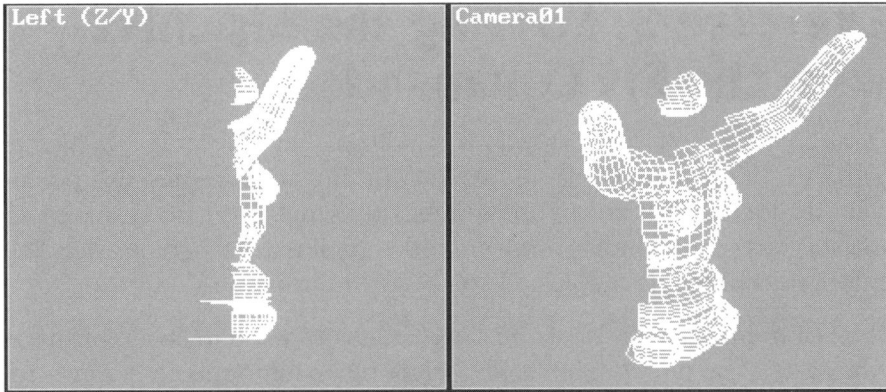

The back of the model was hidden while manipulating selection sets of front vertices to pull in the belly button and add folds of skin.

The torso with vertices modified, rendered in default white. See color plate VI for the finished model, in place on the plunge pool wall.

Exercise 3: Lofting the Lipchitz with the Fit Command

Frank Lloyd Wright often visited his buildings after they were completed, partly to shift around works of art. The Kaufmanns accepted this potentially maddening habit because Wright's unerring eye placed objects in such a way that building and artwork amplified each other, lending emphasis through their adjusted spacial relationship.

The Jacques Lipchitz *Mother and Child* originally stood midway down the long side of the plunge pool wall. Wright moved it to the corner instead, where it gained importance through a confluence of building planes causing it to become a focal point for the east end of the building.

The Lipchitz stands at the corner of the plunge pool.
(Photo courtesy by Donald Hoffmann.)

The following exercise describes a procedure for creating an approximation of the sculpture's basic volume and, by extension, other complex, nonrectilinear objects. For modeling, the Lipchitz can be separated into two types of forms. The torso of the mother is relatively compact, and symmetrical from the front view; it can be lofted in one piece using the Fit command. The figure's arms and breasts are additive volumes. These portions are created separately by modifying 3D primitives.

The available photographs of the Lipchitz were taken from an angle, thus no convenient front and side elevations. The first step in modeling the figure is to make sketches of the two profiles, concentrating on the compact central volume. The sketch doesn't have to be detailed, but should give an indication of the basic contours.

The basic forms of the mother's torso, rendered in a smooth material to better show the geometry.

Make a Fit Shape for the Non Symmetrical Side

The side profile begins with a series of ellipses—sort of like those You-Can-Learn-to-Draw ads. Rather than enter pages of coordinates, you'll have to create the Fit shapes by eye, a not uncommon modeling situation. Don't worry; you don't have to turn in this homework and get graded on it, so have fun in the privacy of your own home or office.

1.   The drawing space uses Architectural units and a Denominator of 4. Snap is set to 1″, Grid to 4″, and Grid Extents to 0 and 44″—the approximate height of the sculpture.

2.   Begin the profile by drawing a stack of six ellipses to form the basic contours for head, neck, upper chest, lower chest, upper pelvis, and lower pelvis.

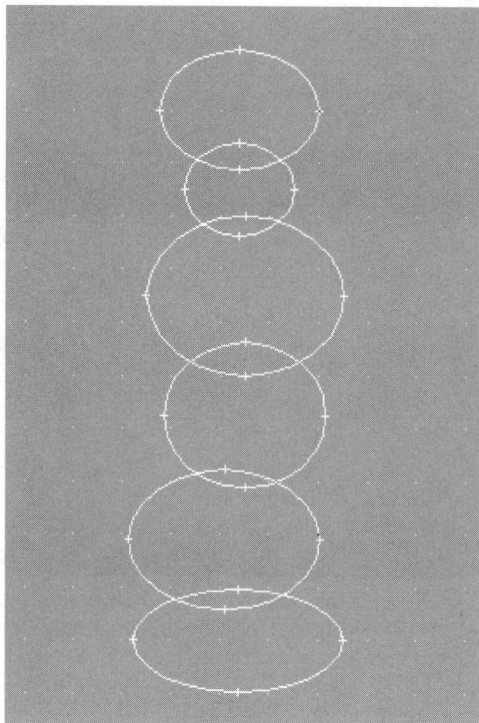

The initial stack of ellipses.

3. Adjust the ellipses in vertical relation to each other, scale them if necessary, and rotate them to match the tilt of the various volumes.

4. Use the Create/Boolean command to Union the ellipses.

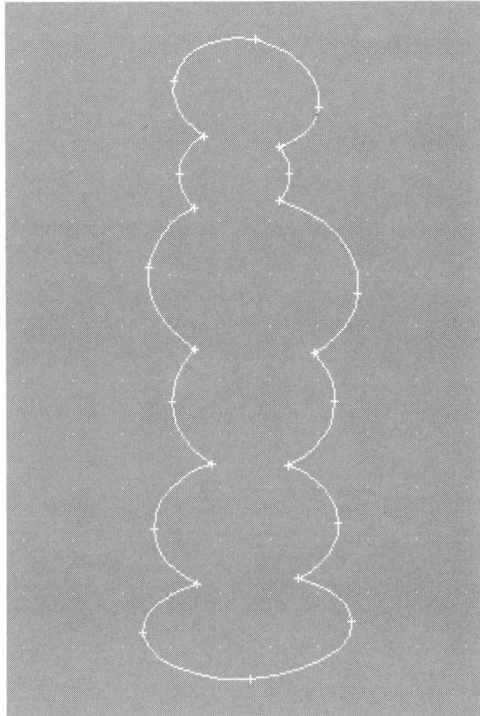

The ellipses moved, rotated, and scaled to more closely
match the volumes, and joined with Boolean Union.

5. Use Modify/Segment/Refine to insert a vertex on either side of the lower curve of the bottom ellipse. Delete the bottom center vertex. Choose Modify/Segment/Linear and pick the segment to flatten it for the base. Use Modify/Vertex/Move to ensure that the two bottom vertices are aligned horizontally.

6. The next step is intuitive and requires a lot of eyeballing. Use the Modify/Segment/Refine command to add vertices to the figure where needed, and use Modify/Vertex/Move to shift vertices where needed. Use Modify/Segment/Linear to straighten segments where needed,

and use Adjust commands for both vertices and segments. Use the Hold button frequently.

7. Adjust the vertices in the Y dimension so that vertices on either side of the profile are at the same height.

Result: The ellipses have been turned into a side profile.

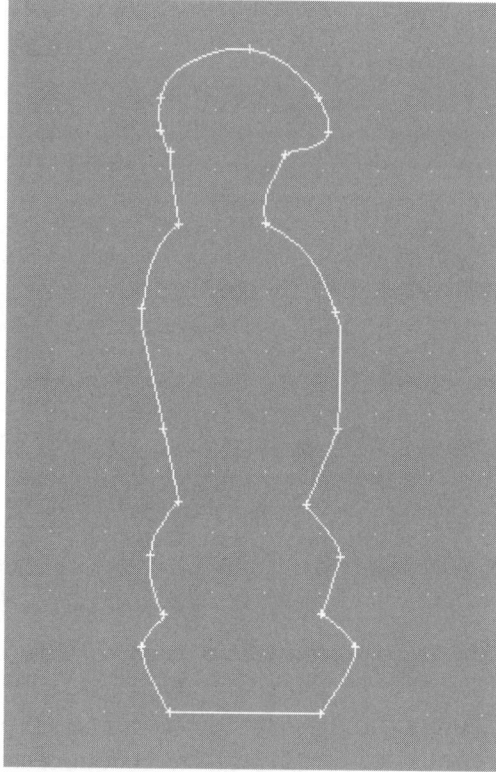

The profile has been refined by adding and moving vertices and using Linear and Curve on segments. It has 23 vertices.

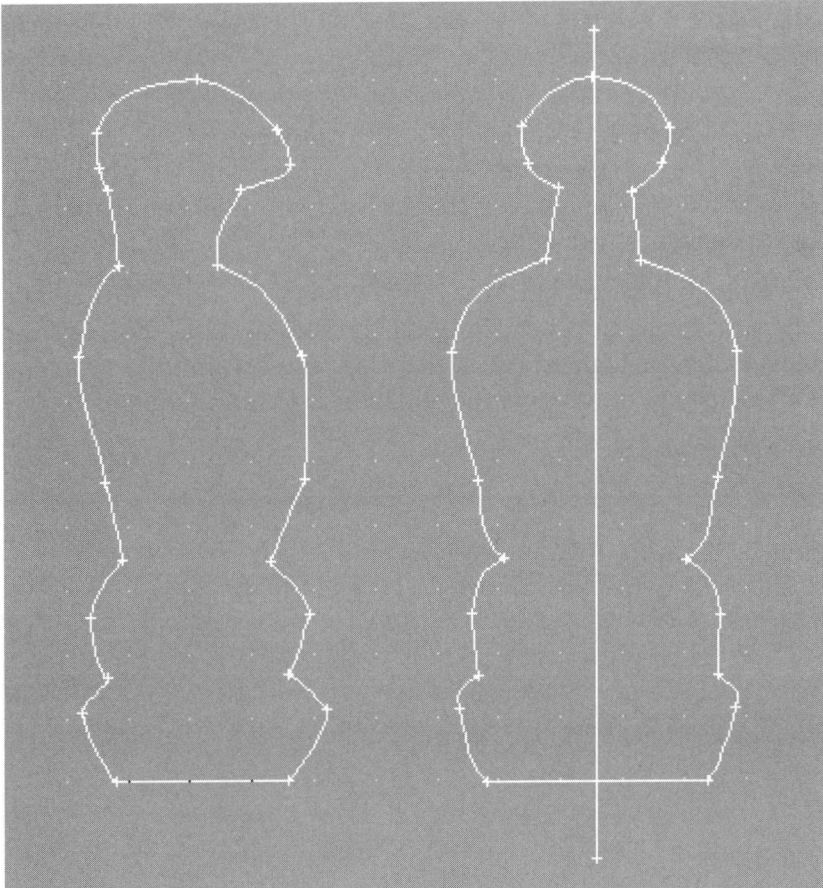

A front profile with 23 vertically matched vertices, created with the same method.

Make a Fit Shape for the Symmetrical Front

This section uses the same techniques to create the symmetrical front profile as you used to create the side profile.

1. Draw a vertical line longer than the height of the sculpture to serve as a centerline.

2. Draw six more ellipses, this time matching the contours of the sculpture as seen from the front and at approximately the same vertical

position as the side ellipses. Adjust the position and size of the ellipses and join them with Boolean Union.

3. Add vertices to refine the figure, as you did with the side profile. If you add a vertex on the left side, match it with one on the right side and locate the pairs of vertices at the same height as vertices in the side profile. Matching vertex height will reduce the complexity of the path generated by the vertices.

4. Zoom in and make sure that there is a single vertex at the highest point of the figure's head on both profiles and that no part of the curvature rises higher. Check that the bases of the two profiles are horizontal and at the same height. Otherwise, the figure won't loft.

Result: The two profiles, with vertices matched in the Y dimension.

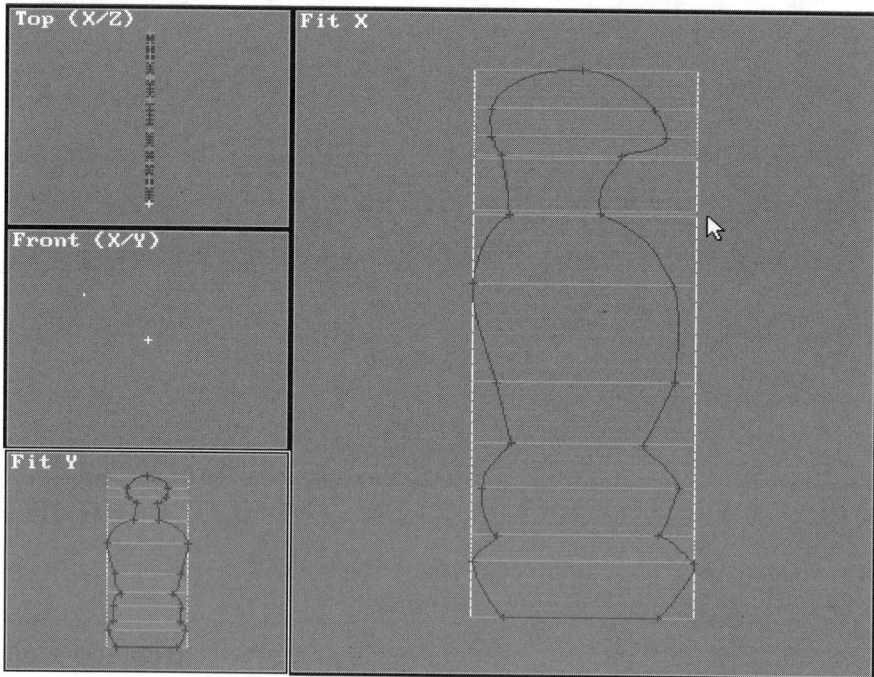

The Fit shapes in the 3D Lofter. The cursor is pointing to multiple path vertices caused by not exactly aligning the shape vertices between the neck and shoulders. If you have the same problem, move the vertices into alignment in the Shaper, re-loft the profile, and pick Deform/Fit/Gen Path again.

Loft with the Fit Command

1. Assign and Check each figure. If one figure has fewer vertices, add vertices to it in a position to match the extra vertices of the other Fit shape.

2. Draw a circle to serve as the lofted shape.

3. Assign the side profile. In the Lofter, choose Deform/Fit/Symmetry/Off. Click on the X-grid window and import the side profile with Deform/Fit/Get/Shaper. Click on the Y-Grid window. In the Shaper, assign the front profile. Import it into the Lofter with Deform/Fit/Get/Shaper.

4. Choose Deform/Fit/Gen Path to create a path adjusted to both shapes. Import the circle with Shapes/Get/Shaper. Choose Objects/Make, turn on the Tween button, and name the object "torso."

5. Get into the 3D Editor and right click Zoom Extents. Toggle on Angle Snap and rotate the torso 90 degrees in the Left viewport so that it stands upright.

Result: The torso is now a three-dimensional object.

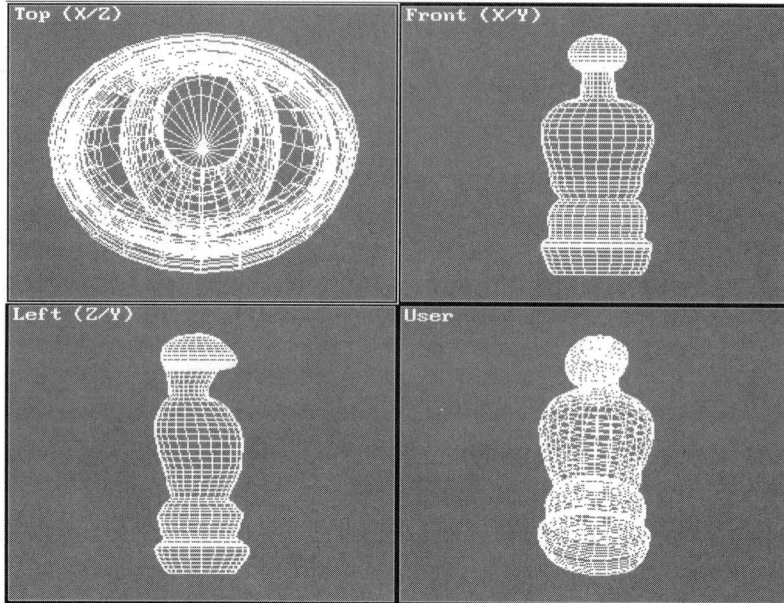

The lofted torso in the 3D Editor.

Model the Arms and Breasts with 3D Primitives, and Render

The arms are formed from long cones capped with hemispheres, then bent at the correct angle. The breasts are modified hemispheres.

1. Choose Create/Cone/Values. Set Sides to 20 and Segments to 10.

2. Choose Create/Cone/Smoothed. Zoom in to an empty space in the Top viewport so that you have a large scale drawing area. Draw a cone with a first radius of $3\frac{3}{4}''$ (0′ 3″3) and a second radius of $2\frac{1}{4}''$ (0′ 2″1). Draw a 2′ 0″ length line.

3. Choose Create/Hemisphere/Values and set the segments to 20. Choose Create/Hemisphere/Smoothed. Still in the Top viewport, draw a hemisphere with a $2\frac{1}{4}''$ radius—the radius must match the smaller cone radius. Move to the Front viewport and toggle on the Local Axis button. Choose Modify/Object/2D Scale, toggle the cursor to vertical arrows, and scale up the hemisphere to 180%.

4. Move the hemisphere to the small end of the cone, checking that the two are exactly aligned in all viewports. You may need to use Modify/Object/3D Scale to exactly match the bottom of the hand to the end of the arm. Use Create/Object/Attach to join the hemisphere and cone.

5. Now you'll turn the cylindrical arm and hand into a slightly oval form. Using a horizontal cursor, in the Top viewport, choose Modify/Object/2D Scale to scale the arm to 80%.

6. Toggle on Angle Snap and the Local Axis button. In the Front viewport, rotate the arm counterclockwise 90 degrees, so that the hand is pointed to the left. Toggle off Angle Snap.

7. The arm flares out widely where it joins the shoulder, so you need to make one more modification. Choose Select/Vertex/Quad and draw a window around the five segments at the larger end of the arm. Choose Modify/Vertex/Taper and pick the Selected button. Using a right cursor, taper the end of the arm out to 130%. Keeping the same selection set, taper the arm the same amount in the Top viewport. Choose Select/None to clear the selection set.

8. Now you'll bend the arm in the vertical plane. Toggle the Front viewport to full screen. Choose Select/Vertex/Quad to select, in turn, the areas shown in the following illustration. When you have selected an area, choose Modify/Vertex/Rotate and then pick the Selected button, rotate the vertices, and use Modify/Vertex/Move to move them. Then pick Select/Vertex/None to clear the selection mode before drawing the next selection quad.

9. When you've finished in the Front viewport, move to the Top viewport to angle the arm in the horizontal plane. Using the same method of quad selection on vertices, modify the arm as shown in the illustration.

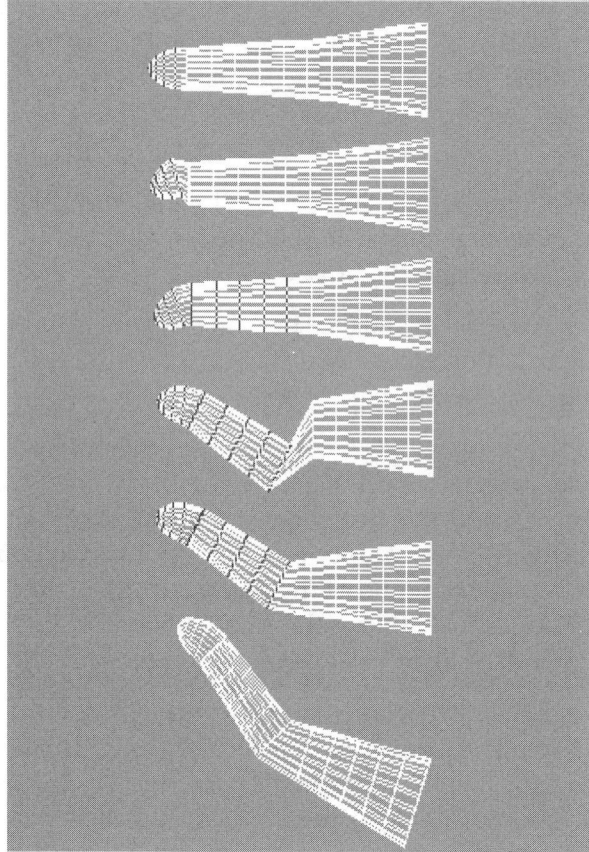

Bending the arm in the vertical plane. From the top down, (1) Select the hand vertices. (2) Rotate the hand counterclockwise 22 degrees. (3) Move the selected vertices down so that the hand bends smoothly. Clear the selection set and then select the hand and the four segments of the forearm. (4) Rotate the forearm clockwise 30 degrees. (5) Move the vertices up so that the forearm bends smoothly. Choose Select/None. (6) Use Modify/Object/Rotate to rotate the entire hand and arm clockwise 20 degrees.

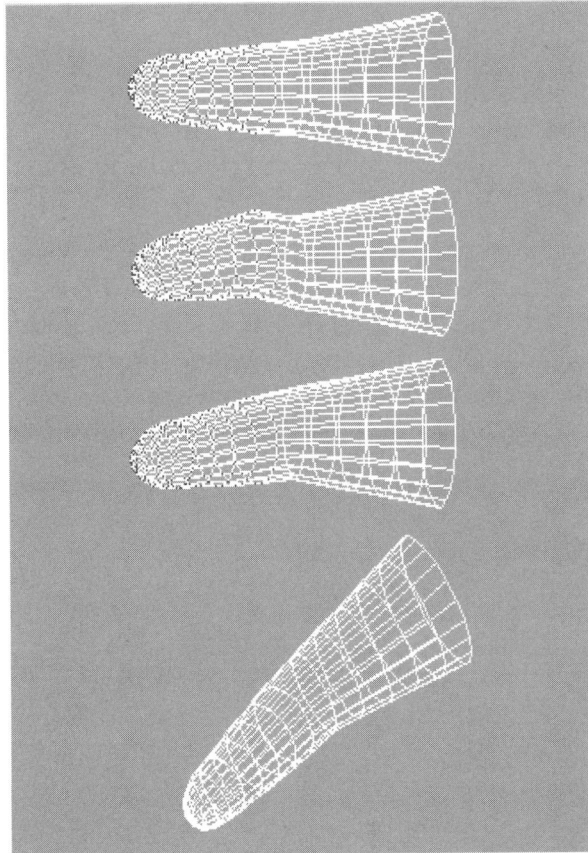

Bending the arm in the horizontal plane. (1) In the Top Viewport, select the hand and forearm vertices. (2) Rotate the selection set counterclockwise 8 degrees. (3) Use Modify/Vertex/Move and move the vertices down slightly to give the elbow a smooth bend. (4) Clear the selection set and rotate the whole arm counterclockwise 32 degrees.

10. Click the Zoom Out button to give yourself some room, and choose Modify/Object/Mirror and toggle to a horizontal cursor. Hold down the [Shift] key and pick the arm to make a mirrored copy. Move the arms into place on the shoulders, checking their position in all viewports, as shown in the following illustration. Use Create/Object/Attach to join the arms to the torso.

11. Zoom in to an empty space in the Front viewport to make the left breast. Choose Create/Hemisphere/Smoothed and draw a hemisphere

with a 2¾″ radius. Choose Modify/Object/Taper and an up arrow cursor. Taper the top of the breast out 150%.

12. Switch to the Left viewport. Using an up arrow cursor, taper the top of the breast down to 75%. Pick the Hold button. Use Modify/Object/Skew with a left arrow cursor, and skew the top of the breast left to an offset of -0′ 0″1.

13. In the Front viewport, choose Create/Cylinder/Values and set the Sides to 10. Choose Create/Cylinder/Smoothed and draw a cylinder with a radius of 0′ 0″3 and a length of 0′ 0″2. Move to the Left viewport and choose Modify/Object/Rotate. Rotate the nipple 10 degrees counterclockwise. Using the Front and Left viewports, move the nipple into place and attach it to the breast as shown in the illustration.

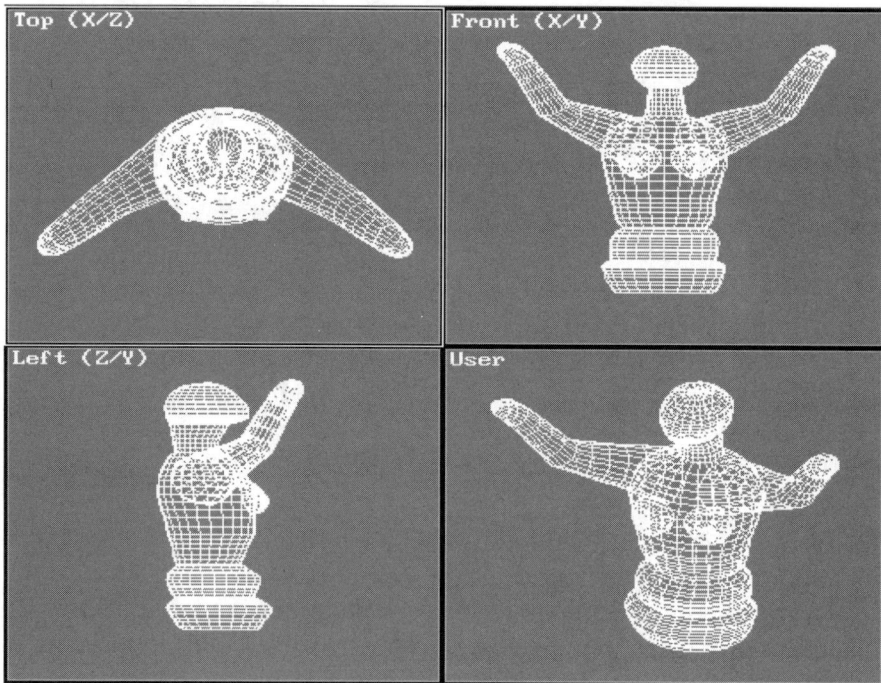

The torso with arms and breasts in place.

14. In the Top viewport, rotate the breast 18 degrees clockwise. Choose Modify/Object/Mirror and toggle to a horizontal cursor. Hold down the [Shift] key and pick the breast to make a mirrored copy.

15. Move the breasts into place using the Top and Front viewports. Choose Display/Hide/Object. In the Top viewport, pick one of the breasts to hide it so that you can see what you're doing. Move the other one into place in the Left viewport, using a horizontal cursor. Make sure that the base of the hemisphere intersects the chest wall all around its perimeter. Unhide the other breast and move it into place. Attach the breasts. (Whew!)

16. Check the proportions of the assembled figure. If you need to modify a portion of it, use a selection set of vertices, as you did when working on the arms.

17. Set up lights and camera similar to the setup used for the barrel chair, and render using 3D Studio's default material. Save the scene with the name **FWLIPCH1.**

Result: This has been a difficult modeling job, and you were left on your own a lot. The object of the exercise is not to produce a rendering for your portfolio, but to familiarize you with a method of creating complex forms. In the next chapter, we'll return to the Lipchitz to add an edited bump-map material.

The child is assembled from modified primitives. It is undefined in the sculpture, melted into the mother's back and hair. If you want to have a go at modeling it, start with the basic volumes.

The arms of the child are formed from a rotated torus, with selection sets of vertices further manipulated to form the hands. The head, neck, and upper and lower torso start from Lspheres. The child's legs are drawn from elongated, bent cones topped with hemispheres, similar to the way the mother's arms were modeled. Selection sets of vertices are pulled in to form the grooves at the ends.

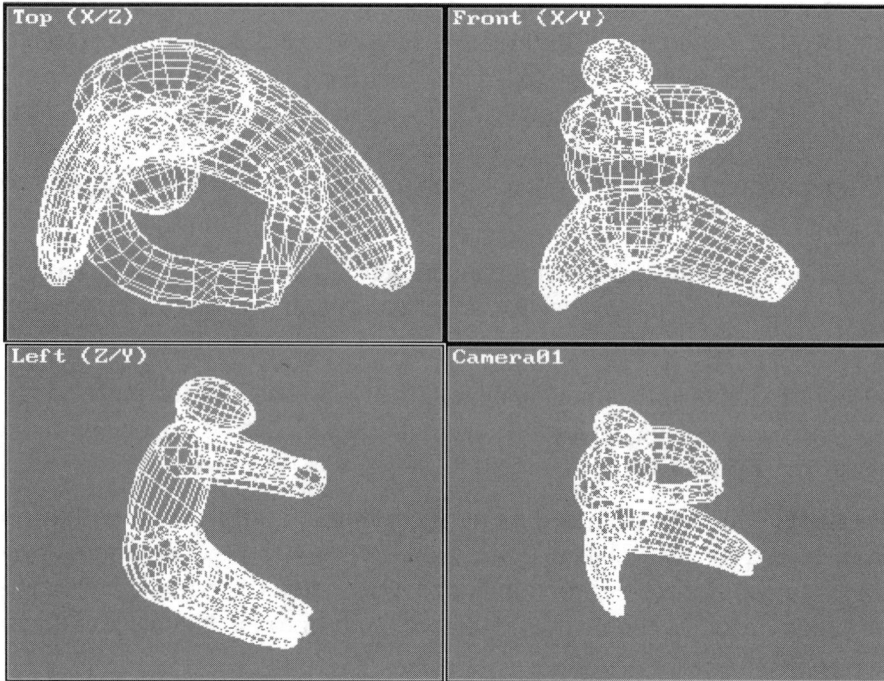

The child's geometry, shown alone.

A rendering of the joined mother and child, from a rear angle.

Summary

This chapter introduced you to some of the workhorse modeling commands. However, many of 3D Studio's modeling techniques are not mentioned here, and the program's capabilities are seemingly limitless. Work with the basics until you have a handle on them, and then study the documentation to increase your ability with the more esoteric commands to model practically anything.

Using 3D Studio Materials

Although it may take months to completely master the Materials Editor, a few hours can give you a grasp of the basics.

Rather than discuss every command, this chapter concentrates on four underlying concepts: the sequence of basic procedures, materials sources, reflected light, and combining the components of a scene. The exercises take you through a wide range of material manipulations:

❏ Glazing the windows

❏ Laying the flagstone and masonry

❏ Bronzing the Lipchitz

The Materials of the House

One reason Fallingwater blends into its setting is that many of its textures were drawn from the immediate surroundings. The stone was quarried on the site, and Wright patterned the masonry coursing on the layering of local outcroppings. Thin layers protrude as much as 2 inches from the faces of walls, casting shadows that strongly affect the appearance of the house. The mortar was struck back to be as unobtrusive as possible.

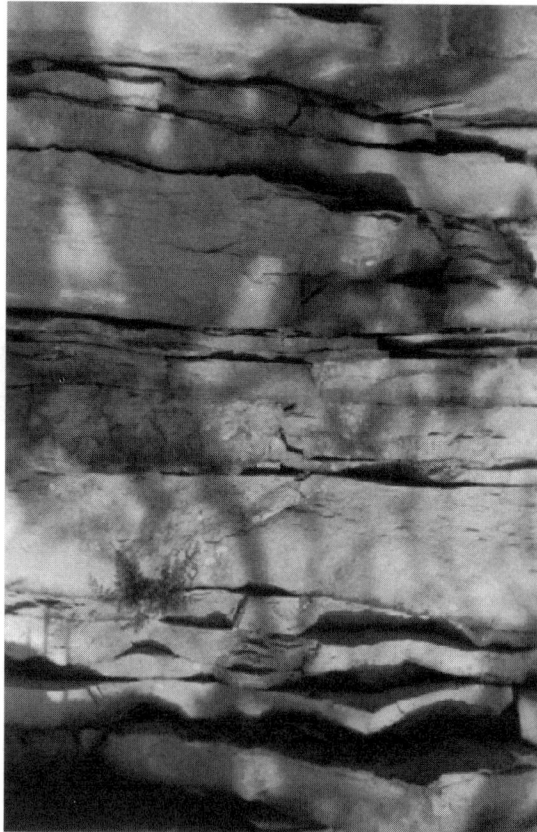

The rock strata in the Bear Run area.
(Photo by Lynda Waggoner, courtesy of Western Pennsylvania Conservancy.)

If great care was taken to match the masonry pattern to the natural local layering, equal care was taken to fit the natural grain of the black walnut woodwork into Wright's vertical and horizontal grid. The Gillen Woodworking Corporation of Milwaukee was awarded the millwork contract, which included doors, cabinets, wardrobes, backboards for beds, built-in seats and desks, radiator casings, shelves, and tables.

Before Gillen began work, Edgar Tafel went to Milwaukee to choose flitches, or planks, for the veneers, looking for pieces in which the lighter sap streak was no wider than 3 or 4 inches. The prominent streak was to run horizontally in cabinets and vertically in doors. Wright accepted the use of veneers to maintain continuity across a series of units (Hoffmann, pp. 70-74).

The wood grain at closet and door.
(Photo by Galen Barton, courtesy of Western Pennsylvania Conservancy.)

At one time Wright considered specially designed carpet for the interior of the house. It was the Kaufmanns who rejected the overly formal carpet and insisted on flagstone to maintain the continuity between interior and terraces.

Applying Fallingwater's dominant textures of masonry, flagstone, dark wood, glazing, and Cherokee red metalwork is the focus of the exercises in this chapter.

Materials Procedures

Materials commands fall into different categories, which are located in different places in different modules. Understanding where commands are located, and the sequence of steps in using them, starts you on the way to mastering materials.

❏ Operations limited to a material itself are in the Materials Editor and its associated dialog boxes.

❏ Material file operations—saving, moving materials to a scene or library—are concentrated in the Materials Editor, with some repeats in the 3D Editor.

❏ Commands that define the material's relation to the object—mapping coordinates, smoothing groups, and material application—are in the 3D Editor's Surface branch.

❏ The appearance of materials is further affected by rendering settings— configuration, shadows, and atmosphere—in the 3D Editor's Renderer/Setup branch.

❏ The final appearance of the material will be affected by the lighting settings in the 3D Editor's Lights branch.

Following are checklists for paths through four basic processes, starting with the simplest.

Choosing and Applying Nonmapped Materials

If you know which nonmapped material you want to use, you can choose and apply it without having to leave the 3D Editor or using mapping commands. Appendix B includes lists of mapped and nonmapped materials

❏ Create or assemble the mesh geometry.

❏ In the 3D Editor, use Surface/Material/Choose to call up a scroll list of materials and select a material.

❏ In the 3D Editor, use Surface/Material/Assign to apply the material to the chosen objects, elements, or faces.

Nonmapped materials are available in 3D Studio's 3DS.MLI and ACADCLR.MLI libraries.

Editing and Applying a Nonmapped Material

If you're changing a material in any way, you need to start in the Materials Editor, to see what you're doing. When you're in the Materials Editor, an edited material may be saved to a library with the Material/Put Material command or applied directly to an object with the Material/Put to Scene command.

❏ In the Materials Editor, use Material/Get Material to choose a material.

❏ In the Materials Editor, adjust the shading limit; the ambient, diffuse, and specular colors; and the material properties as needed.

❏ Use the Render Sample button to check the effect of the adjustments.

❏ To put the new material in a library, choose Material/Put Material, and type in a name for the new material.

❏ Use Library/Save Library to save the chosen library, and thus the new material.

❏ In the 3D Editor, use Surface/Material/Choose to call up a scroll list and pick the new material.

❏ Use Surface/Material/Assign to assign the new material to objects, elements, or faces.

For example, up till now we've used the RED MATTE library material for the window casings. To get the actual color of the Cherokee red semi-gloss enamel that covers the metal work, Ambient color RGB was set to 122, 36, and 16. Diffuse color was set to 143, 41, and 17. Shininess was set to 25 and Shin. Strength was set to 20. You can make the same changes in RED MATTE to apply Cherokee red to your model.

Applying a Bitmapped Material

Using a bitmapped material requires that you first apply mapping coordinates to the mesh objects (description follows) or use the Box mapping or Face mapping commands. Depending on the geometry, you can map the entire object or individual elements or faces.

When you are working on a material, you can use the Materials Editor's View Image button to display the actual material map. The File/Info command calls up a message box with additional information about the bitmap.

❏ In the Materials Editor, use Material/Get Material to call up the material you want and to check which way the pattern runs in the sample window.

❏ In the 3D Editor, use Surface/Mapping/Type to choose a planar, cylindrical, or spherical map.

❏ Use the Surface/Mapping/Adjust commands to fit the map icon to the mesh object.

❏ You can either apply a single instance of the bitmap to the whole object or tile the map so that it repeats at a smaller scale. If you wish to tile the map, one method is to choose Surface/Mapping/Adjust/Tile and set the number of pattern repetitions in the dialog box to a number appropriate for the real-world appearance of the material. For example, suppose you are mapping a 16-foot-long by 8-foot-high concrete block wall, and the texture map pattern is 3 blocks long by 4 courses high. You would need an X dimension repeat value of 4 (4 repeats x 3 blocks x 16 inches = 16 feet) and a Y value of 3 (3 repeats x 4 courses x 8 inches = 8 feet.)

❏ Choose a Surface/Mapping/Apply command and pick the mesh object to receive the mapping coordinates.

❏ Use Surface/Material/Choose to select the mapped material from the scroll list.

❏ Use Surface/Material/Assign to assign the mapped material to the object or element.

Exercises 2 and 3 demonstrate different methods of scaling a bitmap to an object. The first part of exercise 2 applies a mapping icon to a larger object, letting the program automatically set the map repeats. Exercise 3 uses the Surface/Mapping/Adjust/Tile command to specify mapping repeats.

Editing a Texture Map's Color and Material Properties

A library texture may have the right pattern but the wrong color, shininess, or transparency. You can customize the map's color and material properties by using the following procedure.

❏ In the 3D Editor, create or assemble the mesh geometry and apply mapping coordinates, setting tiling repetitions, if necessary.

❏ In the Materials Editor, use Material/Get Material to select the texture map.

❏ Use the Ambient, Diffuse, and Specular color sliders to change the color to more closely match the color you're seeking.

❏ Use the Material Property slider bars to adjust Shininess, Shin. Strength, Transparency, and Trans. Falloff.

❏ The material may need further color editing. The file names of any assigned maps will be listed on horizontal buttons to the right of the Map Types column at the bottom of the Materials Editor. To further change the color of the texture map, click on the "S" button to the right of the map file slot.

❏ In the Mapping Parameters dialog box, click on the RGB Tint button in the Source group. Red, green, and blue color swatches will appear to the right of the button. Each swatch controls the channel for intensity for that component of the material color.

❏ Click on the swatch you want to adjust and a dialog box appears with RGB and HLS sliders for that channel. Adjust the sliders and pick OK.

❏ You may need to pick another swatch to adjust that channel also, and you will need to use the Render Sample button on the Materials Editor screen to check your changes.

❏ When you're satisfied with your edits, choose Material/Put Material and type in a new name. Use Library/Save Library to save the new mapped material.

❏ Go to the 3D Editor and use Surface/Material/Choose and Surface/Material/Assign to assign the edited material to the mesh.

The last exercise in this chapter demonstrates editing bitmaps.

Tip: If you need to check a material's appearance in the rendering while editing, speed up the process by first specifying resolution at 320 x 200 with Renderer/Setup/Configure. To play it safe, make a copy of the .3DS file and use the copy for experimenting. Then choose Renderer/Render Region or Render Object. Go to the Materials Editor and adjust the material. As you make changes, choose Material/Put to Scene or click on the Auto Put button. Then use the Render Last button to check quickly the effect of your material-in-progress applied to the scene.

Exercise 1: Glazing the Windows

Frank Lloyd Wright dismissed the average house as a bedeviled box, with holes. Sketching as he talked, he would describe to apprentices his method of destroying boxiness by dissolving the corners of a structure: first drawing the box with a few wretched holes sketched in for windows, then crossing out the windows and adding support posts moved back from the corners—the most economical way to support a structure—then eliminating the walls, and with them the barrier between the inside of the box and the outside world (Tafel, p. 45).

The glass installers at Fallingwater probably cursed the concept of dissolving corners. Most of the windows turn 90 degrees around corners, with no vertical support member, requiring great effort to miter, butt, and seal the glass.

In this exercise you'll begin to apply realistic surfaces to Fallingwater by glazing the windows—importing a file with panes of glass for a portion of the building and assigning a transparent material.

Load the Model File and Merge a File Containing Glazing, Lights, and Camera

The merged file will establish a camera view looking from the living room toward the hatch and east end of the house. The same view will be used for the next exercise.

1.   Pick File/Load and load the ASSEMB.3DS model file. Save the file with the name **FWSURFAC**.

2. Choose Display/Hide/By Name. Click on the All button, and then click on L1-FLOOR and L1-WINS to deselect these two layers.

3. Choose File/Merge. In the Merge dialog box, leave all the buttons on except Animation. In the Merge a 3DS, DXF, or FLM file dialog box, pick the correct drive button and select the file L1-GLASS.3DS. In the Select Objects to Merge dialog box, click on the All button and OK.

4. Click on the lower right viewport and press [C] to switch to a camera viewport.

Result: The glazing is inserted into the window frames on the east elevation and around the hatch. The glass panes were created in 3D Studio with the Create/Box command. The $\frac{1}{8}$-inch-thick boxes were sized using the model's frame dimensions and coordinates as a guide.

Load the FLW Materials Library, Assign a Transparent Material to the Glazing, and Render

The FLW.MLI library on your distribution disk contains materials for glass, flagstone, masonry, and Cherokee red paint.

1. Choose Surface/Material/Get Library. In the dialog box, click the correct drive button, pick FLW.MLI from the scroll list, and pick OK.

2. Pick Surface/Material/Choose, and select GLASS from the scroll list. Pick OK.

3. Choose Surface/Material/Assign. Press [H] to call up a list of object names, and click on L1-GLASS.

4. Choose Renderer/Setup/Configure and set resolution to 640 x 480. Choose File/Save Project and save your scene as **FWSURFAC.PRJ**. Choose Renderer/Render View and render the Camera viewport.

Result: You have a rendering of the frames and glazing transported to the moon by space aliens.

The hatch area with glazing installed.

Sources for Materials

The easiest way to get a material is to use one somebody else has already created—hence libraries. However, creating almost any material is possible with 3D Studio's array of material operations.

3D Studio Material Libraries

The program includes a 3DS.MLI library of materials, with and without bitmaps. The library is strong on metallic, plastic, glass, wireframe, and matte variations of about ten colors, but weak on different hues. Numerous textures, particularly textile patterns and marble, and texture/bump-map combinations are included. Appendix B lists the 3DS materials and a selection of their settings.

The AutoCAD Color Numbers

The ACADCLR.MLI library of AutoCAD colors contains a wider range of hues within its 256 colors. All of the colors are Phong shaded, 2-sided, and have a shininess value assigned. Choosing ACADCLR.MLI displays a somewhat confusing list of numbers in the scroll box.

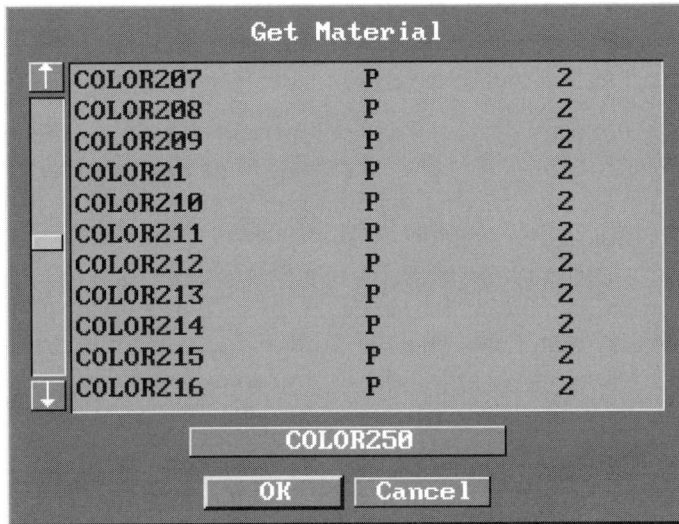

The ACADCLR.MLI scroll list.

The numbers are ASCII-sorted, which "alphabetizes" them rather than arranging them in numerical order. For instance, a random selection of numbers is in the order 201, 21, 212, 22, 224, 23, rather than 21, 22, 23,...201...212...224.

The last digit of each color number is a brightness code which refers to a scale from brightest at 0 to dimmest at 8. The first one or two digits refer to a 24-hue color wheel, with red at 0.

Stealing Materials

The mesh objects in the 3DS files shipped with 3D Studio have been assigned materials. Using the following procedure you can grab these materials to use in your own renderings.

1. Load one of the sample scenes and render it to get a look at the materials.

2. Get back to the 3D Editor and choose Surface/Material/Acquire. Pick the object to which the material is assigned (to verify the name of the material).

3. Go to the Materials Editor and choose Material/Get from Scene. In the scroll box of scene materials, pick the material you want. Use Material/Put Material to save the material to a library.

Warning: Project files do not save bitmaps with a scene, the project file simply directs the program to use a bitmap from a materials library. If you load a project file into another system running 3D Studio, the file will pick up the 3D Studio library materials on that system, but will not be able to render your custom bitmaps. Use the File/Archive command to create a compressed archive file which saves the project and any custom bitmaps used for scene materials. The 3D Studio documentation recommends using PKZIP version 2.04g, a widely available Shareware program, and includes instructions for creating an archive file. (See the *3D Studio Reference Manual,* pp. 3–33.)

Creating Bump Maps

To use an image as a bump map, click on the bump map name slot in the Materials Editor to call up a scroll box of materials. Any bitmap may be used, but black and white images are more predictable than are color ones.

Map Type		Amount		Map		Mask	
Texture 1	−	100	+	ISTONE2.CEL	S	NONE	S
Texture 2	−	100	+	NONE	S	NONE	S
Opacity	−	100	+	NONE	S	NONE	S
Bump	−	40	+	ISTONE2.CEL	S	NONE	S
Specular	−	100	+	NONE	S	NONE	S
Shiness	−	100	+	NONE	S	NONE	S
Self Illum	−	100	+	NONE	S	NONE	S
Reflection	−	100	+	NONE	A	NONE	S

The Mapping Assignment section of the Materials Editor.

A bump map uses the luminance values of the dark and light areas of an image to modify the surface normals of the image; the lighter the area, the more it will seem to protrude from the surface of the image. These "illusionary protrusions" will create shadows according to the placement of lights, as if the surface irregularities were actually part of the mesh geometry.

You can use the same image for both bump and texture maps, as is done in exercise 2. The image as bump map creates the effect of relief, and the image as texture map assigns the color variations. In fact, the power and flexibility (and much of the complexity) of 3D Studio's material operations comes from the capability to combine different types of bitmaps in a single material.

If you're scanning an image to be used as a bump or texture map, keep the following in mind:

❏ Use a head-on photo of the material. to avoid the perspective convergence of lines.

❏ Avoid including very distinctive elements in the image, if you plan to tile it.

❏ Use an image with a clear gradation of image values, with the darkest areas in places that logically will recede.

❏ Images scanned at a higher resolution produce better detail.

Exercise 2: Laying the Flagstone and Masonry

Writing about the interior materials of the house, Edgar Kaufmann junior relates,

> *"On one occasion the rough stone indoors led a lady visitor to ask my mother, after due compliments, 'Tell me, Mrs. Kaufmann, how will you get the wallpaper to stick on these walls?'" (Kaufmann, p. 109)*

The first part of this exercise creates a separate object out of the upper surface of the floor and applies a stock texture that has been edited to match the flagstone at Fallingwater. The second part of the exercise uses box mapping to apply a masonry material created from a video frame of Fallingwater to the walls in the scene.

Separate the Top Surface of the Floor and Assign Mapping Coordinates

In this section, you'll use the Create/Face/Detach command.

1.   Choose File/Load Project and load FWSURFAC.PRJ.

2.   Choose Display/Hide/By Name and pick L1-WINS and L1-GLASS, so that everything is hidden but the floor slab.

3.   Click on the Front viewport and press [W] to assign it as a full screen display.

4.   Choose Select/Face/Quad. Draw an elongated quad around just the top faces of the floor, as shown in the following illustration.

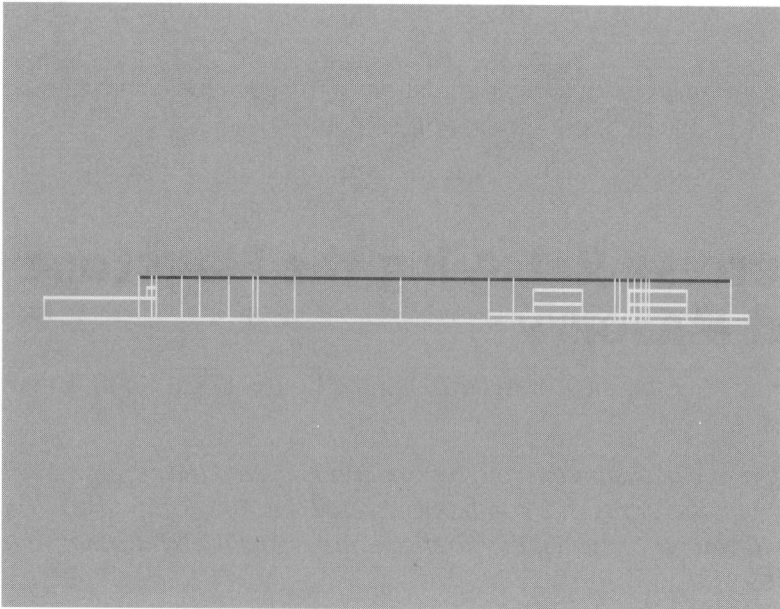

The selected top faces of the floor are displayed in red.

5. Choose Create/Face/Detach. Click on the Selected button and click in the viewport. In the dialog box, type **L1-FLAG** for the object name. Choose Surface/Normals/Object Flip. Press the [H] key and choose L1-FLAG from the scroll list. Press [W] to return to four viewports. Click in the Top viewport and press [W] to toggle it to full screen.

6. Choose Surface/Mapping/Type/Planar and then choose Surface/Mapping/Adjust/View Align to position the mapping icon parallel to the Top view plane. Click in the Top viewport.

7. Choose Surface/Mapping/Adjust/Find to rescale the map icon. Toggle to a free move cursor. Use the Adjust commands Scale and Move to approximately fit the mapping icon to the west terrace area, as shown in the next illustration.

8. Choose Surface/Mapping/Apply Object and press the [H] key. Click on L1-FLAG in the scroll list.

Result: The mapping coordinates are applied to the floor surface. The map will repeat across the floor based on the size of the icon relative to the size of the floor area.

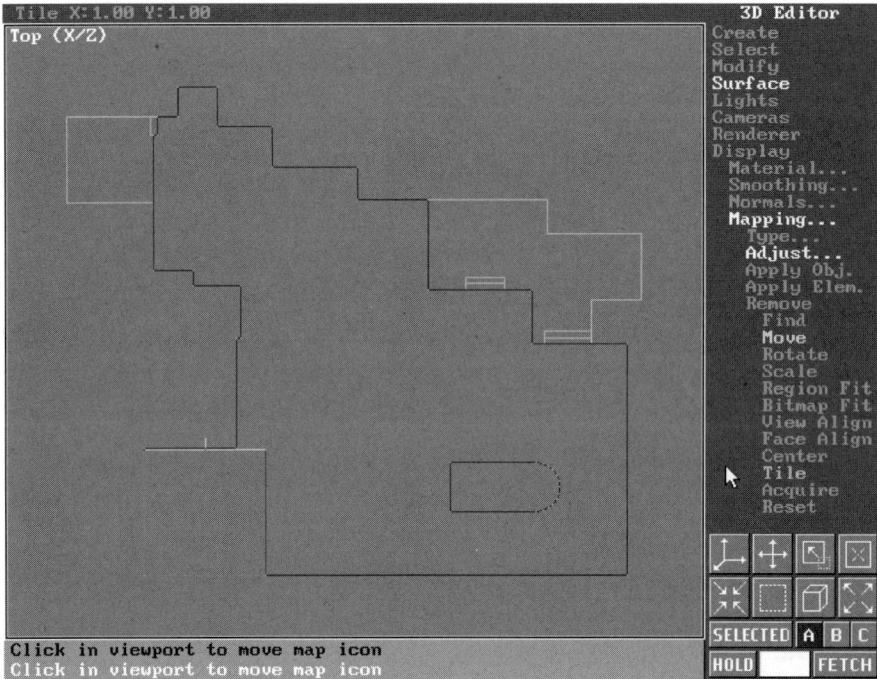

The mapping icon fitted to the west terrace in the lower left corner of the screen.

Apply the Flagstone Texture and Render

The flagstone material consists of a texture map and a bump map generated from the same image, an automatic flat-mirror reflection map, and surface color.

1.   Go to the Materials Editor and choose Library/Load Library. Pick the FLW.MLI library from the scroll list and pick OK. Choose Material/Get Material and click on FLAGSTONE. Note the texture map and bump-map settings and the Diffuse and Ambient color settings.

2.   You can quickly display a bitmap with the View Image button. Click on the Texture 1 Map name slot (FLAGSTONE.TIF), and drag the bounding box over to the View Image button. The original bitmap used for the texture will appear on the screen. Press [Esc] to get back to the interface.

3. Press [F3] to get to the 3D Editor. Pick Surface/Material/Choose and select FLAGSTONE from the scroll list. Choose Surface/Material/Assign/By Name and click on L1-FLAG and OK. Press [W] to switch back to four viewports. Choose Display/Unhide/By Name and select L1-WINS and L1-GLASS from the scroll list.

4. Choose File/Save Project and then choose Renderer/Render View and render the Camera viewport.

Result: The rendering will now include the flagstone.

The flagstone added to the glazing.

Use Box Mapping to Assign a Masonry Texture to the Walls

Box mapping assigns up to six different materials to the top, front, and sides of an object. In this section, you'll assign a single material to the sides of the walls.

1. Choose Display/Hide/All. Then choose Display/Unhide/By Name and click on L1-MWALLS and FOUND to display the masonry walls.

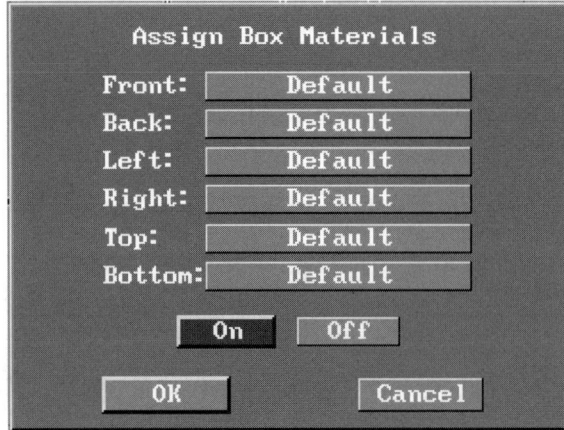

The Assign Box Materials dialog box.

2. Choose Surface/Material/Box/Assign, press [H] and click on L1-MWALLS. The Assign Box Materials dialog box appears.

3. Click on the Front button at the top of the dialog box. The FLW.MLI library scroll list will appear. Pick FW-MASON and click OK. In the Assign Box Materials dialog box, the current material FW-MASON will replace Default as the material for the front of the object.

4. Click the Back button and press [Enter] to assign the masonry texture, and repeat the operation to assign the texture to the Left and Right buttons. Click OK.

5. Press the [H] key and select FOUND from the scroll list. Use the same procedure to assign FW-MASON to the Front, Back, Left, and Right buttons and click OK. The sandstone walls now have FW-MASON assigned, and you're ready to make a test rendering.

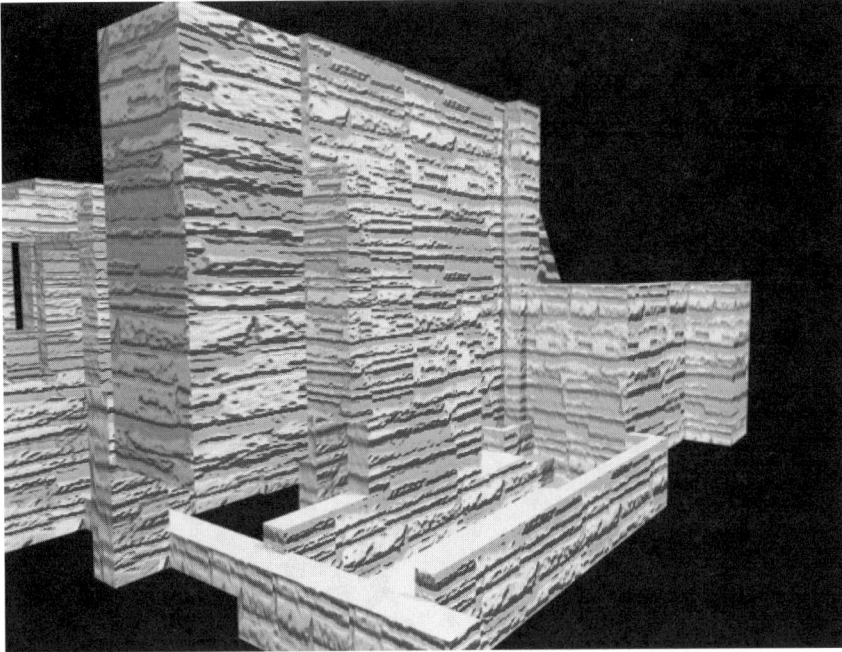

A test rendering of the masonry walls against a black background.

6. Choose Display/Unhide/All to display all parts of the scene. Choose Renderer/Setup/Background and activate the Bitmap button to replace the black background with the TREES.GIF bitmap.

7. Choose File/Save Project to save the scene, and choose Renderer/Render View and render the Camera viewport at 640 x 480.

Result: The fully textured scene is rendered. (The rendering may take over an hour on a 386/33.) See color plate VII.

The scene with all its textures in place.

Lost in the Bouncing-Light Funhouse?

Commands are scattered throughout the 3D Editor and Materials Editor for creating the illusion of reflected light. Remember that you're dealing with three different operations, even though their effects overlap:

❑ Individual specular highlights

❑ Shiny surfaces

❑ Reflections

Specular Highlights

The **location** of individual highlights on an object is determined by the placement of lights in a scene. You can either move a light around to adjust placement or use the Lights/Omni/Place Hilite and

Lights/Spot/Place Hilite commands to choose the highlight location. (The program will move the light to the correct spot.)

The **color** of a highlight is determined by two things: shading limit and specular setting. A Metal shading limit tints the highlight with the color of the metal material on which it falls. A Gouraud or Phong shading limit specifies a white highlight. A white Gouraud or Phong highlight can be tinted by assigning a color to the material's Specular setting.

The **comparative prominence** of a highlight is affected by material color and general light levels. A highlight on a dark material will be more prominent than one on a light-colored material because of the contrast. Increasing the Ambient light setting for a scene makes highlights less prominent.

The **intensity**, or brightness, of a highlight is determined by three things: how close the light is to the object, the luminance value of the material's Specular color, and the Shin. Strength setting assigned to the material. The Shin. Strength slider gives you better control when adjusting highlight intensity.

The **spread**, or area covered by a highlight is determined by the Shininess setting assigned to the material. The higher the value, the smaller and more concentrated the highlight appears.

Beyond tweaking individual highlights with specific controls, bitmaps can be used to control the appearance of highlights throughout a scene. Specular mapping applies the colors of a bitmap only to the specular highlighted area of a material. Shininess mapping alters the intensity of the specular highlight area of a material. So, specular mapping = color; shininess mapping = intensity.

Overall Surface Shininess

The line blurs between manipulating individual highlights and setting surface shininess. Shininess settings affect materials regardless of whether they have been assigned bitmaps. The principle shiny-surface controls are the Shininess slider, which controls the spread of shiny areas, and the Shin. Strength slider, which controls the intensity of the shine.

The geometry of an object affects its apparent shininess. A curved shiny object shows highlights whenever the light in a scene strikes its surface. Shiny flat surfaces usually won't show highlights unless the camera is within the cone of the angle of reflection of a light source. The angle of reflection (the angle at which light bounces off a surface) is equal to the angle of incidence (the angle at which light strikes a surface).

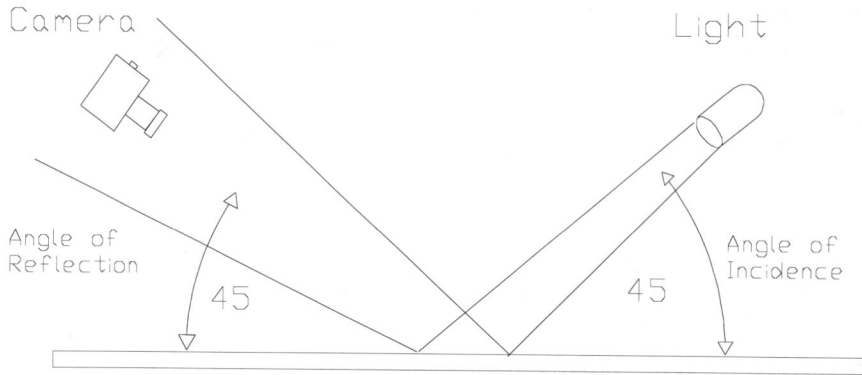

The light hits, and reflects off, the surface at 45 degrees. The camera is within the cone of the angle of reflection and will pick up a specular highlight.

The camera is within the cone of the angle of reflection created by the spotlight on the left, and picks up a highlight. The pool of light on the right is from a spotlight at a different angle.

A shiny surface will not reflect anything but light unless a reflection map has been assigned to it.

Reflection Mapping

Reflection maps and commands create the effect of an image being reflected on a shiny surface. The program includes four types of reflection mapping: spherical, cubic, automatic cubic, and automatic flat mirror.

Spherical mapping does not reflect the surrounding scene geometry. The object to which it is assigned "reflects" the image of the bitmap used, which may have no relation to what would actually be reflected if the surface were mirroring its surroundings. However, spherical mapping can be faster, and require fewer resources, than other mapping techniques.

Cubic mapping reflects a static view of a scene by using six different bitmap views generated from the top, bottom, and four sides of a scene.

The six bitmaps are created by using Renderer/Setup/Make .CUB command, which generates bitmaps from the active camera view.

Automatic cubic mapping is more suitable for animation, because the reflected image changes as the point of view moves. This method combines the qualities of spherical and cubic maps in that the surrounding geometry is reflected as with a cubic map, and any bitmap assigned as a background is also reflected.

Automatic flat-mirror reflection mapping mimics the reflection of scene geometry on a flat shiny surface.

Except for flat-mirror reflection maps, the sharpness of a reflection is controlled by the Reflection Blur Slider in the Material Properties control group of the Materials Editor.

Exercise 3: Bronzing the Lipchitz

The surface of the Lipchitz *Mother and Child* has been corroded by acid rain. The Harvard University Art Museum's Center for Conservation and Technical Studies treated the damage by rubbing the surface of the sculpture with crushed walnut shells to remove the corrosion, and applying several coats of wax for protection, giving the sculpture a darker, more lustrous finish. (*The Friends of Fallingwater Newsletter, Vol. 1, No.1*)

In the last chapter, we left the Lipchitz rendered in default shiny white. This exercise applies mapping coordinates, tiles the bitmap, and edits the color and shine of the material. The MOLDED PLASTIC base material has a texture and bump map, both generated from the same bitmap. Nothing about this material looks like the actual finish of the statue, except for the map pattern when reduced—which is the most critical element. See color plate VI for a finished rendering of the Lipchitz.

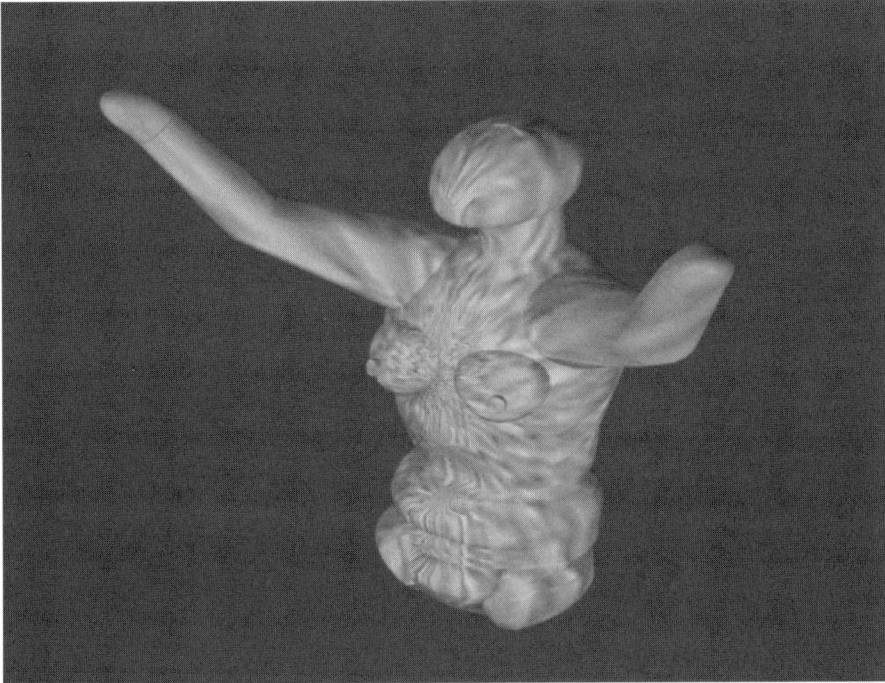

Using Molded Plastic without editing. The original material is spherically mapped to the entire sculpture with no scaling or editing.

Load Geometry and Apply Mapping Coordinates

You'll use spherical mapping for the torso, but apply cylindrical mapping to the arms to prevent the streaking caused by elongation of the map pattern (seen in the illustration).

1. In the 3D Editor, load file FWLIPCH1.3DS. Pick the lower right viewport and press [U] to change it to a user viewport. Choose File/Save and save the file with the name **FWLIPCH2**.

2. Choose Surface/Mapping/Adjust/Tile and set both the X and Y coordinate text boxes to 6. Pick OK.

3. Choose Surface/Mapping/Type/Spherical. Use the Adjust commands Find, Move, Scale, and Rotate to fit the mapping sphere over the torso of the figure as shown in the next illustration.

4. Choose Surface/Mapping/Apply Object and pick the figure.

5. Choose Surface/Mapping/Type/Cylindrical and use the Adjust commands to fit the cylinder over one arm, as shown in the second illustration. Choose Surface/Mapping/Apply Elem. and pick the arm. Use the Top viewport to rotate and move the cylinder to the other arm and repeat the application.

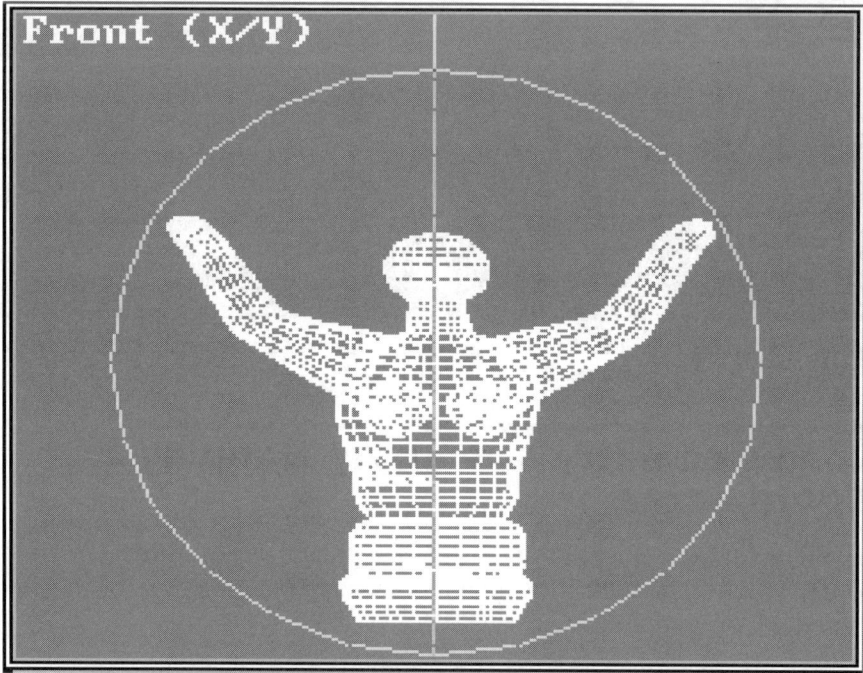

The mapping sphere fitted over the figure.

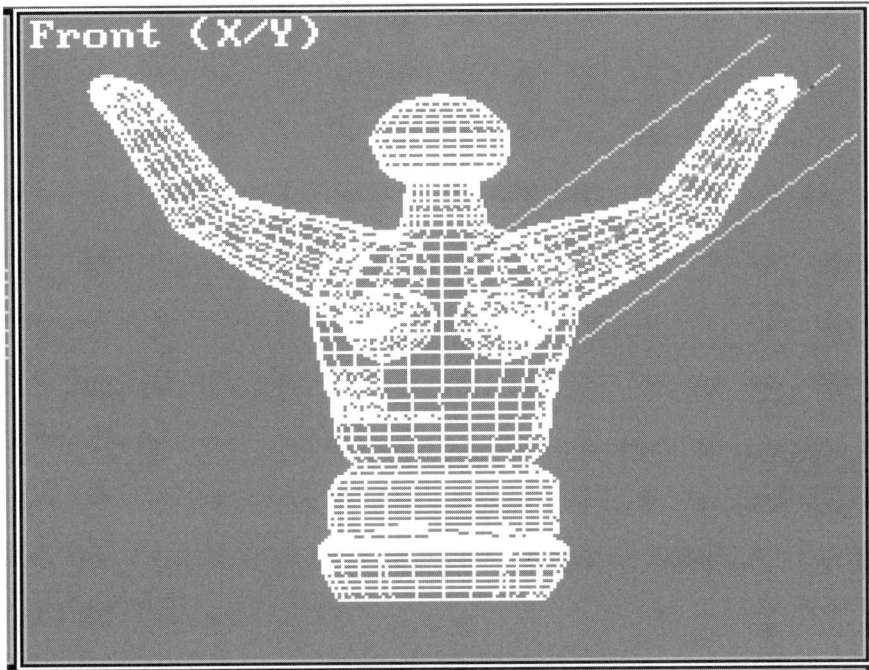

The mapping cylinder fitted over one arm.

Result: The cylindrical mapping replaces the spherical mapping on the arms, so that the pattern will not be elongated on the extended elements.

Edit the Material and Render the Scene

In this section, you'll change the material from the pale original to a shiny bluish-black to match the waxed bronze. First you'll edit the material from the Materials Editor and then from the Mapping Parameters dialog box.

1. In the Materials Editor, pick the 4x4 button in the See Tiling group.

2. Choose Material/Get Material and pick Molded Plastic from the scroll list. Pick the sample window and drag it to the second box. Pick the Current Material button and change the material name to **MOLD-EDLIPCHITZ.**

3. Move the Shininess slider to 30 and the Shin Strength slider to 65.

4. Click on the Ambient button and adjust the color sliders to Red = 1, Green = 7, Blue = 18.

5. Click on the Diffuse button and set the sliders to Red = 5, Green = 50, Blue = 85.

6. Click on the Specular button and set the sliders to Red = 215, Green = 229, Blue = 235.

7. Pick the Render Sample button to see the changes. The sample still doesn't look right—the light gray of the texture map seems to lay a chalky glaze over the dark blue. There are two routes you can take to correct the lightness of the color: use the Map Amount slider to reduce the texture map percentage or edit the texture map's RGB channels in the Mapping Parameters dialog box. We'll do the latter to maintain the full effect of the texture pattern.

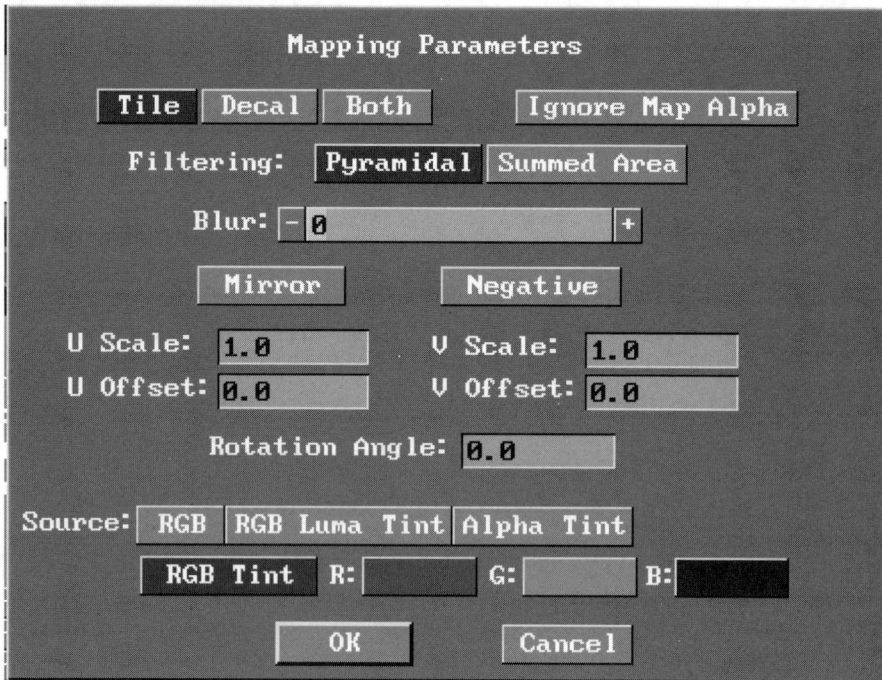

The Mapping Parameters dialog box with the RGB Tint button active.

```
                Define Solid Color
    R  [ - ] [ 8                              ] [ + ]
    G  [ - ] [ 8                              ] [ + ]
    B  [ - ] [   32                           ] [ + ]
    H  [ - ] [                170             ] [ + ]
    L  [ - ] [ 20                             ] [ + ]
    S  [ - ] [              150               ] [ + ]
            [    OK    ]      [  Cancel  ]
```

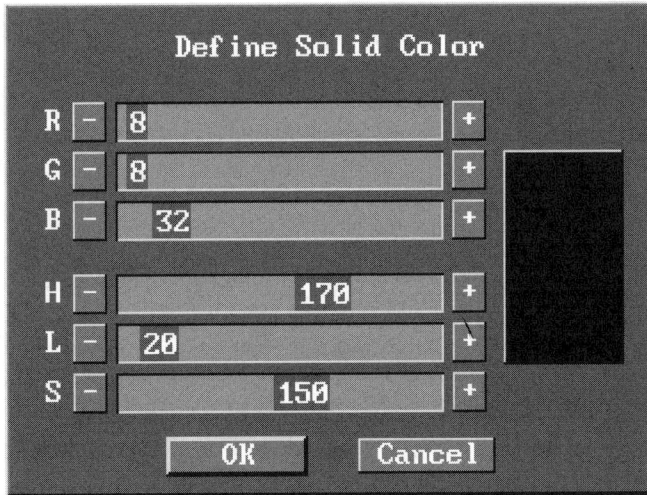

The Define Solid Color dialog box.

8. Pick the S button beside the Texture 1 Map name box. On the Mapping Parameters dialog box, pick the RGB Tint button. Three color swatches appear. You will have to adjust each hue component of the color separately.

9. Pick the red swatch. In the Define Solid Color dialog box, move the Luminance slider to 8 and the Saturation slider to 55, and pick the OK button.

10. Pick the green swatch and move the Luminance slider to 12 and the Saturation slider to 120. Pick OK.

11. Pick the blue swatch and set Luminance to 20 and Saturation to 150. Pick OK twice. Use the Render Sample button to render the material again.

12. To save the material, choose Material/Put Material and then choose Library/Save Library.

13. Go to the 3D Editor, pick Surface/Material/Choose, and pick MOLDEDLIP-CHITZ from the scroll list. Choose Surface/Material/Assign/Object and pick the sculpture to assign the new material to it.

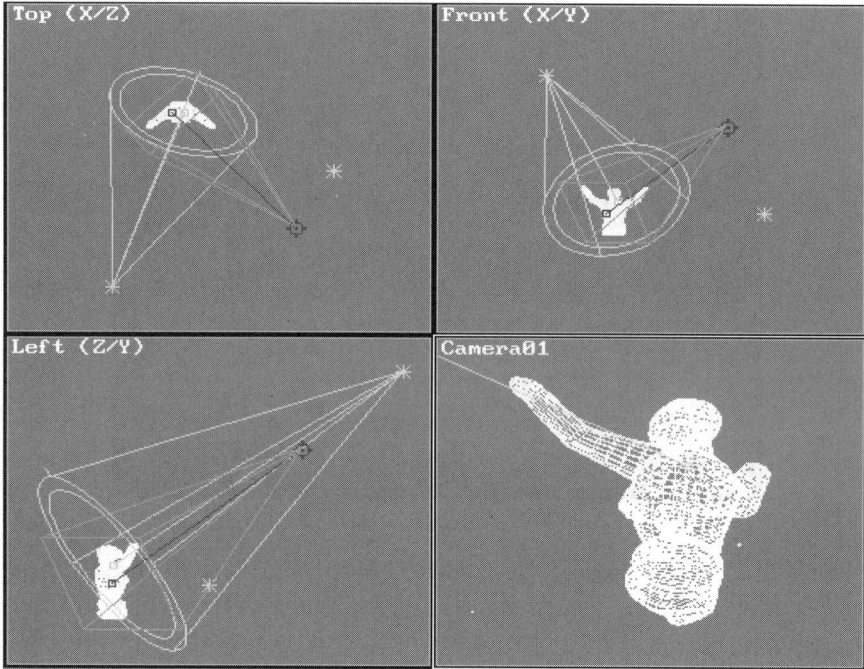

The light and camera setup.

14. Set up a camera in the approximate position shown in the light and camera setup illustration—the angle at which a visitor sees the sculpture when crossing the entry bridge. Click on the lower right viewport and press the [C] key to switch to a camera viewport.

15. Set up a shadow-casting spotlight with a luminance of 170 above and to the left front of the figure. Set up an omni fill light with a luminance of 150 low on the other side.

16. Choose Renderer/Setup/Background and specify a solid color background with HLS values of 16, 105, and 55 to approximate the overall color of the stone.

17. Choose Renderer/Setup/Configure and set resolution at 640 x 480. Choose Renderer/Render View and render the Camera viewport.

Result: The figure approximates the Lipchitz, with a few RoboCop genes thrown in.

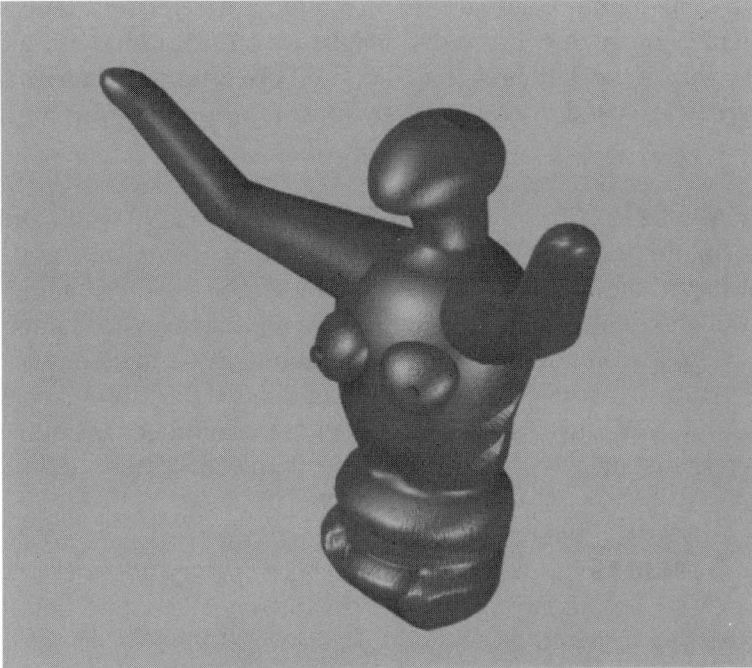

The Lipchitz with the edited material.

Putting It Together

Getting a single material right is one thing, but getting a whole scene right is another. The ultimate appearance of textured objects combined into a rendering is affected both by applications of classic color theory and by the balance among the individual materials.

Sewer World and Cotton Candy World

The principles of traditional color theory apply to computer renderings. Many books on art—both traditional and computer—contain sections dealing with the massive subject of color use. It is helpful to study a reference on handling color to familiarize yourself with the following concepts.

Note: Color terminology varies from reference to reference. **Hue** is used consistently, but **value/intensity/brightness/luminance** are all used for the lightness or darkness of a color, and **chroma/saturation/intensity/purity** are used interchangeably for the proportion of pure hue to gray in a color.

Color Models   Color models are usually illustrated as three-dimensional, mathematically based representations of colors and their relationships. They are composed of color samples arrayed along three intersecting axes indicating hue, saturation, and intensity (or luminance.) Some are based on traditional pigments (the Munsell model), and some are based on light wavelengths (the parabolic C.I.E. Chromaticity diagram). Some versions of the C.I.E. model are useful because they graph the decreasing range of colors that register with eye, camera, and printing inks.

Color Schemes   A color scheme consists of the principal hues used in an image. The primary purposes of color schemes are to limit colors in a rendering to avoid chaos and to aid in the selection of colors that work well together. Schemes are based on the position of colors on a traditional two-dimensional color wheel of hues. The basic ones are:

❏ **One hue with neutrals:** one hue used with neutral gray, white, and black

❏ **Monochromatic:** one hue varied with different intensities and saturations

❏ **Analogous:** adjacent hues, such as red, red-orange, and orange used in different intensities and saturations

❏ **Direct complementary:** hues directly across the wheel from each other

❏ **Near complementary:** a hue and the hue adjacent to its direct complement

❏ **Split complementary:** a hue, and the hues on either side of its direct complement

❏ **Triad:** three hues positioned at equal distances around the wheel

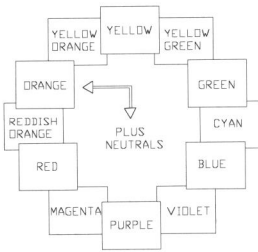

ONE HUE WITH NEUTRALS

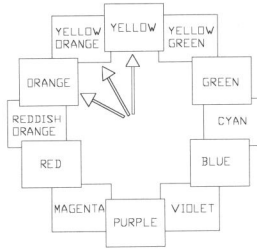

ANALOGOUS

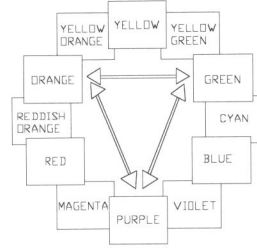

TRIAD

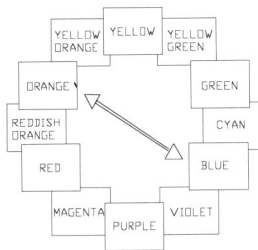

DIRECT COMPLEMENTARY

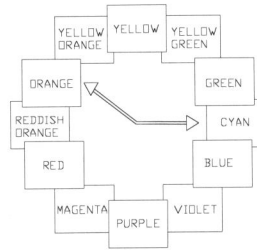

NEAR COMPLEMENTARY

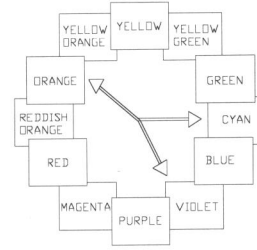

SPLIT COMPLEMENTARY

Basic color schemes, using a red/yellow/blue color wheel.

Well, this is all very fine, but computer colors are based on different color wheel geometry; the computer color wheel is divided into thirds marked by red, green, and blue, instead of red, yellow, and blue. For instance, the direct complement for red is green on an RYB color wheel, but it's cyan on an RGB wheel. Thus, if you're using standard color schemes, pick the colors on a traditional RYB wheel, and then match each color to its RGB-calculated equivalent.

Whether for psychological reasons or because of light wave characteristics, warm color schemes are usually easier to manage than are cool ones. Color schemes based on green are the most difficult. A collection of bright greens can get acidic, and muted green schemes can easily slide into a murky olive-brown Sewer World color scheme.

Color Key   "Color key" refers to the range of intensities used in an image. A full-key image includes intensities that range from white to black.

High, middle, and low keys refer to schemes that limit the overall range of color intensity or luminance. Keys have strong emotional connotations and they affect the quality of reproductions.

Each type has strengths and weaknesses. High-key schemes using light colors can convey an airy, optimistic feeling, but can degenerate into insipid Cotton Candy World renderings. Middle keys play it safe, but tend be bland; the limited contrast eliminates a variety of dramatic effects. Low keys using dark colors can be subtle and disguise a lot, but can tilt over quickly from moody to spooky and depressing. Full key schemes can provide the greatest range and contrast and reproduce well, but can get chaotic.

Balancing Multiple Materials

If your carefully created, color-scheme–obedient materials are still combining into a cluttered scene, the following suggestions may help clean up your rendering. Most are concerned with establishing a dominant object or color and subordinating the rest of the scene.

❏ Lower the saturation of materials that cover large areas, leaving one or two bright colors as highlights in limited areas (Materials Editor, Ambient and Diffuse Saturation sliders).

❏ Subordinate all but one dominant texture by editing color channels (Materials Editor, Texture Map "S" button, RGB Tint button on Mapping Parameters dialog box) or reducing the proportion of bitmaps (Materials Editor, Map Amount sliders).

❏ Adjust lights to highlight selected areas, and keep light levels low in the rest of the scene (3D Editor, Lights commands)

❏ Tone down the shininess of all but one or two materials (Materials Editor, Shininess and Shin. Strength sliders)

❏ Eliminate confusing shadows, or change ambient settings to reduce or increase shadow contrast (3D Editor, Lights commands, or specifying Flat or Gouraud shading limits for individual materials.)

Summary

This chapter concentrated on just the basics of creating and using materials—3D Studio's capabilities are far more extensive and will repay the practice they demand. Start by using the library materials, take a crack at editing them, steal what you can from 3DS scenes and the World Creating Kit, and save the materials you create to build up your own custom libraries.

A Fallingwater
Walkthrough

A walkthrough should simulate, as much as possible, the experience of being in a building—the effect of surfaces, light, and space in relation to human scale. This final chapter concentrates on creating a walkthrough across the bridge and up to Fallingwater's entrance, through the living room, pausing for the hatch to open, and down the stream stairs.

The exercise demonstrates a different method from that used in *3D Studio's Tutorial Guide*. Rather than using a camera and target linked to a dummy object with an assigned path, the exercise gets rid of the dummy and imported path and creates tweened frames between a series of still shots.

Where Are You? What Do You See? What's Moving?

The answers to these questions create the "story line" of your animation.

Where Are You?

Having said in Chapter 6 that animation clarifies building geometry, let us backtrack and qualify that statement. Animation clarifies the building geometry if the viewer can stay oriented in the model's space.

In movies, whenever the location of the action changes, the new sequence often begins with a wide shot of the area surrounding the actors. This establishing shot acquaints viewers with the physical environment of the new scene. When the actors are moving, the camera may track the movement (move along with the actors) or pan from the actors to the space in front of them to indicate the direction in which they're headed. For example, imagine the following movie sequence:

(A) The scene begins with a wide shot of the countryside, with a car traveling along a road.

(B) The camera zooms in to the car, where the hero and heroine are arguing.

(C) The camera view stays in a close-up of the actors as their dialog moves the plot along.

(D) The camera pans away from the actors to show the road ahead, and focuses on a house in the distance.

(E) The camera zooms toward the house at the apparent speed of the car, with voice-over from the actors.

Although the main reason for the scene may be the actors' dialog, most of the camera movement is directed at keeping viewers oriented in space: where the actors are and where they're heading.

The same techniques work for creating animations. (In fact, a basic book about making films or videotapes is helpful for tips on composing and editing animations.) The first frames of the Fallingwater walkthrough show the whole building, orienting the viewer and establishing the subject matter. With the next few frames, the camera moves toward the building on its right side; the changing camera position establishes the direction of travel, along the normal approach to the house.

An early establishing shot from the exercise.

Tip: Be careful, when moving both the camera and target in the same frame. Try moving the target first to establish a new direction, and then moving the camera to resume action, OR move the camera first to start the action, and then move the target to catch up.

Abrupt turns can be confusing in an animation. Whenever the camera/viewer changes direction or level, it's a good idea to insert some type of establishing shot, either a wider view of the area ahead or a pan that signals the direction of travel. The camera follows the natural movement of your eye—it looks where you're going before you start walking. However, using wide shots can conflict with the principle of maintaining a narrow cone of vision to reduce modeling requirements. Try to compromise by limiting the establishing shots to areas that are already modeled.

Tip: If you left out an establishing shot at the beginning of your animation, you can go back and add one with the Slide operation. For instance, to add an 8-frame opening sequence, first pick the Total Frames button and increase the total number of frames by 8. Then pick the Slide button in the camera's Track Info dialog box. Pick the first key in the All track and slide it to the right 8 frames. Then go back and set up a new beginning key for the first 8 frames. You can use the same method wherever the action seems too fast or jerky.

The Background Problem:
What Do You See?

One of the advantages of animated computer graphics is the ability to inspect a building in its proposed setting. However, it is practically impossible to completely replicate an actual environment. So how do you handle the surrounding view? The following approaches move from the quickest to the most time consuming; many animations use a combination of methods to create the background.

Turn Off the Lights   For interior shots, the simplest way to handle the view outside the windows is to make it a night view, the technique used in Chapter 6 for the "spaceship" renderings. However, unless your clients are vampires, this approach gets monotonous.

Nighttime shots also can be used for exteriors; indeed, some of the most spectacular renderings are exterior night scenes. The view angle can be adjusted upward to show little of the foreground or ground plane. Exterior lights and lights shining through windows add the interest and complexity that's lacking from the simplified background.

To add realism to a night scene, you can use a bitmap background (Renderer/Setup/Background) of the night sky, obtained either from a vendor library or by scanning a photo.

Bitmap the Background   Bitmap backgrounds also can be used for daytime scenes. A "generic" bitmap, such as an image of vegetation, hilly terrain, or urban setting that is not taken from the actual building site often works better when only a portion is showing. The more limited the visible area, the more convincing the bitmap. When using a bitmap background, be aware of the apparent distance of the bitmapped image, determined by size and resolution. If the background image seems too close there will be an obvious lack of changing viewpoint as the camera moves. You can control the apparent distance of the bitmap by modeling a semicircular background surface and mapping the image to it instead of simply assigning the image as a background.

Try to match the direction of light in the scene to the light and shadows of the bitmap. (Or try to find a bitmap with lighting that matches your scene lighting.) For instance, the same bitmap of trees was used in the daylighting exercise in Chapter 6 and the materials exercise in Chapter 8. The original photo was taken looking south; the sun was behind the trees and silhouetted them. This unaltered image worked well for the daylighting exercise because the camera view was also toward the south.

However, for the materials exercise the camera view is toward the northeast, requiring a background that shows sun hitting the trees from the front. A paint program was used to increase the luminance and color saturation of the image, creating the more realistic south-facing stand of trees seen in color plate VII.

As a subcategory of using a bitmap background, you can use a photograph of the entire site, matching the camera view of the model to the angle from which the photograph was taken, or vice versa. This will work for a 3D Studio camera that moves straight toward or away from the building or that pans across the front of the building, but not for camera paths that curve around the building—the background will stay the same while the building slides across it.

Use Stylized, Simplified Background Geometry When modeling simplified background geometry, try to match the overall configuration of the terrain's most important features. Keep the level of detail the same throughout, and use fairly low saturation color to make the background unobtrusive. The style of the building itself determines to some extent whether simplified geometry will work. The fussier and more formal the building, the less likely that a simplified background will be convincing.

Simplified background geometry is used for the animation in this chapter. The stream bed and driveway are flat planes. To make the cliff (north of the house), the driveway plane was extruded with Create/Face/Extrude. Then the extruded driveway was subtracted from a large rectangular prism (Create/Box) with Boolean Subtraction. The resulting surface follows the curve of the road to form the face of the cliff. The other surfaces of the box were deleted. Then the "cliff face" was curved back away from the road to match the slope of the original, using the Modify/Object/Bend command, and tessellated.

The slope up from the south side of the stream was created in a similar matter. The streambed plane was extruded into a three-dimensional object, which was then subtracted from a large flattened hemisphere. All of the hemisphere except for the portion along the streambed was then deleted.

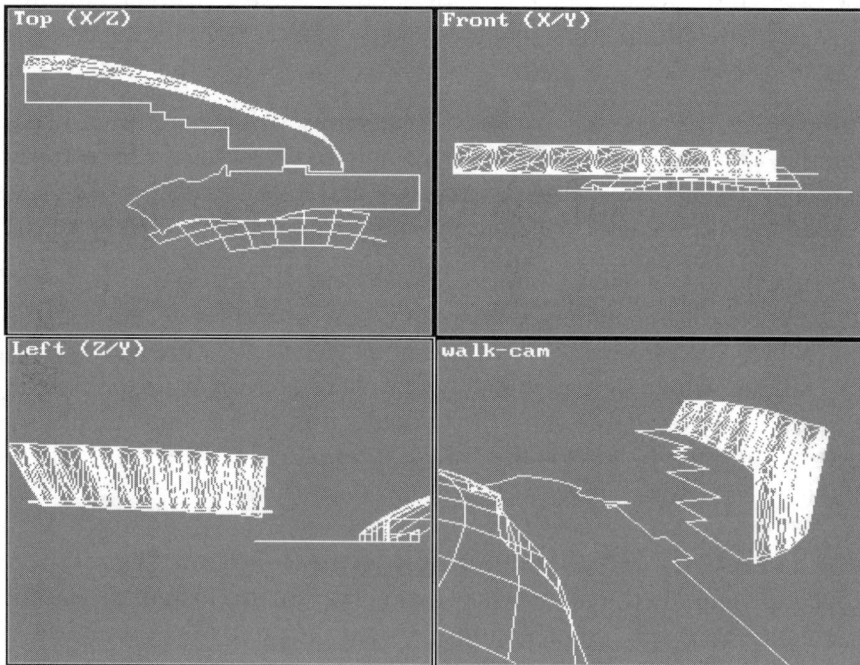

A simplified version of the Fallingwater site.

Once you've modeled the simplified geometry, you can experiment with assigning texture or bump maps to the surfaces. Sometimes the maps increase the realism, but sometimes the contrast between a highly detailed map and the very simple surface to which it's applied emphasizes the fakery. Straight-on views of the mapping tend to work better than views from an acute angle.

Combine a Bitmap "Diorama" with a Modeled Foreground

The ultimate realistic approach combines the bitmapped background and modeled geometry approaches and elaborates on them—sometimes to infinity. In general, start with the largest elements and use mapping instead of modeling whenever possible. For instance, the sequence of operations for Fallingwater would:

❏ Start with a circular "diorama" screen placed around the house at an average distance of about 150 feet. Map it with 360 degrees of photographs of the area, thus taking care of mid- and far distance.

❏ Model a simplified version of the site terrain contours—cliff face to the north, the slope down to the streambed, the rising hill on the south side of the stream. Apply bitmaps of appropriate rock textures, foliage, ground cover, and water to the geometry.

❏ Model the most important "free-standing" site features—the huge boulders at the foundation, the bridge, the rock ledges under the falls. Apply appropriate materials.

❏ Sprinkle a few generic rocks around, and decal-map some trees and bushes to flat transparent planes placed as nearly perpendicular as possible to the principle camera view.

❏ Get really tricky and project a videotaped sequence of the falls onto the streambed geometry, using the Spotlight projector operation, or use an animated bitmap created from a flic file.

❏ Include thick Layered Fog, if all else fails.

Tip: To save rendering time and disk space, you can model entourage objects and then turn the objects into bitmaps to use in the actual scene. First, model the object, then assign it a black background, and render it to disk. Create a plane within the scene and map the file to it as the material. Again, this works better if the camera view is nearly perpendicular to the plane.

What's Moving?

Buildings are, for the most part, static objects. (A roof flying through the air or a structure collapsing are the undesirable exceptions.) Applied to architecture, animation typically simulates the experience of walking around or through the structure. In addition to creating the point of view of a moving visitor, animation possibilities include:

❑ Doors, windows, folding partitions, awnings, and louvers opening.

❑ Elevators and escalators moving.

❑ Light levels changing—either sunlight coming from different angles, as shown in Chapter 6, or lighting fixtures switching on and off.

❑ Entourage (people or cars) moving.

❑ Time lapsing as a building assembles itself.

❑ Cameras flying through the building, as opposed to walking through.

❑ Phantom views showing materials dissolving (Chapter 6).

Creating the Animation

As mentioned earlier, the exercise uses separate paths for the camera and target instead of linking both to a dummy object and assigning the dummy to a path. Unlinking camera, target, path, and dummy allows you to more closely imitate the actual mode of viewing a building and to get more variety in view angle, pans, direction, and speed. The following section describes the complete process of creating the Fallingwater animation. The exercise brings you in at the point of creating the draft animation and editing it.

Plan the Animation

Once again, plan ahead with the following considerations in mind:

❑ **Route.** What do you want to see? Decide on the best views of the building, what has to be shown, and what can be left out. Decide on the shortest, most efficient route that includes everything that you want to show.

❑ **Special features.** An extension of the first consideration: What do you want to slow down and look at, to see from different angles, to show in action? For instance, in the exercise the camera remains stationary while the hatch opens.

❏ **Limitations.** Just as important, what do you want to avoid—perhaps an unfortunate design necessity, or a complicated site, or unmodeled areas? In the exercise, the camera view avoids the unfurnished north end of the living room.

❏ **Main keyframes.** The next step is deciding on the key shots—what they should show, their approximate distance and angle, their sequence, and where establishing shots are needed.

Tip: Unless there's a specific reason not to, keep the camera positioned at eye level. You can establish a consistent eye-level height for the camera by moving the construction plane. Choose Display/Construction/Place and pick an insertion point in the Front or Left viewport about 5 feet above the ground plane. When you create a camera by placing it in the Top viewport, the camera will be placed at the 5-foot height in the Front and Left viewports automatically.

Create the Keyframes

The next step is to create the keyframe shots, just as you would set up the camera and target for a still shot. The program fills in the tween shots to create the draft animation. Accept from the first that you'll have to go back and make changes in camera and target placement and apparent speed once you've seen this first rough version.

Tip: If you're creating an animation that moves from the outside of the building to the inside, once you get inside, turn off the model layers you don't need in order to speed up redraw time.

The animation file you'll import for the exercise was created by setting up an initial camera/target position, advancing the frame slider 4 or 5 frames to the next keyframe and moving the camera and target to the next selected position. The paths (camera and target) are generated automatically from keyframe to keyframe.

Tip: Toggle on Paths/Show-Hide to show the Camera and Target paths being generated as you set up keyframes. An abrupt spike in either path is usually a signal that the movement is too jerky.

The camera and target paths were then adjusted by editing the keyframes with the Paths/Move Key command. Throughout the process, draft frames and draft animation segments were created to check progress. The exercise includes several pages of keyframes created with the flat shaded Preview mode and briefly describes why each keyframe was chosen.

Tip: When creating animations, a lot of your time is spent waiting for the screen to redraw. Often you don't need to see the whole image in each viewport. When a viewport starts redrawing, press the [Esc] key to stop the redraw. The program will start redrawing the next viewport; press [Esc] again to stop the redraw short of a full image, and so on, for each viewport.

Create the Draft Animation

Here's where you will come into the exercise. There are several different methods that you can use to create draft animations at different levels of detail:

❑ **Wireframe:** The quickest, and least informative. Just click on the double right-arrow icon button. The program hasn't yet created and saved the frames—it just redraws the series of tween and keyframe camera views. This method is useful in checking for gross framing and movement problems.

❑ **Flat shaded preview:** Draft animations created with Preview/Make are displayed with no shadows, reflections, or material mapping. All lights are changed to white omni lights. Preview animations provide efficient feedback on the overall level of light, frame composition, and the overall continuity of the animation. Some of the model geometry may disappear from frame to frame when using Preview/Make.

Four drawing modes are available for previews: Faces, Faces + Lines, Lines, and Box. The storyboard sequence in the exercise uses the Faces + Lines mode because of its appealing appearance.

❑ **320 x 200 renderings with a flat shading limit:** Creating an actual rendering at low resolution with flat shading gives you a better idea of actual lighting appearance and renders all model geometry. Surfaces are automatically assigned a white matte material. The following pictures are rendered in this manner. Compare this technique with the same frames in the exercise storyboard.

Frame 0001. Rendering the frames displays cast shadows, which emphasize the recesses of the building geometry.

Frame 0053. The rendering gives you more accurate information than the Preview mode about the luminance of surfaces.

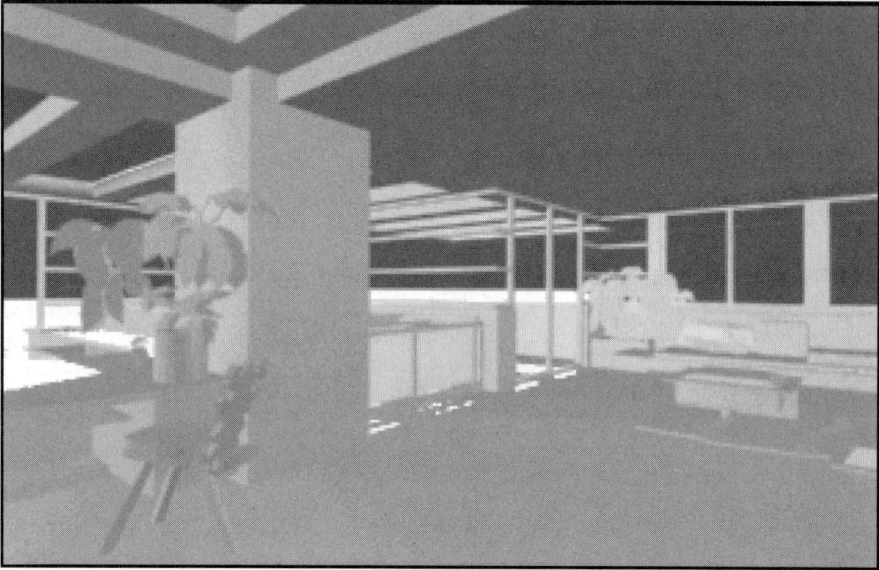

Frame 0086. The rendering includes ceiling geometry that was lost when using the Preview mode.

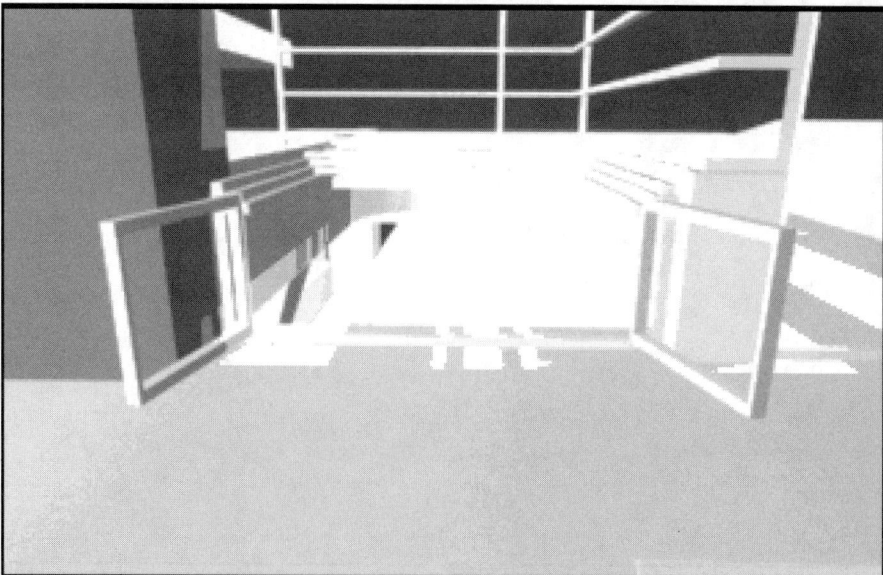

Frame 0101. The rendering gives a more accurate idea of the complex geometry and shadow patterns at the hatch.

❏ **Sample frames rendered at 320 x 200 with materials applied and Phong shading:** Before completely rendering the animation, you should render selected frames to check the appearance of materials and shadows. Rendering a frame of each different area shown in the animation will give you a good idea of the entire sequence. The following illustration is rendered at 320 x 200 with all materials shown. Compare the detail level and lighting with the preceding flat shaded renderings and with the flat shaded preview storyboard.

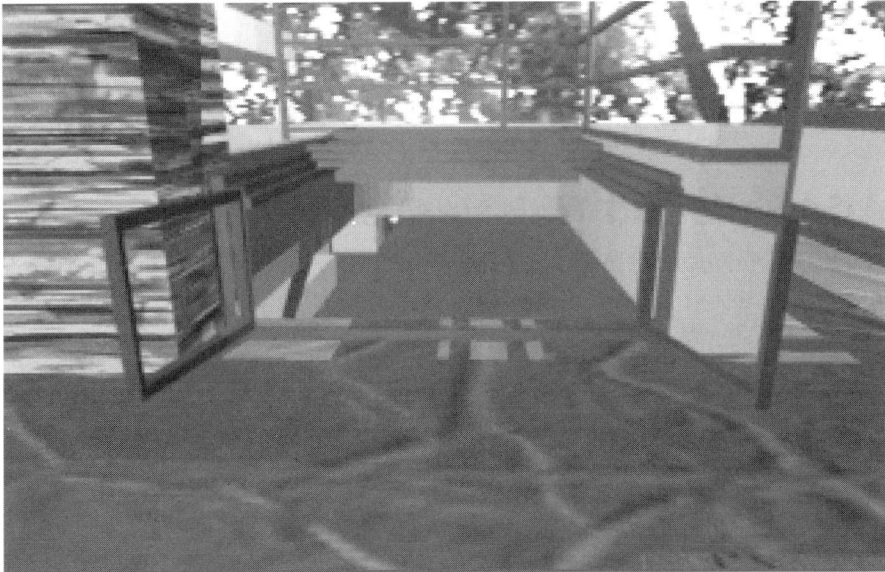

Frame 0101 rendered at 320 x 200 with Phong shading.

Edit the Animation

Once you've viewed a draft animation, you'll have a good idea of what segments need further work. In the Fallingwater animation, the draft animation revealed that transitions were too rapid at the opening view and at the front entrance. More frames were added to slow down and clarify the movement.

Tip: When you're putting together the first-draft animation, leave the camera FOV at the same setting wherever possible. Changing the FOV before viewing the preliminary animation tends to create wild zooms that have to be tracked down later and removed. You can go back and adjust FOV to refine the framing of shots once you've seen the entire sequence.

You want variation in the view, but try to get it with meaningful movement rather than aimless jerking around just to change the view. Any slight wobble in the path is exaggerated in the animation. Be particularly careful when moving up or down stairs. The human body actually bounces up and down at each step, but bouncing the camera for realism is distracting and confusing in the animation. Keep the camera keys on a smooth inclined path.

Tip: If you're panning in one direction and then reversing the pan, hold the end view for two or three frames. Reversing immediately is at best confusing and at worst, makes viewers feel queasy.

Add Bells and Whistles, and Render

Once you have your route polished up, you can go back and add any late inspirations or embellishments and insert furniture. The following illustration shows the south end of the living room with furniture added. The furniture file, FWFURN.3DS, is on the distribution disk.

The south end of the living room, furnished. The profiles for tables, chair, ottomans, sofa, and dishes were drawn in the 2D Shaper and lofted. The cushions and statuette were created from primitives in the 3D Editor.

Exercise 1: Visiting Fallingwater

From the time he encountered the Ho-o-den shrine in 1898 at the Chicago World's Fair, themes based on Japanese architecture recurred throughout Wright's career. He typically used a winding approach path from the edge of a house's grounds up to and through an unobtrusive entry, turning again inside to reach the heart of the house—a concept borrowed from Japanese tradition rather than the Western ideal of a formal, impressive, symmetrical entry sequence (Laseau and Tice, pp. 24–25).

At Fallingwater, a visitor crosses the bridge, turns to pass through the loggia, enters and turns twice again to reach the central space. The contrast achieved by passing through a small, enclosed "tunnel" and emerging into a large open space intensifies the impact of both areas.

In the following script you'll load the model and merge a walkthrough animation that begins on Fallingwater's bridge and ends on the hatch-stair landing. The script includes instructions for creating draft animations and editing the animation.

Load the ASSEMB.3DS Model and Merge an Animation File

The animation file also contains lights, terrain contours, and the Lipchitz.

1. Launch 3D Studio and use File/Load to load the ASSEMB.3DS model. Use Lights/Omni/Delete to delete the existing lights, and the Camera/Delete to delete the camera.

2. Press [F4] to get to the Keyframer and right click Zoom Extents.

3. Choose File/Merge. On the Merge dialog box, make sure all buttons are toggled on and click OK. In the Merge 3DS, DXF, or FLM File dialog box, choose the correct drive button and choose the WALK.PRJ file from the scroll list. Click OK. In the Select Objects To Merge dialog box, click on the All button and OK.

4. Press [Alt] + [L] to toggle off lights, and right click Zoom Extents. Click on the Segment bar (below the Hold and Fetch buttons in the icon panel). In the Define Active Segment dialog box type **0** in the Start Text box, and **130** in the End Text box. Press OK.

Result: The first frame of the animation locates the camera on the bridge, with the target positioned for an establishing shot of the house from the southeast.

Display the Paths and Play the Animation in Wireframe

In this section, you'll check the camera movement along its path and view the draft animation in wireframe mode.

1. Choose Paths/Show-Hide. (This command is a toggle operation that shows the paths if they're hidden or hides them if they're visible.) In the Top viewport, click on the camera.

2. Click on the lower right viewport and press [C] to change to a Camera viewport. Right click Zoom Extents. The screen displays the camera path, with the lower right viewport showing the view at Frame 0000 of the animation.

3. To see the camera move along the path, click in the Top viewport and then click on the Play icon button (the double right-pointing arrows). When you're ready, press [Esc] to stop the playback.

4. To see the animation, click in the Camera viewport and click the Play icon button. The current viewport switches to Full Screen to play the wireframe animation. When you're ready, press [Esc] to stop the playback.

Result: The draft animation is displayed in a series of wireframe redraws, the quickest way to check for bad shot framing or other gross composition problems.

Create Test Frames and a Preview Animation

In this section, you'll move up to the next level of display and create flat shaded preview animations of a single frame, a segment of the animation, and the full animation.

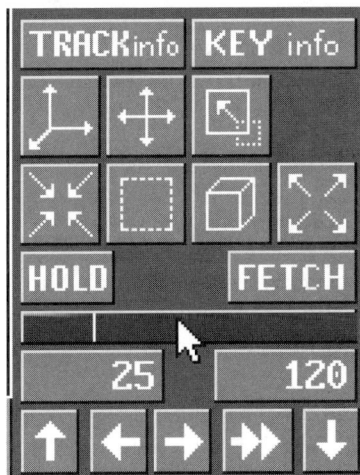

The Keyframer icon panel. The cursor is pointing at the Segment bar, just above the Current Frame Field and Total Frames Field buttons.

1. Click on the Current Frame Field button (left button in the second row up from the bottom) in the icon panel. The Go To Frame dialog box will appear. Type **10** in the text box for the frame number.

2. Choose Preview/Make and click on the Camera viewport. The Make Preview dialog box will appear. Click on the Faces + Lines button in the Draw group. Click on Yes in the Numbers group. Click on Yes in the Two-Sided group. Click on the Single button in the Frames group and check that Size is set to the default 320 x 200. Click on the Preview button.

3. In a few seconds the Preview rendering of the frame will appear. Press [Esc] to return to the interface. (Preview renderings can be screen captured with Pizazz Plus® or other screen capture utilities and printed to create a storyboard of the animation sequence.)

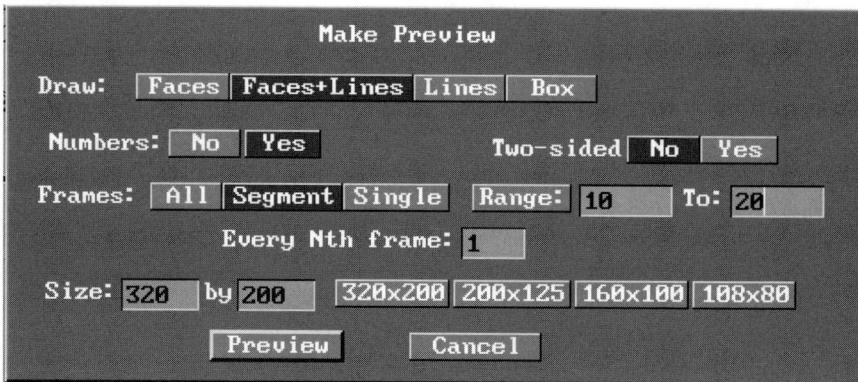

The Make Preview dialog box.

4. To refine a portion of the animation without creating a preview of the whole sequence, you can define an active segment and limit the preview to that range of frames.

5. Click on the Segment bar in the icon panel. The Define Active Segment dialog box appears. Type **10** in the Start text box and **20** in the End text box. Pick the OK button.

6. Choose Preview/Make and click in the Camera viewport. When the Make Preview dialog box appears, click on the Segment button in the Frames group and click on the Preview button. Shortly, the animation of frames 10 through 20 will appear.

7. Next you'll make an animation of the entire sequence. First, click on the Segment bar. When the Define Active Segment dialog box appears, click on the All button to clear the previous segment setting. Click on OK.

8. Choose Preview/Make. When the Make Preview dialog box appears, click on the All button in the Frames group and click on OK.

Result: In a few minutes the preview animation will appear on screen. On the keyboard press the left arrow key until the animation plays back at a reasonable speed. Try using the other keys to control movement: The down arrow pauses and resumes the animation. The right arrow speeds up the animation or advances it one frame if it's paused. The up arrow defaults to a 20-frames-per-second speed. You can also use the Preview/Set Speed command to control speed.

The animation simulates the way that a visitor might tour one of the many interesting routes through the house. The camera and target positions were arranged to include several panning shots woven into the general movement from the bridge to the stream stairs. The following illustrations, created with Preview/Make using Faces + Lines mode, show selected keyframes.

Frame 0001. An establishing shot from the southeast with the target centered on the house. Enough of the south bank of the stream is visible to indicate the width of the streambed.

Frame 0012. The target has been placed on the Lipchitz, and the camera is beginning to move across the bridge.

Frame 0022. The camera and target are lined up directly to the east of the house. As the camera moves around the house, action slows down to keep the viewer oriented.

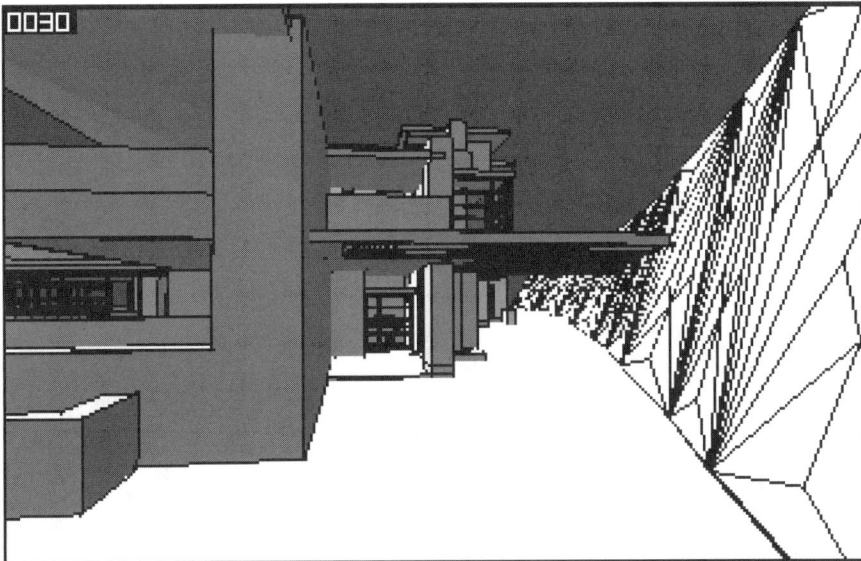

Frame 0030. The camera and target swing out to make a wider turn than is necessary to head directly for the door. The position gives a better view of the driveway and upper levels of the house.

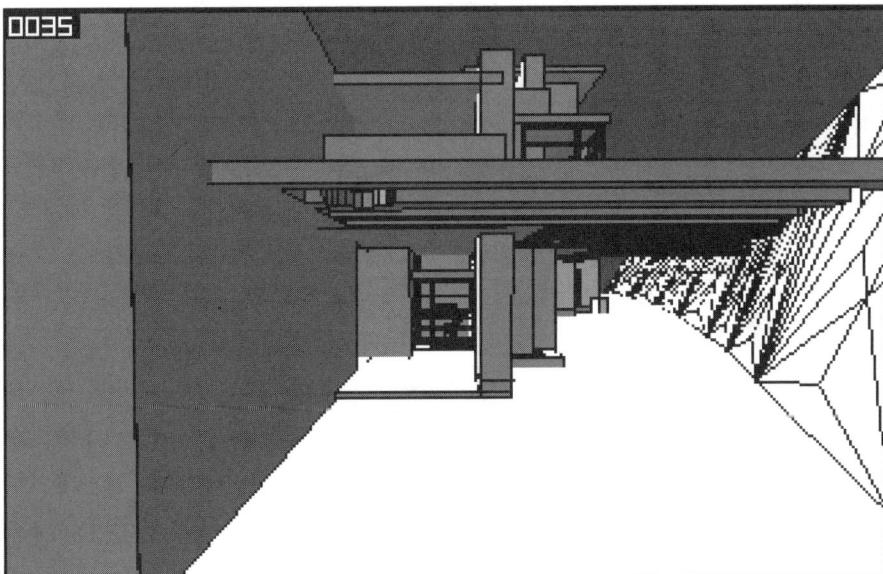

Frame 0035. The target is now centered on the door, and the camera is moving toward the loggia.

Frame 0043. The camera continues to move toward the door. The sense of motion is intensified by the masonry wall sections rushing toward the camera.

Frame 0050. The door begins to open.

Frame 0053. Moving into the entry with its chair, lamp, and reception desk. The stepped shape to the right of the entry is the stairway to the second floor.

Frame 0054. The camera begins panning to the left to show the living room before entering. The wall between the entry and living room blocks the view of the unfurnished part of the room.

Frame 0061. Moving across the living room toward the south end. Surfaces of the ceiling geometry are missing. It happens regularly with the Preview mode; don't panic.

Frame 0081. The camera is still moving in the same direction. The target is moving left toward the hatch.

Frame 0087. The target is at the hatch, and the hatch doors are beginning to open. Note the plant on the desk at the left. It is a collection of planar shapes. The plant was rotated between frames 0081 and 0087 to avoid an edge-on view.

Frame 0094. The hatch doors are fully open. The camera and target remain stationary as the top of the hatch slides back.

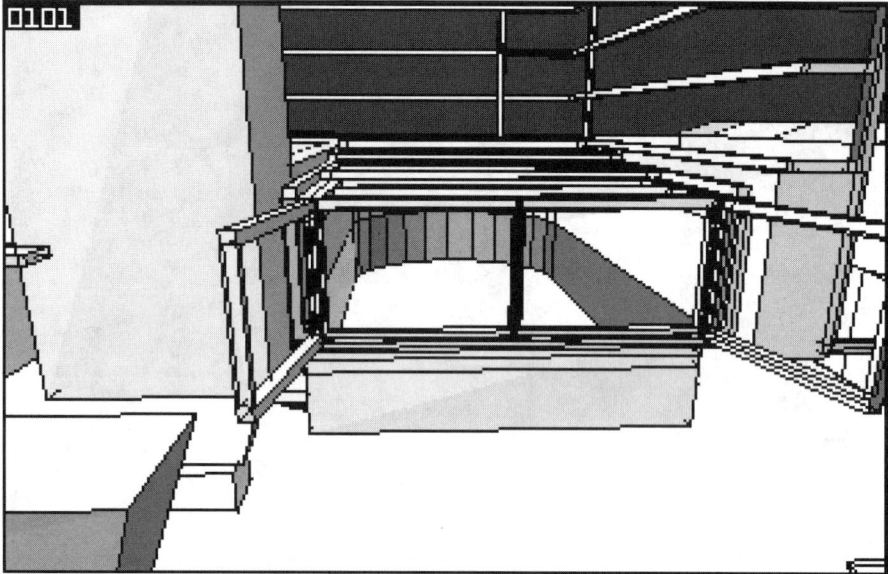

Frame 0101. Moving toward the hatch to start descending the stream stairs.

Frame 0120. Halfway down the stairs, the target moves to the Lipchitz.

Frame 0125. Standing on the stair landing looking toward the plunge pool.

Animate the Front Door

In the preview, you crashed right through Fallingwater's glass-paneled front door. In this section, you'll use the Rotate command to open the door politely before entering.

1. Click on the Current Frame Field button and type **54** in the Go To Frame dialog box. (This is the frame for the door completely opened.)

2. Click on the Top viewport and zoom in on the front door.

3. Choose Hierarchy/Object Pivot. Press the [H] key and pick FRONT-DOOR from the scroll list and click on OK. Everything on the screen will disappear except the door.

4. In the Top viewport, use the mouse to place the cross-hairs on the upper left corner of the door where the hinge would be.

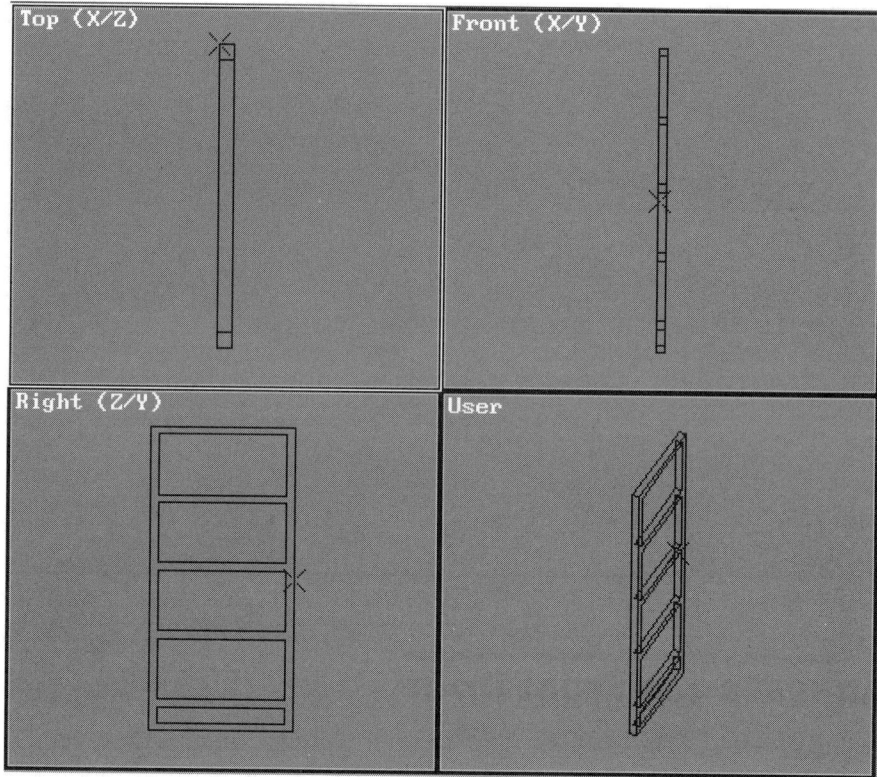

The cleaned-up screen, zoomed in on the front door, with the pivot mark positioned correctly.

5.   Press [A] to toggle on Angle Snap. Choose Object/Rotate and pick the door. Press the [Tab] key twice to specify the Y-axis. Move the mouse to rotate the door 90 degrees so that it is fully opened.

6.   To confine the door rotation to six frames, first click on the Track Info button and then click on the door.

7.   In the Track Info dialog box, click on the Move button. Click on the key in the first frame of the Rotation track and use the mouse to drag it to Frame 48 and click again. Click on the OK button. Moving the first frame key to frame 48 brackets the rotation between frames 48 and 54.

8. To test the door swing animation, first click on the Segment bar. In the Define Active Segment dialog box, type **45** for the Start frame and **55** for the End frame and click the Preview button.

9. Choose Preview/Make and click in the Camera viewport. In the Make Preview dialog box, click on Segment in the Frames group and click OK.

Result: In a minute, a 10-frame preview will appear, showing the door opening.

Render the Animation

Rendering the entire 130-frame animation, even at 320 x 200, can take from 3 to 12 hours, depending on your system. Therefore, this section includes directions for rendering a single frame and for rendering the entire animation. (See color plate X from the finished animation.)

You can render the images with either a blue background or the bitmap of trees and sky used in previous exercises. First, choose Renderer/Setup/Background.

❑ To use a blue background, pick the Solid Color button in the Background Method dialog box and then pick the color swatch. Use the color sliders in the Define Solid Color dialog box to define a sky-blue color and pick OK twice.

❑ To use the bitmap background, pick the button to the right of the Bitmap button in the Background Method dialog box. A file selector will appear. Pick the correct drive button for your floppy drive and pick the *.GIF wildcard button. Select SKY1.GIF from the scroll list.

To add furniture to your rendering, choose File/Merge. In the Merge dialog box, toggle off all but the Mesh Objects button. In the Merge .3DS, .DXF, or .FLM File dialog box, select the correct drive button for your floppy drive and pick FWFURN.3DS from the scroll list. In the Select Objects To Merge dialog box, pick the All button.

Warning: Currently, a merged file does not always retain Box mapping. You may need to re-map the tables and desk once you've merged the furniture file. Use the Box mapping method described in Chapter 8 to reassign WOOD-MED. ASH to the tables, ottomans, and desk.

1. To render a single frame of the animation, pick the Current Frame Field button in the icon panel and type the number of the frame you want. Choose Renderer/Setup/Configure and specify 320 x 200 resolution.

2. Choose Renderer/Render View and click on the Camera viewport. In the Render Animation dialog box, set the Shading Limit to Phong and pick the Single button in the Frames group. Verify that Shadows is set to On and that Background is set to Tile if you're using the bitmap background. Click on the Disk button in the Output group if you wish to save the rendering to disk. Click the Render button.

3. To render the entire animation, click on the Segment bar in the icon panel. In the Define Active Segment dialog box, click the All button and click OK.

4. Choose Renderer/Render View and click on the Camera viewport. In the Render Animation dialog box, click on the All button in the Frame group. (You can render every other frame of the entire animation by clicking the Every Nth Frame button and typing 2.) Click on the Render button.

Result: As Wright once said (when confronted with a complete refutation of a statement he'd just made),

"Well, there you are!" (Gill, pp. 24–25).

Summary

3D Studio is a deep and complex program, but the reward for mastering it is the ability to create and animate an almost limitless range of images. We hope this book has given you a grasp of the basics and the ability to create useful renderings—a platform from which to expand your skills.

Appendix A
3D Studio
Pull-Down and
Screen Menu Maps

The following pages provide diagrams of the 3D Studio menu structure.
If you are a new program user, you may wish to copy the pages and tape
them up somewhere until you learn your way around.

The Pull-Down Menus

Each of the program modules except the Materials Editor displays menu bar entries for Info, File, Views, Program, and Network pull-down menus. The same items are listed regardless of which module is active. Items may be disabled and shown in black type, depending on which operations have been performed and which module is active. If a command has a keyboard alternate, it is shown to the right of the command listing.

INFO	FILE	VIEWS	PROGRAM	NETWORK
About 3D Studio... !	New N	Redraw '	2D Shaper F1	Slave
Current Status ?	Reset	Redraw All ~	3D Lofter F2	------
Configure *	Load ^L	-----------------	3D Editor F3	Configure
System Options	Merge ^M	Viewports ~V	Keyframer F4	Edit Queue
Scene Info	Replace Mesh ^R	Drawing Aids ~A	Materials F5	
Key Assignments	Save ^S	Grid Extents E	DOS Window F10	
Gamma Control	Save Selected	Unit Setup ~U	Text Editor F11	
		-----------------	PXP Loader F12	
	Load Project ~J	Use Snap S		
	Save Project ~P	Use Grid G		
	Merge Project ~G	Fastview V		
	Archive	Disable D		
	----------------	Scroll Lock I		
	File Info	Safe Frame @E		
	Rename	See Backgrnd @G		
	Delete ~D	Adj Backgrnd		
	----------------	-----------------		
	Quit Q	Vertex Snap @V		

		Save Current [		
		Restore Saved }		
		Angle Snap A		

The Materials Editor

The Materials Editor screen differs from the other modules. The Info and Program pull-downs are the same, but the File, Views, and Network pull-downs have been replaced by menus for Library, Material, and Options, shown in the next illustration.

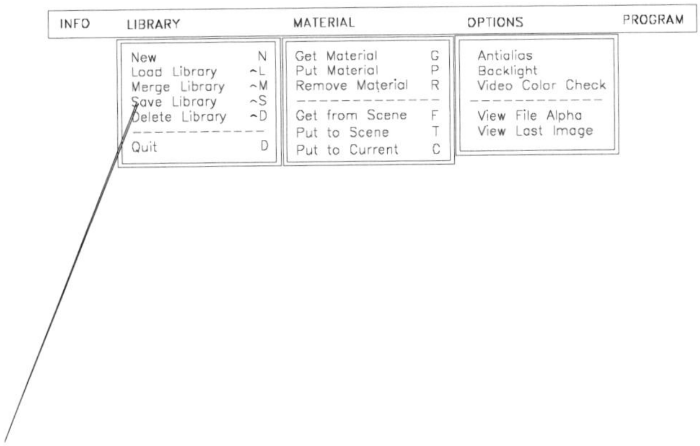

The Screen Menus

The following pages show the screen menus for the 2D Shaper, 3D Lofter, 3D Editor (shown on two pages), and Keyframer. Menu branches that include a default command show the default in **boldface** type, preceded by an asterisk. Commands that call up a dialog box are indicated by a boldface **D** to the right of the command.

The 2D Shaper Screen Menu

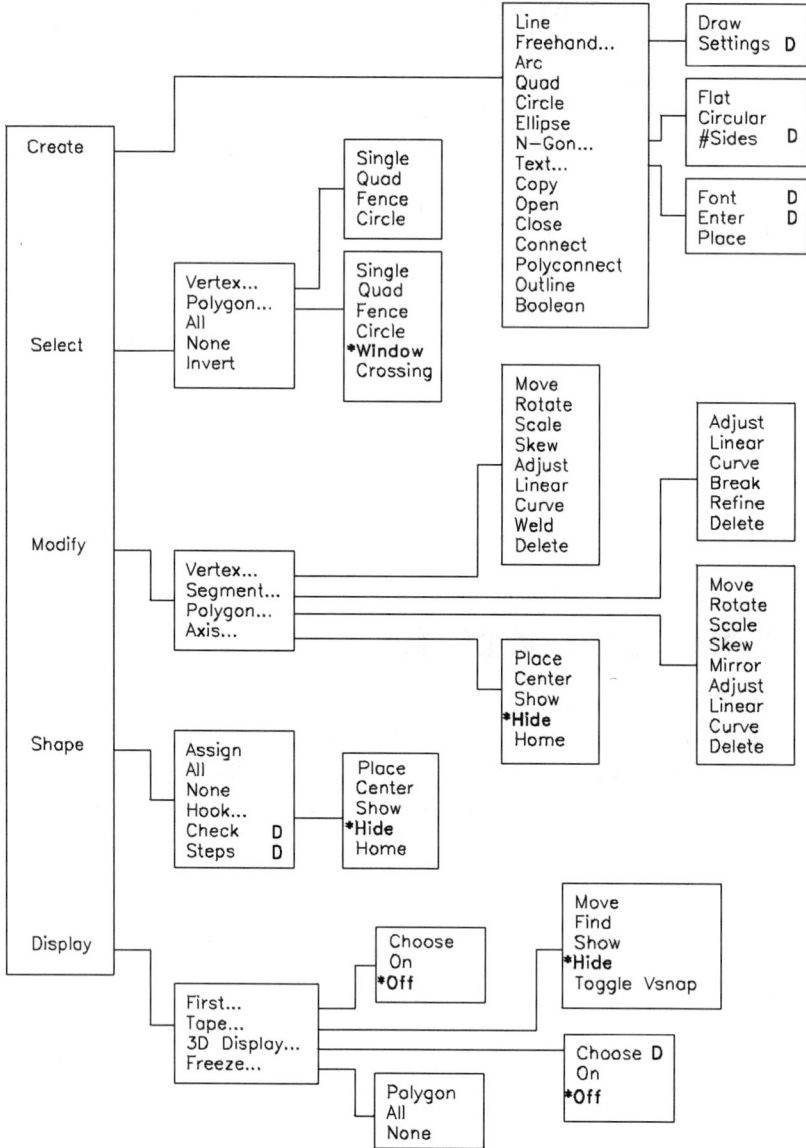

```
Create ─────────────┐                    Line        ┌── Draw
                     │                    Freehand...  │   Settings  D
                     │                    Arc          │
                     │                    Quad          │── Flat
                     │                    Circle         │   Circular
                     │                    Ellipse        │   #Sides   D
                     ├── Single           N-Gon...       │
                     │   Quad             Text...        │── Font      D
                     │   Fence            Copy            │   Enter     D
                     │   Circle           Open            │   Place
                     │                    Close
        Vertex...    ├── Single           Connect
        Polygon...   │   Quad             Polyconnect
Select  All          │   Fence            Outline
        None         │   Circle           Boolean
        Invert       │  *Window
                     │   Crossing

                                         Move              ┌── Adjust
                                         Rotate            │   Linear
                                         Scale             │   Curve
                                         Skew              │   Break
                                         Adjust            │   Refine
                                         Linear            │   Delete
                                         Curve
Modify                                   Weld
                                         Delete            ── Move
        Vertex...                                             Rotate
        Segment...                                            Scale
        Polygon...                                            Skew
        Axis...                          Place               Mirror
                                         Center              Adjust
                                         Show                Linear
                                        *Hide                Curve
                                         Home                Delete
Shape   Assign
        All                              Place
        None            Place            Center
        Hook...         Center           Show
        Check   D       Show            *Hide
        Steps   D      *Hide             Home
                        Home

                                         Move
                        Choose           Find
Display                 On               Show
                       *Off             *Hide
                                         Toggle  Vsnap
        First...
        Tape...                          Choose D
        3D Display...                    On
        Freeze...                       *Off
                        Polygon
                        All
                        None
```

The 3D Lofter Screen Menu

Shapes — Get... / Put... / Pick / Move / Rotate / Scale / Compare / Center / Align... / Delete / Steps D

Shaper / Disk D / Level

Shaper / Disk D / Level

Left / Right

Path — Get... / Put / Move Vertex / Move Path / Insert Vertex / 2D Scale / 3D Scale / Skew / Mirror / Refine / SurfRev D / Helix D / Rotate / Default Angle / Straighten / Default Path / Open / Delete Vertex / Steps D

Shaper / Disk D

Move / Insert / Refine / Delete / Limits D / Reset / Swap / Symmetry...

*On / Off

Move / Insert / Refine / Delete / Limits D / Reset

Deform — Scale... / Twist... / Teeter... / Bevel... / Fit... / Preview D

Move / Insert / Refine / Delete / Limits D / Reset / Swap / Symmetry...

*On / Off

Move / Insert / Refine / Delete / Limits D / Reset

Get... / Put / Refine / Reset / Swap / Symmetry... / Gen Path

Shaper / Disk D

On / Off

3D Display — Choose D / On / *Off / Constr... / Tape... / Speed...

Place / Show / *Hide / Home

Fastdraw / *Fulldraw / Set Fast D

Move / Find / Show / *Hide / Toggle Vsnap

Objects — Make D / Preview D

The 3D Editor Screen Menu, I

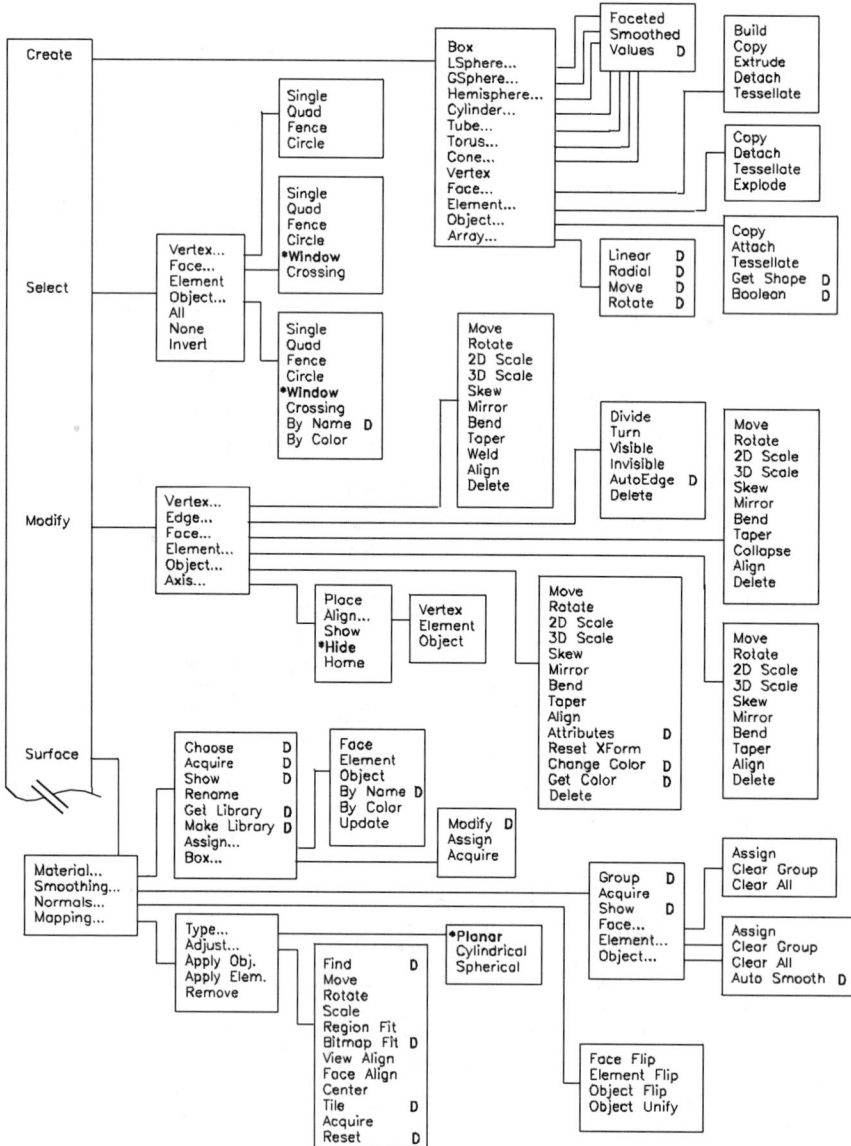

The 3D Editor Screen Menu, II

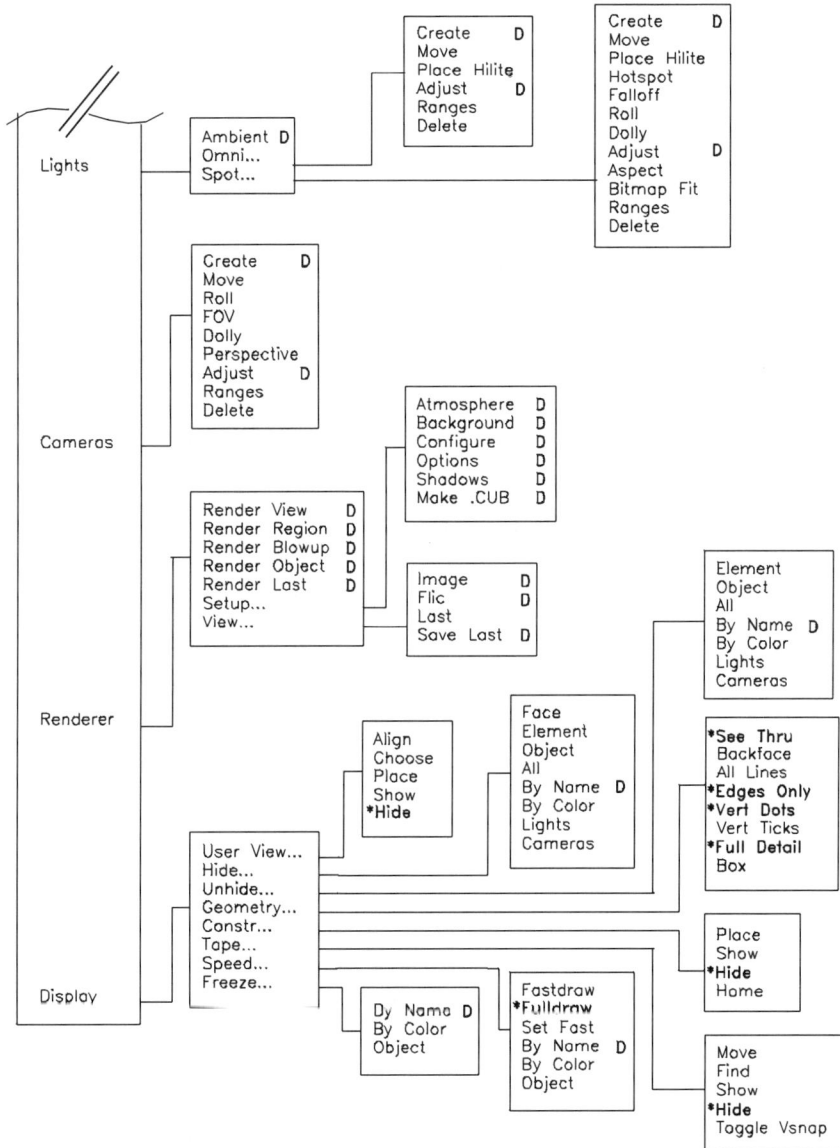

```
Lights ──┬── Ambient D
         ├── Omni...
         └── Spot...
```

Ambient / Omni menu:
```
Create       D
Move
Place Hilite
Adjust       D
Ranges
Delete
```

Spot menu:
```
Create       D
Move
Place Hilite
Hotspot
Falloff
Roll
Dolly
Adjust       D
Aspect
Bitmap Fit
Ranges
Delete
```

```
Cameras ──
```

Cameras menu:
```
Create       D
Move
Roll
FOV
Dolly
Perspective
Adjust       D
Ranges
Delete
```

```
Renderer ──
```

Renderer menu:
```
Render View    D
Render Region  D
Render Blowup  D
Render Object  D
Render Last    D
Setup...
View...
```

Setup submenu:
```
Atmosphere   D
Background   D
Configure    D
Options      D
Shadows      D
Make .CUB    D
```

View submenu:
```
Image      D
Flic       D
Last       D
Save Last  D
```

```
Display ──
```

Display menu:
```
User View...
Hide...
Unhide...
Geometry...
Constr...
Tape...
Speed...
Freeze...
```

Hide/Unhide submenu:
```
Element
Object
All
By Name D
By Color
Lights
Cameras
```

Geometry submenu:
```
*See Thru
Backface
All Lines
*Edges Only
*Vert Dots
Vert Ticks
*Full Detail
Box
```

Constr / Align submenu:
```
Align
Choose
Place
Show
*Hide
```

```
Face
Element
Object
All
By Name D
By Color
Lights
Cameras
```

Tape submenu:
```
Place
Show
*Hide
Home
```

Freeze submenu:
```
By Name D
By Color
Object
```

Speed submenu:
```
Fastdraw
*Fulldraw
Set Fast
By Name D
By Color
Object
```

```
Move
Find
Show
*Hide
Toggle Vsnap
```

The Keyframer Screen Menu

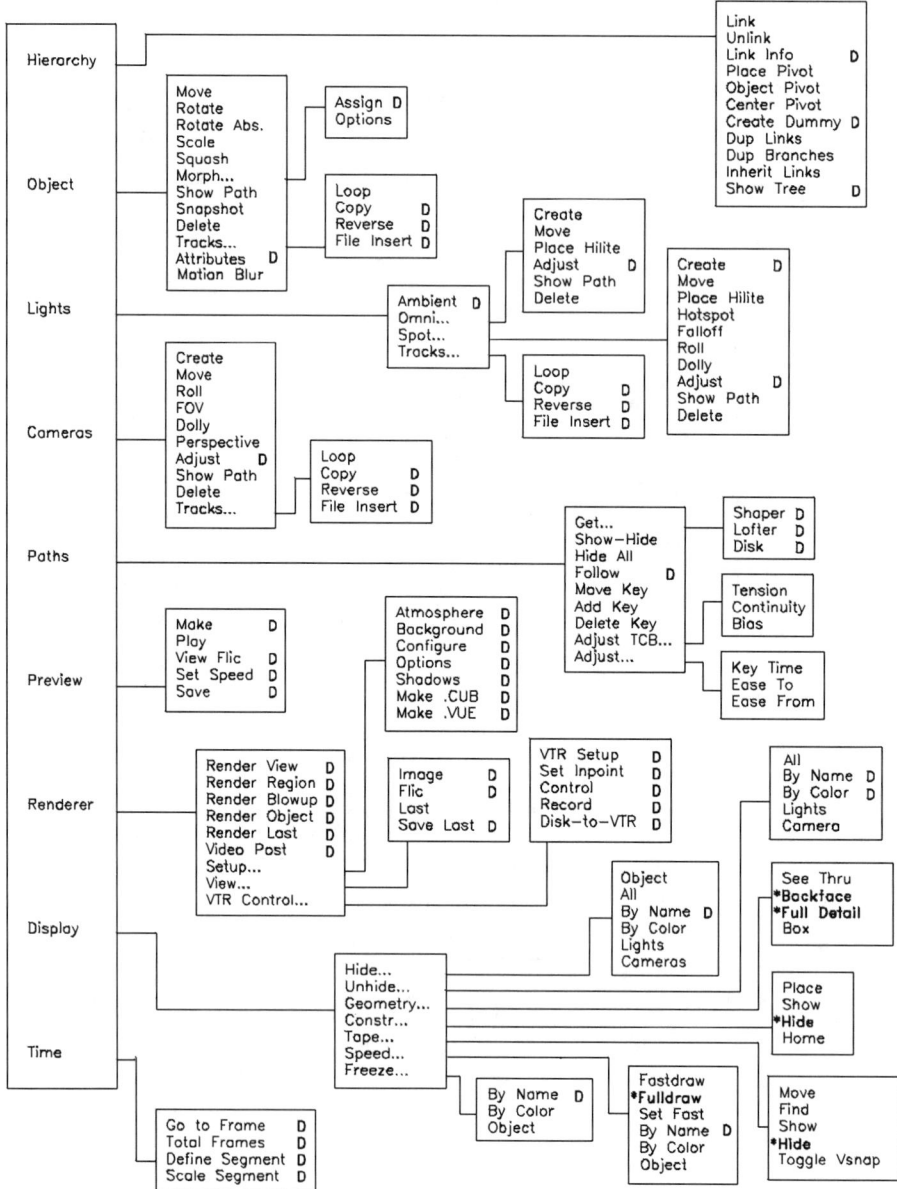

Hierarchy
- Link
- Unlink
- Link Info   D
- Place Pivot
- Object Pivot
- Center Pivot
- Create Dummy   D
- Dup Links
- Dup Branches
- Inherit Links
- Show Tree   D

Object
- Move
- Rotate
- Rotate Abs.
- Scale
- Squash
- Morph...
- Show Path
- Snapshot
- Delete
- Tracks...
- Attributes   D
- Motion Blur

  - Assign   D
  - Options

  - Loop
  - Copy   D
  - Reverse   D
  - File Insert D

Lights
- Ambient   D
- Omni...
- Spot...
- Tracks...

  - Create
  - Move
  - Place Hilite
  - Adjust   D
  - Show Path
  - Delete

  - Loop
  - Copy   D
  - Reverse   D
  - File Insert D

  - Create   D
  - Move
  - Place Hilite
  - Hotspot
  - Falloff
  - Roll
  - Dolly
  - Adjust   D
  - Show Path
  - Delete

Cameras
- Create
- Move
- Roll
- FOV
- Dolly
- Perspective
- Adjust   D
- Show Path
- Delete
- Tracks...

  - Loop
  - Copy   D
  - Reverse   D
  - File Insert D

Paths
- Get...
- Show–Hide
- Hide All
- Follow   D
- Move Key
- Add Key
- Delete Key
- Adjust TCB...
- Adjust...

  - Shaper   D
  - Lofter   D
  - Disk   D

  - Tension
  - Continuity
  - Bias

  - Key Time
  - Ease To
  - Ease From

Preview
- Make   D
- Play
- View Flic   D
- Set Speed   D
- Save   D

  - Atmosphere   D
  - Background   D
  - Configure   D
  - Options   D
  - Shadows   D
  - Make .CUB   D
  - Make .VUE   D

Renderer
- Render View   D
- Render Region   D
- Render Blowup D
- Render Object   D
- Render Last   D
- Video Post   D
- Setup...
- View...
- VTR Control...

  - Image   D
  - Flic   D
  - Last
  - Save Last   D

  - VTR Setup   D
  - Set Inpoint   D
  - Control   D
  - Record   D
  - Disk–to–VTR D

  - All
  - By Name   D
  - By Color   D
  - Lights
  - Camera

Display
- Object
- All
- By Name   D
- By Color
- Lights
- Cameras

  - See Thru
  - *Backface
  - *Full Detail
  - Box

- Hide...
- Unhide...
- Geometry...
- Constr...
- Tape...
- Speed...
- Freeze...

  - Place
  - Show
  - *Hide
  - Home

  - By Name   D
  - By Color
  - Object

  - Fastdraw
  - *Fulldraw
  - Set Fast
  - By Name   D
  - By Color
  - Object

  - Move
  - Find
  - Show
  - *Hide
  - Toggle Vsnap

Time
- Go to Frame   D
- Total Frames   D
- Define Segment D
- Scale Segment   D

Appendix B
3D Studio
Materials

3D Studio ships with three materials libraries: 3DS.MLI, ACADCLR.MLI, and TUTORIAL.MLI. The ACADCLR.MLI library contains 256 nonmapped colors with numerical names. The 3D Studio Tutorial library contains 19 materials, most of which are variants of the 3DS library materials.

The 3DS library contains more than 150 materials listed alphabetically in the Materials Selector dialog boxes. The dialog box display is handy for selecting a material if you already know its name, but not too helpful for choosing materials by type. The following tables list the materials separated by type of mapping.

NonMapped Materials		
Material Name	**Diffuse RGB**	**Shin./Shin. Str./Trans.**
Aqua Glaze	0-59-56	80/95/0
Beige Matt 2s	129-92-58	0/0/0
Beige Matte	129-92-58	0/0/0
Beige Plastic	129-92-58	31/47/0
Black Matte	0-0-0	9/14/0
Black Plastic	0-0-0	69/88/0
Blue Glass	7-13-118	52/73/67
Blue Matte	0-0-97	0/0/0
Blue Metalic	0-0-5	25/38/0
Blue Plastic	0-0-63	43/63/0
Blue Plastic 27	0-0-63	27/41/0
Blue Plastic 50	0-0-63	50/71/0
Blue Plastic 77	0-0-63	77/94/0
Blue/Green/Cyan	0-255-241	63/84/0
Bright Olive	21-45-14	20/31/0
Brown Matte	50-2-0	0/0/0
Copper	16-3-1	28/43/0

NonMapped Materials		
Material Name	**Diffuse RGB**	**Shin./Shin. Str./Trans.**
Cream Plastic	104-110-20	50/71/0
Cyan Matte	0-93-93	0/0/0
Cyan Metalic	0-2-6	23/35/0
Dark Brown Matte	5-0-0	0/0/0
Dark Gray Luster	0-0-0	21/32/0
Dark Gray Matte	1-1-1	0/0/0
Dark Olive Matte	2-3-0	0/0/0
Glass	14-14-14	46/66/93
Gold	37-13-1	23/35/0
Gray Matte	67-67-67	0/0/0
Gray Semigloss	67-67-67	18/28/0
Gray/blue Paint	27-46-75	11/17/0
Green Glass	13-116-7	52/73/80
Green Matte	1-6-0	0/0/0
Green Neon	0-255-0	43/63/0
Green Plastic	3-125-5	69/88/0
Maroon Pearl	28-6-17	34/51/0
Metal Cherry Red	39-0-0	34/51/0
Olive Drab	4-9-2	10/16/0
Olive Metal	7-10-1	25/38/0
Orange Matte	255-40-0	0/0/0

NonMapped Materials		
Material Name	**Diffuse RGB**	**Shin./Shin. Str./Trans.**
Orange Plastic	140-35-0	60/81/0
Pink Plastic	210-55-55	52/73/0
Purple Metal	1-0-2	33/50/0
Purple Plastic	35-0-104	69/88/0
Red Faceted	134-0-0	34/51/0
Red Glass	92-2-2	52/73/67
Red Gouraud	134-0-0	37/55/0
Red Matte	134-0-0	0/0/0
Red Neon	255-0-0	52/73/0
Red Plastic	140-0-0	52/73/0
Violet Plastic	122-0-122	52/73/0
White Glass	113-110-113	52/73/67
White Glass Flat	113-110-113	0/73/80
White Matte	255-255-255	0/0/0
White Neon	125-183-255	52/73/0
White Plastic	129-129-129	52/73/0
White Plastic 2S	63-63-63	69/88/0
Yellow Glass	113-110-6	52/73/67
Yellow Plastic	122-82-1	61/82/0

Wireframe Materials		
Material Name	**Diffuse RGB**	**Shin./Shin. Str./Trans.**
Blue Wireframe	0-0-183	0/0/0
Gold Wireframe	45-18-0	0/0/0
Green Wireframe	0-102-1	0/0/0
Red Glass Wireframe	186-0-0	0/0/0
Red Wireframe	186-0-0	0/0/0
White Wireframe	255-255-255	0/0/0

Materials With Texture Maps Only			
Material Name	Map File	Map Amount	Shin./Shin Str./Trans.
3D Cel Texmap	3d.cel	100	0/0/0
4 Way Bar Pattern	pat0150.tga	100	17/16/0
Amoeba Pattern	pat0107.tga	100	17/16/0
Ape	ape.cel	100	57/58/0
Beige Pattern	pat0111.tga	100	17/26/0
Blue Marble	graymarb.gif	55	34/51/0
Blue Planet	blplanet.cel	66	0/0/0
Bluestripe Pattern	pat0084.tga	100	17/26/0
Brown Brick	brnbrick.cel	100	31/47/0
Brown Brick 2S	brnbrick.cel (2)	100	0/0/0
Camouflage	camoflag.cel	75	17/26/0
Checker Texture	checkers.cel	100	0/0/0
Clover Pattern	pat0007.tga	100	17/26/0
Color-x Pattern	pat0149.tga	100	17/26/0
Concrete Tile	conctile.cel	100	0/0/0
Crosshatch Patrn	pat0094.tga	100	17/26/0
Cruiser	cruiser.gif	100	0/0/0
Dark Wood Inlay	idkwood.cel	100	17/26/0
Eyeball Pattern	pat0148.tga	100	17/26/0
Gray Marble	graymarb.gif	100	34/51/0

Materials With Texture Maps Only			
Material Name	**Map File**	**Map Amount**	**Shin./Shin Str./Trans.**
Jupiter Texmap	jupiter.gif	100	23/35/0
Marble – Green	marbteal.gif	100	87/98/0
Marble – Pale	marbpale.gif	100	43/63/0
Marble – Tan	benediti.gif	100	77/94/0
Mosaic Pattern	pat0019.tga	100	17/26/0
Mottled Plastic	gravel1.cel	44	28/43/0
Palm Frond	palmfrnd.cel	100	0/0/0
Pat0003	pat0003.cel	100	0/0/0
Pink Grid Pattern	pat0153.tga	100	17/26/0
Pink Marble	pinkmarb.cel	100	0/0/0
Polkadot Pattern	pat0106.tga	100	17/26/0
Red Tile Pattern	pat0039.tga	100	17/26/0
Sand Texture	sand.cel	100	0/0/0
Semicircle Pattern	pat0027.tga	100	17/26/0
Southwest Pattern	pat0003.tga	100	17/26/0
Square Dot Pattern	pat0134.tga	100	17/26/0
Stitched Pattern	pat0127.tga	100	17/26/0
Stone Tan	stonetan.gif	100	0/0/0
Tan Tile Pattern	pat0110.tga	100	17/26/0

Materials With Texture Maps Only

Material Name	Map File	Map Amount	Shin./Shin Str./Trans.
Tile Goldgranite	tile0016.tga	100	32/48/0
Tile Graygranite	tile0020.tga	100	32/48/0
Tile Pinkgranite	tile0003.tga	100	32/40/0
Tile Tan Granite	tile0009.tga	100	32/48/0
Tile White	tile0011.tga	100	32/48/0
V Pattern	pat0006.tga	100	17/26/0
Wood – Dark Ash	ashsen.gif	53	23/35/0
Wood – Dark Red	bubinga.gif	100	23/35/0
Wood – Med. Ash	ashsen.gif	100	15/23/0
Wood – Teak	teak.gif	100	17/26/0
Wood – White Ash	whiteash.gif	100	18/28/0
Wood Inlay – A	inlay4.tga	100	22/34/0
Wood Inlay – B	inlay3.tga	100	17/26/0
Y-Grid Pattern	pat0158.tga	100	17/26/0
Zigzag Pattern	pat0035.tga	100	17/26/0

Materials With Opacity Maps Only

Material Name	Map File	Map Amount	Shin./Shin. Str./Trans.
Checker Opac Pur	bwcheckr.cel	100	36/54/0
Checker Opacity	bwcheckr.cel	100	36/54/0

Materials With Bump Maps Only

Material Name	Map File	Map Amount	Shin./Shin. Str./Trans.
Ape Bump	ape.cel	80	28/43/0
Bumpypatrn Glass	pat0027.tga	44	29/44/41
Leaded Bmp Glass	gravel1.cel	52	52/73/67
Squig Red/Vio	squig.cel	100	41/60/0
Squig Red/Vio 5	squig.cel	20	41/60/0

Materials with Reflection Maps Only

Material Name	Map File	Map Amount	Shin./Shin. Str./Reflt. Blur
Brass Gifmap	refmap.gif	53	42/61/36
Brass Valley	valley_l.tga	58	39/57/38
Chrome Blue Sky	sky.gif	100	48/68/25
Chrome Chaos Sky	cloud.gif	70	46/66/25
Chrome Gifmap	refmap.gif	100	61/82/36
Chrome Lake	biglake.gif	100	60/81/25
Chrome Pearl	house2_l.tga	95	35/52/60
Chrome Sky	cloud.gif	70	46/66/25
Chrome Sunset	sunset.gif	100	48/68/25
Chrome Tutorial	house2_l.tga	100	94/100/0
Chrome Valley	valley_l.tga	93	37/55/10
Chrome Victorian	house2_l.tga	95	40/59/10
Old Metal	refmap.gif	87	44/64/30
Soap Bubble	blplanet.cel	15	53/74/40

Materials With Two Maps			
(T = Texture, B = Bump, O = Opacity)			
Material Name	Map 1 File/Amount	Map 2 File/Amount	Shin./Shin. Str./Trans.
Blue Rings	T/ringtex.cel/100	O/ringopac.cel /100	0/0/0
Brown Bumpybrick	T/brnbrick.cel/100	B/brnbricb.cel/36	7/11/0
Bumpy Camouflage	T/camoflag.cel/81	B/camoflab.cel/4	17/26/0
Bumpy Grid	T/grid.cel/70	B/brnbrick.cel/80	54/75/0
Bumpy Metal	T/imetal.cel/100	B/imetab.cel/20	46/66/0
Bumpy White Stone	T/istone2.cel/100	B/lstone2.cel/40	7/11/0
Dark Wood Tile	T/iltwood.cel/57	B/iltwood.cel/1	10/16/0
Green Vines	T/ivines1.cel/89	B/ivines1.cel/20	9/14/0
Light Wood Tile	T/iltwood1.cel/ 100	B/iltwood.cel/4	10/16/0
Light Wood Shingles	T/shingl2.cel/100	B/ishingl2.cel/40	7/11/0
Molded Plastic	T/gravel1.cel/63	B/gravel1.cel/8	28/43/0
Mottled Marble	T/imarble1.cel/ 100	B/imarble1.cel/0	10/16/0
Palm Tree Trunk	T/treetrnk.cel/100	B/treetrnk.cel/40	0/0/0
Pitted Metal	T/imetal.cel/100	B/imetal.cel/72	46/66/0

Materials With Two Maps			
(T = Texture, B = Bump, O = Opacity)			
Material Name	Map 1 File/Amount	Map 2 File/Amount	Shin./Shin. Str./Trans.
Slate L-Pattern	T/ipavers.cel/100	B/ipavers.cel/20	46/66/0

Appendix C
Minimum
Hardware and
Software

The following list of minimum hardware and software required to run Release 3 is taken from the *3D Studio Installation Guide.* Consult the guide for further details about system components.

COMPAQ® Deskpro 386™, 80386SX, IBM® PS/2® models 70 or 80, Hewlett-Packard® 80386™ systems, or a true 80386-compatible (80386 CPU must be step D0 or higher). The 80486DX™, 80486DX2, 80486SX, 80486SL, and Pentium® CPUs are also supported, although performance has not been optimized for Pentium CPUs.

A math coprocessor, which can be an Intel® 80387, or an 80387-compatible coprocessor, such as a Cyrix D87 for 80386-based systems. For 80486SX-based systems, you must either upgrade your CPU to an 80486DX or add an 80487SX math coprocessor. On the 80486DX, 80486DX2, and Pentium, the coprocessor is an integral part of the chip. The Weitek 3167 and 4167 math coprocessors are not supported in Release 3.

Eight megabytes of random-access memory (RAM). Using the 386|DOS-Extender from Phar Lap™, 3D Studio has direct access to all the conventional and extended memory available in your computer. In addition, 3D Studio also uses 386|VMM™ (Virtual Memory Manager). This creates a virtual memory system that lets 3D studio use a memory space larger than the available RAM of the computer.

A hard disk with at least 20 MB of free capacity. We recommend an additional 20 MB of free disk space.

A 1.2-MB or 1.44-MB floppy disk drive.

DOS operating system, Version 3.3 or later.

An SVGA or Video Electronics Standards Association (VESA)–compatible display capable of displaying at least 256 colors in 640 x 480 resolution, or an RCPADI-capable display.

A Microsoft-compatible mouse, a Summagraphics® Summa-Sketch®-compatible digitizing tablet, or a DGPADI-capable pointing device.

A CD-ROM drive for accessing the World-Creating Toolkit® library of texture maps, images, geometry files, and flics included with 3D Studio (not necessary for normal operation of 3D Studio).

Appendix D
References

Callender, John H., ed. *Time-Saver Standards for Architectural Design Data, 6th ed*. New York: McGraw-Hill, 1982.

Gill, Brendan. *Many Masks: A Life of Frank Lloyd Wright*. New York: Ballantine Books,1987.

Hoffmann, Donald. *Frank Lloyd Wright's Fallingwater: The House and Its History, 2d ed*. New York: Dover Publications,1993.

Kaufmann, Edgar, Jr. *Fallingwater: A Frank Lloyd Wright Country House.* New York: Abbeville Press, 1986.

Laseau, Paul, and James Tice. *Frank Lloyd Wright: Between Principle and Form.* New York: Van Nostrand Reinhold, 1992.

Ramsey, Charles G., and Harold R. Sleeper. *Architectural Graphic Standards, 8th ed.* New York: John Wiley & Sons, 1988.

Tafel, Edgar. *Years with Frank Lloyd Wright: Apprentice to Genius.* New York: Dover Publications, 1979.

Index

F

Z

More
OnWord Press Titles

Pro/ENGINEER Books

INSIDE Pro/ENGINEER
Book $49.95 Includes Disk

The Pro/ENGINEER Quick Reference
Book $24.95

The Pro/ENGINEER Exercise Book
Book $39.95 Includes Disk

Interleaf Books

INSIDE Interleaf
Book $49.95 Includes Disk

Adventurer's Guide to Interleaf Lisp
Book $49.95 Includes Disk

The Interleaf Exercise Book
Book $39.95 Includes Disk

The Interleaf Quick Reference
Book $24.95

Interleaf Tips and Tricks
Book $49.95 Includes Disk

MicroStation Books

INSIDE MicroStation 5X. 3d edition
Book $34.95 Includes Disk

MicroStation Reference Guide 5.X
Book $18.95

The MicroStation Productivity Book
Book $39.95 Optional Disk $49.95

MicroStation Bible
Book $49.95 Optional Disk $49.95

Adventures in MDL Programming
Book $49.95

Programming With MDL
Book $49.95 Optional Disk $49.95

Programming With User Commands
Book $65.00 Optional Disk $40.00

101 MDL Commands
Book $49.95
Optional Executable Disk $101.00
Optional Source Disks (6) $259.95

101 User Commands
Book $49.95 Optional Disk $101.00

Bill Steinbock's Pocket MDL Programmer's Guide
Book $24.95

MicroStation for AutoCAD Users
Book $29.95 Optional Disk $14.95

MicroStation for AutoCAD Users Tablet Menu
Tablet Menu $99.95

MicroStation 5.X Delta Book
Book $19.95

Managing and Networking MicroStation
Book $29.95 Optional Disk $29.95

The MicroStation Database Book
Book $29.95 Optional Disk $29.95

The MicroStation Rendering Book
Book $34.95 Includes Disk

INSIDE I/RAS B
Book $24.95 Includes Disk

The CLIX Workstation User's Guide
Book $34.95 Includes Disk

Build Cell
Software $69.95

SunSoft Solaris Series

The SunSoft Solaris 2.* User's Guide
Book $29.95 Includes Disk

SunSoft Solaris 2.*for Managers and Administrators
Book $34.95 Optional Disk $29.95

The SunSoft Solaris 2.* Quick Reference
Book $18.95

Five Steps to SunSoft Solaris 2.*
Book $24.95 Includes Disk

One Minute SunSoft Solaris Manager
Book $14.95

SunSoft Solaris 2.* for Windows Users
Book $24.95

The Hewlett Packard HP-UX Series

The HP-UX User's Guide
Book $29.95 Includes Disk

HP-UX For Managers and Administrators
Book $34.95 Optional Disk $29.95

The HP-UX Quick Reference
Book $18.95

Five Steps to HP-UX
Book $24.95 Includes Disk

One Minute HP-UX Manager
Book $14.95

HP-UX for Windows Users
Book $24.95

CAD Management

One Minute CAD Manager
Book $14.95

Manager's Guide to Computer-Aided Engineering
Book $49.95

Other CAD

CAD and the Practice of Architecture: ASG Solutions
Book $39.95 Includes Disk

INSIDE CADVANCE
Book $34.95 Includes Disk

Using Drafix Windows CAD
Book $34.95 Includes Disk

Fallingwater in 3D Studio: A Case Study and Tutorial
Book $39.95 Includes Disk

Geographic Information Systems

The GIS Book. 3d edition
Book $34.95

DTP/CAD Clip Art

1001 DTP/CAD Symbols Clip Art Library: Architectural
Book $29.95

DISK FORMATS:
   MicroStation
DGN Disk $175.00 Book/Disk $195.00

AutoCAD
DWG Disk $175.00 Book/Disk $195.00

CAD/DTP
DXF Disk $195.00 Book/Disk $225.00

Networking/LANtastic

Fantastic LANtastic
Book $29.95 Includes Disk

The LANtastic Quick Reference
Book $14.95

One Minute Network Manager
Book $14.95

OnWord Press Distribution

End Users/User Groups/Corporate Sales

OnWord Press books are available worldwide to end users, user groups, and corporate accounts from your local bookseller or computer/software dealer or from HMP Direct: call 1-800-526-BOOK or 505-473-5454; fax 505-471-4   ; e-mail to ORDERS@BOOKSTORE.HMP.COM; or write to High Mountain Press Direct, 2530 Camino Entrada, Santa Fe, NM 87505-8435.

Wholesale, Including Overseas Distribution

We have international distributors. Contact us for your local source by calling 1-800-ONWORD or 505-473-5454; fax to 505-471-4424; e-mail to ORDERS @BOOKSTORE.HMP.COM; or write to High Mountain Press/IPG, 2530 Camino Entrada, Santa Fe, NM 87505-8435, USA.

Comments, Corrections, and Bug Fixes

Your comments can help us make better books. If you find an error in our products, or have any other comments, positive or negative, we'd like to know! Please contact our e-mail address: READERS@HMP.COM, or write to us at the address below.

OnWord Press, 2530 Camino Entrada, Santa Fe, NM 87505-8435 USA